THE
UNITED STATES
AFTER THE
WORLD WAR

By

JAMES C. MALIN

Associate Professor of History

University of Kansas

GINN AND COMPANY

GINN AND COMPANY

BOSTON · NEW YORK · CHICAGO · LONDON
ATLANTA · DALLAS · COLUMBUS · SAN FRANCISCO

FOREWORD

THE year 1928 marked the passing of the first decade after the World War, and by coincidence it was also a presidential election year. Circumstances indicated that the next administration must assume responsibility for a marked degree of reshaping of public policies. It seems an appropriate time, therefore, to make some evaluation of what has happened in these ten years. It is not only appropriate; but, since the World War, the public demands that history be brought down to the present.

In the selection of materials no two persons would agree on what should be included. Neither would there be agreement on the method of treatment. Time and space impose their limitations also. The author has chosen to depart from the traditional narrative methods of presentation and has treated each line of policy by tracing its development through the period as an individual problem. By this method the direction of change is more definitely revealed. Social and cultural aspects of history as such have been omitted, but not because of any lack of appreciation of their importance. It is only by limitation of subject matter that reasonably adequate space is available for treatment of such material as has been included.

In writing a history of so recent a period one must necessarily depend much upon the writings of others — such books as have been written on particular problems, periodical literature, pamphlets, and newspapers. No footnotes have been used, and no attempt has been made to give complete bibliographies. The specialist would want more than could be given, and the more general student would not need them. The indexes of United States government publications are so complete that there is no particular point in including an array of those sources. Such bibliographies as are given at the end of some of the chapters list some of the best available material on the particular subject and serve also (where the author has used them in the preparation of the chapter) as acknowledgments. The McKinley Publishing Company has kindly given permission to use parts of the series of articles prepared by the author for the *Historical Outlook* for October and November, 1927, and January and February, 1928. The author's greatest obligation, however, is to Professor Frank H. Hodder. Without his loyal support and encouragement it would have been necessary to abandon the writing of this book.

JAMES C. MALIN

CONTENTS

The United States after the World War

◄ PART ONE ►

The United States and the Establishment of International Government

CHAPTER I

THE LEAGUE OF NATIONS: THE MAKING
OF THE COVENANT

DURING the nineteenth century much had been done toward evolving machinery of international coöperation and government. Most of the elements necessary to a League of Nations existed in solution before the outbreak of war in 1914. The prime necessity was to precipitate or crystallize these into concrete institutions in order to provide machinery not only to function in settling disputes at times of crisis, but to provide the means of promoting the interests of the world at peace.

The United States had not been concerned directly in the events which led to the outbreak of the World War. Woodrow Wilson as president of the United States accepted this view from the beginning; as late as May, 1916, he still held that "with its causes and objects we are not concerned." The post-war revelations of European diplomacy, as bearing upon the immediate and the more remote causes of the war, confirmed his position. It was more evident afterwards than in 1914 that both belligerent groups must bear an approximately equal responsibility for the tragedy. The American neutrality proclamation, dated August 4, 1914, defined the legal position of the United States with respect to the participants in the war.

Wilson's first important expression of the principles which should underlie a permanent world peace is to be found in his address of May 27, 1916, but at that time he had no expectation of participating in the making of the treaty which would close the European war. It was at this time that he first publicly indorsed a League of Nations. The next step

in the development of the American position on the question
of a league is contained in the naval appropriation act of
August 29, 1916, which authorized and requested the President to call a conference not later than the close of the European war to bring about some organization for international
peace. Later in the year Wilson considered the possibility that
should the belligerent groups state their war aims fully and
frankly it might pave the way for the opening of peace negotiations. It would also inform public opinion in the United
States as to the issues involved should the United States be
drawn into the conflict. Accordingly on December 18, 1916,
he addressed notes to the belligerent powers asking "that
an early occasion be sought to call out from all the nations
now at war such an avowal of their respective views as to
the terms upon which the war might be concluded and the
arrangements which would be deemed satisfactory as a guarantee against its renewal or the kindling of any similar
conflict in the future as would make it possible frankly to
compare them." The President "takes the liberty of calling
attention to the fact that the objects, which statesmen of
the belligerents on both sides have in mind in this war, are
virtually the same, as stated in general terms to their own
people and to the world." Furthermore, he pointed out his
hope that after the peace "a concert of nations" would be
"immediately practicable."

The replies of the belligerents were made the occasion of
an address to the Senate on January 22, 1917, which stands
as a landmark in the development of war aims. President
Wilson pointed out that "in every discussion of the peace
that must end this war it is taken for granted that that peace
must be followed by some definite concert of power which
will make it virtually impossible that any such catastrophe
should ever overwhelm us again." The conditions upon
which the American people could be asked to adhere to such
a League for Peace were a concert of power; a just peace;
equality of nations; recognition of the principle of govern-

ment with the consent of the governed; direct outlets to the sea; freedom of the sea; limitation of armament; and the Monroe Doctrine as the doctrine of the world, "that no nation should seek to extend its policy over any other nation or people. . . ."

During the next three months affairs moved rapidly. The United States entered the war April 6, 1917, in defense of American neutral rights. In coöperating with the Allies in the war against Germany the United States did not become one of them, but was designated as an "Associated Power." During October and November the Bolshevist revolution occurred, which took Russia out of the war, and the Bolshevists' publication of Allied secret treaties challenged the sincerity of Allied war aims. The Bolshevists also announced their own peace terms in the slogan "No annexations, no indemnities, self-determination." Allied morale was seriously undermined. Lloyd George, the British prime minister, met the situation with his war-aims speech of January 5, 1918. He stood for the restoration of Belgium and occupied territories, for self-determination, for disposition of the German colonies according to the wishes and interests of their inhabitants, for a just and permanent peace, for a League of Nations, for sanctity of treaties, for reduction of armaments, and for reparation for violations of international law. Wilson made a similar statement in his Fourteen Points speech (January 8, 1918). The Fourteen Points were as follows:

I. Open covenants of peace, openly arrived at, after which there shall be no private international understandings of any kind, but diplomacy shall proceed always frankly and in public view.

II. Absolute freedom of navigation upon the seas, outside territorial waters, alike in peace and in war, except as the seas may be closed in whole or in part by international action for the enforcement of international covenants.

III. The removal, so far as possible, of all economic barriers and the establishment of an equality of trade conditions among all the nations consenting to the peace and associating themselves for its maintenance.

IV. Adequate guarantees given and taken that national armaments will be reduced to the lowest point consistent with domestic safety.

V. A free, open-minded, and absolutely impartial adjustment of all colonial claims, based upon a strict observance of the principle that in determining all such questions of sovereignty the interests of the populations concerned must have equal weight with the equitable claims of the government whose title is to be determined.

VI. The evacuation of all Russian territory and such settlement of all questions affecting Russia as will secure the best and freest coöperation of the other nations of the world in obtaining for her an unhampered and unembarrassed opportunity for the independent determination of her own political development and national policy, and assure her of a sincere welcome into the society of free nations under institutions of her own choosing; and, more than a welcome, assistance also of every kind that she may need and may herself desire. The treatment accorded Russia by her sister nations in the months to come will be the acid test of their good will, of their comprehension of her needs as distinguished from their own interests, and of their intelligent and unselfish sympathy.

VII. Belgium, the whole world will agree, must be evacuated and restored, without any attempt to limit the sovereignty which she enjoys in common with all other free nations. No other single act will serve as this will serve to restore confidence among the nations in the laws which they themselves have set and determined for the government of their relations with one another. Without this healing act the whole structure and validity of international law is forever impaired.

VIII. All French territory should be freed and the invaded portions restored, and the wrong done to France by Prussia in 1871 in the matter of Alsace-Lorraine, which has unsettled the peace of the world for nearly fifty years, should be righted in order that peace may once more be made secure in the interests of all.

IX. A readjustment of the frontiers of Italy should be effected along clearly recognizable lines of nationality.

X. The peoples of Austria-Hungary, whose place among the nations we wish to see safeguarded and assured, should be accorded the freest opportunity of autonomous development.

XI. Rumania, Serbia, and Montenegro should be evacuated; occupied territories restored; Serbia accorded free and secure access to the sea; and the relations of the several Balkan States to one another determined by friendly counsel along historically established lines of allegiance and nationality; and international guarantees of the political and economic independence and territorial integrity of the several Balkan States should be entered into.

XII. The Turkish portions of the present Ottoman Empire should be assured a secure sovereignty, but the other nationalities which are now under Turkish rule should be assured an undoubted security of life and an absolutely unmolested opportunity to autonomous development; and the Dardanelles should be permanently opened as a free passage to the ships and commerce of all nations under international guarantees.

XIII. An independent Polish State should be erected which should include the territories inhabited by indisputably Polish populations, which should be assured a free and secure access to the sea, and whose political and economic independence and territorial integrity should be guaranteed by international covenant.

XIV. A general association of nations must be formed under specific covenants for the purpose of affording mutual guarantees of political independence and territorial integrity to great and small states alike.

Six of these points, the first five and the fourteenth, were general in their application and are therefore of direct importance to American history. The remaining eight referred to specific European settlements. The Fourteen Points speech was followed on February 11 by an address to Congress which outlined the Four Principles:

First, that each part of the final settlement must be based upon the essential justice of that particular case and upon such adjustments as are most likely to bring a peace that will be permanent;

Second, that peoples and provinces are not to be bartered about from sovereignty to sovereignty as if they were mere chattels and pawns in a game, even the great game, now forever discredited, of the balance of power; but that

Third, every territorial settlement involved in this war must be made in the interest and for the benefit of the populations concerned, and not as a part of any mere adjustment or compromise of claims amongst rival states; and

Fourth, that all well-defined national aspiration shall be accorded the utmost satisfaction that can be accorded them without introducing new or perpetuating old elements of discord and antagonism that would be likely in time to break the peace of Europe and consequently of the world.

A further statement of war aims was enunciated in a speech delivered July 4 at Mount Vernon. The Four Objects for which the associated nations were fighting were as follows :

I. The destruction of every arbitrary power anywhere that can separately, secretly, and of its single choice disturb the peace of the world; or, if it cannot be presently destroyed, at least its reduction to virtual impotence.

II. The settlement of every question, whether of territory, of sovereignty, of economic arrangement, or of political relationship, upon the basis of free acceptance of that settlement by the people immediately concerned, and not upon the basis of the material interest or advantage of any other nation or people which may desire a different settlement for the sake of its own exterior influence or mastery.

III. The consent of all nations to be governed in their conduct towards each other by the same principles of honor and of respect for the common law of civilized society that govern the individual citizens of all modern states in their relations with one another; to the end that all promises and covenants may be sacredly observed, no private plots or conspiracies hatched, no selfish injuries wrought with impunity, and a mutual trust established upon the handsome foundation of a mutual respect for right.

IV. The establishment of an organization of peace which shall make it certain that the combined power of free nations will check every invasion of right and serve to make peace and justice the more secure by affording a definite tribunal of opinion to which all must submit and by which every international readjustment that cannot be amicably agreed upon by the peoples directly concerned shall be sanctioned.

These great objects can be put into a single sentence. What we seek is the reign of law, based upon the consent of the governed and sustained by the organized opinion of mankind.

The last important address on war aims was the statement of the Five Particulars (September 27) :

First, the impartial justice meted out must involve no discrimination between those to whom we wish to be just and those to whom we do not wish to be just. It must be a justice that plays no favorites and knows no standard but the equal rights of the several peoples concerned;

Second, no special or separate interest of any single nation or any group of nations can be made the basis of any part of the settlement which is not consistent with the common interest of all;

Third, there can be no leagues or alliances or special covenants and understandings within the general and common family of the League of Nations.

Fourth, and more specifically, there can be no special, selfish economic combinations within the League and no employment of any form of economic boycott or exclusion except as the power of economic penalty by exclusion from the markets of the world may be vested in the League of Nations itself as a means of discipline and control.

Fifth, all international agreements and treaties of every kind must be made known in their entirety to the rest of the world.

War Aims as the Basis of Peace

Germany made overtures for peace in a note dated October 4. It was received by Wilson on October 6, 1918. He laid down three stipulations as a condition of further discussions of peace terms: acceptance of the Fourteen Points and subsequent addresses as the basis of peace, immediate withdrawal from invaded territory, and assurance that the German government was speaking for the German people and not for the authorities who had been conducting the war. These conditions being met, the question was submitted by Wilson to the Allied governments, and he so notified the German government on October 23. The Allied answer was transmitted by Wilson on November 5. The Fourteen Points and the principles stated in subsequent addresses were accepted by the Allies as the basis of peace, with two reservations: (1) the freedom of the seas; (2) an interpretation of Wilson's statement on restoration of invaded territories to the effect that "by it they understand that compensation will be made by Germany for all damage done to the civilian population of the Allies and their property by the aggression of Germany by land, by sea, and from the air." With these principles as a basis the armistice terms were formulated and signed November 11, 1918. By this time the German revolution had taken place, and the Kaiser had abdicated and fled to Holland.

The Austro-Hungarian armistice was negotiated separately, but was based upon the Fourteen Points and the Four Principles of the address of February 11, and it was agreed that the "viewpoints" of the address of September 27 (the Five Particulars) were also to "be taken into account." The tenth point was modified to permit self-determination. These negotiations were begun on September 16, and the armistice was signed on November 3.

The preparations for the Peace Conference next occupied the minds of all concerned. The mid-term elections were at hand in the United States, and Wilson issued a call on October 25 for the return of a Democratic Congress. The appeal in itself was not unusual; it was the use made of it by the President's enemies which gave it exceptional character. Republicans, forgetting similar action on the part of Republican presidents, denounced the President in the strongest terms. Roosevelt, who had himself made similar calls in 1906 and 1908, led the attack in a speech (October 26). The elections were a defeat for Wilson. This meant that the last two years of Wilson's administration, which included the peace negotiations and post-war reconstruction, must be conducted with a Republican Congress in opposition to a Democratic president.

With the signing of the armistice such restraints on partisanship as the war had imposed were largely removed. The world had been keyed up to a high emotional pitch for four years, and in desperation had promised things which apparently were not seriously meant. Now that the war was over, the almost universal question was What do we get out of it? By some miracle world peace would be established which would be a peace of justice and end all war, but which would still give to the Allies the spoils of the conqueror, crushing indemnities, and a peace of revenge. In the United States, Roosevelt would have divided up most of the world into spheres of interest among the great Allied and Associated Powers. Henry Cabot Lodge in the Senate (December 21) demanded that Germany pay heavy indemnities instead of reparations, and that "in these indemnities the United States must have its proper and proportional share." Senator William E. Borah wished to establish the isolation of the United States. War aims and peace aims often presented sharp contrasts.

Wilson announced on November 18 that he would attend the Peace Conference, although he might not remain for the whole of its deliberations. The members of the peace commission were Robert Lansing, Secretary of State, Henry White, former ambassador to France, E. M. House, and General Tasker H. Bliss. Mr. White was a Republican, but the Senate was not represented. It was the opinion of the opposition that the President should stay at home and carry out national reconstruction. Republicans were incensed that such men as Root, Taft, or Roosevelt were not chosen for the peace commission. Fuel was added to the flames by the announcement on November 20 that the cables would be taken over by the government.

Wilson's annual message to Congress was delivered December 2, shortly before his departure. Foreign policy was omitted, except for a recommendation for the ratification of the treaty with Colombia in settlement of the old Panama-revolution controversy. It was the President's opinion that "so far as our domestic affairs are concerned the problem of our return to peace is a problem of economic and industrial readjustment." He said that no "general scheme" of reconstruction he had seen was acceptable, and he warned particularly against too much government interference in economic reconstruction. He said, further, that war controls should be removed as rapidly as possible and information and experience acquired by the government be placed at the disposal of business men; that public works should be pushed and plans elaborated for development of unused resources; that such a program would serve two purposes — it would help to meet the unemployment problem as well as conserve natural resources (the Secretary of the Interior would present a definite program); that marine shipping controls should be continued; and that the naval building program should be resumed. A general program of tax revision was outlined for the years 1919 and 1920, the purpose of which was to remove uncertainties in business adjustments. The President recommended that the railroads should be returned to private operation and that government control should be provided, but on a plan different from pre-war policy. He further recommended a comprehensive national transportation policy which should include railroads, waterways, highways, and countryside roads. At the end of the message came an explanation of his mission to Europe: since the peace was to be based upon his Fourteen Points and other messages, he felt the obligation of making every possible effort to insure the realization of the ideal which they expressed. Censorship of cables had been removed by the British and French at his request, and news channels were to be open without discrimination so far as existing facilities permitted; but to insure adequate facilities for the government service and the least possible interference with other uses, the government had taken over the control of cables.

Wilson did not attempt to outline a foreign policy in his annual message, possibly because he was dealing with that himself, but he had made elaborate preparations for the work just ahead. In September, 1917, a United States committee of inquiry was organized by E. M. House with headquarters at the American Geographical Society's offices at New York.

The results of the investigations made by this committee had supplied the basis for part of the Fourteen Points. As the Peace Conference approached, the personnel and organization were expanded so that the whole American delegation at Paris numbered about thirteen hundred persons. Wilson's plan of territorial settlements was contained in the Black Book drawn up by these experts under his direction.

In Europe the "slump in idealism" was more pronounced than in the United States. In the last analysis it was fear that had held the Allied powers together behind Wilson's war aims rather than any genuine belief in the principles embodied therein. The victory in the war removed that overwhelming fear, and the powers tended to revert to the imperialistic policies that had been the underlying cause of the war. Probably, in view of the secret treaties, it would be more accurate to say that they came out openly in advocating policies which they had never given up. Lloyd George won the Parliamentary elections of December 14 on the slogan "Hang the Kaiser and make the Germans pay the cost of the war." In Paris *Le Temps*, an administration organ, said, "Let us reconstruct central Europe in accordance with French interests." It seemed to be generally understood that the peace would be made in accordance with the secret treaties.

The general nature of the most important of these secret treaties is indicated below. The treaty of London, concluded April 26, 1915, brought Italy into the war on the Allied side by promising to her territories on the Adriatic and the right to a share in Turkey and in German colonies. This treaty was first published by the Bolshevist government on November 17, 1917. The treaty with Rumania was concluded August 18, 1916, and brought that power into the Allied combination by offering compensations in territory taken from other states. The Franco-Russian agreement on the dismemberment of Germany (concluded March 11, 1917) gave Russia a free hand to draw the eastern boundaries of

Germany and Austria, and France and Great Britain a free hand to draw the western boundary. This arrangement was made after the war-aims notes of January, 1917, declaring for self-determination. By the Anglo-Japanese secret treaty of February 16, 1917, Great Britain agreed to support Japanese claims to the German rights in Shantung and to German colonies in the Pacific north of the equator, and the British were to receive similar support in respect to the German islands south of the equator. On the question of the Straits, Constantinople, and the partition of Turkey, there were at least six separate agreements by April, 1917, the last of the group being signed after the entrance of the United States into the war. Negotiations continued throughout the war and even throughout the Peace Conference itself. The question has frequently been asked why the United States government did not know of these secret treaties, or, if it knew, why no action was taken on the knowledge. No adequate explanation has been made.

Wilson arrived in Paris on December 14, 1918. He was received with an ovation, possibly without parallel, in his subsequent tour of France, Italy, and England. Among the representatives of governments he appears to have met the general assumption that the peace terms would be framed with due consideration of the commitments of the secret treaties. The war aims of the Allied and Associated Powers as expressed in the Fourteen Points and Wilson's subsequent addresses had been officially accepted by the Allies as well as by Germany as the basis of the armistice. The legal and moral obligations of the armistice terms are inescapable. When in the negotiations with the Germans in May and June, 1919, the Germans charged the Allied and Associated Powers with violating their pledges, the Allied reply admitted in full the obligations of the armistice agreement, but denied categorically that there was any failure to fulfill them. Probably no two historians will agree regarding the terms of the peace treaty, but all attempts to evaluate it must recognize three major factors: the ideal statement of principles as laid down by Wilson, the practical difficulties and in some cases impossibilities of applying these fully, and, last but not least, the commitments embodied in the secret treaties.

Wilson's disillusionment in December, 1918, seems to have had a profound effect upon the course which he followed during the Peace Conference. It completed the evolution of his ideas as to the relation of the project of the League to the world settlement. It is essential to trace the course of development of this problem in Wilson's mind before it is possible to understand his line of action in the Peace Conference and in the campaign in the United States to secure ratification of the treaty by the Senate. Ray Stannard Baker has pointed out four stages in the problem. First, in the address to the League to Enforce Peace (May 27, 1916), Wilson assumed that peace would be made by the belligerents (the United States had not yet become a party to the war) and that the United States would join an association of nations which should be made after that event. The peace was first; the League would come later. Secondly, in his address to the Senate January 22, 1917, he stressed the point that the peace must be a just peace, and that unless it was a peace of justice the United States would not enter the League. The peace was first, but it must be a just peace. Thirdly, in his Metropolitan Opera House address (September 27, 1918) he insisted that "the constitution of that League of Nations and the clear definition of its objects must be a part, in a sense the most essential part, of the peace settlement itself," and the treaty must contain "impartial justice in every item of the settlement." Here the stress was for the first time placed on the League as possibly the most important part of the settlement. Fourthly, in his Guild Hall and Manchester speeches (December 28 and 30, 1918), after his arrival in Europe, he began to realize that the hope of a just peace had vanished. Under these circumstances he said "the key of the peace was the guarantee of the peace, not the terms of it." "I am not hopeful that the individual terms of the settlement will be altogether satisfactory." The League would "provide the machinery of adjustment, . . . the machinery of good will and friendship." He repeated the same idea at the plenary session of the Peace Conference (January 25, 1919) when he said: "We can set up permanent processes. We may not be able to set up permanent decisions." By the time he entered the Peace Conference his position was the reverse of what it had been three years before. The League was now first in importance; the peace, second. The paramount object of the conference was the creation of the League as a permanent system of international government and adjustment.

PROVISIONS OF THE COMPLETED COVENANT

The Covenant of the League of Nations as finally adopted provided the following general scheme of organization and powers: Membership in the League is open to all self-governing states, dominions, and colonies, and admission is accomplished by a two-thirds vote of the Assembly. Any member may withdraw upon two years' notice (Article 1). The machinery of government is composed of three branches: a permanent Secretariat, which performs all routine functions, a Council made up of five major states with permanent seats and four minor states [1] with elective seats, and an Assembly composed of representatives of all member states. Each state is entitled to one vote in the Assembly (Articles 2, 3, 4, and 6). The seat of the League is fixed at Geneva (Article 7). Decisions, with certain exceptions, are arrived at by unanimous vote in either the Council or the Assembly (Article 5). Certain obligations are assumed by the members. First, the members undertake to reduce armament to the standard of national safety, to exchange information con-

---

[1] The original provision for four nonpermanent members continued until 1922. From 1923 to 1926 there were six nonpermanent members; after 1926 there were nine. Germany received a permanent seat in 1926.

cerning military plans, and to establish a commission to advise the Council concerning armament problems. The Council should formulate plans for reduction of armament, such plans to be subject to revision every ten years (Articles 8 and 9). Second, "the members of the League undertake to respect and preserve as against external aggression the territorial integrity and existing political independence of all members of the League. In case of any such aggression the Council shall advise upon the means by which this obligation shall be fulfilled" (Article 10). This guaranty is indirectly qualified by the last paragraph of Article 11, which provides that questions threatening international peace may be brought to the attention of the League. It was qualified also by Article 19, which makes similar provision for treaties that have become inapplicable or international conditions that might endanger peace. Third, the members undertake to refrain from war pending attempts at peaceful settlement of disputes. The methods of peaceful settlement are (1) arbitration, (2) inquiry by the Council, and (3) adjudication by an international court (Articles 11–15). Domestic questions are specifically reserved from the jurisdiction of the League (Article 15). The means of enforcement of decisions of the League are economic blockade with a possible use of international military action (Article 16). Treaties to be valid and binding must be registered with the League (Articles 18 and 20). "Nothing in this Covenant shall be deemed to affect the validity of international engagements, such as treaties of arbitration or regional understandings like the Monroe Doctrine, for securing the maintenance of peace" (Article 21). Enemy colonies and territories of dismembered enemy states, such as Turkey, where incapable of self-government, are to be administered by member states as mandatories under the supervision of the League (Article 22). Declarations of international policy are contained in Articles 23 and 25. Members of the League endeavor to secure fair and humane conditions of labor.

They undertake to secure just treatment of native inhabitants under their control. The League undertakes to supervise execution of agreements regarding traffic in women and children and traffic in drugs, and to supervise trade in arms and ammunition with countries where such traffic is of common interest. The members agree to make provisions to secure freedom of communications and of transit and "equitable" treatment of commerce, and to endeavor to prevent and control disease and promote Red Cross organizations for the betterment of health, the prevention of disease, and the mitigation of suffering throughout the world. International bureaus and unions were to be consolidated at Geneva under League administration (Article 24). Amendments to the Covenant were to become effective only when ratified by the states which compose the Council and by a majority of the members of the Assembly (Article 26).[1]

ORIGIN OF THE PROVISIONS OF THE COVENANT

There are two primary sources to which the provisions of the Covenant can be traced : the British Empire and the United States. In the United States the League to Enforce Peace was organized in 1915. Its plan included the submission of disputes to arbitration or conciliation and a pledge that the nations would agree to enforce such submission against nations refusing to accept these methods of peaceful settlement. The methods of enforcement included economic blockade and the use of military force. A second very important plan supported by American opinion was the convention drafted at the Second Hague Conference for establishing a permanent Judicial Arbitration Court. Elihu Root and William H. Taft were closely associated with this scheme. A third plan was Wilson's Pan-American plan of January 6, 1916, in which he contemplated a league of American states to guarantee "to each other absolute political independence

[1] The text of the Covenant is printed in Appendix A.

and territorial integrity." Such a guaranty was to be qualified in certain respects to prevent inflexibility to changing
conditions. Here are the American origins of several articles
of the Covenant (9, 10, 11, 12, 14, 16, and 19).

In Great Britain sentiment for the League was probably
stronger than in the United States. Several organizations
were carrying on propaganda. In 1918 the British government appointed the Phillimore committee to formulate a
draft for consideration. The resulting plan was a compila-
tion of current ideas brought together into a coherent scheme.
It was reported on March 29, 1918, and was sent to the
Dominions and to Wilson. In content it was similar in many
respects to the plan of the League to Enforce Peace. The
only administrative machinery provided was occasional conferences of the Allied States at which unanimous decisions
would be required to secure action. There was an early
French plan also, but it is not known whether this influenced
Wilson's draft of a covenant.

The Phillimore draft may be taken as the concrete starting
point of Wilson's experiments. He discussed the League
question with House and instructed him to formulate a
plan, which was submitted July 16, 1918. Several things
not contained in the Phillimore draft were included: a
permanent secretariat, a world court, enforcement by economic blockade alone, reduction of armaments, publicity of
military questions, and manufacture of war materials by
governments only. Wilson revised House's draft later in
the summer. He omitted the world court, but provided for
obligatory arbitration, reduced armament to a standard of
"domestic safety," and restored armed force as a last resort
in the enforcement of international obligations. The guaranty of territorial integrity was left much as House drafted
it (adapted from the Pan-American scheme) and included
the flexible clause to allow for adjustments. This is the
draft which Wilson took to Europe in December, and is the
first of a series of four.

In Europe he met with new plans, particularly those of Lord Robert Cecil of England, General Jan Smuts of South Africa, and of France. The official French plan did not contemplate the establishment of an international political state or even a confederation : it provided for an international council composed of all member states or representatives, with power to bind the states to observe decisions, and a permanent delegation to carry on routine work. The methods of peaceful settlement included were mediation and conciliation, arbitration through the Hague Tribunal, and adjudication by an international court. Enforcement was to be provided by economic blockade binding upon all members and by military action through an international army and navy supplied by members under the direction and plans of an international general staff. National military establishments were to be coördinated as far as possible in methods of training, organization, and recruiting under plans of the general staff.

The Cecil and Smuts plans contained several points which Wilson used in his second draft. Both included the provision for a Council and an Assembly. From the Smuts plan he adapted the arbitration features which were substituted for obligatory arbitration, the abolition of conscription, the adjustment of war material in proportion to military forces, the mandatory system [1] (with modifications) for administering enemy territory incapable of self-government, and the provisions relating to labor. This plan was printed and distributed for comment January 10, 1919. Many suggestions were presented, and a third draft was prepared January 20. Two additional points in this third draft should be emphasized : (1) the provision that treaties, to be binding and valid, must be published (this point seems to have originated with Lansing and Miller) ; (2) that there should be no discrimination among nations in fiscal and economic regulations.

[1] Wilson had the mandatory principle in mind before the Smuts draft was printed, but the Smuts plan gave it concrete expression.

The British official draft was presented to Wilson on January 19. It had been prepared with reference to his second draft, but it contained several new or different elements: the representation of the Dominions, an international court, and rights of minorities. It is here that the international court, which Wilson had always discounted, was brought back into League plans. These plans (Wilson's and the British) were referred to the legal advisers of the two delegations, — Sir Cecil Hurst for the British and David H. Miller for the United States, — and these worked out a compromise which was presented on February 2. During the same day Wilson, in consultation with Miller, framed a fourth draft which he hoped to have adopted as the basis of discussion in the League of Nations Commission. At the last moment, however, the Hurst-Miller draft was substituted, and served as the basis of deliberations. It is clear that Wilson contributed very little of his own to the content of these drafts of the Covenant, but he was responsible for two things: he acted as chief compiler of ideas, and he was determined that the League should be established as a part of the immediate peace settlements.

The Peace Conference and the League of Nations

The Council of Ten, made up of heads of states, met for the first time on January 12, 1919. The first plenary session of the Peace Conference met January 18. The order in which subjects were to be considered was presented by Wilson and accepted by the Council of Ten (January 13). The list is as follows: the League of Nations, reparations, new states, territorial adjustments, and colonial possessions.

Wilson's own peace program was by that time quite clearly before the Conference. It provided first, a League of Nations; secondly, that the League must be an integral part of the general treaty of peace; thirdly, that the armistice terms were to be applied to the peace settlement.

The question of the relation of the League to the general treaty of peace was determined by a resolution presented to the Council of Ten by Balfour, amended by Wilson, and accepted by the Council on January 22. The resolution was adopted by the second plenary session of the Peace Conference on January 25. It created a League of Nations Commission, whose duty it was to draft the Covenant, and declared that "this League' should be created as an integral part of the general treaty of peace, and should be open to every civilized nation which can be relied upon to promote its objects." Clemenceau said at the time, "The program of the Conference has been laid down by President Wilson." The League of Nations Commission met February 3, chose Wilson chairman, and completed the draft of the Covenant so that it could be adopted by the third plenary session of the Peace Conference (February 14).

The subject of the disposition of the German colonies was brought up by Lloyd George, out of order, on January 23. In the following days the powers all presented their claims for annexations. Wilson opposed dealing with the question until after the Covenant of the League was finished, and insisted upon the acceptance of the mandatory system instead of annexations. He pointed out (January 27) the bad effect that the annexation program would have upon public opinion : it "would discredit the Conference." Eventually the question was referred to the League of Nations Commission (January 30), and the mandatory system was incorporated into the Covenant as Article 22.

UNITED STATES PUBLIC OPINION REGARDING A LEAGUE OF NATIONS, JANUARY–FEBRUARY, 1919

Wilson disapproved the discussion of the details of a draft of a League of Nations before the framing of the Covenant at the Peace Conference. It was his opinion that if public opinion were crystallized on specific questions this would make it difficult if not impossible to secure the acceptance of the final Covenant, which of necessity must be the product of common agreement and compromise among all the nations at the Peace Conference. For this reason supporters of the League, in their advocacy of the idea, restricted themselves rather definitely to the general question and did not undertake the formulation of particular details of organization and machinery. Various aspects of the peace settlement were discussed in the United States during the winter of 1918–1919 and before the Covenant of the League was completed and published. Ex-President Taft was one of the most prominent advocates of a League, and his activity indicates substantially the character of this phase of the movement. He toured the country during February discussing the project along the lines proposed by the League to Enforce Peace. He also urged a codification of international law which should become binding upon all members of the League. This program was more drastic than Wilson's, a fact which Taft pointed out later when members of the League to Enforce Peace opposed the Covenant.

Theodore Roosevelt, shortly before his death on January 6, 1919, announced his program for a League, but admitted that he had not made up his mind fully on its details. First, he said, "the league would have to be based on the combination among the Allies of the present war, . . . together with such peoples as the Czechoslovaks." Secondly, each nation would retain absolute rights over economic policy, tariff, immigration, citizenship, and form of government. Thirdly, the world would be divided up into "spheres of interest to be reserved to each nation or group of nations" — the Caribbean for the United States, eastern Asia for Japan, and northern Africa for Europe. "Everything outside of what is thus reserved . . . should be decided by some species of court." Fourthly, the League states must maintain adequate armament for use "against the nations and hordes which represent despotism, barbarism, and anarchy." The

United States should establish "universal obligatory military training for all our young men." Fifthly, treaties for universal arbitration between the United States and the British Empire might be adopted. The sharp contrast between Roosevelt's plan and Wilson's is clear. The Roosevelt scheme is more nearly comparable to the French plan. Henry Cabot Lodge did not formulate a plan of his own, but was in accord with Roosevelt's views. He explained his position in his debate with A. Lawrence Lowell, president of Harvard University, at Boston on March 19, 1919: "The line I have followed in the Senate and elsewhere was the one he [Roosevelt] wished to have followed."

Of the extreme nationalists, later called the irreconcilables, Senator William E. Borah was among the most conspicuous. He was absolutely opposed to any League. He attempted to discredit Wilson, Taft, and the League to Enforce Peace by linking their program with the request of the Secretary of the Navy for a naval appropriation of $600,000,000. This, he said, was "militarism in its most pronounced form." "If the Savior of men would revisit the earth and declare for a League of Nations, I would be opposed to it. . . . It is a question of policy for my government, and I will decide regardless of individuals. . . . What we need in this country is the fostering and strengthening of the national spirit." The League is the "first step in internationalism and the sterilization of nationalism."

THE LEAGUE OF NATIONS, FEBRUARY 15 TO APRIL 28; WILSON'S CONCESSIONS

Wilson left Paris on February 15 for a month in the United States to close up the business of the session of Congress ending March 4. He landed at Boston on February 24 and two days later met the Senate Committee on Foreign Relations in conference at the White House for discussion of the Covenant. Senators Borah and Fall refused to attend. The question now was not *a* League, but *the* League. The discussion was transferred from the general to the particular. Opposition in the Senate crystallized around Lodge, presently to become the chairman of the Committee on Foreign Relations. On March 4 he asked the Senate for unanimous consent for the introduction of a resolution refusing its consent to the Covenant as it stood and requesting that immediate peace be made with Germany, after which the project of a League should be considered. Unanimous consent was refused. Lodge then stated that he had the signatures of thirty-seven senators and senators-elect to the Sixty-sixth Congress approving the resolution. Since thirty-seven senators constituted more than one third of the Senate, this meant that the League was defeated before it was submitted for ratification unless amendments could be framed and adopted which would win over enough senators from the thirty-seven to make a two-thirds majority in its favor.

In the closing days of the session a filibuster in the Senate blocked appropriation bills as well as other important legislation. Its purpose was to force an extra session in order that Congress might follow up the President's activities in Paris. The Republican caucus voted against the filibuster, and Lodge attempted to stop it; but three individual senators persisted until noon of March 4, when Vice President Marshall declared the Senate adjourned *sine Deo* ("without God"). Wilson refused to call the expected extra session until the work of the Peace Conference was done.

Outside of Congress the discussion of the Covenant was active. Taft defended it; Hughes and Root, who supported a League in principle, advocated amendments. Rumors came from Paris that the League was sidetracked. In a farewell at the Metropolitan Opera House, New York City, where Wilson and Taft spoke for the League, Wilson restated his determination to carry out the project as an integral part of the peace. On his return to Paris he attacked the problem of amendments to the Covenant. Suggestions made by the congressional committees, together with amendments cabled from Taft, Lowell, and Root, were used as the basis of these changes. Wilson was assured that these amendments would conciliate the moderate Republicans, who were then supporting Lodge.

Wilson adopted the substance of the five Taft amendments, three in very nearly the original language. These provided (1) that withdrawal from the League should be possible on two years' notice; (2) that armament standards should be revised every two years; (3) that unanimous consent should be required for decisions in the Council and the Assembly; (4) that the Monroe Doctrine should be reserved from the jurisdiction of the League; and (5) that domestic questions should be reserved from the jurisdiction of the League. Lowell's suggestions were used in making some adjustments of details in the modified Taft amendments.

The Root amendments provided for obligatory arbitration or adjudication of cases of justiciable character, codification of international law, reservation of the Monroe Doctrine, the right to terminate Article 10 after five years, definite inspection of national armament, and revision of the Covenant in from five to ten years. Part of these amendments duplicated the Taft amendments. In the article on international arbitration important changes were made in the direction of the Root suggestions but not going the full length of the Root amendment. On other points Wilson felt that either the original language or the amendments made covered all points sufficiently. This point of view is reasonably defensible except on two points: the codification of international law and the termination of Article 10. Considering the extent of the American changes and the difficulties of securing agreement of the other powers to the peculiar American national sensibilities, it must be left to history to answer whether it was not a remarkable performance to carry out the American amendments so completely. The other powers possessed their own groups of peculiar national sensibilities which they felt should be allowed for either in the Covenant or in the treaty settlement. With France it was a matter of security, or, in other words, fear, which must be considered above all other things. Part of the price of the foregoing amendments was the signing of treaties between France and Great Britain and the United States by which Great Britain and the United States were to go to the aid of France in case she was attacked by Germany. For France the guaranty in Article 10 was not strong enough; it had to be supplemented by the security treaties. This is a matter which must be taken into account in dealing with the Lodge reservations in the Senate later. It took time to work out these adjustments, and the revised Covenant was not ready for adoption by the Conference until April 28.

SUMMARY OF THE TREATY

The Political Settlements

The peace settlements and territorial adjustments are matters primarily connected with European history and must be summarized very briefly here. In a vivid sense the Franco-German frontier settlements were first in the minds of the Conference. France wished to separate the left bank of the Rhine from the remainder of Germany permanently. The theory was that whoever controls the Rhine controls Germany, and in the interest of French security France was determined to exercise that power. Great Britain and the United States opposed this extreme settlement in the interest of justice and the future stability of Europe. They feared the creation of another Alsace-Lorraine question. A compromise was at last arrived at, and the Rhineland Commission of five civilians was created to exercise Allied occupation of the territory for fifteen years. French security was further guaranteed by Article 10 of the Covenant and by the treaties entered into with Great Britain and the United States. France was forced also to surrender the plan for annexation

of the Saar coal field, and a plebiscite was arranged to be
held after fifteen years to determine whether the area should
be annexed to France or to Germany or whether the existing
régime should continue.

On the question of German reparations the British and the
French asked for the cost of the war; the United States
objected that the Fourteen Points as accepted and interpreted by the Allies in the agreement for the armistice were
a binding pledge to the Germans. These provided only for
"compensation for all damage done to the civilian population of the Allies." The result was a compromise which
included pensions, allowances, and the like. The United
States wished a fixed maximum sum, but in the end the
British and French refused. This left the greatest uncertainty in Germany in regard to future financial adjustments.
The reparations question was to be administered by an Interallied Commission.

Italy demanded the control of the Adriatic, including the
port of Fiume; Wilson demanded that Fiume must be open
as an outlet to the sea for the countries of central Europe
and be free from Italian control. Italy withdrew from the
Conference in protest. The matter was indefinitely postponed. The Japanese crisis threatened even more serious
results. Japan demanded fulfillment of the secret treaty
concerning Shantung and the German colonies. Wilson was
opposed. He wished the return of Shantung to China and
the release of China from the twenty-one demands which
had been imposed upon her in 1915. In the treaty, however,
he was obliged to consent to what were substantially the
terms of the secret treaty; but Japan gave assurances that
it would be her immediate policy to restore Shantung to
China in full sovereignty, retaining only the economic privileges granted to Germany and the right to establish a settlement under the usual conditions at Tsingtau, to withdraw
Japanese troops at the earliest possible time, and to use
Chinese for railway police.

The Economic Settlements

The economic settlements brought before the Conference two general types of problems. The first was the relation between the Allied and Associated Powers and the enemy powers. This was, properly speaking, the real work of making peace. The second was the future relations between the Allied powers and even between all powers after the peace. This may not seem at first sight to be a necessary part of a peace settlement; but the further this aspect is studied, the more vital it becomes. What was the use of making peace terms and repairing past maladjustments if future arrangements were omitted for preserving the new adjustments? At one of the early meetings of the Council of Ten (January 27) Wilson pointed out that he might meet difficulty in the Senate in securing ratification of the treaty if it went beyond the first type of problems. This was an indication of what was to follow so far as American policy was concerned.

It was on economic settlements that the Americans were least prepared. Wilson apparently did not expect to have to meet the question of post-war economic policies at the Conference. His conception of the settlement was primarily political — to make the immediate peace settlements and to set up machinery of future adjustment and international co-operation. As the Conference progressed, however, he was required more and more to meet problems of economic policies. Here the American record at the Conference is least defensible. Wilson was only partly to blame. When the more fundamental questions were stated to the Council of Ten as indicated above, he had given warning that the Senate would not readily agree to a treaty in which these problems were settled. Wilson had to reckon with American nationalistic economic policies, which were at variance with European practice on too many points, and on points where Americans were peculiarly sensitive and selfish.

The economic problems of the Conference can be divided on this basis into two general types : problems of immediate settlements and problems of permanent policy. In the first group were those questions relating to Germany : reparations, removal of blockade, famine relief, raw materials, and placing industry on a productive basis. Germany could not be expected to pay reparations unless she were granted the other points. In international finance a nation's capacity to pay depends upon its international trade. France stood out against these essential concessions to Germany. There was also the problem of territorial adjustments between France and Germany, especially the coal and iron territory. France stood for the full measure of punishment for Germany, and felt that if concessions were to be made they should be in colonies or world-trade privileges. This was particularly opposed by the British, who, of course, would have to sacrifice something. They urged France to make concessions. The upshot was that no comprehensive settlements were made, and the problems have been working themselves out gradually since.

Of the questions of permanent policy, the question of Allied debts was one which the Americans refused to meet, and additional credits were limited to the minimum by American policy. The other powers wished adjustment in the Peace Conference.

The question of equality of opportunity for trade, the removal of economic barriers, and freedom of transit opens up some of the most serious of post-war economic problems, especially as they relate to American policies. The third of Wilson's Fourteen Points included the first two phases of the question. It was promptly attacked in the United States by Republicans, who interpreted Wilson as proposing the abolition of the protective-tariff system. Wilson's answer was clear : that he intended only the establishment of conditions under which all nations should enjoy equal privileges. It was not intended to deprive a nation of full control over its own economic policy so long as this policy was applied equally to all. Even here Wilson was on dangerous ground, in view of the preferential tariff relations existing between the United States and Cuba. In his first two drafts of the Covenant of the League of Nations he omitted these points, but they appeared in modified form in the third. The British took up the Wilson program and added to it the question of freedom of transit, and in this form they and the United States supported it. France was opposed, as were other powers. It is true that in view of the economic position of the English-speaking powers, their international trade would be benefited by the adoption of these principles. Interest and idealism happened to fit together for them; but for some other powers (especially France) they did not. In its final form in the Covenant, "equal treatment" gave way to "equitable treatment," which is quite a different idea. The statement of principle was the most important thing accomplished with respect to these problems. The application was largely passed on for later negotiation and adjustment.

The whole American principle embodied in these policies may be summarized in two propositions: (1) the minimum of government association with international economic matters (laissez faire); (2) the establishment of conditions where individual enterprise might function freely and fully on a basis of equality. In Wilson's annual message in 1918 a very similar idea was outlined with respect to domestic policy. In all financial discussions this point of view was foremost, and this was the theory behind the principle of equal treatment and of removal of economic barriers. Government policy was essentially negative, and the removal of obstructions was left to individual initiative. It was on this point that the inadequacy of the American program was most evident, and in the post-war period the requirement of more positive action through international coöperation was increasingly recognized. Within this field of international economic coöperation there was, however, a most important aspect which must not be ignored. What form was such coöperation to take, and what was to be its purpose? National economic imperialism had proved most dangerous and unjust. If international coöperation meant merely international economic imperialism as a substitute for national imperialism, just where lay the advantage to civilization? Wilson was rightly very suspicious of certain French proposals on this general ground. The weakness of his position was that on most of these problems the Americans had little to offer except postponement.

By May 7 the first stage of the Peace Conference was over. The Allied and Associated Powers had agreed to the terms to be imposed upon defeated Germany. To this date the Germans had not been consulted. It had been strictly an Allied conference. Between May 7 and June 28 the negotiations with Germany were completed, and on the latter date the treaty was signed.

CHAPTER II

THE LEAGUE OF NATIONS: THE SENATE AND THE TREATY; THE TEST OF STRENGTH

(March 15 to November 19, 1919)

THE TREATY IN THE UNITED STATES: ORGANIZATION OF THE FORCES, MARCH 15 TO JUNE 28

WHILE the Peace Conference was engaged in the revision of the Covenant and in the completion of the terms of the treaty, the different factions in the United States were discussing the treaty and especially the League of Nations. They were organizing their forces and crystallizing public opinion on the subject. The defense was represented by such men as Attorney-General Palmer, Senator G. M. Hitchcock of Nebraska, and ex-President Taft. The ratification of the treaty was urged by prominent organized groups, such as business men, women's organizations, labor, and the Federal Council of Churches. In the opposition Senator Lodge declared that the amendments to the Covenant made it worse than before. Most of the criticisms mentioned earlier were still urged. Borah attacked it because it did not provide disarmament. He also criticized the position of the British Empire in the League and rehearsed the Irish question. Racial antipathies played their part. Senator Phelan (California, Democrat) opposed the League because of the Japanese question. James A. Reed (Missouri, Democrat) urged Jews to oppose it and also declared it a colored League, with yellow and brown races predominating.

What attitude would political parties take on the issue? Wilson addressed the Democratic National Committee at the White House on February 29, 1919, saying, "We ought not even to create the appearance of trying to make that [the League] a party issue." He suggested that the national and state committees get in touch with Republican committees, come to an understanding, and issue public statements of the course to be followed by both parties. Wilson stated his position on March 4, and on May 10 the Republican National Committee announced their intention that consideration of the treaty should be nonpartisan. From this time until after the test vote taken in November both parties adhered to the pledge, at least outwardly, although the actual alignment on the treaty followed party lines very closely. Borah and other irreconcilables were always, of course, exceptions which emphasize the prevalence of the rule. Borah announced on May 26 that the League should be made a party issue, and on June 21 stated that if such action were not taken he would bolt the party and organize a new one through which the people could express their sentiments.

The approach of the day set for the signing of the treaty at Paris (June 28) and Wilson's return, when the treaty would be officially presented to the Senate, tended to bring issues to a focus. Compromises had been made all along the line by all the countries concerned, to a point where the collapse of the whole Peace Conference seemed imminent. Wilson felt that it was a question of the whole treaty or none, and that changes by the United States Senate would be improper. "We ought either to go in," he said, "or stay out."

THE TREATY BEFORE THE SENATE, MAY 19 TO NOVEMBER 19, 1919

Wilson delayed the call for the special session of Congress until after the completion of the treaty and its presentation to the Germans on May 7. The call was issued May 8 for the meeting May 19. Although the treaty was not officially before the Senate, an unofficial copy was secured by Borah and read into the *Congressional Record* June 9. In this manner the country was familiarized with the terms of the treaty, especially as interpreted by its enemies.

The next important step was the presentation of a resolution by Philander C. Knox (Pennsylvania, Republican) June 10, providing for the separation of the League from the treaty. Knox had served in the cabinets of Presidents Roosevelt and Taft. He was now a member of the Senate Committee on Foreign Relations and chairman of the Committee on Rules. It was reported that the resolution had been drafted in consultation with Lodge. The essential points in the resolution were declarations that the Peace Conference had exceeded its authority in creating a League; that the Covenant should therefore be separated from the treaty, and in lieu thereof a declaration of policy should be made to the effect that if in the future the peace of Europe should be threatened the United States would regard such a situation with grave concern and as a menace to its own peace and freedom and would consult with the other powers with a view to devising means for the removal of the menace. Senator Hitchcock, for the Democrats, announced that he would filibuster against the resolution if there were any attempt to act on it before the treaty was officially presented. Lodge reported it from committee favorably on June 12.

A new turn was given to affairs by a letter from Elihu Root to Lodge dated June 19 but made public June 21. Root believed that the League and the treaty should be separated, and he therefore approved the Knox resolution; but he believed that in the absence of such action, there should be reservations to ratification which would protect America. He wrote:

Nothing has been done to provide for the establishment and strengthening of a system of arbitration or judicial decision upon questions of legal rights. Nothing has been done toward providing for a revision or development of international law. In these respects principles maintained by the United States without variation for half a century are still ignored, and we are left with a program which rests the hope of the world for future peace in a government of men and not of laws, following the dictates of expediency, and not of right.

The letter continued a catalogue of sins of omission: nothing was done to limit Article 10; the article on withdrawal left doubt concerning the fulfillment of obligations necessary for withdrawal; "the clause which has been inserted regarding the Monroe Doctrine is erroneous in its description of the doctrine and ambiguous in meaning." He considered immigration an American question which should be reserved. In his opinion the reservation of domestic questions was not broad enough, and Article 10 really should be omitted altogether. "On the other hand, it still remains that there is in the Covenant a great deal of high value that the world ought not to lose." He included in the letter a draft of a reservation and understandings which he considered necessary to remedy the defects of the Covenant:

This reservation and these expressions of understanding are in accordance with long-established precedent in the making of treaties. When included in the instrument of ratification they will not require a reopening of negotiations, but if none of the other signatories expressly objects to the ratification with such limitations, the treaty stands as limited between the United States and the other powers.

If any doubt were entertained as to the effect of such action, the doubt could be readily dispelled by calling upon the four other principal powers represented in the Council to state whether they do in fact object to the entrance of the United States into the League with the understanding and reservations stated in the resolutions.

The text of the Root reservation and understandings included in the letter follows:

The Senate of the United States advises and consents to the ratification of the said treaty with the following reservations and understandings to be made a part of the instrument of ratification; namely:

1. In advising and consenting to the ratification of the said treaty, the Senate reserves and excludes from its consent the tenth article of the covenant for the League of Nations, as to which the Senate refuses its consent.

2. The Senate consents to the ratification of the said treaty, reserving Article X, aforesaid, with the understanding that whenever two years' notice of withdrawal from the League of Nations shall have been given, as provided in Article I, no claim, charge, or finding that international obligations or obligations under the covenant have not been fulfilled will be deemed to render the two years' notice ineffectual or to keep the power giving the notice in the League after the expiration of the time specified in the notice.

3. Inasmuch as, in agreeing to become a member of the League of Nations, the United States of America is moved by no interest or wish to intrude upon or interfere with the political policy or international administration of any foreign State, and by no existing or anticipated dangers in the affairs of the American continents, but accedes to the wish of the European States that it shall join its power to theirs for the preservation of general peace, the Senate consents to the ratification of the said treaty, excepting Article X, aforesaid, with the understanding that nothing therein contained shall be construed to imply a relinquishment by the United States of America of its traditional attitude toward purely American questions, or to require the submission of its policy regarding questions which it deems to be purely American questions to the decision or recommendation of other powers.

The political significance of Root's letter was almost immediately recognized. The Knox resolution had placed the Republicans in an awkward position, and the Root plan gave them an avenue of escape — as one senator put it, "a mattress for the Republicans to fall on." It was rumored that Lodge would drop the Knox resolution for the Root plan. The next day (June 22) Lodge issued a statement in which he approved the Knox resolution:

I should like to bring the Knox resolution to a vote at once, but, after consultation with Senator Knox this afternoon, I have come to the conclusion that in the present situation of the appropriation bills, and especially the army bill, now before the Senate, we ought not to press the Knox resolution at this moment, because it will lead to debate, and nothing should be allowed to interfere with the passage of the appropriation bills before July 1. We propose to pass them before that date and shall sit night and day if necessary.

I am more willing to accept this postponement because the resolution is growing stronger daily, and the absolute necessity of amending the League, if it is to be made safe for the United States and for the cause of peace, has just been freshly demonstrated in Senator Root's letter with extraordinary force.

From this point the Knox resolution remained in the background. The procedure outlined in Root's letter became the Lodge plan of action. The second plan suggested by Root, that of securing the acceptance by four principal powers of the American reservations, was adopted in the preamble to the Lodge resolutions in November, 1919, and the first plan was adopted in the preamble of March, 1920. The Root reservation and understandings found their way in modified form into the Lodge reservations in November.

Wilson returned to the United States on July 8, and on July 10 presented the treaty officially to the Senate, asking for ratification. He pointed out that it was the result of compromise. "The treaty," he said, "as a result is not exactly what we would have written. It is probably not what any one of the national delegations would have written. But results were worked out which on the whole bear test." He indicated that at a later time he would present the special treaty of security with France.

There were essentially four points of view represented in the Senate and in the country at large, although no hard-and-fast classification of individuals can be made. The administration opposed any amendments, but it did not oppose reservations which would not modify the meaning of the treaty, provided such reservations should not be made a part of the instrument of ratification. Senator Hitchcock acted as administration leader. The opposite extreme was represented by the irreconcilables, — William E. Borah, Robert M.

La Follette (Senior), Hiram Johnson, James A. Reed of Missouri, and their associates. They opposed ratification in any form. Between the two extremes were two other factions. One was represented by Lodge, chairman of the Senate Committee on Foreign Relations. They advocated drastic changes in the form of amendments or reservations or both. The majority of the Republican members of the Senate were to be found here. The other faction believed in explanatory or interpretative reservations which would obviate any possibility of misunderstanding certain articles of the treaty. These men may be called mild reservationists. They included Republicans and Democrats, but among them were some distinct differences regarding the reservation on Article 10 and the Monroe Doctrine. Senator Porter J. McCumber (North Dakota) led the Republicans, and in the later stages of the campaign Hitchcock led the Democrats when unconditional ratification became impossible.

The activities of leading men outside the Senate had a bearing on the subject. The views of Charles E. Hughes are of particular interest because he later held the office of Secretary of State under Harding and Coolidge. His attitude was brought to public notice by a letter from Senator Hale of July 18 which Hughes answered July 24. The correspondence was published on July 29. Hughes favored a League; and although in his opinion the Covenant did not provide adequately for certain aims, nevertheless it went far enough to be worth supporting with proper definition and reservation. If the reservations were reasonable, they would place responsibility for rejection upon the opposition. They must then be accepted by the President. Four reservations were submitted as being suitable: two were similar to the Root understandings, and a third specified immigration and tariff as domestic questions which were to be reserved from the jurisdiction of the League. Hughes agreed with Root that Article 10 should be omitted altogether, but he differed from him in believing that it could be adequately clarified by the interpretative reservation which he was offering. Borah commented favorably on Hughes's letter and reservations but insisted that Article 11 was more dangerous than Article 10.

Hoover spoke strongly for the League in Paris on July 27, in New York on September 16, and, at the special request of Taft, at Palo Alto on October 2. He admitted that the treaty was not perfect,— that it could not be expected to be when it was realized that it was the product of five hundred minds; but, making due allowances, he maintained that "greater things were accomplished by this conference than any other in history," that the League was founded upon the intent to settle problems without military force, and that "the treaties themselves cannot be carried out without the League. If the League falls, the treaties also fall."

The story of the various issues on which the League and the treaty were attacked is too long to present in full, but in addition to the arguments which have already been indicated three others are referred to briefly at this point. Borah, for instance, made a vigorous attack on the League as an organ of big business and bankers. On June 30 he denounced a Republican round robin, signed by twenty-six men (including such men as Taft and Wickersham), as a Wall Street move to coerce New York senators to vote for the treaty. He charged Henry P. Davison, the chairman of the governing board of the World League of Red Cross Societies and a partner of J. P. Morgan, of securing a copy of the treaty from Thomas W. Lamont, a member of the American peace commission and also of the Morgan firm, before it was published in the United States, for the purpose of using such advance information for business purposes. Davison explained that his copy of the treaty was obtained because of his connection with the Red Cross work, which was affected by it, and that no member of his banking firm had seen the treaty or discussed it with him. Borah also charged that the Export Finance Corporation, then being organized, was started under government supervision as a "combination to exploit the natural resources of Europe." Senator W. E. Edge (New Jersey, Republican) explained that the purpose of the institution was to help meet the emergency of financing post-war exports during the disturbed transition period.

The question of China, Japan, and Shantung was another point of attack. Japan had publicly declared her intention to return Shantung to China. In the Peace Conference the German concessions were turned over to Japan with the definite understanding that the pledge would be fulfilled. These facts were made public during the Conference and were restated by the Japanese government in a public announcement on August 3. Nevertheless the question persisted, and appeared in the Senate reservations to the treaty in November.

The voting power of the British Empire was one of the most persistent of all points of argument against the League. The Covenant provided that self-governing colonies and dominions might be members. This gave the British Empire six votes in the Assembly. The United States had not granted self-government to its colonies and so was limited to one vote. This voting question and the agitation for self-government in Ireland were used as arguments against the League by all factions with anti-British proclivities.

Wilson presented his point of view to the Senate in a series of conferences with senators which began on July 17, and later (on August 19) he received the Senate Committee on Foreign Relations. He discussed the objections raised against the Covenant. It was explained that there was no objection to interpretative reservations so long as they were not made a part of the instrument of ratification. The Senate opposition presented its point of view in speeches and hostile requests for information, and later in public hearings between July 31 and September 12. In these hearings all phases of the President's activities at Paris were probed. It was on the last day of these hearings that

William C. Bullitt, a former member of the American delegation at Paris, testified that Secretary of State Lansing had said, "I believe that if the Senate could only understand what this treaty means, and if the American people could really understand, it would unquestionably be defeated, but I wonder if they will ever understand what it lets them in for." This statement, made while Wilson was in the West, was not publicly denied, although Lansing sent Wilson an explanation which denied it in part.

By the end of August the President had decided that it was useless to discuss the question further with the Senate and determined upon an appeal to the country. A tour of the Middle West and Far West was arranged, beginning September 3 and closing September 29. Borah, Johnson, and Reed trailed him, making opposition speeches. Wilson's health gave way on September 26, and the remaining speaking dates were canceled. From this time on, illness handicapped and even prevented his leadership of the remainder of the treaty fight. This fact must be remembered in dealing with the history of the succeeding months. It is always a question how far the President's health permitted him really to follow the details of developments.

The majority report of the Senate Committee on Foreign Relations was made by Lodge on September 10 and recommended forty-five amendments and four reservations. The reservations covered the right of withdrawal, Article 10, domestic questions, and the Monroe Doctrine. A minority report was presented September 11 without amendments or reservations. A third report was made by McCumber on September 15 with "mild reservations" only. It included six reservations, four of which were substitutes for the four majority reservations and the other two on Shantung and the voting power. Lodge had gone too far and was obliged to compromise with his faction. On October 24 he reported from committee fourteen reservations together with a preamble, dropping the question of amendments. On November 6 he moved the adoption of the revised report. Twelve of the fourteen reservations were adopted, two were rejected, and two new ones presented by McCumber and Lenroot were substituted by November 19.

The resolution of ratification is summarized below. The preamble provided that the ratification of the United States should not take effect until the American reservations were accepted by an exchange of notes by three of the four principal Allied powers. Reservation No. 1 made the United States sole judge as to whether its obligations have been fulfilled in case of withdrawal. No. 2 referred to Article 10 and declared that Congress alone had power to declare war or authorize the use of the military forces of the United States. No. 3 prohibited the acceptance of a mandate without the consent of Congress. No. 4 declared that the United States possessed the exclusive right of determining what questions are within its domestic jurisdiction. No. 5 declared that the Monroe Doctrine is interpreted by the United States alone, and questions relating to it as an element of foreign policy are reserved from the jurisdiction of the League. No. 6 withheld the assent of the United States to the Shantung settlement. No. 7 prohibited the appointment of representatives to any League position without the consent of the Senate. No. 8 repudiated any authority of the reparations commission to regulate trade between the United States and Germany without the consent of Congress. No. 9 denied any obligation to contribute to any expenses of the League or its agencies except with the consent of Congress. No. 10 reserved the right of the United States to increase its armament at will whenever it is threatened with invasion or engaged in war. No. 11 declared the right of the United States to regulate commercial relations with the nationals of a covenant-breaking state residing outside the state violating Article 16 of the Covenant. No. 12 was intended to protect the rights of American citizens under Articles 296 and 297 of the peace treaty. These articles have to do with debts and claims arising out of the war situation. No. 13 withheld consent to the section of the treaty creating the international labor organization unless Congress should act at a later time in the matter. By No. 14 the United States refused to be bound by any decision in which any empire should have cast more than one vote.

Just before the treaty came to a vote (November 19) Wilson sent to Hitchcock a letter in which he took the ground that the Lodge resolution of ratification "does not provide for ratification but rather for nullification of the treaty. . . . I trust that all true friends of the treaty will refuse to support the Lodge resolution."

On November 19 four significant votes were taken. The first was on the treaty with the Lodge reservations. The result was 39 for and 55 against the treaty with the reservations attached. As this was less than two thirds, the resolution of ratification was defeated. On reconsideration Hitchcock presented five reservations of a purely interpretative character. He moved to refer the treaty to the committee of the whole with instructions to report them back. His motion was lost by a vote of 41 to 50. These reservations had been previously indorsed by the Democratic party caucus. They covered the questions of withdrawal, domestic questions, the Monroe Doctrine, Article 10, and voting power. The third vote was a second attempt to ratify the treaty with the Lodge reservations attached, the vote being 41 for and 51 against. The fourth and last vote was on Underwood's motion to ratify the treaty without reservations. It was defeated 38 for to 53 against.

An analysis of the votes shows that the reservations themselves were adopted by votes which varied little from an average of 53 to 40. The irreconcilable senators voted consistently for the reservations. Their strength varied from 12 to 15, but for the most part stood at 14. In this way they made the resolution of ratification as objectionable as possible to supporters of the administration and mild reservationists. The irreconcilables did not want the treaty ratified in any form. In the votes of November 19 these men voted against the treaty with the reservations attached. The division of the Senate as revealed by this analysis gives from 38 to 41 votes to the supporters of the treaty with the Lodge reservations, from 31 to 41 to the supporters of the administration, and from 12 to 15 to the irreconcilables. With the Senate split three ways, it is clear that no group had so much as a majority and that a two-thirds majority was out of the question.

For the men of the generation then in power the decision on the League of Nations was the most important that any of them had ever been called upon to make. All groups showed unnecessary irritation, and personal animosities undoubtedly complicated the situation. It was not one group that was guilty, but all groups. Yet, considering the momentous nature of the decision to be taken, all groups were entitled to hold their respective positions until the issue was clearly and unequivocally joined and an indisputable answer rendered on each point. Logically, then, since all had failed to carry their points, a compromise was in order.

CHAPTER III

THE LEAGUE OF NATIONS: AN OPPORTUNITY FOR COMPROMISE

(November 19, 1919, to March 19, 1920)

THE REPUBLICAN ATTITUDE

ON THE status of the treaty after the votes of November 19 Lodge took the position that it was no longer in the hands of the Senate; that it was dead unless it was resubmitted by the President. The Senate had no further responsibility for it. This view was definitely expressed on at least two occasions — November 27 and December 8. This position seems indefensible. The Senate had not voted to return the treaty to the President. On the basis of Lodge's argument, if the treaty was no longer in the hands of the Senate after the three defeats of November 19, by what right did the Senate vote to reconsider it after one defeat or after two defeats?

It was Lodge's wish to submit the treaty to the voters as the campaign issue of 1920, and on November 21 he issued an appeal. He said, "There is no room for further compromise between Americanism and the supergovernment presented by the League." On November 23 moderate Republicans answered him by indicating that they disapproved of making the treaty a political issue. They expected a compromise and felt that compromise and ratification were necessary. The Republican National Committee was scheduled to meet December 7, and the Democratic soon after. Political questions would then begin to shape themselves.

Lodge answered (November 26) that the treaty would be ratified with the reservations when Wilson submitted it.

The procedure would be for the Committee on Foreign Relations to withhold the treaty until the Democrats had agreed as to its support in the Senate. "I have always stood for peace with Germany," he insisted, "and a League of Nations; but I stood for an honorable and victorious peace and a League of Nations that would not sacrifice America, its Constitution or its sovereignty." This treaty "would hand the United States over to a foreign tribunal to steer its political and economic course." "I am fighting Woodrow Wilson; that I am willing to admit." He also indorsed Calvin Coolidge, governor of Massachusetts, for president in 1920. On November 30 he stated that the treaty would have been ratified on November 19 except for Wilson's interference. He again defended the Senate reservations. "They do not nullify the treaty. They simply Americanize it." "They constitute the irreducible minimum." On December 18 he called a meeting of the Senate Committee on Foreign Relations for December 20, and restated his position on reservations. On December 23 he predicted that the Democrats would come over to his position.

Again Lodge had gone too far, not only for the Democrats but for the moderate Republicans. On December 18 press reports indicated that he was the only senator, except the irreconcilables, who assumed so extreme an attitude. The next day it was reported that Taft was working for a compromise independent of Lodge and Wilson, and had stated the basis of agreement in a letter to a senator, but what senator was not indicated. Root also was reported (December 23) as working for a compromise. On December 26 matters came to a crisis. Senator I. L. Lenroot (Wisconsin, Republican) was sent as envoy to serve notice on Lodge that unless he would make concessions and take action to assist in bringing about a compromise the moderate Republicans would repudiate his leadership and act for themselves. This was the status of affairs in the Republican camp at the end of the year.

THE DEMOCRATIC ATTITUDE

In Hitchcock's opinion the status of the treaty was that the votes on the treaty did not remove it from the jurisdiction of the Senate and that it was still in their hands awaiting final disposition. Hitchcock (November 21) disapproved the making of a political issue of the treaty. He said :

It appears to have become a question between patriotism and politics. The patriotic thing to do is to work out a compromise. . . . The vote would have been the same even if the President had not written his letter. I do not mean to say that the letter did not have some influence, but there would have been enough Democrats anyway to vote against the Lodge ratification resolution. . . . I do not think in this crisis that politics should be the issue when the interests of the country and the world are to be considered. The Democrats will work for a compromise. They will take the stand that the passage of the treaty is their supreme duty.

The next day he explained, further, that the Lodge reservations were not framed to ratify the treaty but to defeat it, that it was the irreconcilables who made these reservations possible, and that if the senators who wanted the treaty ratified got together it could be done.

After a visit to Nebraska, Hitchcock attacked the problem again. His conference with Wilson was postponed, but from previous conferences he felt confident (November 29) that Wilson would accept some modification of Article 10, which was the center of the whole issue. He said : "I do not know that Senator Lodge actually wants the treaty ratified. If he does, it can be done early in the next session by yielding by both sides. If the Republicans really desire it, they can save the treaty." On December 13 it was reported that Wilson was immovable, but Hitchcock proposed a committee on conciliation to work out an agreement before the treaty was called up in the Senate. He had proposed five reservations to Wilson, but on December 18 he had heard nothing. Smith of Georgia suggested a bipartisan conference to which Lodge and Hitchcock should not be invited.

The situation in the Democratic party was unfavorable to any immediate action, however. The death of Senator Martin had left the question of leadership in the Senate open, and Hitchcock and Underwood were rivals. This question would not be decided until January 15, and until that time Democratic action was difficult. It became known (December 31) that Wilson was gathering information for the purpose of determining his position, and Joseph P. Tumulty, the President's private secretary, on his own responsibility interviewed Hitchcock. It became a question whether Wilson had abandoned his hands-off policy regarding the treaty. The answer came January 8 in Wilson's letter to the Jackson Day dinner. He was unable to attend, but his message stated his views : "If there is any doubt as to what the people of the country think on this matter, the clear and single way out is to submit it for determination at the next election to the voters of the nation, to give the next election the form of a great and solemn referendum." Bryan took issue with this point of view in his speech at the dinner. He insisted that the treaty should be ratified immediately by compromise. The party could not go before the country on the issue raised by Article 10 ; and since the Republicans were in control he insisted that they should be given the responsibility for action — either ratification or defeat. "A majority of Congress," he said, "can declare war. Shall we make it more difficult to conclude a treaty than to enter a war?"

THE BIPARTISAN CONFERENCE TO EFFECT A COMPROMISE, JANUARY 15–30, 1920

By the middle of the month the situation began to crystallize. Senators Robert L. Owen (Oklahoma, Democrat) and William S. Kenyon (Iowa, Republican) started a movement to secure the appointment of eight senators from each party to work out a compromise. Hitchcock was consulted and went with the proposal to Lodge, who agreed to a bipartisan conference of a less formal nature. On the next day Hitchcock, Owen, Simmons (North Carolina), McKellar (Tennessee) and Walsh (Montana), Democrats, went to Lodge's office, where they met him and three of his associates,— Lenroot, Kellogg (Minnesota), and New (Indiana). The Lodge reservations were made the basis of discussion. It was January 21 before they reached Article 10, and then it was said that the conference would have broken up but for the action of Simmons, who secured an adjournment because of the acuteness of the situation. The next day, reports indicated that there was hope of agreement; but before the next meeting there was another crisis, which possibly changed the situation.

The irreconcilable senators Hiram Johnson (California, Republican) and William E. Borah interpreted the reports of the near agreement of January 22 as meaning that Lodge was about to surrender on Article 10. A protest meeting was arranged to convene in Johnson's office at the hour of the next bipartisan conference. It was attended by Johnson, Borah, L. Y. Sherman (Illinois), Knox, F. B. Brandegee (Connecticut), G. H. Moses (New Hampshire), Medill McCormick (Illinois), and Miles Poindexter (Washington). Lodge was sent for. He excused himself from the bipartisan meeting, telephoning later that he could not meet them at all that day. This was Friday. On Saturday the meeting was again postponed, and no meeting was held until Monday, January 26. Lodge then made a definite statement which was interpreted as an ultimatum that the Lodge reservations as adopted must be accepted on Article 10 and the Monroe Doctrine, and without change. The session ended. No further meeting was held until Thursday, January 29. On the day before this meeting Hitchcock made public the tentative agreements which had been accepted for purposes of negotiation so far as the conferences had gone. They showed that there had been distinct progress toward compromise. The irreconcilables met again Friday, January 30. Hitchcock read Taft's compromise reservation on Article 10. Lodge refused to consider it. The conferences then ended quietly.

Had there been any genuine intention of compromise, or was it all just a comedy played out to the end for the entertainment of the audience and, incidentally, for the improvement of strategic political positions?

Hitchcock's position seems reasonably secure. He had three propositions any one of which he appears to have been willing to adopt, and the evidence available seems to confirm his sincerity. First, there were his reservations of November. These he had submitted to Wilson, and they were accepted in a letter January 26. Secondly, he submitted the reservation on Article 10 which was thought to be so near acceptance on January 22 by the bipartisan conference. Wilson answered: "To the substance of it I, of course, adhere. . . . But I think the form of it very unfortunate." The text of this resolution follows:

The United States assumes no obligations to employ its military or naval forces or the economic boycott to preserve the territorial integrity or the political independence of any other country under the provisions of Article 10, or to employ the military or naval forces of the United States under any article of the treaty for any purpose, unless in any particular case the Congress, which, under the Constitution, has the sole power to declare war, or authorize the employment of the military or naval forces of the United States, shall by act or joint resolution so provide. Nothing herein shall be deemed to impair the obligation in Article 16 concerning the economic boycott.

Hitchcock's third compromise was the Taft reservation:

The United States declines to assume any legal or binding obligation to preserve the territorial integrity or political independence of any other country under the provisions of Article 10, or to employ the military or naval forces of the United States under any article of the treaty for any purpose. But the Congress, which under the Constitution has the sole power in the premises, will consider and decide what moral obligation, if any, under the circumstances of any particular case, when it arises, should move the United States in the interest of world peace and justice to take action therein, and will provide accordingly.

Lodge's case is more complicated. It will be remembered that in December the mild Republicans had served notice of the necessity of compromise. Then when Lodge was approached by Hitchcock in January he consented. The *New York Times* correspondent had some interesting remarks on the second day's proceedings. The Democrats, he said, were given to understand that some points were discussible and that some, like Article 10, were not. "Mr. Lodge's attitude appeared to be that of tolerance and amusement about the whole matter. He indicated that he would do nothing to stop the pleasant conferences, now proceeding, by becoming blunt." But this observer may have been prejudiced. One Democratic senator criticized the selection of Republicans, giving it as his opinion that only one of them even wished to see the treaty ratified. A Lodge senator a few days later explained that Lodge could not refuse to hold conferences and would not break them up. He could not afford to be placed in a position where it would appear that he would not compromise. The conferences must go on until the Democrats became fully convinced that he stood just where he had always stood and until the Democrats broke off negotiations. A mild reservationist is quoted as saying: "We are going to give those 'impossibles' who are meeting in Senator Lodge's office a day longer. They can't agree in a thousand years." Did the protest meeting of the irreconcilables, then, change Lodge's position? Lodge himself said not. His explanation was that his "ultimatum" to the Democrats did not represent a change in position, that they were not near an agreement, and that he had told them from the very beginning that there could be no yielding in principle. After

the conference broke up on January 30 he issued the following statement of his position :

Speaking for myself alone, I have only this to say, that I was
unable to agree to any change in reservations Nos. 2 and 5, dealing
with Article 10 and the Monroe Doctrine. In my opinion reservation No. 2, which provides that we shall assume no obligation of
any kind under Article 10, except the one mentioned in the treaty,
that we should ourselves respect the boundaries of other nations,
cannot possibly permit change.

The change proposed in reservation No. 5 in regard to the Monroe
Doctrine was an absolutely vital one because it was asserted as an
official interpretation by the representatives of Great Britain that
the Monroe Doctrine under the treaty was to be interpreted by the
League. To this I for one could never assent, and in view of the
statement made in Paris by the British delegation, to which I have
referred, I regard the line which it was proposed to strike out as
absolutely necessary.

The United States has always interpreted the Monroe Doctrine
alone. It is our policy. No one else has ever attempted to interpret
it, and it is something which in my judgment ought never to be permitted even by the most remote implication.

If we should strike out that phrase now after it has been accepted
by the Senate, it would lead to a direct inference that we left that
question open. The right to interpret the Monroe Doctrine [as]
pertaining to the United States alone must never be open to question.

The mild reservation Republicans warned that they would
not wait for Lodge and threatened (January 26) to call up
the treaty in the Senate. Their position seems consistent.
Again, what of the irreconcilables? Why had they become
the self-appointed guardians of the Lodge reservations when
they opposed the treaty in any form? One of them explained
that eventually they expected to see the Democrats come
over to the Lodge reservations and ratify the treaty. In
that case they could not consent to see anything less than
the Lodge program accepted.

RECONSIDERATION IN THE SENATE

As early as January 28, Hitchcock indicated that if the compromise conferences broke up he would move the reconsideration of the treaty in the Senate. This notice to call up the treaty on February 10 was formally given January 31 by Walsh of Montana in the absence of Hitchcock. Lodge countered this move by announcing in the press (February 2) that he would call up the treaty. His notice was given to the Senate on February 3 to call up the treaty on February 9.

With the date set for action, negotiations were rushed among the various groups to determine their respective lines of action. On February 7 Hitchcock presented to the Democratic caucus the January correspondence with Wilson in which the latter accepted Hitchcock's reservations and expressed approval in substance of the bipartisan scheme submitted. This seemed to offer a solid basis of compromise, if the interpretation placed upon Wilson's letter was correct. On this point, however, there is serious doubt. Hitchcock would probably also present part or all of his November resolutions.

The moderate Republicans were meeting in a room adjoining the Democrats. They prepared their drafts of reservations regarding Article 10 to present to Lodge, and it was understood that they would work with him and would not negotiate directly with the Democrats or offer their reservations independently. It was reported that the irreconcilables Moses, Sherman, and McCormick agreed to vote with Lodge if the mild Republicans would coöperate. Lodge's program was to refer the treaty to the Committee on Foreign Relations for immediate report with his reservations of the previous November. The purpose of the move was purely technical, to remove the cloture imposed in November. He would then move some modifications of the November resolutions, probably in line with those considered by the bipartisan conferences. He held that they had agreed on five of the nine tentatively accepted reservations — the preamble, domestic questions, Shantung, the appointment of American representatives, and disarmament, — but not on withdrawal, expenses, the treatment of nationals, and voting power. As to this report of progress, however, there was some disagreement.

During the ten days in which these preparations were being made, an unusual element had been suddenly injected into the situation. Lord Grey, special ambassador to the United States, had been very much interested in the treaty. On January 1 the press had commented on a report that Henry White, former member of the peace commission, who had just returned from Europe, had stated that the reservation on voting had caused such opposition in the British dominions that pressure was being exerted on the government at London. Hitchcock is reported to have consulted Grey on the subject. On February 1 the *New York Times* printed a letter of Lord Grey, who meanwhile had returned to England. In this letter he analyzed the American situation, pointing out that there should be no charge of bad faith because of the slowness of American action. Two factors ought to be taken into consideration : the force of American tradition and the peculiar nature of the American Constitution. He considered that the aid of the United States was essential and hence that even though some of the Senate reservations were material changes of the terms of the Covenant, they should be accepted by the powers, with one exception. On the question of the voting powers of self-governing dominions and colonies he said Great Britain can admit "no qualification whatever of that right." It was known that Grey was officially accredited to the United States in a diplomatic capacity, but was technically on leave. His letter was explained as being written in a private capacity and as an expression of personal views. It was pointed out by observers, however, that such a letter would hardly have been published by Grey unless it had been shown to the British government and approved.

The letter was generally interpreted in the United States as being an encouragement to the Lodge faction, and little was said of the exception respecting voting. Rumors then circulated freely that senators had had assurances from both Great Britain and France some weeks earlier that those governments would accept the Lodge reservations. In one case a senator is reported as quoting what he alleged to be a telegram from Lloyd George accepting the Lodge reservations. On February 6 an official denial was made from London.

It is difficult to estimate what influence the Grey episode had in the treaty situation, if any. Some reports said that it was the Grey letter which prompted Lodge to give notice to call up the treaty. On this point, however, it should be remembered that Hitchcock had already made such an announcement, and reports indicated that moderate Republicans would support such a move. If the treaty was to be considered at all, it was to Lodge's advantage to have charge of it, with such support as he could get from the moderate Republicans and irreconcilables.

On February 9 unanimous consent to reconsider the treaty was blocked by Borah. The consent of the Senate was then secured by suspension of the rules by a vote of 63 to 9. Lodge moved to refer the treaty to the Committee on Foreign Relations, with instructions to report it back immediately with the resolutions adopted in November. Hitchcock objected, and asked that the reference be changed to report without recommendations. Lodge then stated his position so definitely that there should have been no misunderstanding it: "Whatever we do in the Senate will be done through modification of the reservations formerly adopted." Lodge had his way, and on February 11 the treaty was so reported.

It was rumored on February 12 that Wilson had sufficiently recovered his health to resume direction of the executive offices and meet his cabinet. This was followed almost immediately by the dismissal of Lansing on February 13, announced the same day. The correspondence between Wilson and Lansing, from February 7, when Wilson inquired as to the truth of the reports that Lansing had held cabinet meetings, to the acceptance of Lansing's resignation, was published in full. The whole episode was used against Wilson and the treaty. During the succeeding weeks the Italian crisis was pending, and this furnished further opportunities of attack.

During the period of reconsideration the Canadian government lodged protest with London in regard to the acceptance of the reservation on voting; and on three other occasions responsible government officials expressed themselves publicly to the effect that if such changes as were contemplated in the Lodge reservation should be accepted by the League, Canada would immediately withdraw.

At the opening of the reconsideration Lodge presented certain amendments to the resolutions adopted in November. The Democrats presented (February 13) two drafts of reservations on Article 10, together with a statement signed by twenty-eight Democratic senators pledging support to either draft. The Republicans were asked to make their choice. The two drafts presented were the bipartisan draft and the Taft draft of January. Hitchcock warned that debate would be futile unless they first agreed on the reservations dealing with Article 10. Lodge answered that he would let the debate go on awhile. It was reported February 28 that Wilson would refuse to deposit ratifications of the treaty if it should be adopted with the Lodge reservations. Borah announced on February 29 that he with his associates would bolt if concessions were made on Article 10. Meanwhile the debate was going on, and between February 21 and March 19 the voting on reservations proceeded. Again Wilson wrote a letter to Hitchcock (March 8) in which he declared that Article 10 was the heart of the Covenant, and that without it the Covenant was hardly more than a scrap of paper, as ineffective as the Belgian treaty had been in 1914. The new reservations contained seven of the November resolutions unchanged, three amended, four substitutes, and one additional reservation which expressed sympathy with the aspirations of Ireland. The preamble was amended to provide that the treaty should become effective if no objections were made to the reservations before the deposit of ratifications.

The final vote on the treaty with the reservations was had March 19 and resulted in 49 for ratification and 35 against, twelve senators being absent. The vote was made up of twenty-eight Republicans and twenty-one Democrats in the affirmative and twelve irreconcilables and twenty-three Democrats in the negative. Here again the irreconcilables had voted for the reservations in order to secure their adoption and then voted against the treaty with the reservations attached.

Immediately after the vote Lodge moved a resolution to return the treaty to the President. The resolution was adopted 47 to 37. Robinson of Arkansas moved a reconsideration. The moderate Republicans joined the Democrats in defeating an attempt to table the motion, and it was defeated 34 to 42. Cummins, in the chair, ruled Robinson's motion out of order. Lodge then offered to move to reconsider if the Democrats would agree to vote immediately. Hitchcock asked for a few days for a cooling-off period. Lodge refused. Robinson again offered his motion, with a request that the President should resubmit the treaty. The moderate Republicans refused to coöperate further, and the resolution was withdrawn. The Senate adjourned. Lodge announced after adjournment, "If the President desires to make a campaign issue on the treaty, the Republicans are willing to meet that issue."

Would the European powers have accepted the American ratification on the basis of the Lodge reservations? It is evident that the British Empire would not have accepted the fourteenth reservation. There is good reason to believe, although the evidence is not specific, that France would not have accepted the reservations on account of the question of

French security; it should be remembered that in the Peace Conference she had insisted that the pledges in the Covenant were not sufficient guaranty for her security, and it had been necessary for Great Britain and the United States to make additional pledges contained in the security treaties. By these agreements both states pledged to go to the assistance of France in case she were attacked. The fight in the United States on the peace treaty made it evident that a ratification of the security treaty was out of the question. If there is any reliable evidence that France would have accepted this situation as a price of the entrance of the United States into the League with reservations attached, it has not been made public.

Peace by Resolution (?)

Having failed to ratify the peace treaty with the Lodge reservations, the Republicans decided that a treaty was not necessary, after all, since the country was really at peace. A joint resolution was introduced in the Senate by Knox in December, 1919, and later a similar one in the House. The House resolution was passed April 9 by a vote of 242 to 150. In the Senate it was redrafted by Knox, and on April 30 was favorably reported from committee by Lodge on a partisan vote. The resolution repealed the declaration of war against Germany and declared the state of war to be at an end. All enemy property was to be retained until a treaty was made providing suitable arrangements for the settlement of all claims against the German government. The President was directed to negotiate a treaty immediately. The effective date of this resolution was to become the official date for fixing the time at which war and emergency legislation should cease to be in effect. The resolution also declared that the United States does not "waive any of the rights, privileges, indemnities, reparations, or advantages to which it or its nationals have become entitled" under the terms of the armistice or the Treaty of Versailles. The last section of the resolution declared the termination of the war with Austria, American rights to be reserved.

On May 13 the paragraph requesting the negotiation of a separate treaty with Germany was dropped from the resolution on Lodge's motion, and two days later (May 15) the resolution was adopted by a vote of 43 to 38. On May 21 the House adopted the Knox version by a vote of 228 to 139. It was said that this haste in passing the resolution was intended to force a veto before the Republican convention should meet. If that was the intention it succeeded, for Wilson returned the measure with his veto on May 27. The House failed to pass it over the veto.

Wickersham, in an article in *Current History* for June, 1920, criticized the resolution from the standpoint of international law. If it had stopped short with a mere declaration of the end of the war, it could not have been seriously challenged; but the provisions in regard to enemy property were contrary to recognized international law respecting civilized warfare and especially contrary to American traditions. This objection was the more serious in view of the purpose of the United States in entering the war in defense of its nationals and their property from unlawful destruction or seizure in time of war.

There was also a separate attempt to repeal war legislation by fixing a date which should be interpreted as the end of the war for the purpose of terminating such statutes as were to expire by limitation at the end of the war. Two measures were excepted from this provision, the Lever Food and Fuel Act and the Trading with the Enemy Act. The House passed the joint resolution June 3 by a vote of 343 to 3, and the Senate June 4 by a viva voce vote. The President failed to sign it, and Congress adjourned the next day; so the resolution was lost.

CHAPTER IV

THE LEAGUE AND THE CAMPAIGN OF 1920

WHEN the campaign was well under way, Wilson wrote a letter to Oregon Democrats in which he declared "that the party should at once proclaim itself the uncompromising champion of the nation's honor . . . and indorse and support the Versailles treaty and condemn the Lodge resolutions. . . ." The Democratic platform announced that its party favored the League of Nations: "We advocate the immediate ratification of the treaty without reservations which would impair its essential integrity." The Republican platform declared:

The Republican party stands for agreement among the nations to preserve the peace of the world. . . . We believe that all this can be done without the compromise of national independence. . . . The Covenant signed by the President at Paris failed signally to accomplish this great purpose, and contains stipulations not only intolerable for an independent people but certain to produce the injustice, hostility, and controversy among nations which it proposed to prevent. The senators performed their duty faithfully. We approve their conduct and honor their courage and fidelity.

Cox, the Democratic nominee, accepted the League as an issue and advocated its ratification with or without reservations. The element of doubt that was left in his program throughout the campaign was the exact extent of the reservations he would be willing to accept.

The chief point of interest in the campaign was the position of Harding and the Republican party. The mystery was not explained even to the day of election. Harding, in a statement of July 13, accepted Cox's challenge to make the campaign a referendum on the League. In his formal speech of acceptance (July 22) he seemed to stand on the Lodge reservations in that he indorsed the action of the Senate; but he said also:

It will avail nothing to discuss in detail the League Covenant, which was conceived for world supergovernment, negotiated in misunderstanding, and intolerantly urged and demanded by its administration sponsors, who resisted every effort to safeguard America, and who finally rejected it when such safeguards were inserted.

He did not repudiate the League specifically if American nationality were properly safeguarded, neither did he say definitely that he would accept it with the Lodge reservations. On August 20 he referred to the work of Root and the drafting of the statute of the World Court. It was hinted that this might become the center of his program for an association of nations. Apparently Harding did not understand that it was a League commission which was at work on the Court. In another speech (August 28) he went into the question further, but he shifted his ground:

The Democratic nominee has flatly said he is in favor of going in [the League]. I am not. This is the whole difference between us. But it is a most vital one, because it involves the disparity between a world court of justice supplemented by a world association for conference on the one hand, and the Council of the League on the other.... It [the League] has already been abandoned by Europe.

Harding said that his scheme would be worked out in consultation with a committee of the Senate or of the leading minds of the country, and that he would take such parts of the Hague Tribunal and of the League of Nations as he could "use properly and advantageously."

I would take and combine all that is good and excise all that is bad from both organizations. This statement is broad enough to include the suggestion that if the League, which has heretofore riveted our considerations and apprehensions, has been so entwined into the peace of Europe that its good must be preserved in order to stabilize the peace of that continent, then it can be amended or revised.

The two paragraphs quoted are contradictory, but they illustrate the way in which Harding's campaign speeches were constructed. The speeches thus far in the campaign did not satisfy the irreconcilable element in the party, and it was considered necessary to bring them into the canvass in full force. Harding declared at Des Moines : "I do not want to clarify these obligations ; I want to turn my back on them. It is not interpretation, but rejection, that I am seeking." The public was confused, and rightly so, as to just what Harding did stand for beyond his desire to be elected. He attempted to clear up the matter in a statement (October 12) summarizing his position as expounded in the series of speeches on his Middle Western trip. The only definite point in the summary was the sentence "I am unalterably opposed to going into the League of Nations as that particular proposition now stands." The next day he declared, "There has been and will be no change from the position of August 28," adding that "if read in full" the Des Moines speech is "in complete harmony."

The test of campaign speeches is in the effect that they have on the voters and not in their substance or logical consistency. The extreme differences in point of view within the Republican party made any definite stand on the League impossible. Taft chose to support Harding not because he opposed the League, but because he thought Harding would stand for ratification in some form. The Senate would be Republican without doubt, and a Republican president, he thought, would be in a stronger position than a Democratic one to secure the approval of the treaty. This statement was made during the first week in August. Hoover, also a strong League advocate, entered the campaign very late (October 9) in a speech at Indianapolis. His ground was that the party was pledged to put the ideal of the League into effect, and he believed it could be trusted. He said, "I do not believe it would fail, or I would not be here this moment" ; that the League was so entwined in the world's affairs that "Republican statesmanship must build upon the foundations of the existing treaty, and include in it the great step forward in international justice now settled by Senator Root." A group of thirty-one friends of the League, among them Hoover, Hughes, Lowell, Root, and Wickersham, published a signed statement dated October 14 pledging support to Harding. They based their decision on Harding's promises in the speech of August 28.

The irreconcilables were in even greater difficulty. Borah received Harding's speech of acceptance in silence. He refused to comment when his views were asked by reporters. He declared the Des Moines speech to be a "great speech." Johnson on July 19 expressed a hope that Harding would not evade the issue in his speech of acceptance, and after the speech he expressed his full approval of Harding's position. He did not enter the campaign, however, until after the Des Moines speech. Then it was announced from Chicago that he would enter actively.

In the election in November the Harding plurality over Cox was approximately six million votes. Of course the question arose whether the election was a repudiation of the League or an indorsement of it. Harding interpreted it, in his special message to Congress of April 12, 1921, as a positive repudiation of the League. He said, "There can be no misinterpretation and there will be no betrayal of the deliberate expression of the American people." To all intents and purposes he had gone over to the irreconcilable position. With Coolidge, the vice president, the case was different. He said : "I doubt if any particular mandate was given at the last election on the question of the League of Nations. . . . You can't say there was a preponderance of votes against the League of Nations."

In repudiating the League and the treaty outright it was necessary to do something in regard to the relations between the United States and the enemy powers. Harding recommended a declaratory resolution by Congress "to establish the state of technical peace" and to confirm American rights and interests as already provided in the peace treaty. For the purposes of terminating war legislation an act had been passed March 3, 1921, establishing that date as the end of the war. All emergency war acts, unless otherwise provided, would automatically expire. This had been done at the end of the Wilson administration. Knox's peace resolution was now revived and received the approval of the President (July 2, 1921). It was drafted in two parts, to apply separately to Germany and Austria. There were three principal provisions : (1) the declaration of the end of the war, (2) the reservation to the United States of all rights and advantages to which it was entitled under the Treaty of Versailles, and (3) the retention of all enemy property until treaties were negotiated with Germany and Austria in settlement of claims. Such treaties were ratified by the Senate on October 18, 1921. In ratifying the German treaty a reservation was added prohibiting the president from appointing representatives to serve on any League commission or agency without the consent of the Senate. This proviso was an expansion of a similar restriction imposed upon the president's conduct of foreign affairs by a rider on the general deficiency appropriation act of 1913. At that time it was provided that "hereafter the Executive shall not extend or accept any invitation to participate in any international congress, conference, or like event, without first having specific authority of law to do so."

The primary arguments against the League had been (1) violation of national sovereignty, (2) violation of the Monroe Doctrine, and (3) violation of the constitutional right of Congress to declare war. In support of the argument for isolation Washington's Farewell Address was used probably more frequently than any other document except the Monroe Doctrine. Although the emotional appeal to the public was most effective, it contains little historical basis. In evaluating Washington's expressions of this type it is necessary to bear in mind the position of the infant republic. What bearing that situation had upon the problems of one hundred and twenty-five years later is very remote. The propagandist naturally quotes only such things as serve his purpose, whatever else there may be to the contrary. About the time of the address Washington said also that, given ten years of peace, the United States could hold its own with the nations of the world. At another time he said that when American institutions were firmly established, the United States "might safely and perhaps beneficially take part in the consultations held by foreign states for the advantage of the nations."

In addition to the arguments, there was the personal element — an extreme hostility to Wilson. This was due partly to the inevitable reaction against the abnormal powers exercised by the president in time of war (Lincoln had suffered most acutely from such hostility and abuse); partly to Wilson's individual peculiarities, which alienated or infuriated his opponents; and partly to petty partisan rancor of Republican against Democrat.

While the League controversy was being waged in the United States other nations ratified the peace treaty. The French government (January 10, 1920) certified that sufficient powers had ratified to meet the stipulated requirements for the completion of organization. Wilson, as had been provided, issued the official call on January 13 for the first meeting of the Council. On January 16 the Council met, and the League became a reality. Practically all the states except the United States, Russia, Turkey, Mexico, and a few small powers joined the League. The League being the only available instrument of world government, most of the international problems after 1920 were conducted through its machinery. The United States was obliged to coöperate in some manner with the League.

After Wilson's death, on February 3, 1924, a tablet was erected at Geneva inscribed "To the memory of Woodrow

Wilson, Founder of the League of Nations." Upon him alone, among citizens of the United States of America, could such an international distinction be conferred. Washington and Lincoln are peculiarly national heroes; Woodrow Wilson belongs not to America only, but to the world.

SELECTED BIBLIOGRAPHY

NOTE. The books are arranged as nearly as practical in the order in which the subject matter appears in the chapter.

GOOCH, G. P. History of Modern Europe, 1878–1919. Henry Holt and Company, 1923.

BUELL, RAYMOND LESLIE. Europe: a History of Ten Years. The Macmillan Company, 1928.

TEMPERLEY, H. W. V. A History of the Peace Conference at Paris. 6 vols. Oxford University Press, London, 1920.

BAKER, RAY STANNARD. Woodrow Wilson and the World Settlement. 3 vols. Doubleday, Page & Company, 1922.

WILSON, WOODROW. Public Papers. 6 vols. Harper & Brothers, 1925–1927.

MILLER, DAVID HUNTER. The Drafting of the Covenant. 2 vols. G. P. Putnam's Sons, 1928.

HOUSE, E. M. The Intimate Papers of Colonel House. Arranged by Charles Seymour. 4 vols. Houghton Mifflin Company, 1926, 1928.

HOWARD-ELLIS, C. The Origin, Structure, and Work of the League of Nations. Houghton Mifflin Company, 1928.

LANSING, ROBERT. The Peace Negotiations. Houghton Mifflin Company, 1921.

HASKINS, C. H., and LORD, R. H. Some Problems of the Peace Conference. Harvard University Press, Cambridge, 1920.

HOUSE, E. M., and SEYMOUR, CHARLES. What Really Happened at Paris. Charles Scribner's Sons, 1921.

BARUCH, BERNARD M. The Making of the Economic Sections of the Treaty. Harper & Brothers, 1920.

BASSETT, JOHN SPENCER. The League of Nations. Longmans, Green & Co., 1928.

KELLOR, FRANCES, and HATVANY, ANTONIA. Security against War. 2 vols. The Macmillan Company, 1924.

LODGE, HENRY CABOT. The Senate and the League of Nations. Charles Scribner's Sons, 1925.

Pamphlets of the American Association for International Conciliation (later International Conciliation Series of the Carnegie Endowment for International Peace, New York) and of the World Peace Foundation, Boston. The latter organization is agent in the United States for the publications of the League of Nations and of the Permanent Court of International Justice.

CHAPTER V

THE PERMANENT COURT OF INTERNATIONAL JUSTICE: ORGANIZATION

INASMUCH as there is great confusion concerning the differences between the several methods of peaceful settlement of disputes, a brief explanation will somewhat clarify the following discussion. *Mediation* is friendly action on the part of third parties taken with a view to bringing the disputants together on some common ground of understanding and to making possible the settlement of their differences with each other. The essential point to remember here is that the settlement remains in the hands of the disputants. The second and third methods, *arbitration* and *adjudication*, are not so easily defined. In the earlier literature on international peace there was no clear distinction, and there is some confusion or indefiniteness yet. There is, however, a very fundamental difference in the principles offered, whatever the terminology. James Scott Brown makes the following distinction:

In arbitration the parties define the question and submit the issue to arbiters of their own choice; in a judicial settlement each party states its case to the court, which frames the issue and decides it by judges chosen in advance and without reference to the dispute. In arbitration both parties must appear before the tribunal; in judicial procedure one party may submit the case, present the facts, argue the law, and obtain judgment against the other party duly summoned but not appearing.

Other points may be added to these. Arbitration, as practiced, requires special agreements between the parties, and the principles to be applied by the arbiters may be specially defined by the disputants for the purpose of the particular case and in terms which are quite at variance with international law as it would be applied by a court. In arbitration the arbiters may be men of limited training in international law, and the political considerations involved may result in the arbiters' acting more as diplomats than as judges. There is a lack of stability in the personnel and a lack of continuity in procedure and legal principles, inasmuch as each arbitration court is created separately for each dispute. In a permanent court, continuity and unity of action are more fully realized. Root made a general distinction that is worth remembering. Mediation and arbitration represent a government of men in international affairs, whereas the purpose of a permanent court is to establish a government of law. According to these distinctions it is clear that the Hague Tribunal is not a court in the strict sense. Each nation was authorized to nominate judges (a maximum of four), from which nations might choose boards of arbitration for particular disputes. The so-called court is only a panel of about one hundred and twenty men, from which arbiters may be selected on occasion. In the very nature of the case, few of this number were ever called upon to serve.

The Covenant of the League contained the following provisions, which have a direct bearing upon the Permanent Court of International Justice. The second and third paragraphs of Article 13 defined the nature of disputes which were considered suitable for arbitration. Here the term "arbitration" is evidently intended to include both arbitration and adjudication. Article 14 provided that "the Council shall formulate and submit to the members of the League for adoption plans for the establishment of a Permanent Court of International Justice." The Council undertook the fulfillment of the obligation promptly. Its first meeting was held January 16, 1920, and on February 13 the Advisory Committee of Jurists, ten in number, was set up. Among those selected was Elihu Root, of the United States. This committee met June 16 at the Hague and ended its work July 24. The basis of discussion, on Root's suggestion, was the draft scheme for a permanent Judicial Arbitration Court drawn up at the second Hague Conference in 1907. The completed draft statute of the Court was submitted by the committee to the Council and transmitted to the members of the League under the date of August 5. At the meeting of the Assembly of the League later in the year the statute was amended, and on December 13 it was adopted.

The amendment was important. The draft statute had provided for compulsory submission of all cases falling under the classification of justiciable questions, using the definition incorporated in Article 13, paragraph 2, of the Covenant.[1] However, both Article 13 and Article 14 of the Covenant provided only for voluntary submission of cases. The commission had exceeded its authority, and its draft statute was accordingly amended. A provision was made, however, for the incorporation of an optional clause by which states so desiring could accept the pledge of compulsory submission of all cases of justiciable character. In specifying voluntary submission of cases the League was falling short of the ideal of a court of adjudication, but as a practical consideration the change was necessary to the ratification of the statute.

In justice to the advisory committee it must be recorded that it had in mind the linking of compulsory jurisdiction with a codification of international law, and the new code would be the law to be applied by the Court. This codification proposal also went farther than seemed practicable for immediate realization.

Article 14 of the Covenant provided that the statute should be submitted to the members of the League for adoption. This provision is of great importance. If the statute had been adopted by the League acting as an organized body either through the Council or through the Assembly, or through both, then the Court might very properly be considered as a League court; that is, as an agency of the

[1] Compare the text of the Covenant (Appendix A).

League itself. The proviso that the statute must be submitted to the members meant that each state must act upon it as an independent document, and that the court resulting from their ratification became an institution independent of the League. Furthermore, membership in the Court was independent of membership in the League. In view of this the Assembly provided a Protocol of Signature, an international or multilateral treaty, to which the statute was attached. This protocol was opened formally on December 16, 1920, for signature by the states of the world.

The statute was to become effective, as provided in the Assembly's resolution of December 13, when it had been ratified by a majority of the members of the League. This was accomplished by September, 1921. The election of judges was held September 14–16. The preliminary organization took place during an extraordinary session, lasting from January 30 to March 24, 1922. Officers were elected, and rules of procedure were drafted. The rules were promulgated on March 24. It remained for the Council to take final action for setting the new machinery in motion. This was done by a resolution of May 12, when the Court was declared open not only to the members of the League but to all nations of the world. The first ordinary session was held June 15 to August 12, 1922, when the Court handed down three advisory opinions.

The provisions of the statute may be summarized as follows:[1] "This Court shall be in addition to the Court of Arbitration organized by the Conventions of the Hague of 1899 and 1907, and to the special Tribunals of Arbitration to which States are always at liberty to submit their disputes for settlement." The Court is composed of eleven judges and four deputy judges with a term of nine years. The judges are eligible for reëlection and may not be removed except by unanimous action of the Court itself. They shall not be chosen with regard to nationality, except that not more than

---

[1] The text of the statute is printed in Appendix B.

one judge of any one nationality may be a member. It is provided, however, that the "electors shall bear in mind that . . . the whole body should represent the main forms of civilization and the principal legal systems of the world." If either or both of the parties to a suit do not have a judge on the Court, such party or parties may choose a judge or judges to sit during the particular case. In this manner the number of judges may be in excess of eleven.

The election of judges shall be held by the Assembly and Council of the League voting separately on the list of candidates presented. A majority vote in both bodies is essential to an election. The list of candidates is made up from persons nominated by the national groups in the Hague Court of Arbitration. "No group may nominate more than four persons, not more than two of whom shall be of their own nationality."

The sessions of the Court shall begin annually on June 15 at the Hague, and extraordinary sessions may be called by the president whenever necessary. Nine judges constitute a quorum unless otherwise provided. Special chambers, composed of three judges for summary procedure, may hear cases with consent of the parties in order to secure speedy action. A chamber of five judges is provided every three years to hear labor cases. These judges are assisted by four technical assessors who have no vote. A similar chamber is provided to consider problems of transit and communications. "The expenses of the Court shall be borne by the League of Nations, in such a manner as shall be decided by the Assembly upon the proposal of the Council."

The competence of the Court is outlined as follows: Only states, not individuals, can be parties in cases before the Court. It shall be open to League members and to states mentioned in the Annex to the Covenant (this includes the United States). It may be open to other states on terms laid down by the Council (this was defined by the resolution of the Council of May 12). The Court is open to any state which accepts the jurisdiction of the Court in accordance with the Covenant and the statute and undertakes to carry out in full good faith the decisions of the Court. Article 36 of the statute says, "The jurisdiction of the Court comprises all cases which the parties refer to it and all matters especially provided for in Treaties and Conventions in force." There is also the compulsory clause (which is open to acceptance by the states) providing for the submission of any or all of the following classes of legal disputes:

a. The interpretation of a Treaty.

b. Any question of international law.

c. The existence of any fact which, if established, would constitute a breach of an international obligation.

d. The nature or extent of the reparation to be made for the breach of an international obligation.

In the event of a dispute as to whether the Court has jurisdiction, the matter shall be settled by a decision of the Court.

The law applied by the Court is specifically defined in Article 38:

1. International conventions, whether general or particular, establishing rules expressly recognized by the contesting States.

2. International custom, as evidence of a general practice accepted as law.

3. The general principles of law recognized by civilized nations.

4. Subject to the provisions of Article 59, judicial decisions and the teachings of the most highly qualified publicists of the various nations, as subsidiary means for the determination of rules of law.

This provision shall not prejudice the power of the Court to decide a case *ex æquo et bono*, if the parties agree thereto.

The procedure of the Court as provided in the statute recognizes French and English as the official languages. When a case is brought to the Court all parties are notified. "The hearing in Court shall be public, unless the Court shall decide otherwise, or unless the parties demand that the public be not admitted." "The deliberations of the Court shall take place in private and remain secret." Decisions

shall be made by a majority vote and shall contain the name
of the participating judges. "The judgment shall state the
reasons on which it is based." Dissenting judges may present separate opinions. The judgment "shall be read in open
Court." Articles 59 and 60 state: "The decision of the Court
has no binding force except between the parties and in respect of that particular case. ... The judgment is final and
without appeal." However, an application for revision may
be made within a limited time when it is "based upon the
discovery of some fact of such a nature as to be a decisive
factor. . . . Unless otherwise decided by the Court, each
party shall bear its own costs." In addition to the framework of rules of procedure outlined in the statute, the Court
provides the details of application necessary. The Court
has no power to enforce its judgments; but under Article 13,
paragraph 4, of the Covenant the failure to carry out an
award would bring the matter before the League in cases
affecting members, and "the Council shall propose what
steps should be taken to give effect thereto." Inasmuch as
few states are not members of the League, this provision
would in practice be almost universal in its application.

The Protocol of Signature was signed by fifty-four states
and ratified by forty-two, including all the great powers eligible except the United States. The compulsory clause was
signed by forty-two states and was ratified by fourteen.
The optional clause was put into force by some states without ratification. In all, then, it was binding upon twenty-one
states. In several states the ratification was for a five-year
period, and must be renewed. No great power ratified the
compulsory clause except Germany. These figures include
all action taken prior to October, 1929.

The general position of the Court in the system of international government is now before the reader. It is seen
that while the League and the Court are independent of
each other in the sources of their authority — the Covenant
and the statute — and are independent of each other within

their own respective jurisdictions, they are complementary to each other and are closely coördinated at certain points. A state may be a member of either organization without being a member of the other. This has actually occurred. Several members of the League did not join the Court, and Brazil withdrew from the League in 1928 but retained membership in the Court.

David Jayne Hill, in his book "The Problem of the World Court," attacks the independence of the Court, basing his argument on legal distinctions in international law. He takes the ground that a protocol is not a treaty but "a supplementary document necessary to the execution" of a treaty, and that in this case the protocol of signature to which the statute is annexed is merely a "supplementary document necessary to the execution of the Treaty of Versailles "; that "no plenipotentiaries are named, no seals are attached"; that "the document is merely signed by the members of the League of Nations, in whose name alone it is drawn, and deposited in its archives"; and that the document is not therefore an "independent treaty," and the Court created by it is not an independent court. In this Hill is right up to a certain point, but there are several objections to this extreme view.

In the first place, there is no hard and fast definition of the word "protocol," and an argument based on a fixed definition breaks down. Hill insists, for example, that the Protocol of Signature is not a treaty in international law; but later in his book he states that the Draft Protocol contained in the Final Act of the conference of the signatories at Geneva is not a protocol: "It is clear that in substance it is a project of a formal treaty." In the second place, the use of multilateral treaties during the nineteenth and the early twentieth century developed certain practices peculiar to this type of instrument. Where a large number of states are signatories of a multilateral document, it is not possible to expect unanimous consent to amendments.

Two other methods are possible: to specify that changes or additions may be made by less than unanimous consent (as was the case in the Covenant of the League) or to make new multilateral agreements which may be ratified separately from the original treaty and which become binding only on the parties ratifying. The new agreement may be substantially a substitute for the first or it may be additional to any matter contained in the first. Both documents continue in force until abrogated by mutual consent. Thus, while the statute of the Court was drafted and put into operation by the League in pursuance of Article 14 of the Covenant, the protocol to which it was attached stands as a separate agreement ratified separately by each state which becomes a member of the Court. This brings the argument back to the simple statement of facts already mentioned. The two institutions derive their powers from separate documents, separately ratified, and are therefore independent of each other, each within its own sphere of action. The really fundamental connection which exists between them is the fact that substantially the same states are members and sponsors of both. For these two agencies of international action to coöperate and coördinate their activities where it seems desirable is a natural adjustment; for them to do otherwise would be absurd.

The government of the United States had no part in the making of the statute of the World Court, as it is called in America. The participation of Elihu Root was individual, and his selection was by the Council of the League. When the judges of the Court were elected, one of the regular seats was filled by John Bassett Moore, an American. The possibility of the participation of the United States was broached during the campaign of 1920, but Harding evaded commitment on the issue. After the election (December 13) it was reported in the press that Root was urging Harding to consider ratification, but the new administration chose the policy of isolation instead.

SELECTED BIBLIOGRAPHY

Materials Favorable to the World Court

HUDSON, MANLEY O. The Permanent Court of International Justice and the Question of American Participation. Harvard University Press, Cambridge, 1925.

BUSTAMENTE, ANTONIO SANCHEZ DE. The World Court. Translated from the Spanish by the American Foundation. The Macmillan Company, 1925.

WRIGHT, QUINCY. The Permanent Court of International Justice. American Conciliation Pamphlet No. 232, Carnegie Endowment for International Peace.

HUDSON, MANLEY O. The World Court, 1922–1928. World Peace Foundation Pamphlet, Vol. XI, No. 2.

JESSUP, PHILIP C. The United States and the World Court. World Peace Foundation Pamphlet, Volume XII, No. 4.

Materials Opposed to the World Court

HILL, DAVID J. The Problem of the World Court. Longmans, Green & Co., 1927.

KELLOR, FRANCES, and HATVANY, ANTONIA. Security against War. 2 vols. The Macmillan Company, 1924.

KELLOR, FRANCES, and HATVANY, ANTONIA. The United States and the International Court. Albert and Charles Boni, 1925.

◀ PART TWO ▶

Domestic Policies after the World War

CHAPTER VI

THE CONSERVATIVE REVOLUTION

ALTHOUGH not many Americans have formed the habit of thinking of political issues in terms of systematic theories concerning the scope and functions of government, it is almost necessary to do this in order to achieve a coherent orientation in the multiplicity of facts, opinions, and prejudices. The laissez faire theory of government assumes that government shall govern as little as possible, leaving the individual free to work out his own destiny on the assumption that what is good for the individual is also good for society as a whole. The "progressives" hold that this view is not necessarily true, and that the public interest often requires the limitation of individual action. In case of a conflict between the interest of the individual and that of society, the latter should predominate. Their dogma can be stated as popular control of government, and government control of economic and social problems in the interest of society. Both these theories are based upon the concept of private property. Socialism differs both as to the ownership of property and as to the position of the individual, vesting the control of both in the group. During the years immediately preceding the World War, the "progressive" theory was dominant in both domestic and foreign policy and also in both the Democratic party and the Republican party.

Regulation by the Federal government seemed to promise a solution of all difficulties. The development of big business had created economic power which had been misused to the detriment of society. Regulation by the government had been advanced as the solution. Business had opposed government regulation for some time; but when the movement became too strong, business attempted to control government to neutralize regulation. "Progressive" elements then demanded reorganization of the machinery of government and the addition of devices of direct democracy in order to restore the control of government to the people. These new devices were the secret ballot, popular election of senators, the initiative, the referendum, the recall, direct primaries, and presidential-preference primaries.

One effect of the war was to drive people to extremes: either to the right, toward conservatism, or to the left, toward extreme radicalism. Conservatives became reactionary, liberals became conservative, and socialists returned to the capitalist system or turned to the left — extreme syndicalism or communism. The overwhelming drift was toward conservatism. Liberalism and moderate socialism found relatively few supporters. Men who shouted for Roosevelt, Wilson, or La Follette in 1912, demanding the adoption of the Progressive program to save the nation from Wall Street plutocracy, insisted with similar vehemence on the opposite policy in 1928. The most amazing fact in the situation from the logical point of view is that both times they were firmly convinced that they were right. The only error would be to admit that they were in error. While it is more or less trite to say that the post-war decade was a period of conservatism, that alone does not answer the question. Just what did conservatism mean in terms of specific measures? In just what respects did this conservatism differ from previous periods of conservatism?

POLITICAL THEORIES AFTER 1919

The general spirit of the post-war decade may be indicated quite clearly from presidential messages, speeches of public men, and the organized activities of various types of societies. Five different aspects of political ideas may be selected to illustrate significant tendencies: exaggerated nationalism, laissez faire, government assistance to business, self-government in business, and states' rights.

Exaggerated nationalism was to a great extent a product of war psychology: war hates, war rivalries, militarism, "one hundred per cent Americanism," race antagonisms, and so on. Campaigns for military preparedness were conducted by the more extreme elements in the army and navy, by soldiers' organizations, and by such bodies as the Security League. There were also movements to dictate or control education, especially the teaching of history, sponsored by bar associations, the American Legion, the Sons of the American Revolution and other patriotic societies, as well as by racial groups (Irish, Germans, Italians, etc.). In certain states laws were passed placing control of history textbooks in the hands of politicians. The American Legion and other groups sponsored an American history which was to tell American history "truthfully," but the instructions to the committee on preparation required that the truth be told "optimistically." The Ku-Klux Klan carried on nationalist propaganda in a different manner. It was organized in 1915 in Alabama, but it did not become of any consequence until 1918 in the South and 1920 in the North. The slogan of the Klan was "one hundred per cent Americanism," which was interpreted to mean law and order (enforced by night-riding, whippings, and so on by masked men), white supremacy, anti-Catholicism, and anti-Semitism. National sentiment had been successfully mobilized for military purposes; but one of the most difficult phases of post-war reconstruction was to demobilize it and to prevent its degenerating into fanaticism. It seemed impossible to view problems of domestic or foreign policy except in terms of nationalism. This was the primary element in the defeat of the League of Nations. Harding declared in his special-session message of April 12, 1921: "We recognize no super-authority."

The second phase of the post-war conservatism is the reversion (or, at least, attempted reversion) to laissez faire. In Wilson's fifth annual message (December 2, 1918) he expressed the opinion that "our people . . . do not want to be coached or led. . . . Any leading strings we might seek to put them in would speedily become hopelessly entangled. . . . All we can do as their legislative and executive servants is to mediate the process of change here, there, and elsewhere as we may." Harding, as was to be expected, went much farther in his special message to Congress of April 12, 1921. He repeated from his campaign statements, "I have said to the people we meant to have less government in business as well as more of business in government." Coolidge's third annual message of December 8, 1925, said, "The age of perfection still is in the somewhat distant future, but it is more in danger of being retarded by mistaken government activity than it is from lack of legislation." The expressions of private citizens were in much the same spirit. Edward W. Bok's thousand-dollar Harvard award for the most distinguished single advertisement "most effective in the use of text" was granted in 1925 to *The Nation's Business*, the official organ of the Chamber of Commerce of the United States, for an advertisement entitled "Let Washington Do It." The theme of the text was this: "As a people, we have come to expect the Federal government to perform economic miracles. 'Pass a law' has become the national panacea."

Not only was serious argument used in the attack upon government regulation, but ridicule was in some respects more effective. The editor of *The Nation's Business* exploited a mythical organization advocating a law to suppress the back collar button. Another story was told of a man in Kansas who wrote to the Department of Agriculture at Washington for information on 'how to put on a shirt, eat an apple, peel potatoes, adjust a dog collar, shovel coal, wash a dog, and pick a chicken." Although the department had three thousand advisory pamphlets, it was compelled to admit that it could not give assistance except on the point how to pick a chicken.

The third phase of post-war conservatism is the justification of Federal government assistance to business. The editor of the *Review of Reviews* (July, 1926) presented the frankest possible exposition of one aspect of this political philosophy:

> The world was moving rapidly in the direction of a better and happier mode of life for the vast majority, when foolish and criminal leaders precipitated the World War of 1914. . . . Since governments were chiefly responsible for the war and its incalculable disasters, it becomes necessary for governments to aid the forces of business in restoring economic life to a normal routine, on higher social levels. . . . It was a wholly new conception — a very recent one too — that there might be wealth enough to go around, and that the luxuries of the few might become conveniences of the many. To work for the success of this ideal is the new conservatism.

Wilson pointed out in his fifth annual message (December 2, 1918) that "never before have there been agencies in existence in this country which knew so much of the field of supply, of labor, and of industry as the [government war agencies]. . . . It has been the policy of the Executive . . . since the armistice . . . to put the knowledge of these bodies at the disposal of the business men of the country and to offer their intelligent mediation at every point and in every matter where it was desired." On November 19, 1925, Coolidge told the New York State Chamber of Commerce that "the American policy toward business has been to cherish the general structure of business while holding its avenues open to the widest competition so its opportunities and benefits might be given the broadest possible participation. Those who are so engaged, instead of regarding government as their opponent and enemy, ought to regard it as their vigilant supporter and friend."

A second aspect of government assistance to business was derived from the argument of military preparedness.

D. F. Davis, Secretary of War, writing in *Current History* (February, 1926), said that "industrial preparedness now occupies as important a place as man-power preparedness in the scheme of national defense. Mobilization of munitions and man-power have to be synchronized." He insisted that the development of essential war industries for military ends means close coöperation between the government and business in peace and will result in increased efficiency and more rapid industrial progress which "will not only help America to be self-sustaining but will add materially to the wealth of the world and the value and happiness of life." He thought the nation should support this stabilizing influence.

A fourth phase of the new conservatism is the development of the theory of self-government in business. Harding pointed out in his special message of April 12, 1921, that the government "has a right to expect the coöperation of . . . legitimate business in stamping out the practices which add to unrest and inspire restrictive legislation." Coolidge voiced the opinion before the New York State Chamber of Commerce that it was desirable to have "the largest possible independence between government and business"; that "each ought to be sovereign in its own sphere." William M. Jardine, Secretary of Agriculture, made one of the clearest statements of the theory on August 14, 1927:

> Groups of producers and sections of the country are bound together in an increasingly complex relationship, which demands some form of control over economic forces. What shall be the nature of this control? Shall it be, as some would have it, control by political government attempting to legislate prosperity to this group or that? Or shall it be self-control by men organized along lines of mutual interest, with political government, backed by an informed public opinion, protecting the public interest by prescribing broad rules of conduct? I am one of those who believe our hope lies in the latter form of control.

A clear warning to business men was sounded by John W. O'Leary, president of the Chamber of Commerce of the

United States, in addresses to business men in various parts of the country. On March 24, 1926, he said :

If the government is not to resort to regulation, business must keep its own house in order. We have protested against government interference in the past and we seek to avoid it in the future. There is no better way to accomplish this purpose than by assuming without reserve the responsibility for self-regulation. Our failure to accept it will mean more drastic government regulation than we have ever had before or ever dreamed of having.

The movement which O'Leary was leading came to a definite head in the fourteenth annual meeting of the Chamber of Commerce of the United States in Washington, May 10, 1926, when the central theme of the meeting was the discussion of this problem of self-regulation of American business in contrast to government control.

The fifth aspect of the new conservatism is a certain revival of states' rights, as opposed to nationalization and centralization. Coolidge definitely voiced the policy of limiting the scope of activity of the Federal government in favor of the states and other local units. The first statement was in his Memorial Day address in 1925, and a similar view was repeated in his annual message in December, when he said that "society is in much more danger from encumbering the national government beyond its wisdom to comprehend, or its ability to administer, than from leaving the local communities to bear their own burdens and remedy their own evils." Probably the most conspicuous single line of agitation was associated with the campaign against national prohibition. Governor Smith of New York and Governor Ritchie of Maryland, for example, made this a very important part of their advocacy of states' rights.

CHAPTER VII

PUBLIC FINANCE

ECONOMY

THE World War left a tragic heritage of ethical demoralization, economic deflation, debt, and taxes. In the midst of the controversy over the peace treaty Wilson began the formulation of a program for the reduction of the cost of living, for economy, and for orderly expenditure. The message of December 2, 1919, recommended an audit not only to determine the legality of expenditures but to examine into efficiency and economy of expenditures. The annual message of December 7, 1920, emphasized "rigid economy." "I cannot overemphasize the necessity of economy in government appropriations and expenditures."

Harding, in his special-session message of April 12, 1921, said that economy was to be made "an outstanding and ever-impelling purpose in both legislation and administration. The unrestrained tendency to heedless expenditure and the attending growth of public indebtedness, extending from Federal authority to that of state and municipality and including the smallest political subdivision, constitute the most dangerous phase of government today." Each annual message, thereafter, of Harding and of Coolidge reiterated the term, which became a Republican slogan.

The primary method recommended by Wilson for achieving the desired result was the inauguration of a Federal budget. This was advocated in the annual message of December 2, 1919. His plan was to vest in the Executive the responsibility for the formulation of a comprehensive plan of appropriations each year. In Congress no additions to the budget were to be made except by a single committee on appropriations in each house. Congress passed a measure, but Wilson vetoed it on constitutional grounds. In the House of Representatives the desired amendment was made, and in his annual message of December 7, 1920, Wilson urged the repassage of the bill in this new form. Harding continued the general policy, and in his special-session message of April 12, 1921, urged a similar program. The Budget and Accounting Act was passed and approved June 10, 1921. It provided that on the first day of each regular session the president should submit to Congress a budget, which should include estimates of expenditures and receipts for the ensuing year, together with estimates for the current and last fiscal years. The president should also present a complete financial statement of the condition of the government. When necessary he should submit recommendations for revision of taxes, for loans, or for other financial measures. Except on special request of either house of Congress, no request for appropriation or financial recommendation should be made by any officer except through the budget. The Budget Bureau was created in the Department of the Treasury. The procedure of budget preparation was for each bureau to submit its own estimates to the Budget Bureau by October 15 and for the Bureau to study these and to prepare the budget under the direction of the president. The last division of the act provided for the General Accountancy Office, separate from the departments of government and under the direction of a new officer — the Comptroller General of the United States. The accountancy divisions of the different departments were transferred to this office, and all claims against the government and all accounts with it were to be settled there. The tenure of the Comptroller General was set at fifteen years. He was eligible for reappointment, and could be removed only by joint resolution of Congress for certain stated reasons or by impeachment. Although this budget did not measure up to the best ideals of budget practice as worked out in England, it was a very distinct improvement over previous usage in the United States. It provided, for the first time, for definite coördination of income and expenditure; but it did not prevent Congress from disregarding executive recommendations.

Cost of Government

The high cost of government came to be one of the chief questions of public interest. The cost of all the branches of government — Federal, state, and local — was estimated at $2,919,000,000 in 1913 and $11,125,000,000 in 1925. This did not allow for the depreciation in the value of the dollar from 100 to 64 for the period. With this adjustment the ratio for the two dates was 3 to 7. The per-capita cost increased from $30 to $96. The national income for 1924 was estimated at approximately double that of 1913, and taxation increased from 6.9 per cent to 12.5 per cent of the total national income. Other estimates were even higher. The Chamber of Commerce of the United States published estimates for 1926 at the same figure, 12.5 per cent.

Federal expenditures in 1921 were 60 per cent of the total, but by 1925 they were reduced to about 33 per cent. Exclusive of debt, interest charges, and military establishment, the actual cost of the Federal government was reduced but slightly after the immediate post-war adjustments had been made.

State-government expenditures increased rapidly: in 1915 the total was $494,907,000, in 1923 it was $1,310,333,000, and in 1925 it was $1,614,562,000. The per-capita debt of the states was $4.31 in 1915 and $11.12 in 1925. A great portion of this represented road-building.

Local government showed even greater increase in cost. In 1913 it stood at $1,844,000,000, in 1923 at $5,136,000,000, and in 1925 at $6,184,405,000. In later years the rate of increase was somewhat diminished.

DISTRIBUTION OF FEDERAL EXPENDITURE AND INCOME

A survey of the distribution of Federal expenditures is an illuminating but usually neglected phase of public finance. In 1913 war (present defense and past wars) consumed 73 per cent of Federal money, leaving less than 27 per cent for all civil functions. The average annual expenditures over the ten-year period 1910–1919 (exclusive of the cost of war) and for the years 1920, 1922, 1923, and 1924 were as follows:[1]

	1910–1919	1920	1922	1923	1924
Primary government functions (legislative, executive, and judicial)	15.98%	3.9%	6.6%	7.0%	6.0%
Research, education, and development	4.21	1.0	1.9	1.9	2.0
Public works (including the Panama Canal)	11.75	1.5	4.0	5.6	6.0
Total civil expenditures . .	31.94%	6.4%	12.5%	14.5%	14.0%
Army and navy	39.67%	23.7	17.1%	16.9%	20.2%
Pensions and care of soldiers . .	24.76	5.8	18.9	24.6	26.0
Special activities pertaining to the recent war		28.7	−1.0	4.9	.4
Interest	3.63	16.3	25.6	28.3	26.7
Retirement of public debt . . .		19.1	26.9	10.8	12.7
Total national defense and past wars	68.06%	93.6%	87.5%	85.5%	86.0%

According to Coolidge's budget message of December, 1928, the estimates for 1929, exclusive of refunds and trust funds, assigned 79.2 per cent to war and 20.8 per cent to civil functions. When it is understood that only 14 per cent to 20 per cent of the total Federal expenditures were devoted to civil affairs, it can be realized how little the program of post-war economy in the conduct of government could affect the rate of taxation. This is further emphasized by the fact that

[1] The figures in the first two columns are from E. B. Rosa's study "Expenditures and Revenues of the Federal Government," *The Annals of the American Academy of Political and Social Science* (May, 1921), Vol. XCV, pp. 1–113. The figures in the last three columns are drawn from compilations of the Bureau of Efficiency based on Rosa's method.

after 1922 the total number of government employees, as indicated by Commissioner Morgan, increased slightly rather than decreased. The war charges were relatively fixed except for reductions in debt and in interest. The militarist element would have absorbed a large part of this saving in the competition for armament. The limit of economy was reached in 1925, according to the budget message of that year. The Sixty-eighth Congress (1923–1925) appropriated $7,935,000,000, but the Seventieth Congress (1927–1929) appropriated $9,291,000,000.

According to the Treasury statements the public debt of over $26,000,000,000 in 1919 was reduced to a little more than $17,000,000,000 in 1928. Except for increasing national income, reduction of the debt was the only source from which substantial tax reductions came after the immediate post-war adjustments. Coolidge resisted the demands of the extreme militarists, thereby preventing the expenditure of part of this saving in interest charges.

The changing sources of Federal income are also a matter of special interest. In 1909, before the new tariff went into effect, 47.7 per cent of revenue came from customs and 40 per cent from internal revenue. By 1913 and before the revenue act of that year, customs had fallen to 44 per cent, and internal revenue (which included the new corporation tax of 1909) had increased to 47.5 per cent. The disturbance to commerce resulting from the World War, together with the revenue act of 1913, further reduced customs by 1916 to 27 per cent and increased internal revenue (including the income tax) to 65.8 per cent. For 1923, customs yielded only 14 per cent, whereas internal revenue produced 65.5 per cent. The returns from income and excess-profits taxes alone yielded over 41 per cent. For 1928, customs yielded 14.75 per cent, income tax 53.78 per cent, and other internal revenue 15 per cent, making a total of 68.78 per cent from internal revenue. These figures show the revolution which took place in public finance after the beginning made by

Taft's insistence upon the corporation tax in 1909. From the standpoint of public revenue the tariff became a relatively unimportant political question; its chief significance in post-war finance lay in its protective features for the promotion of a national industrial system and for purposes of international economic warfare.

INTERNAL REVENUE

Tax revision was one of Wilson's chief concerns in domestic policy after the armistice. In his annual message of December 2, 1918, he asked that in order to remove business uncertainties Congress should immediately approve a tax policy for the years 1918, 1919, and 1920.

For the steadying and facilitation of our own domestic business readjustments nothing is more important. . . . As much of the burdens of taxation must be lifted from business as sound methods of financing the government will permit, and those who conduct the great essential industries of the country must be told as exactly as possible what obligations to the government they will be expected to meet in the years immediately ahead of them. It will be of serious consequence to the country to delay removing all uncertainties in this matter a single day longer than the right processes of debate justify. It is idle to talk of successful and confident business reconstruction before these uncertainties are resolved.

He estimated that taxes payable in 1919 could be reduced from the war figure of $8,000,000,000 to $6,000,000,000, and that $2,000,000,000 of this could be raised from excess taxes on "war business," which would leave $4,000,000,000 to be raised from regular taxation. The estimate for taxes payable in 1920 was reduced from $6,000,000,000 to $4,000,000,000. He warned that "an immediate rapid decline in the expense of the government is not to be looked for."

The revenue act of 1918 was approved February 24, 1919; but in his special-session message of May 20, 1919, Wilson continued discussion of the subject of taxation. He asked for simplification of schedules and administration, and expressed the hope that the war debt could be lifted within one generation. Holding the belief that the aim of taxation should be constancy in revenue-yielding power, with the lightest possible burden upon the taxpayer, he said of the Federal revenue, "I take it for granted that its mainstays will henceforth be the income tax, the excess-profits tax, and the estate tax." He urged that further changes be made in the rates and method of collection of the income tax, that the excess-profits tax be made a permanent system which should reach undue profits without discouraging enterprise, that the estate tax be made permanent but be adjusted in relation to the states, and that the so-called nuisance taxes (for example, taxes on theater tickets, telegrams, club dues, and the like) be abandoned. In his message of December 2, 1919, Wilson again asked for simplification of taxes. The rates, he urged, should not be disturbed for taxes of the calendar year 1920 payable in 1921, but Congress should consider peace-time rates on income and excess profits which should yield revenue without discouraging enterprise and producing stagnation. Congress still took no action, though the President's tax program was fully before it. The annual message of 1920 repeated the earlier recommendations.

Harding's special-session message of April 12, 1921, attacked the problem somewhat differently:

The most substantial relief from the tax burden must come for the present from the readjustment of internal taxes and the revision or repeal of taxes which have become unproductive and are so artificial and burdensome as to defeat their own purpose. A prompt and thoroughgoing revision of the internal tax laws, made with due regard to the protection of the revenues, is, in my judgment, a requisite to the revival of business activity in this country. . . . We are committed to the repeal of the excess-profits tax and the abolition of inequalities and unjustifiable exasperations in the present system.

The most distinct difference between Wilson and Harding here was on the excess-profits tax. The revenue act of 1921 was approved by Harding on November 23, 1921. In his annual messages of 1921 and 1922 he added another item of importance to his program — the advocacy of the abolition of tax-exempt securities. No action was taken, however.

Coolidge outlined a more comprehensive policy in his annual message of December 6, 1923. He went so far that he practically reversed the principles laid down by Wilson. He advocated reduction on moderate incomes and on surtaxes, and the abolition of the excess-profits tax and of tax-exempt securities through constitutional amendment. He opposed the estate tax, although he did not specify this in the message. His argument was that these were war taxes which were not suitable for peace times; that they were such a burden on capital as to make it unproductive and to prevent its proper growth and increase to meet the requirements of industry; and that the tax-exempt securities, in conjunction with high rates, drove capital out of productive enterprise and contributed to municipal extravagance. The revenue act of 1924, as passed on the eve of a presidential election, did not suit Coolidge. He approved it under protest, June 2, 1924. The Democrats and insurgent Republicans combined to produce a law quite at variance with presidential policies. Accordingly, immediately after signing the bill, Coolidge issued a long statement in which he subjected the bill and the methods by which it was passed to scathing criticism. Inasmuch as he outlined the whole internal-taxation policy very forcibly in this document, there is justification for summarizing it at some length.

"The passage of the new revenue bill was required for two reasons, the reduction of taxation and the reform of taxation. The bill as passed provides a certain amount of tax reduction. It improves some of the features of administration. But it not only is lacking in tax reform: it actually adds some undesirable features to the present law. As a permanent expression of government fiscal policy, this bill contains provisions which, in my opinion, are not only unsatisfactory but are harmful to the future of the country.

"The reduction of high surtaxes from 50 to 40 per cent is quite immaterial to accomplish a real improvement in the law." Congress failed to pass the constitutional amendment abolishing tax-exempt securities. " With some twelve billion of tax-exempt securities now outstanding and one billion of new issues each year, it is idle to propose high surtaxes. . . . This does not mean wealth in existence is taxed; it is not. It escapes. It does mean, however, initiative and new enterprise are throttled."

" The principles applicable to high surtaxes apply similarly to high estate taxes. The bill raises the estate tax to 40 per cent. As a concomitant is added a gift tax, which is a further invasion of the rights of citizens, both unusual in nature and of doubtful legality. When there is added to this the inheritance taxes levied by the states, it amounts to a practical confiscation of capital." The tax was a war measure and should not be kept in time of peace. It belongs primarily to the states.

Congress had provided for publicity of income-tax returns. "For the needs of revenue, publicity is unnecessary." "It is not alone in the unwarranted interference with the right of the citizen to privacy that these provisions are hurtful." It will drive millions of income into concealment.

" Provision should be made for the prompt and final determination of a taxpayer's liability and such was the purpose in the suggestion for a board of tax appeals." As framed the provisions hamper procedure, reduce terms to too short a duration and reduce salary to such an extent as to defeat its purpose and make the securing of competent men difficult.

"The excess-profits tax and income-tax laws of the war period were new in principle and exceedingly complicated in practice. . . . We must consider, therefore, the establishment for the future of such a policy of taxation as will insure the maintenance of the sources of taxation without the aid of these reservoirs which soon will be empty. This means the policy must be framed so it will encourage the creation of income subject to tax, will close the most obvious methods of avoidance, will not diminish by excessive estate taxes the very values upon which the Federal and state governments must rely for revenue and will bring about a reduction in the high cost of living as a means of meeting world competition." He was much concerned over "the increased cost of capital for new industrial enterprises." "When other countries return to productivity and become again the serious commercial rivals of our people, and we experience those periods of depression which normally follow periods of prosperity, we should have our house in order by establishing our tax system so its economic effects will be beneficial and not harmful."

"The bill represents tax reduction, not tax reform. . . . We must adjust our taxes upon an economic and not a political basis. . . . As I have said, the bill does not represent a sound permanent tax policy, and in its passage has been subject to unfortunate influence which ought not to control fiscal questions. . . . A correction of its defects may be left to the next session of Congress. I trust a bill less political and more truly economic may be passed at that time."

In the fall of 1925 the Committee on Ways and Means met early and drafted a tax bill which closely accorded with the recommendations of the Treasury. It was announced (November 20) that Congress would open in December with a political spectacle without parallel. The Republicans and Democrats were united in support of the measure as a bipartisan tax program. On November 24 it was stated in the press that both President Coolidge and Andrew W. Mellon, Secretary of the Treasury, approved the bill. Coolidge, in his annual message of December 8, approved the bill in principle as embodying many sound policies which would remedy many of the defects injected into the act of 1924 as well as many inherited from war time. He pointed out that in the bill as projected excessive surtaxes and estate taxes were reduced, that the gift tax and publicity were repealed, that miscellaneous taxes were lowered or abandoned, and that the board of customs appeals was strengthened. He did not fully commend the extent of the increased exemptions. He was most gratified by the nonpartisan character of the bill and the promise that such effort would result in prompt action. The House passed the bill, and the Senate amended it to more nearly the Coolidge ideal. The inheritance tax was repealed. Other taxes repealed were those on passenger motor cars, admissions and dues, and capital stock. The surtax rate on incomes between $24,000 and $100,000 was reduced, and the corporation tax was increased 1 per cent. The measure was passed by a vote of 58 to 9 on February 12, 1926. The conference committee worked out a compromise. The inheritance tax was reduced to 20 per cent as a maximum, and with a proviso of allowance to states of 80 per cent instead of 25 per cent. A retroactive clause was included applying the rates of 1921 on inheritances in place of the 1924 rates; the exemption was raised from $50,000 to $100,000. The surtax rates on incomes of $24,000 to $100,000 were reduced, the tax on capital stock was repealed, the corporation tax was increased $\frac{1}{2}$ per cent for one year and 1 per cent thereafter, and the passenger motor-car tax was reduced from 5 per cent to 3 per cent. A retroactive reduction of the tax on gifts was voted, applying the inheritance tax rates of 1921 to gifts before January 1, 1926, after which date the tax was repealed. The conference report was accepted in the House on February 23 by a vote of 354 to 28 and in the Senate the next day by a vote of 61 to 10. The bill was signed by the President on February 26, 1926, without comment.

By the autumn of 1926 it was evident that there would be another large surplus, and public demands spoke for further reduction. Coolidge stood his ground against the movement until after the congressional elections, which were unfavorable to the administration. He then announced (on November 5) that he favored a tax refund of 10 or 12 per cent, but not a change in the law itself. Four days later he asked for nonpartisan support for this proposal such as had been given to the revenue act of 1926. In his annual message this position was restated. In 1927 the Treasury, with the approval of the President, proposed a new tax bill carrying a reduction of $225,000,000. The Chamber of Commerce of the United States asked for $400,000,000. The Committee on Ways and Means drew a bill for a reduction of $236,000,000, later reduced to $232,000,000. The House passed the bill providing for a reduction of $290,000,000, and the Senate finance committee postponed consideration of the measure until after March 15, 1928.

After the tax returns were in, the Treasury decided to revise its estimates of possible reduction. Instead of a reduction of $225,000,000, the figure was placed at a maximum of $201,000,000. The Chamber of Commerce still insisted upon greater reduction. The Senate passed the tax bill in a form which would provide a reduction of $205,000,000. In conference committee in May a compromise between the House and the Senate figures was worked out. The total reductions were estimated at $225,295,000, and increases of $2,800,000 were allowed in rates affecting nonresident stockholders and prize-fight tickets. Thus the net tax reduction was $222,495,000. The measure was signed by the President on May 29, 1928. There were two major items of reduction: the tax on corporations was reduced from $13\frac{1}{2}$ per cent to 12 per cent (this one item accounted for $123,450,000), and the tax of 3 per cent on sales of automobiles was repealed (this meant a reduction in revenue of $66,000,000). The inheritance tax was retained. The explanation given in the press for this move was that a bargain was struck between the administration and the insurgent Republicans by which the insurgents voted for the relief of corporations in return for the retention of the inheritance tax. This situation is explained by the fact that the administration did not have a majority in the Senate without the insurgents.

The provisions of the revenue acts can now be summarized most successfully in a comparative chart. With the foregoing historical sketch of policy and the chart (on pages 104–105) before the reader, a very few interpretative comments are sufficient. It will be remembered that the revenue act of 1913 introduced the income tax into United States public finance, but tariff was still a substantial source of revenue. The collapse of import trade in the early stages of the European war forced a rapid development of the internal-revenue system — a more rapid development than normal circumstances would have permitted. It is in this light that the emergency revenue act of 1916 must be viewed, because government income lost from tariff had to be made up from the newer sources. Then followed the entrance of the United States into the conflict, and the extremes of war finance. The act of 1916 provided a general increase in rates, including what was thought at that time to be a rather sharp graduation of rates on large incomes. The high tax on munitions was the beginning of the excess-profits tax. In 1918 the rates were all high; but they bore very heavily on great wealth, although corporations were given some relief for 1919 and after. The act of 1921 cut normal income rates one third, but left surtaxes as before for one year, with some reductions thereafter. The corporation tax was raised for 1922, the only increase made. The act of 1924 cut normal income rates one fourth, except on smaller incomes, which were reduced one half. Surtaxes were cut only moderately. The maximum on estate taxes was increased from 25 per cent to 40 per cent, the only increase in this act. The tax on gifts was added to prevent evasion of the high estate tax, and publicity was incorporated. This was the last stand of the "progressive" point of view in taxation, and the form which it took was inconsistent on some points. The act of 1926 represented the victory of the conservative point of view — the removal of high taxation of wealth. The surtaxes and estate taxes were cut drastically, the taxes on gifts were repealed, exemption was raised, and occupational taxes were repealed. The corporation tax was raised, — a point which seemed inconsistent with the remainder of the program. The corporation tax in a conservative régime was $13\frac{1}{2}$ per cent as against 2 per cent in 1916, and $1\frac{1}{2}$ per cent higher than the highest war rate. This was the reason that corporate business made such a determined drive on tax reduction in the winter of 1927–1928, and explained why the corporations were the chief beneficiaries of the revenue act of 1928, which reduced their rate to 12 per cent and increased their income exemption from $2000 to $3000.

TARIFF

Post-war trade conditions caused much uncertainty in some quarters as regards foreign competition in American markets. Wilson took the view in his special-session message of May 20, 1919, that "there is, fortunately, no occasion for undertaking in the immediate future any general revision of our system of import duties. No serious danger of foreign competition now threatens American industries." In his regular annual message of December 2, 1919, he pointed out that the position of the United States was fundamentally changed now that the United States was a creditor country : European trade balances could be paid in three ways, — by gold, by credits, or by goods; further importations of gold were undesirable; it was time for government loans to be curtailed or stopped, and the payments must therefore be by goods. "If we want to sell," he insisted, "we must be prepared to buy."

While Wilson was upholding this view the world-wide depression and deflation of 1920 gave encouragement to the opposite contention. High protective tariff was advanced as a major remedy : first, an emergency tariff to assist agriculture, and then as soon as possible a general revision of the tariff upward. Hearings were commenced in January,

Revenue Acts, 1916–1928

	Act of 1916	Act of 1918	Act of 1921	Act of 1924	Act of 1926	Act of 1928
Individual income Normal tax	2%	For 1918 6% on first $4000 12% on remainder For 1919 4% on first $4000 8% on remainder	Same as for 1919	2% on first $4000 4% on second $4000 6% on remainder	1½% on first $4000 3% on second $4000 5% on remainder	Same as for 1926
Surtax	1% on $20,000–$40,000 2% on $40,000–$60,000 . . . . . . 13% above $2,000,000	1% on $5000–$6000 2% on $6000–$8000 . . . . . . 52% on $100,000–$150,000 65% above $1,000,000	1921 Same as for 1919 For 1922 1% on $6000–$10,000 2% on $10,000–$12,000 . . . . . . 48% on $100,000–$150,000 50% above $200,000	1% on $10,000–$14,000 2% on $14,000–$16,000 . . . . . . 37% on $100,000–$200,000 40% above $500,000	1% on $10,000–$14,000 2% on $14,000–$16,000 . . . . . . 20% above $100,000	Same as for 1926
Exemption	$1000 for single person $3000 for married person or head of family	$1000 $2000	$1000 $2500	Same as for 1921	$1500 $3500	Same as for 1926
Corporation tax	2%	For 1918, 12% For 1919, 10%	For 1921, 10% After 1921, 12½%	12½%	13% for 1925 13½% for 1926	12%

REVENUE ACTS, 1916–1928 (CONTINUED)

	Act of 1916	Act of 1918	Act of 1921	Act of 1924	Act of 1926	Act of 1928
Estate tax	1% below $50,000 2% on $50,000–$150,000 . . . . 10% above $5,-000,000	Same as for 1916 Same as for 1916 . . . . 25% above $10,-000,000	Same as for 1916 Same as for 1916 . . . . Same as for 1918	1% on first $50,-000 2% on second $50,000 3% on third $50,-000 . . . . 40% above $10,-000,000	Same as for 1924 Same as for 1924 3% on second $100,000 . . . . 20% above $10,-000,000	No change
Exemption	$50,000	$50,000	$50,000	$50,000	$100,000	No change
Munitions tax	12½% of income in addition to income tax					
Excess-profits tax		20%–40%	30%–40% of income in excess of 20% on capital			
Automobile			5% on passenger 3% on trucks	3%	3% on passenger	Repealed
Publicity of returns				Publicity	Repealed	
Occupational taxes	Imposed				Repealed	

1921, before the Wilson administration ended. The emergency measure was passed and vetoed March 3, the day before Wilson left office. His veto message was a caustic lecture on economic policy:

Very little reflection would lead anyone to conclude that the measure would not furnish in any substantial degree the relief sought by the producers of most of the staple commodities which it covers. This nation has been for very many years a large exporter of agricultural products. [He then gave figures on wheat, corn, cotton, milk, sugar, and wool.]

It is obvious that for the commodities, except sugar and wool, mentioned in the measure, which make up the greater part of our agricultural international trade, the imports can have little or no effect on the prices of the domestic products. This is strikingly true of wheat and corn. . . .

What the farmer now needs is not only a better system of domestic marketing and credit, but especially larger foreign markets for his surplus products.

Clearly, measures of this sort will not conduce to an expansion of the foreign market. It is not a little singular that a measure which strikes a blow at our foreign trade should follow so closely upon the action of Congress directing the resumption of certain activities of the War Finance Corporation, especially at the urgent insistence of representatives of the farming interests, who believed that its resumption would improve foreign marketing. Indeed, when one surveys recent activities in the foreign field and measures enacted affecting the foreign trade, one cannot fail to be impressed with the fact that there is consistency only in their contradiction and inconsistencies.

We have been vigorously building up a great merchant marine and providing for the improvement of marketing in foreign countries by the passage of an export trade law and of measures for the promotion of banking agencies in foreign countries. Now it appears that we propose to render these measures abortive in whole or in part.

I imagine there is little doubt that while this measure is temporary, it is intended as a foundation for action of a similar nature of a very general and permanent character. If there ever was a time when America had anything to fear from foreign competition, that time has passed. . . .

If we wish to have Europe settle her debts, governmental or commercial, we must be prepared to buy from her, and if we wish to assist Europe and ourselves by the export either of food, of raw materials, or finished products, we must be prepared to welcome commodities which we need and which Europe will be prepared, with no little pain, to send us.

Clearly, this is no time for the erection here of high trade barriers. . . .

This measure has only slight interest so far as its prospective revenue yields are concerned. . . .

The rates, however, have a peculiar interest. In practically every case they either equal or exceed those established under the Payne-Aldrich Act, in which the principle of protection reached its high-water mark, and the enactment of which was followed by an effective exhibition of protest on the part of the majority of the American people. . . .

Such a policy is antagonistic to the fundamental principles of equal and exact justice to all, and can only serve to revive the feeling of irritation on the part of the great masses of the people and lack of confidence in the motives of rulers and the results of government.

Wilson's statement was so inclusive that the full import of it may not be apparent at the first reading; but as the details of domestic and foreign policies are presented, each paragraph will take on a new or fuller significance. It was a clear statement of principles which would, for the most part, have established domestic and foreign policies consistent with each other.

Harding's special message of April 12, 1921, took the opposite point of view: "The urgency for an instant tariff enactment, emergency in character, . . . cannot be too much emphasized. I believe in the protection of American industry, and it is our purpose to prosper America first." In his annual message he urged permanent tariff legislation and the inclusion of a flexible device which would authorize the president to increase or decrease tariff rates in order to preserve a continuous and adequate standard of protection. The emergency measure was passed by the new Republican Congress and signed by Harding on May 27, 1921. Professor Taussig said of it, "As a means of meeting the emergency of the time it was hardly more than an amiable gesture"; but it was of tremendous political importance for the agricultural section, which was largely responsible, because that section was thereby "committed to a policy of high and even ruthless protection." They could not then oppose similar high rates to the manufacturers when the permanent tariff came up for consideration.

The hearings on the permanent measure began in January, before Wilson's term expired. The bill was introduced in the House on June 29 and was passed July 21. The Senate did not pass the bill until August 19, 1922, over a year later, and it did not become law until September 19. The Senate dominated the situation and, in characteristic fashion, increased duties. Agricultural duties were as follows:

	1909	1922
Wheat	25 cents a bushel	30 cents a bushel
Rye	10 cents a bushel	15 cents a bushel
Corn	15 cents a bushel	15 cents a bushel
Beef	1½ cents a pound	3 cents a pound
Lamb	2 cents a pound	4 cents a pound

Agricultural implements were placed on the free list, but this had no economic significance, inasmuch as the United States was an exporter of this product. Sugar was taxed 2.206 cents per pound; the former rate had been 1.25 cents per pound. Since Cuba received a 20 per cent reduction, the effective duty on Cuban sugar was 1.7648 cents and 1 cent per pound respectively. The Cuban sugar crop had increased to such an extent during the war that it supplied all the foreign sugar imported. Wool was given a duty of 15 cents per pound in the emergency tariff and of 31 cents in the permanent tariff. The method of calculation was changed, however: before 1922 the duty was on wool "in the grease"; the new rate was based on "cleaned wool." Taussig calculated that the effective increase in duty was from 40 per cent to 111 per cent, largely owing to the change in method.

Woolens were given a compensating duty of from 37 cents to 45 cents per pound in order to equalize the tariff on wool of 31 cents. The ad valorem duty on woolens was fixed at 50 per cent as against 55 per cent in 1909, but the concealed protection in the compensating duty offset the apparent reduction. The effect of the new schedules was to establish a prohibitive duty on all but the finest grades of woolen fabrics. The duties on cotton goods were largely changed from ad valorem to specific duties, but they were left at about the same level as in 1909 and were prohibitive on all but the finest grades. Plain white chinaware was charged 60 per cent, common jewelry 80 per cent, toys 70 per cent, cotton gloves about 75 per cent, laces 90 per cent, and cutlery from 75 per cent to 400 per cent. There was little change in the free list. Chemicals and dyes were substantially increased, the argument being primarily national and military in order to prevent recapture of the trade by Germany.

The administrative section of the act was commended by everyone, except such features of it as had to do with methods of valuation. The tariff commission had been working for several years on the problem of classification, technical form, phraseology, and methods of administration. Thus in the chemical schedules the body of the act was written by the commission, Congress doing little more than fill in the rates and determine the policy. In administrative methods some changes had been made in 1913; now a complete recodification was effected, the first complete revision since the establishment of the government. Supplementary administrative legislation was provided in an act of March 4, 1923.

The recommendation concerning the flexible machinery was incorporated into the act of 1922. The president was authorized to increase or decrease the tariff on particular articles by as much as 50 per cent in order to equalize cost of production at home and abroad, or, if that was not sufficient, to fix duties on the basis of an American valuation. The tariff commission was required to provide the necessary information, and the executive action would be exercised by proclamation. The constitutionality of the flexible provision was upheld by the court of customs appeals in a decision handed down February 24, 1927.

Under the flexible clause, changes were made on seventeen articles by presidential proclamation by the close of the fiscal year ending June 30, 1927. There were fourteen increases and three decreases. Six increases were on chemicals; three on agricultural products — wheat, flour, and butter; and five on manufactures — taximeters, cheap straw hats, print rollers, gold leaf, and pig iron. Ten of the increases were the maximum of 50 per cent, two were slightly less, and two were increased by fixing the duty on the basis of American selling price. The three decreases were on bobwhite quail, paintbrush handles, and mill feeds such as bran and shorts. The proclamations cited the principal competing countries. For the articles increased Germany was named seven times, Canada twice, and Norway, Switzerland, Denmark, Italy, and India once each; for the articles decreased Canada was named twice and Mexico once (for bobwhite quail).

The tariff law provided that the tariff commission should make the investigations and furnish the facts upon which the president was to base his action. All did not go well with the commission under this injunction. The high-tariff and low-tariff men seemed prone to find facts which supported their particular economic theory, and the difference in point of view became little less than open warfare over the sugar report of 1924. Political party membership seemed to make little difference. Marvin (chairman), Burgess, and Glassie favored a raise; Culbertson (vice chairman), Costigan, and Lewis favored a reduction of 50 per cent. It was reported in December, 1924, that Coolidge had under consideration a reorganization of the board and that Culbertson, the Republican member in the opposition, might be appointed to a diplomatic position. The appointment was made, as had been predicted, during the next spring, and Culbertson went to Rumania as minister. Brossard of Utah, a high-tariff man, was appointed in his place. Lewis, a low-tariff Democrat, whose term had expired and who was serving for a time under a recess appointment, was replaced by Dennis of Maryland. This made a high-protectionist majority.

On March 6, 1926, Robinson of Arkansas, Democratic floor leader, proposed a resolution to appoint a committee to investigate the tariff commission. The insurgent Republicans joined the Democrats and passed the resolution March 11. The investigation began March 23 with Taussig, the first chairman of the commission, as first witness. He expressed disapproval of Glassie's sitting on the sugar case when his wife held a hundred shares in a sugar company. He called the appointment of Burgess and of Brossard unfortunate: Burgess because he had long been known as a representative of the Potters' Association, and Brossard because of lack of training. Dennis charged Marvin, Glassie, Brossard, and Baldwin (a new appointee) with administering the commission with the intention of breaking it up. Burgess assailed Culbertson, who had criticized Glassie for sitting on the sugar investigation because his wife had sugar interests; he said that Culbertson had taken an active part in the wheat investigation when his wife owned a quarter of a section of Kansas wheatland from which she received $275 per year, or twice as much as Mrs. Glassie. He also charged Culbertson with using the commission staff to prepare his outside lectures, for which he was paid, and with using the staff and commission information for writing magazine articles and books for which he took the credit. Culbertson appeared before the committee May 19. He said in part:

While I disagreed at times with the President on the tariff and tariff-commission matters, I agreed with his foreign policy and was glad to accept under him the post of minister to Rumania. I resigned from the tariff commission, therefore, not because I was forced off, not because I was tempted off, but because I wanted to leave. To stay on the tariff commission was worse than futile: it was to continue to lend my name as a sanction to a situation which for me had become intolerable.

Senator Norris charged that Coolidge had attempted to get Culbertson to hold up the sugar report during the 1924 campaign. Costigan of the commission testified to this also and based his statement upon a letter of Culbertson's to William Allen White. Culbertson answered this to the effect that Coolidge's request was only to hold the report until he could get some other work out of the way. This reply to the charges, however, did not express his views fully, as was shown by a letter of Culbertson's written to Costigan from Bucharest in July, 1925, in comment on the appointment of Brossard and on the sugar situation.

I can hardly believe it, but it's in the *Emporia Gazette*, so it must be true. It's not much of a compliment to me that Brossard is selected to fill my place. If this appointment is to be regarded as a revelation of the President's policy, I feel justified in leaving the commission. They were certain to put you and me in a minority, and I would have been driven by the force of circumstances to break with my party without saving the commission.

How does Dennis take the appointment? This will test his professions to me. I didn't suppose that Coolidge would do the thing so rawly if he did it at all.

Evidently our suspicions were correct, and Brossard had been playing with the sugar lobby, and now he has his reward.

I can imagine the effect on the staff. They must feel that honesty is not the best policy. Write me through the pouch what the liberal elements will do about the confirmation. If they can defeat Warren this raw case ought to be easy.

My work here will not be less exciting than in Washington and, I hope, more satisfactory. I shall miss your wise advice and friendly sympathy. More power to your arm in the fight you are in.

It was obvious that Culbertson was seriously embarrassed by both the testimony and the letter. The whole investigation, however, was most illuminating as to the conditions which surrounded scientific tariff-making.

The report of the Senate committee was submitted on May 29, 1928. The majority report was signed by Joseph T. Robinson (Arkansas, Democrat), by William C. Bruce (Maryland, Democrat), and by Robert M. LaFollette, Jr. (Wisconsin, Republican insurgent). It held that the flexible provision of the tariff law should be repealed, that the record of the tariff commission was disappointing and it should be required to report its findings to Congress instead of to the president, and that the commission should be distinctly a congressional agency. The minority report was signed by Senator James W. Wadsworth (New York, Republican) and David A. Reed (Pennsylvania, Republican), who took essentially the opposite view. It should be noted that the personnel of the committee included two regular members from each party, with an insurgent Republican holding the balance of power.

Again (March 14, 1928) the tariff commission was in the newspaper headlines. Costigan's resignation was accepted. He addressed a letter of explanation to Senator Robinson, Democratic floor leader and chairman of the Senate investigating committee, in which he denounced the Marvin group as "reckless on occasions in their treatment of facts and law." He further charged that Coolidge had refused to act on decisive evidence that rates should be lowered, and that it was this course on the part of the President, together with the "manipulation of the commission since 1922," that had "helped to wreck the commission's usefulness."

Coolidge stood solidly on the tariff, refusing to sanction any revision by Congress. In his annual messages of both 1926 and 1927 he analyzed the effect of the tariff upon imports. He reported that 65 per cent of imports entered free; that of the 35 per cent paying duty, 23 per cent were luxuries and agricultural products and only 12 per cent were manufactures. It was only this last 12 per cent, he insisted, that could be considered in any discussion of tariff reduction. In his 1926 message, in commenting on prosperity, he declared that in his opinion "this whole development has been predicated on the foundation of a protective tariff." The historian, however, cannot help wondering if it was really true that American post-war prosperity was based upon so insecure a foundation as a mere act of Congress.

In the Congress that passed the act of 1922 the Democrats were in a hopeless minority, and the agricultural sections of the Republican party were extreme protectionists. By 1927–1928 the situation had changed: the parties were about evenly divided in the Senate, and the agricultural West, which supplied the largest group of insurgent Republicans, was deserting the tariff. The Democratic program was outlined by Cordell Hull, of the House of Representatives, in November, 1925. There were three principal points in his scheme: certain high rates must be cut drastically; the flexible clause must be repealed, and also the countervailing clause providing that any article on the free list should be protected if a duty were placed upon that article in another country. His argument was similar to Wilson's, that domestic and foreign economic policy must be coördinated.

The question of agricultural relief stirred up the most serious opposition to the tariff. Senator McMaster (South Dakota, Republican) announced a resolution in December, 1927, proposing a general and immediate downward revision of the tariff. The resolution was passed by the Senate January 16, 1928, by a vote of 54 to 34. On the whole, it was a combination of the South and the West against the industrial East; politically, it was a combination of insurgent Republicans and low-tariff Democrats. McMaster denounced the tariff on farm products as a farce and a fraud, and insisted that everything the farmer was required to buy was taxed.

The only way agriculture can win relief is by arousing the industrial East. I want to see the industrial group placed on the defensive just as agriculture has been on the defensive for the last seven years.

The West must strike industry where it hurts to get any necessary relief. I know no better way to bring the East to its senses than to tamper with the tariff.

The farmer is determined in this. They must either get the benefits of the tariff or they must be relieved of the burdens of the tariff.

The regular Republicans opposed any revision of the tariff on the eve of a presidential election. In the House, where the industrial East had the balance of power, they tabled the resolution January 17 by a vote of 183 to 164. Viewing the matter from the standpoint of history, agriculture should have considered these questions in 1921 and 1922 rather than in 1928; for instance, they might profitably have read Wilson's message of March 3, 1921, vetoing the emergency tariff, because after seven years they had in many respects come back to his position on this point.

SELECTED BIBLIOGRAPHY

TAUSSIG, F. W. Tariff History of the United States (Seventh Edition). G. P. Putnam's Sons, 1924.

NOYES, A. D. The War Period of American Finance, 1908–1925. G. P. Putnam's Sons, 1926.

MORGAN, H. E. "The Growing Burden of Government Costs in America," *Current History* (January, 1927), Vol. XXV, pp. 504–508.

CHAPTER VIII

BANKING, CURRENCY, AND INDUSTRIAL FINANCE

THE Federal Reserve Act was approved on December 23, 1913. The preamble called it "an act to provide for the establishment of Federal Reserve Banks, to furnish an elastic currency, to afford means of rediscounting commercial paper, to establish a more effective supervision of banking in the United States, and for other purposes." The country was to be divided into from eight to twelve districts, and a Reserve Bank was to be established in each district, incorporated for twenty years. National banks were required to become members of the Reserve Bank in their district, and state banks and trust companies might join if they met the conditions. The control of the system was placed in the hands of a Federal Reserve Board of seven men. The Secretary of the Treasury and the Comptroller of the Currency were ex officio members; the remaining five were appointed by the president with the consent of the Senate. The Federal Reserve Banks were governed by a board of nine members divided into three groups: class A represented member banks; class B, the commercial, industrial, and agricultural interests of the district; and class C, the Federal Reserve Board. One of the members representing the Federal Reserve Board was to act as Federal Reserve agent. A Federal advisory council was provided, to be made up of one man from each district, appointed by the board of directors of each Federal Reserve Bank. This council was to meet quarterly and report advice and recommendations to the Federal Reserve Board. Conferences of governors of the Federal Reserve Banks and of the Federal Reserve agents could be called to meet with the Board.

Commercial paper drawn for commercial, industrial, and agricultural purposes might be discounted by Federal Reserve Banks for member banks. Agricultural paper must be secured by staple agricultural products or live stock and have a maturity of not more than six months. The maximum time of maturity for other discounts was ninety days. No discounts should be made to finance investment or trading in stocks, except government securities. Member banks were permitted to accept drafts and bills of exchange growing out of import or export of goods and with not more than six months to run. Such acceptances could be discounted at Federal Reserve Banks with a maximum maturity of three months. Reserve Banks could engage in open-market operations, buying and selling cable transfers, bankers' acceptances, and bills of exchange; they could deal in bullion or coin at home or abroad; they could buy and sell government bonds and securities of nation, state, or other subdivisions with not more than six months to run. Foreign accounts and agencies could be established with the consent of the Federal Reserve Board. Discount rates were to be fixed by the Reserve Banks with the approval of the Federal Reserve Board.

National banks were permitted to lend money on improved lands for terms not exceeding five years. Under certain conditions permits to engage in trust business might be granted. Banks with a capital and surplus of a million or more might be permitted to establish foreign branches.

A new currency system was provided. Upon deposit of gold and commercial paper, member banks might receive Federal Reserve notes to be used as currency. The gold deposits were relatively stable, but the commercial paper running not more than ninety days supplied a flexible element in the system. The amount of commercial paper presented, and correspondingly the amount of currency received for circulation, tended to vary with the volume of business transacted in each district.

The new elements in the system may be summarized as follows: The Federal government was given general and constant supervision of the system. The Federal Reserve Banks were made fiscal agents of the government, displacing the independent treasury system established in the eighteen forties. Gold reserves were decentralized in twelve Reserve units. A discount market was established. Agricultural credits were introduced in a limited form. Control of discount rates provided a means of regulating the volume of credit and, closely associated with it, the volume of currency. Foreign commercial operations and banking were authorized to finance growing foreign trade and investments. The system ushered in a new era in American banking and credit policy, and on this foundation post-war financial stability and leadership were made possible.

The Federal Reserve system went into operation November 16, 1914. By that time the World War had begun. The financial disturbances attending its outbreak were met by the emergency credit provisions of the act of 1908, which had been extended by the Federal Reserve Act until the new system should be under way. After nearly two years of experience an act of September 7, 1916, provided many amendments of details and some extensions of the scope of operations, but did not change fundamental principles. There were modifications of the discount system, of the trust privileges of national banks, of loan privileges to include loans on city property for one year, and several other details.

Since the system went into operation under the abnormal war conditions, its initial policies and precedents were determined by such factors rather than by normal banking principles. The discount policy in particular was subordinated to the needs of the Treasury after the United States had entered the war. Liberty Bonds were marketed at from $3\frac{1}{2}$ per cent to $4\frac{1}{4}$ per cent interest, and discount rates were kept not more than half of one per cent above that mark. Preferential discount rates of half of one per cent were fixed on paper drawn to finance purchases of government securities. The commercial rates of interest were much above these figures. During 1915 and 1916 there were heavy importations of gold, and during this period the Reserve Banks followed a policy of hoarding gold. In this way gold reserves were built up to a high standard. Not only was the volume of gold in the country increased, but the currency was also increased. Between July 1, 1914, and September 1, 1918, money expanded 65 per cent. These unusual features were increased by an abnormal rise in prices.

The immediate period of post-war adjustments involved problems of unusual difficulty. The abnormal conditions did not concern the United States alone: they were world-wide. The country was obsessed by various economic illusions. The experience of the past in the course of post-war depressions should have been a warning, but experience was ignored. Prices were high and were going higher. It was generally conceded that there was underproduction and that the remedy was to increase production. The Wilson administration was not alone in this analysis. It was thought that the world would purchase larger and larger amounts of goods; but a large part of the world was devastated. It was thought that credit could be extended still further when there was little prospect of prompt liquidation of credits already outstanding. Speculation was general.

It was one of the purposes of the Federal Reserve system to provide means of discouraging undue expansion of credit. The Board considered the question of advancing discount rates in April, 1919, but the Treasury Department intervened and nothing was done. In September the Federal advisory council advised an advance, and the Treasury asked postponement until January 1, 1920. It must be remembered that the policy of the Federal Reserve Board was not determined during this period by the economic requirements of the banking situation but by the Treasury Department's policies in financing the war. The Victory Loan had been authorized by Congress in March, 1919, and was floated in May at 4¾ per cent. It was thought that in justice to the purchasers of war bonds the rate should be kept as near to the Liberty Bond level as possible. At that time money rates on the New York market were from 6 per cent to 8 per cent. Installment payments on Victory Bonds would be completed in November; then the discount rates could follow the requirements of credit control.

The success of the Victory Bond issue further stimulated speculation. In August a Senate resolution was urged directing an investigation of inflation and the advisability of restricting it by legislation. W. P. G. Harding, at the time governor of the Federal Reserve Board, subsequently pointed out that some of these same senators eighteen months later led the attack on the Board for permitting increases in discount rates. In November, 1919, slight increases were allowed in discount rates; and in January, 1920, the New York rate was increased to 6 per cent and in June to 7 per cent, where it remained until May, 1921. Credit expansion, however, increased in the face of these rates.

Deflation began during 1920. The causes were both foreign and domestic. Early in the year exporters were faced with the sudden cancellation of contracts and refusals of goods shipped. At home buyers' strikes were organized. Overall clubs and old-clothes clubs were formed as protests against high prices. New Orleans declared a holiday called Old-Clothes Day. New York held an economy parade. The collapse came first in Japan. The buyers' strike in March, 1920, crippled the inflated silk market. The crash came in April. Prices declined 17 per cent to 35 per cent in six weeks. There was no immediate effect in the United States, but on May 3 the Wanamaker stores announced a 29 per cent reduction of prices in their New York stores. Soon after, the deflation of prices verged on panic. Wholesale prices of all commodities fell from a level of 231 in 1920, based on the five-year average of 1910–1914, to a level of 150 in 1921.

It was then that the Federal Reserve Board was charged with causing the depression by enforcing a policy of deflation of credits and currency, and it was argued by critics that relief could come only through reduction of discount rates. The Federal Reserve conference of May 18 became the "crime of 1920." The conference had discussed the question of further advance in discount rates and warned against further expansion. There was no decision either to increase discount rates or to deflate credit or currency. Such a decision would have been beyond the competency of the conference. The stringency in credit came rather through a collapse in the values upon which the credits were based. The reduction in discount rates did not begin until April, 1921, and continued rapidly until the close of the year to between 4 per cent and $4\frac{1}{2}$ per cent. It was not until the second half of 1924 that rates reached a normal 3 per cent to $3\frac{1}{2}$ per cent.

The years 1922–1924 were a period of great imports of gold, giving the United States over half the world's supply. This had an important influence on currency and credits during the period of recovery from the depression of 1920–1921. In spite of charges of deflation Federal Reserve notes increased in amounts until October, 1920. During this period they were based to a considerable extent upon commercial paper. With the great importation of gold beginning in 1922, gold tended to displace paper as security. Instead of hoarding gold, as in 1915–1917, the Federal Reserve Banks attempted to force it into circulation. Correspondingly, Federal Reserve notes continued to decrease relatively as circulating medium.

During the period of immediate post-war adjustment numerous changes were made in details of the Federal Reserve system, especially in regard to loans and liability. No summary need be made here, because they were of little general interest. An act of March 1, 1921, repeated a familiar post-war requirement to the effect that directors of national banks must be citizens of the United States. An act of June 3, 1922, increased the membership of the Federal Reserve Board to eight, with a view to giving representation to agriculture. An act of March 4, 1923, allowed the states to tax shares, dividends, or income of national banks, the act being amended March 25, 1926. The Intermediate Credits Act of March 4, 1923, extended the time of maturity on agricultural paper from six to nine months. These amendments made no sweeping changes; but with the stabilization fairly well worked out by 1924, a definite campaign was opened for more fundamental changes in the national banking system.

The Federal Reserve law of 1913 was purposely designed to fix strict limitations on banking in the interest of stability, but during the first decade of its operation many changes had taken place. In the opinion of many bankers, trust and investment business became more profitable than the regular business, or became necessary to the fullest development of their banking business. National banks were restricted in these fields. The act of 1913 authorized the Board to permit national banks to engage in trust business. The banks were handicapped, however, by twenty-year charters, which raised the question of accepting trusts running beyond their charter limits. An act of July 1, 1922, granted ninety-nine-year charters as a step toward remedying this situation. The reports indicated that 1140 banks conducted a trust business. The investment business was not clearly recognized under the act of 1913, but a liberal interpretation had been placed upon the phrase authorizing national banks to deal in notes, drafts, bills of exchange, "and other evidences of debt." Under this vague clause, bond departments had been established in many banks.

The public had become accustomed to the tendency of business enterprises to combine into gigantic units in the industrial and commercial fields, but little attention had been given to the relation of this development to the banking field. The banking laws provided, however, that a national bank should not make loans to any one customer in excess of 10 per cent of the bank's capital and surplus. Thus, a bank with a capital of $1,000,000 was limited to $100,000 as the maximum loan that could be made. The loans permissible under the rule were clearly inadequate, but the rule itself was regarded as essential to sound banking. The only alternative was larger banks. The giant post-war business combinations were therefore forcing a corresponding merger movement among banks in order to provide adequate banking facilities for industry.

Branch banking gained rapidly, bringing about a serious competition between the small local banks and the branches of the large banks. In this rivalry the branch banks claimed greater stability on account of greater resources. In 1911 Attorney-General George M. Wickersham ruled that branches of national banks were not authorized under existing law. There was no judicial pronouncement until after the World War. In 1922 a St. Louis bank established a branch. The test case (the First National Bank in St. Louis *v.* State of Missouri) was decided adversely by the Supreme Court on January 28, 1924. In the case of certain state banks' becoming national banks the law permitted them to retain and operate their branches. In this way there were 248 branches in existence in 1924. All these new features of the business placed a greater emphasis upon large resources, which could be secured only through mergers of smaller institutions. The reports of the Federal Reserve Board on failures also emphasized the greater stability of the larger institutions. In the two years 1924 and 1928 there were a total of 1389 bank failures, with deposits of $386,444,000. In New England and the East, where there was one bank for 7300 population, there were only 21 failures. In the Middle West and the West there were 1003 failures. In North and South Dakota there was one bank for 800 population. In the South there were 312 failures. Over half the failures of the country were in the more sparsely populated

states of the Middle West, where there were a large number
of small banks: Minnesota, Iowa, North and South Dakota,
and Oklahoma. Eighty per cent were in these states together with Nebraska, Kansas, Montana, Wyoming, and
New Mexico in the Middle West, and North and South Carolina, Georgia, and Texas in the South. The average bank in
the United States had a capital of $40,000 and deposits of
$280,000. Ninety-six per cent of the failures were in towns
of less than 25,000 population.

The tendency toward mergers developed throughout the
country both among the small banks and among the largest banks. The merger of the Chase National and the
Mechanics and Metals National, announced February 11,
1926, was an example of the large bank merger. The new
institution became the second largest bank in the United
States. The National City Bank was credited with resources
of $1,215,000,000; the enlarged Chase National Bank, with
$1,025,000,000.

Another element of uncertainty in the national situation
was the rechartering of the Federal Reserve Banks. The
charters of these institutions were to expire in 1934. In
1925 and 1926 the American Bankers' Association and the
Chamber of Commerce of the United States asked for recharter. The agricultural sections, because of their convic-
tion that the Federal Reserve system was responsible for
the deflation of 1920 and was at the bottom of their credit
difficulties, opposed the recharters unless they should be
accompanied by drastic changes. During the campaign of
1926 the question was injected into politics, and some
thought there was serious danger of its becoming a political
issue. During the year 1925 banking was immensely profitable. The price of stock in New York banks and trust
companies was reported to have increased 100 per cent.
These profits were largely attributed to development of the
investment end of the business. The branch banking privileges in some states were attractive, and the uncertainty

arising out of the question of recharter added its quota of dissatisfaction. There developed a rivalry between the national and state banking systems. Many national institutions surrendered their charters for state charters. For the year ending October 1, 1926, 87 banks left the national system and only 29 state banks entered, making a net loss of 58. This decrease in the membership began in 1922 and had continued steadily. Bankers were allured by large profits, broader scope of business, and less stringent regulation. Continued losses would endanger the whole Federal Reserve system.

The Agricultural Credits Act of 1923 had lowered the immediate capital requirements for state banks, to induce them to join the Federal Reserve system, but with little or no result. This act also directed an investigation into the reasons why state banks did not join. In 1924 the membership of the Federal Reserve system (including national and state banks) embraced 33 per cent of all banks and 70 per cent of all banking resources of the country. Only about 10 per cent of the state banks were members.

The McFadden banking bill was introduced into Congress February 11, 1924, but it was delayed for three years. One of the most serious causes of difficulty was the Hull amendment eliminating branch banking. The amendment was indorsed by the American Bankers' Association in 1924, but they reversed their action in 1926. The recharter provisions were not in the original bill, but were inserted during the session of 1925–1926. In February, 1927, the bill came to a deadlock in the Senate. At the same time the McNary-Haugen agricultural bill was also blocked. Vice President Dawes was interested in both bills; in fact, his brother, Henry M. Dawes, one-time Comptroller of the Currency, was credited with the genesis of the bill. An agreement was worked out by which the Eastern supporters of the bank bill would assist in bringing the agricultural bill to a vote in return for the support of their bill. Cloture was voted on both bills February 3. In this manner the bank bill was passed by the Senate 71 to 17. It was then passed by the House 298 to 22. Coolidge approved the bill February 25, 1927. The provisions of the act warrant a rather full summary. Consolidations of national banks had been authorized by the act of November 17, 1918; the present act made possible the direct consolidation of a state bank and a national bank. Safe-deposit business was legalized. Real estate could be held by a bank in anticipation of future needs. Adjustment was made of the amount of discounts allowed to a Federal intermediate credit bank in order to remedy an omission in the act of 1923. National banks were granted indeterminate charters instead of ninety-nine-year charters as provided in 1922; this was to accommodate long-time trusts. Dealing in investment securities was directly authorized, but dealing in stocks was excluded. Loans on city real estate might be made for a maximum of five years. Savings departments were legalized. The maximum time of maturity of agricultural loans was increased from nine months to ten. Branch banking was authorized in states permitting branch banking by state institutions. On January 1, 1926, twenty-one states permitted branch banking, seventeen states prohibited it, and ten states had no provision. Only ten states permitted state-wide branch banking. Lastly, and possibly most important of all, the Federal Reserve Banks were rechartered. With these changes the Federal Reserve system entered upon a new era in its history.

SELECTED BIBLIOGRAPHY

Noyes, A. D. The War Period of American Finance, 1908–1925. G. P. Putnam's Sons, 1926.

Goldenweiser, E. A. The Federal Reserve System in Operation. McGraw-Hill Book Company, Inc., 1925.

Harding, W. P. G. The Formative Period of the Federal Reserve System. Houghton Mifflin Company, 1925.

Reed, H. L. The Development of Federal Reserve Policy. Houghton Mifflin Company, 1922.

Preston, H. H. "The McFadden Banking Act," *American Economic Review* (June, 1927), Vol. XVII, pp. 201–218.

CHAPTER IX

TRANSPORTATION AND COMMUNICATION SYSTEMS

RAILROADS

WAR–TIME government control over railroads, ocean and coastwise shipping, inland waterways, express, telegraph, cable, and wireless demonstrated the value of unified control and coördination of transportation and communication systems, not only for military purposes but for economic and public purposes in time of war. The lesson was impressed indelibly upon the country. The pervading spirit of national and military self-sufficiency indicated the continuation and development of this phase of policy, embracing all mediums — land, water, and air. In the pre-war period the government had approached many of these problems from the standpoint of restriction. The resulting policy was negative and was critical of the prevailing economic tendencies. In the post-war period the approach was from the standpoint of constructive assistance to business, and the resulting policy recognized and accepted as an obligation the promotion of such a national transportation and communication system.

Wilson's annual message of December 2, 1918, was the first official proposal of the new post-war policy. He had no definite plan, but he said that in fairness to the roads and to the public something must be provided. He indicated three possibilities: return to the old conditions, complete government control or even ownership, or modified government control under a unified and affirmative policy of public regulation.

The one conclusion that I am ready to state with confidence is that it would be a disservice alike to the country and to the owners of the railroads to return to the old conditions unmodified. Those are conditions of restraint without development. There is nothing

127

affirmative or helpful about them. What the country chiefly needs is that all its means of transportation should be developed — its railways, its waterways, its highways, and its countryside roads. Some new element of policy, therefore, is absolutely necessary — necessary for the service of the public, necessary for the release of credit to those who are administering the railways, necessary for the protection of their security holders. The old policy may be changed much or little, but surely it cannot wisely be left as it was.

Public opinion also generally condemned a return of the railroads to pre-war conditions. The Plumb plan (a socialistic proposal supported by the railroad brotherhoods) was even more positively rejected. Wilson's third proposal was the only approach to a common agreement in principle; an agreement in detail came only through a long process of debate and delay. The bill was finally passed and was approved by Wilson on February 28; it is known as the Transportation Act of 1920.

On March 1, 1920, the government returned the railroads to private operation under the terms of the act. Government assistance was extended to meet the adjustment of immediate financial difficulties. In rate-making policy the act inaugurated new principles in the relations between the government and the railroads. The Interstate Commerce Commission was expressly enjoined to make rates with a view to allowing the roads, either as a whole or as groups, under good management, a fair return of $5\frac{1}{2}$ per cent, plus — at its discretion — $\frac{1}{2}$ per cent for improvements. After February 28, 1922, the Commission was to fix what it considered a fair return. Under previous legislation the railroads were protected in rate-fixing policy only by the due-process-of-law clause in the Fifth Amendment to the Constitution. The railroads were now relieved of the burden of proof of the reasonableness of any proposed advance in rates unless they were at the time receiving a fair return. Upon the Commission was now placed the responsibility not only of providing rates adequate to assure a fair return on the investment, but of providing the nation with an adequate transportation system. To accomplish this end it was necessary to empower the Commission to fix intrastate rates where these influenced interstate rates, to pass upon new construction and upon the abandonment of roads, and even to require the building of new lines. New issues of securities, regulation of service and traffic, and pooling were placed under its supervision. The control of one road by another through lease or purchase of stock or otherwise might be permitted with its consent. The climax of the whole scheme was a mandate to work out a plan for consolidation of all railroads in the United States into a limited number of competing groups.

The labor provisions of the act also presented matters of unusual interest. The law recognized three methods of settling difficulties: (1) by direct negotiation between railroads and employees; (2) by railroad boards of adjustment to be formed voluntarily by the railroads and the employees, with jurisdiction over disputes not involving wages; (3) by the Railroad Labor Board, created by the statute, with jurisdiction over wages in the event of failure of direct negotiations and with jurisdiction over other disputes if the boards of adjustment were not organized or if they failed to reach a settlement. This board was not given power to enforce decisions. It was constituted in a form which was very popular at the time: three members were chosen to represent the railroad executives, three to represent labor, and three to represent the public.

In the application of the act the problems of rates and wages were interrelated and required immediate adjustment. During the last days of government operation the railroads were running at a loss; but the administration decided to supply the deficit out of public funds for the time being, rather than increase rates. The appropriation to cover the deficit was continued for six months, under private operation, and in the meantime the Interstate Commerce Commission was working out adjustments in rates and wages.

The rate decisions were dated July 29, 1920, effective August 26, based on a temporary valuation of $18,900,000,000 to yield $5\frac{1}{2}$ per cent plus $\frac{1}{2}$ per cent for improvements; they authorized increases of from 25 per cent to 40 per cent in freight rates, of 20 per cent in passenger fares, and of 50 per cent (to accrue to the railroad) in sleeping-car fares. In spite of the opposition of the states these increases were applied to intrastate commerce as well as to interstate commerce; this was upheld by the Supreme Court (February 27, 1922) in the Wisconsin Passenger Fare case. These increases in rates likewise took into consideration the fact of labor adjustments. The Railroad Labor Board decisions of July 20, 1920, authorized wage increases of approximately 22 per cent retroactive to May 1. This added a burden to railroad operation of approximately $600,000,000.

Post-war deflation began definitely in May, 1920, as indicated by the fall of wholesale prices. Its effect on the railroads was not particularly apparent until November; it touched bottom in February, 1921. This deflation deprived the railroads of the adequate income anticipated by the Interstate Commerce Commission in authorizing the rate increases. It also tended to lower general operation costs and living expenses and led to the reopening of the controversies over wages and rates. Two other problems complicated the situation during 1921: the creation of the railroad boards of adjustment and the adoption of agreements respecting rules governing working conditions. On both these questions the basic differences were similar: the employees wanted national adjustment boards and national agreements; the railway executives wanted local boards and local agreements. The failure to arrive at an understanding between themselves threw the whole burden of decision on the Railroad Labor Board.

The controversy over agreements in respect to rules governing working conditions dated from the war period, when agreements had been made with certain groups. The Labor

Board postponed a decision on this question until the more pressing questions of wages and rates were disposed of. A decision was reached and new rules were promulgated between August and November, 1921. In the meantime the wage controversy led to a decision (July 1, 1921) fixing decreases which averaged about 12 per cent. This left the wage level about 7 per cent above that of March, 1920. The railway executives asked (October 14) for further reductions to the level of March, 1920, and then the four brotherhoods threatened a strike. The whole matter was postponed through an announcement that no further wage reductions would be considered until the question of rates was settled.

Rate reduction after the deflation began in August, 1921, on live stock and was extended to grain in October and to other products in January, 1922. On May 16 the Commission ordered a 10 per cent horizontal reduction for all rates, to be effective on July 1. This was based upon the new standard of fair return, fixed by the Commission at $5\frac{3}{4}$ per cent.

Wage reductions were then adjusted in conjunction with the new rates. During May and June decisions were announced providing wage reductions to be effective July 1. The new scale was practically the level of March, 1920, except for the brotherhoods. The shopmen called a strike in protest against the wage reductions and the board's rules governing working conditions. The strike was lost on all points. The effect of the strike on the Railroad Labor Board, together with the quarreling between factions on the board, was decisive in discrediting it with labor and to a great extent with the public. Harding, in his annual message of December 8, 1922, recommended "the substitution of a labor division in the Interstate Commerce Commission." This indicated that he still favored the continuance of a government agency.

The amendment of the labor provisions of the Transportation Act became only a matter of the time necessary to come to an agreement on a substitute. Coolidge gradually responded to the newer conservative philosophy of economic self-government. In his annual message of December 8, 1925, he reported:

> I am informed that the railroad managers and their employees have reached a substantial agreement as to what legislation is necessary to regulate and improve their relationship. Whenever they bring forward such proposals, which seem sufficient also to protect the interests of the public, they should be enacted into law.
>
> It is gratifying to report that both the railroad managers and railroad employees are providing boards for the mutual adjustment of differences in harmony with the principles of conference, conciliation, and arbitration. The solution of their problems ought to be an example to all other industries. Those who ask the protection of civilization should be ready to use the methods of civilization.

The principle of self-constituted adjustment boards had been included in the Transportation Act of 1920 to a limited degree, but with the government board occupying the major position. The new scheme approved by the President turned practically all disputes over to this self-constituted machinery.

The measure referred to was presented to Congress as the Watson-Parker Bill. It passed the House on March 1, 1926, by a vote of 381 to 13, and the Senate on May 11 by a vote of 69 to 13. The unusual procedure by which the bill passed excited a marked degree of comment. One editorial stated that "instead of Congress devising a law to keep the peace between the railroads and their workers, we are witnessing the strange phenomenon of railroad managers and labor leaders putting their heads together to draw up a plan for settling wage disputes complete in every detail and asking Congress simply to sign on the dotted line — which Congress does, with exactly thirteen dissenting votes in each house." The act abolished the Railroad Labor Board. It provided for (1) the creation of boards of adjustment "between any carrier or group of carriers, or the carriers as a whole, and its or their employees"; (2) a permanent board of mediation of five members appointed by the president; (3) a board of arbitration consisting of three members, one chosen by each of the parties and a third selected by the other two. If each of the foregoing devices failed in turn, and the dispute threatened to "interrupt interstate commerce to a degree such as to deprive any section of the country of essential transportation service," then the president might appoint an emergency board to investigate and make report. During the investigation, and for thirty days after the report, neither party should make any change in conditions out of which the dispute arose, except by agreement. The whole machinery was voluntary and was kept in the hands of the interested parties except for the appointment of the boards of mediation and investigation. It must be kept clearly in mind that there was no government machinery involved which was vested with authority to hand down decisions. This was an example of economic self-government sanctioned by the political government.

In accordance with the Transportation Act of 1920 the Interstate Commerce Commission attacked the problem of formulating a plan of consolidations; Professor Ripley of Harvard assisted in it. A scheme proposing nineteen systems was announced in 1921 as a basis of public discussion. Little headway was made, but many possible combinations were offered. Two examples excite a particular historical interest. The combination of the Southern Pacific and the Central Pacific was attacked by the government in 1911 under the pre-war antitrust acts. The case came to the Supreme Court. It was decided in 1922, and orders were issued to dissolve the combination. The Interstate Commerce Commission's consolidation scheme (announced the preceding year) included this very combination as a part of its plan. In view of this the Commission (February 6, 1923) declared the combination valid, and the circuit court of appeals upheld its action. The second case was the Northern Pacific and Great Northern railroads, which jointly owned the Chicago, Burlington and Quincy. These roads had been combined by means of the National Securities Company, which was dissolved by the Supreme Court in 1904. It was largely on this case that Roosevelt achieved fame in his trust program. In 1921 joint refunding operations of these roads were approved by the Interstate Commerce Commission, and in 1927 preparations were being made to secure the Commission's approval for outright consolidation. The press comment on this proposal was quite favorable.

Several important difficulties stood in the way of carrying out the intention of the Transportation Act with regard to consolidations. It provided for the possibility of voluntary consolidation, or consolidation according to a Commission plan. The Commission and the railroads were unable to agree, inasmuch as a proposal which would be favored by the railroads as a profitable business transaction would not meet the Commission's ideas with regard to public interest. Strong roads, as a rule, would not choose to combine with weak roads. Another difficulty was that the Commission did not adopt a final plan. This problem was linked with a mandate of the act requiring that the securities issued in a combination should not exceed the combined values of the property. The valuation work of the Commission had not been completed. A third difficulty was the provision of the act that roads might acquire control of other roads by means other than consolidations; so that until consolidation plans were finally adopted, the two lines of action might conflict with each other.

In his annual messages after 1923 Coolidge urged that Congress enact legislation to facilitate consolidation, completion of physical valuation under the act of 1913, and revision of the general structure of freight rates. He repeatedly pointed out that there was no satisfactory remedy for the defects of the rate structure until the consolidation of railroads had been effected. It was manifestly impossible to frame any rate structure which would insure a fair return to roads of all classes, strong and weak. The plan incorporated in the Transportation Act instructing the Commission to follow the rule of fair return as a basis of rate-making was scarcely practicable until the roads were grouped in combinations of approximately equal earning power.

The process of physical valuation of the railroads was begun under the act of 1913. It provided that the Commission should determine the original cost, the cost of reproducing the property new, the cost of reproduction less depreciation, the original cost and present value of land, and other values. Some parts of these instructions proved impossible to execute. The opinion of the Supreme Court expressed in the Minnesota Rate Cases was as follows:

> The ascertainment of . . . value is not controlled by artificial rules. It is not a matter of formula but must be a reasoned judgment, having its basis in a proper consideration of all the relevant facts.

After detailed study of the methods employed by the Commission in determining final values expressed as single sums, D. P. Locklin, an authority on railway economics, summed up the matter as follows:

> The final values do not vary greatly from the cost of reproduction less depreciation, plus the present value of carrier lands, plus 5 per cent of the two preceding figures, plus an allowance for working capital. Nothing is added for the intangible elements of value unless the 5 per cent can be so considered.

The prices used for valuation purposes were those of June 30, 1914, except for expenditures after that date. The first final valuation was completed on July 11, 1922; by October 31, 1927, the Commission had made final valuations on six hundred and eight cases, covering about 21 per cent of the total railroad mileage.

The results of the constructive policy of the post-war period were quite favorable to the railroads. The earnings of the first-class roads in 1921 were 3.3 per cent. This was during the period of greatest depression. In 1922, in spite of the shopmen's strike, earnings were 4.1 per cent; in 1923 they rose to 5.1 per cent. *The Railway Age* in 1928 made estimates for first-class roads which were somewhat lower than those of the Commission; they were as follows:

1921 . . . . . . 3.09%	1925 . . . . . . 5.22%
1922 . . . . . . 3.86%	1926 . . . . . . 5.5%
1923 . . . . . . 4.83%	1927 . . . . . . 4.74%
1924 . . . . . . 4.69%	

The railroads complained that the Commission continued to order reductions of rates in the face of the falling off of earning power after 1926. Under the recapture clause, half the earnings above $5\frac{3}{4}$ per cent were turned over to the government. This was to create a fund from which loans were to be made to the weaker roads. The constitutionality of the clause was upheld by the Supreme Court on January 7, 1924; but difficulties were encountered in applying it, and litigation ensued involving the methods of valuation.

The impatience of the public (especially the agricultural sections) with the failure of the Commission to make readjustments of the structure of railroad rates was finally voiced in the Hoch-Smith resolution of January 30, 1925. The Interstate Commerce Commission was directed to give consideration in rate-making to the conditions which prevail at any given time in the several industries of the country. It was to conduct an investigation of the rate structure with respect to localities and sections of the country, as between the various classes of traffic and as between the various classes and kinds of commodities, and to make adjustments to correct any defects that might be found to exist. The market value of commodities should be considered as a factor in rate-making. The last paragraph gave special consideration to agriculture as an emergency case. The resolution was directed primarily at agricultural rates, but its provisions were also of general interest. The only thing that was really new was the mandate to consider the financial conditions which prevailed in an industry in rate-making. Other factors provided in the Transportation Act and established by judicial decisions limited the scope of this new rule so narrowly that it could not greatly modify the prevailing practice.

The Interstate Commerce Commission objected strenuously to the growing tendency for different interests to bring pressure to bear upon the Commission in order to influence its action. Although the statement of B. H. Meyer of the Commission was probably directed particularly at the farm pressure for favors in rates for agricultural products, it applied also to other organized groups. At Madison, Wisconsin (May 17, 1928), he said:

I say without the slightest hesitation that if the Interstate Commerce Commission is to be influenced and controlled by external and political suggestions rather than by the considerations which have hitherto always controlled its official acts, it should be abolished.

Methods of transportation such as express, pipe lines, and parcel post can be passed over with very brief comment, and thus leave more space for considering policies of relatively larger significance to the period. In accordance with the war policy of consolidation the four great express companies were combined in May, 1918, into one system, and on November 16 they were taken over by the government. When they were returned to private operation, in 1920, they were transferred as a single organization, the American Express Company, the legality of the consolidation being confirmed by the Transportation Act of 1920. Pipe lines have come to occupy a tremendously important place in the transportation of oil. By 1925 there were 65,000 miles of pipe line, representing an investment of $518,500,000. In parcel-post policy there was little change except a reduction of rates. Highway policy presents more that is new.

SELECTED BIBLIOGRAPHY

LOCKLIN, D. P.   Railroad Regulation since 1920.   A. W. Shaw Company, 1928.

JONES, ELIOT.   Principles of Railway Transportation.   The Macmillan Company, 1924.

MCVEAGH, ROGERS.   The Transportation Act, 1920.   Henry Holt and Company, 1923.

WOLF, H. D.   The Railroad Labor Board.   The University of Chicago Press, 1927.

Report of the Committee on Recent Economic Changes of the President's Conference on Unemployment, including the Reports of a Special Staff of the National Bureau of Economic Research.   2 vols.   McGraw-Hill Book Company, 1929.

CHAPTER X

TRANSPORTATION AND COMMUNICATION SYSTEMS
(CONTINUED)

HIGHWAYS AND MOTOR TRANSPORTATION

THE automobile had been working an economic and social revolution in the life of the people. By about 1910 the experimental period of the industry had passed, and by about 1925 mechanical perfection had been developed to such a degree in standard makes of cars that on that basis there was comparatively little choice between cars in any particular price class. The manufacturers had come to emphasize economy of operation, color, design of body, and special features, rather than mechanical details. In 1906 there were about 48,000 cars in the United States, and in 1914 there were 1,700,000; the registration of passenger cars in 1920 was 8,225,859 and of trucks 1,006,082; the 1928 registration was 21,630,000 and 3,120,000 respectively. This meant a passenger car for every five and a half persons. Only 540 foreign cars were imported during the year. The United States owned about 78 per cent of the world's automobiles.

Transportation has been one of the most important and constant factors in American history. Each method of locomotion presented its problems: in the early nineteenth century those of highways and canals, later those of railroads, and in the twentieth century those of motor highways and of airplane landing fields and airway markers. The Federal government was appealed to for aid, with success in each case. By 1916 the campaign for motor highways had reached a stage where the first Federal highway act was passed and approved (July 11). The act was called a Rural Post Roads Act, and for the purpose of the act the term "rural post road" was construed "to mean any public road over which the United States mails are now or may hereafter be transported. . . ." The Secretary of Agriculture was designated to administer the act and was to coöperate with the states. A total of $75,000,000 was authorized over a five-year period to be apportioned to the states on the basis of area, population, and mileage of rural and star mail routes. The states were to submit plans for road projects. These were to be subject to the approval of the Secretary of Agriculture, and when they were approved the United States government would bear half the expenses up to a maximum of $10,000 per mile, exclusive of bridges of over twenty feet of span, provided the state would advance the other half. The payments were not to be made until construction was completed in accordance with the specifications. Maintenance expenses were to be met by the states; in case they were not, further road projects were prohibited. A total of $10,000,000 was also authorized to build roads in national forests. Although the act was based upon the postal clause, it was administered by the Secretary of Agriculture. It was evident that the postal clause was merely a device incorporated into the act to establish its legality, because otherwise it would be difficult to find constitutional authority for such Federal activity unless it could be done under the war power.

During the preparedness campaign before the entrance of the United States into the World War the military character of highway policy was conspicuous. In the Army Appropriation Act of August 29, 1916, the Council of National Defense was created. Among its numerous activities it was charged with the duty of making investigations and recommendations for the location of frontier railroads and "the coördination of military, industrial, and commercial purposes in the location of extensive highways and branch lines of railroad; the utilization of waterways etc."

After the war the conception of a transportation system for military and commercial purposes was an ever-present element in the plans for reconstruction. As has already been pointed out, Wilson in his annual message for 1918 recommended the development of highways as well as waterways and railroads.

Under the legislation of 1916 the Federal government had expended $75,000,000 for roads by 1921. Secretary Meredith, in his annual report of January, 1921, recommended annual expenditures of $100,000,000 by the Federal government. Harding, in his special message of April 12, 1921, recommended further appropriations and amendment of legislation. The new act was approved November 9, 1921. It adopted the new title "Federal Highway Act." The powers of the Council of National Defense over roads were transferred to the Secretary of Agriculture. Surplus army road materials also were transferred and distributed among the states, except 10 per cent which the secretary might reclaim to expend on roads under his jurisdiction. The new conception of a national transportation system was definitely incorporated into the law. In giving approval to road projects the Secretary of Agriculture was instructed to give preference to those making a connected system of interstate highways. Roads designated as Federal-aid highways should not exceed 7 per cent of the roads in any state and were to be divided into primary and secondary classes. Primary roads were those forming interstate systems, and were not to exceed three sevenths of the mileage nor more than 60 per cent of the appropriations; secondary roads were connecting roads. More definite administrative provisions were incorporated, based on five years of experience. The maximum Federal expenditure per mile was fixed at $20,000. After the 7 per cent was completed, additional projects might be approved by the secretary. The appropriation for 1922 was $75,000,000, or a sum equal to the amount authorized in 1916 for five years. This became the standard annual appropriation. For roads and trails in national forests the appropriations were $5,000,000 and $10,000,000 for 1922 and

1923, but in the following years the regular annual appropriation was fixed at $7,500,000.

By the end of 1926 the total expenditure of Federal and state governments on road construction amounted to $1,051,403,098, of which the Federal government had provided $473,558,553. The mileage completed was 55,000, with some 10,000 under construction to be completed in 1927. Coolidge, in his annual message of December 6, 1927, took the ground that "national participation should be confined to trunk-line systems." This was a departure from the statement of policy incorporated in the act of 1921, which limited primary systems to three sevenths of the state mileage authorized to receive aid.

Between the years 1895 and 1926 the total number of persons killed by motor cars was estimated at 170,612. Before 1910 the figures were estimates; after that date they were exact. This was approximately half the number of men killed in all American wars, the total of which was given as 323,702. In 1925, according to Hoover, 23,900 were killed and approximately 600,000 injured. This was approximately half the American casualties during the World War. In 1928 there were about 27,000 killed and 800,000 injured. The National Automobile Chamber of Commerce reported for the years 1919–1926, inclusive, 120,050 deaths and over 3,500,000 injuries. Of these 26 per cent were children under fifteen years of age. The Department of Commerce held annual conferences on street and highway safety, beginning in 1925, the most concrete result being the drafting of three model state laws which were adopted by several states in order to establish uniform motor-traffic codes. The Federal government enacted a law (approved October 29, 1919) providing for the punishment of car thieves in interstate and foreign commerce. The question of a national registration system was pending.

The building of roads brought the development of motor-coach passenger lines and motor-truck lines. The report of the Interstate Commerce Commission indicated that at the end of 1926 there were 28,368 coaches in operation as common carriers in line and terminal service, and the line routes over which passengers and goods were carried totaled 352,800 miles. This was more than the total railroad mileage of the United States. Railroads in class 1 reported 502 coaches operating under railroad control in line service totaling 6838 miles; motor-transport companies operated 20,352 coaches, with a mileage of 345,962 in line service. Motor trucks numbered 43,432 in line service, with a mileage of approximately 600,000. The motor coach became a permanent adjunct to the railroad business as well as a competitor. In the case of electric interurban railroads the motor proved disastrous. The National Automobile Chamber of Commerce reported that 2500 miles of electric lines had been replaced by motors in ten years. The Interstate Commerce Commission reported in 1928 that the ton mileage of railroads in 1925 was 414,139,835,000 and of motor trucks 16,356,526,667. If half this load was carried on rural roads, it would mean that motor-truck ton mileage equaled 1.9 per cent of the load of the railroads.

In the propaganda for the building of the interstate highways the demands were insistent that the matter was one of national significance, and that the aim, as stated in the act of 1921, was to give preference to the development of interstate traffic-ways. This was one side of the story. The motor-coach passenger lines and motor-truck lines operated over Federal highways. Who had jurisdiction over the traffic over these? At a national conference of motor-coach operators in May, 1925, resolutions were passed asking for a restriction of the powers of the Interstate Commerce Commission over motor transportation, on the ground that coach lines were primarily local and intrastate, not interstate. The question of state jurisdiction over interstate motor-highway traffic was settled by two decisions of the Supreme Court on March 2, 1926. States did not have authority to restrict operation of motor coaches or trucks in interstate commerce where such regulation was not primarily for the purpose of safety and for conservation of the highways. After that date no regulation of this traffic was exercised except in rail terminal services. To cover this field of transportation several bills were introduced into Congress, but they failed to pass.

In dealing with questions relating to coach and truck service the Interstate Commerce Commission was embarrassed by a lack of legislation. The entry of railroads into the motor field raised a question of the legality of such service. Under the Transportation Act any new railroadbuilding or additional service or abandonment of lines was under the jurisdiction of the Commission. Would this authority apply to motor service to supplement rail service or as a substitute for it? In view of the numerous difficulties and the irresponsibility of many of the motor lines acting as common carriers in interstate commerce, the Commission decided that to meet these new problems adequately it must act under its authority to make investigations and to recommend new legislation. The investigation was ordered and was begun under the direction of Leo J. Flynn, June 15, 1926. It continued through the years 1926 and 1927, hearings being held in all parts of the United States. The final report was made public January 16, 1928.

The recommendations of the Commission's report outlined the following policy: Original jurisdiction in regulation of motor-coach and truck traffic in interstate and foreign commerce should be vested in state regulatory bodies who would consent to act; otherwise the Commission should be given jurisdiction. Where commerce was carried on in two or more states, joint boards made up of representatives of state regulatory bodies should be authorized to act. When the Interstate Commerce Commission was acting for a state agency it should be included in the joint board. In both these cases the right of appeal to the Interstate Commerce

Commission should be provided. The prerequisite for a common carrier entering such commerce should be a certificate of the convenience and necessity of the service, issued by the proper authority, and provision for liability insurance or indemnity bonds or other satisfactory assurance of financial responsibility. In granting certificates full consideration should be given to the relation of the new service to existing services by other means. It should also be made a condition that the carrier assume the obligation of increasing service facilities at the request of the regulatory body as traffic requirements expanded. Rates should be reasonable, and proper accounting, reports, and bills of lading should be required. Brokerage in motor transportation should be prohibited except for persons possessing required certificates.

This report seemed an attempt to conciliate the post-war advocates of states' rights as well as to meet the outspoken opposition of the operators of motor-transportation facilities. In the light of experience in railroad regulation it was doubtful whether this decentralized system would work effectively. The coach and truck operators, nevertheless, denounced the plan as another step in Federal encroachment on business and on states' rights.

CHAPTER XI

TRANSPORTATION AND COMMUNICATION SYSTEMS
(Continued)

Inland Waterways

DURING the World War the inland waterways were brought under Federal-government control, as were other transportation facilities. A director-general was appointed February 16, 1918. In his annual message of December 2 after the armistice, Wilson indorsed the coördination of rail, water, and highway facilities. In the Transportation Act of 1920 Congress took definite steps to make such a policy effective. In Section 500 a declaration of policy was made: "It is hereby declared to be the policy of Congress to promote, encourage, and develop water transportation, service, and facilities, in connection with the commerce of the United States, and to foster and preserve in full vigor both rail and water transportation."

Federal control over transportation systems was revoked by the same act, including the powers of the president to purchase, construct, or acquire boats, barges, and tugs, canal and coastwise waterways, or terminal facilities, and to utilize and operate canals. Such of these facilities as were owned by the government were transferred to the Secretary of War. He was directed to construct terminal facilities to provide for the interchange of traffic between the transportation facilities operated by him and other transportation facilities, whether rail or water. He might make loans to a state or, according to an amendment of March 4, 1921, to any municipality or transportation company, subject to the approval of the Interstate Commerce Commission. He was, further, to operate the facilities owned by the United

States on the Mississippi River above St. Louis. Such transportation facilities operated by the Secretary of War were to be subject to the Interstate Commerce Act and the shipping act of 1916, and the vessels were to be subject to the laws governing the merchant marine.

The Secretary of War was still further directed to investigate the most appropriate types of boats for different classes of waterways, to investigate water terminal facilities for water and rail service, to advise with the communities and cities regarding the location of terminals, to investigate existing service on inland waterways, and to collect and distribute information and statistics. For the purpose of this act inland waterways were to include the Great Lakes. The act included the New York Barge Canal, but this was unintentional and was repealed by a joint resolution approved February 27, 1921.

President Harding accepted the policies already outlined. In his special message of April 12, 1921, he restated the formula in his own words: "Linked with rail and highway is the problem of water transportation — inland, coastwise, and transoceanic." Again in his second annual message he said, "Manifestly we have need to begin on plans to coördinate all transportation facilities. . . ." Coolidge subsequently indorsed the same program in successive messages. This was the situation at the beginning of the period, together with executive declarations of policy. It remains to trace briefly the policies followed out in the improvement of waterways and in development of the traffic on them under government encouragement. One of the particular difficulties in treating water transportation is the overlapping of services. Inland traffic was often associated with coastwise business; ocean facilities often engaged in part-time coastwise trade. The Great Lakes – Atlantic waterway project would bring ocean traffic into the greatest of the inland waterways. The present discussion is limited primarily to the inland-waterway phase of the problem.

Interest centered upon two great projects: the Great Lakes–Atlantic waterway and the Mississippi River system. The former project was agitated continuously after the war and even before. The Middle West favored the St. Lawrence River outlet through Canada; New York insisted upon an all-American route which among other things would direct all traffic through the port of New York. There were two possible New York routes: the Erie Canal to Albany from Lake Erie and the Oswego-Albany Canal from Lake Ontario. Through an agreement between the United States and Canada (April 22, 1925) a study of the international aspect of the project was authorized.

The reports on the investigation were made by the Department of Commerce in January, 1927. Hoover, Secretary of Commerce, recommended the St. Lawrence outlet, which would admit ocean ships into the Great Lakes by a series of locks and would develop five million electric horse power. At the direction of Congress engineers of the War Department made a survey which agreed with the report of the Department of Commerce. The St. Lawrence outlet would be cheaper to construct and would require only nine locks, whereas the New York route would require twenty. The former would necessitate 25 miles of restricted navigation; the latter, 128 miles. The distance of haul from the Great Lakes to New York City would be 1550 miles greater by the St. Lawrence River than by the New York route, but to Europe it would be 625 miles shorter. The St. Lawrence route could be completed in ten years. The initial traffic was estimated at from nineteen to thirty-four million tons annually. The proposed twenty-seven-foot channel would admit 81 per cent of ocean tonnage. The savings in freight on a bushel of wheat shipped from Duluth to Liverpool would be $6\frac{1}{2}$ cents.

The improvement of the Mississippi River system not only involved the maintenance of the channel but was complicated by the problem of flood control. For the present purposes flood-control policy may begin with the act of March 1, 1917. The Secretary of War was authorized to carry out the plans of the Mississippi River Commission for control of floods and improvement of the river from the mouth of the Ohio to the head of the Passes. For this purpose an appropriation of $45,000,000 was authorized, not more than $10,000,000 to be expended in any one year. Levee work was authorized as far up the river as Rock Island, Illinois. Federal money was to be expended only when plans for levee construction by local authorities were approved and half the expenditure was provided by such authorities. Levees must be maintained by local interests. The Sacramento River improvement was also provided on the same plan. The fifty-fifty plan of Federal and state financing was similar to the highway policy of the same period.

After the act of 1917 there were regular appropriations as well as extensions of the scope of the work. In 1922 work was extended above Cairo, and surveys of the problem of control near the mouth of the Mississippi were made in 1926. An act of March 4, 1923, authorized annual appropriations of $10,000,000 for six years beginning in 1924. The unusual floods of 1927, especially on the lower course of the river, raised the question of broader plans and larger appropriations. The flood began April 22. The damage was estimated at $300,000,000, and two hundred and forty-six lives were lost. Relief work cost $34,800,000; of this amount $7,500,000 was spent by the Federal government, $10,000,000 by the states, and $17,300,000 by the Red Cross. The army engineers' plan of flood control called for $296,400,000, excluding tributaries and reservoir projects. Eighty per cent of the cost was the maximum which should be assumed by the Federal government. The Mississippi River Commission (created 1879) presented a plan of much broader scope, the cost of which was estimated at $775,000,000. Coolidge stood for a distinct limitation of Federal responsibility; Congress seemed to be disposed to go to the other extreme. In the conference between the two Houses the President's point of view was accepted on some points: the extent of liability for flood control was limited, no expenditure being made for right of way on natural flood ways. Press reports indicated that Congress was given to understand that the bill would be vetoed unless these changes were made. The act as approved May 15, 1928, provided for a further strengthening of the levee system; this was a continuation of the work under the flood acts of 1917 and 1923. Three flood ways and a spillway were to be built to carry excess water at times of flood. The cost was to be borne by the Federal government, except the cost for levee foundations, which was to be provided by the states. The estimated cost to the Federal government was $325,000,000 and to the states $500,000. The War Department reported January 3, 1929, that the project could be completed in ten years at the rate of progress maintained during the first year.

The scope of channel improvement was indicated in a general way by the administration, as in Coolidge's third annual message (1925), where he stated that "a modern channel connecting Chicago, New Orleans, Kansas City, and Pittsburgh should be laid out, and work on the tributaries prosecuted. Some work is being done of a preparatory nature along the Missouri, and large expenditures are being made in the lower reaches of the Mississippi and its tributaries which contribute both to flood control and navigation. . . . Work on the Ohio River will be completed in about three years." Again (November 22, 1926) Secretary Hoover, speaking for the administration, urged that the Mississippi waterway improvement should be taken up as a whole. It could be completed in five years at a cost of $150,000,000. The bill authorizing this project was signed by Coolidge on January 21, 1927. As enacted, it carried all the earmarks of pork-barrel methods, especially in its efforts to conciliate the upper Missouri valley farm bloc. The major appropriations required to carry out the project were yet to be made.

The last phase of the inland waterways to be treated here is the operation of transportation facilities by the government after their transfer to the Secretary of War in 1920. During the first four years the secretary operated them directly; but by an act of June 3, 1924, an Inland Waterways Corporation was created "for the purpose of carrying out the mandate and purpose of Congress as expressed in Sections 201 and 500 of the Transportation Act." The corporation was chartered in the District of Columbia and was capitalized at $5,000,000, the whole of which was subscribed by the government. The act provided that the Secretary of War should direct and govern the corporation in the exercise of its functions, but should consult with an advisory board of six men appointed by himself, and he should appoint a chairman to manage the corporation. The duties of the corporation were to carry on the operations of government-owned inland, canal, and coastwise water-transportation facilities (including terminals) and to develop these to a point where the system could be transferred to private operation to the best advantage of the government. As soon as the improvement of the channel permitted, a line was to be established on the Mississippi River above St. Louis. There was to be no discontinuance or addition of other lines except at the direction of Congress. The system was made subject to the provisions of the Interstate Commerce Act and the shipping act of 1916.

On February 12 the Secretary of War announced that the Inland Waterways Corporation, operating Federal barges on the Mississippi and Warrior rivers, had made agreements with one hundred and sixty-five railroads effecting cheaper transportation of freight for forty-one states. It was announced in May, 1927, that the barge line had made a profit in 1926 for the first time since its organization in 1920. The report also stated that although private capital could operate barges with a profit on the lower river, the conditions did not permit profitable operation on the upper Mississippi, and government support would be necessary to continue demonstration and experimentation. Savings in freight enjoyed by the public were estimated at $20,000,000 per year. The Interstate Commerce Commission (July 30, 1927) ordered railroads to make joint rates with barge lines on the upper Mississippi, allowing a 15 per cent differential under the rail rates. This extended the principle previously applied to the lower river and set a precedent for the Missouri River when improvements should be completed.

The river interests demanded further legislation, and an act to extend the system was approved May 29, 1928. The capital of the Inland Waterways Corporation was increased from $5,000,000 to $15,000,000. The service of government barge lines was directed to be extended to the tributaries of the Mississippi (except the Ohio) as soon as improvements permitted and when such operation appeared to be in the public interest. The powers of the Interstate Commerce Commission were extended with respect to development of through routes and joint rates and to fair division of traffic over railroads and inland waterways. The policy of the government was stated to be to continue the barge service under government operation until suitable channels and terminals should be provided on the tributaries, and the barge services should not be turned over to private interests until such time. When the Mississippi River and the Warrior River services were disposed of they should be sold separately. In this manner the government was attempting to make the inland-waterways transportation an integral part of the national transportation system as outlined in the Transportation Act of 1920. Here nationalism and the principle of assistance to business outweighed the principle of "less government in business."

CHAPTER XII

TRANSPORTATION AND COMMUNICATION SYSTEMS
(CONTINUED)

AVIATION

AIRCRAFT was the product of the pre-war period in both the major forms — dirigibles and planes. The use of aircraft during the war brought about a rapidity of development which could not have occurred in a like period of peace. By the end of the war a stage of perfection had been reached which made air commerce a practical, though experimental and speculative, business. Up to the close of the war the major use of aircraft had been military, and it was natural that under such circumstances governments should have been vitally interested in promoting civil air service as well as military air service. There was a marked contrast, therefore, between the governmental interest in automobile development, for instance, and in aviation. In the former the initiative and risks were assumed wholly by private enterprise; in the latter, after the World War, promotion was undertaken with active government encouragement and some assistance. The army and navy services were of vital importance to the development of civil air service, both directly and indirectly.

The first field of government activity in civil aviation was the establishment of air-mail service between Washington and New York in May, 1918. This was owned and operated by the government. In 1919 the first division of transcontinental service was opened from Chicago to Cleveland, and during the next year the Cleveland–New York division and the Chicago–San Francisco division. Until 1924, when night flying was begun, the service was by train and plane.

Chicago was made the center of midcontinental service, lateral lines being established by 1928 with St. Paul, St. Louis, Cincinnati, Detroit, San Antonio, and Galveston by way of Kansas City and Dallas. Salt Lake City became the center of mountain service, with radiating lines, by 1928, through Boise to Pasco (Washington) to Great Falls (Montana) and to Los Angeles. Pacific-coast lines connected San Francisco north to Seattle and south to Los Angeles. Atlantic-coast lines reached New Orleans and Miami.

Air-mail postage was fixed by act of Congress (May 10, 1918) at not to exceed twenty-four cents an ounce or a fraction thereof. The service was operated by the Postmaster-General until 1926. The prevailing sentiment against government operation, except in the experimental stage, when the government was to bear the losses, dictated a transfer to private operation. An act of February 2, 1925, was passed "to encourage commercial aviation and to authorize the Postmaster-General to contract for air-mail service." Rates of postage were to be not less than ten cents an ounce. Contracts with private operators were not to exceed four fifths of the revenue collected for air mail and were not to exceed four fifths of the revenues from other first-class mail. The contract price was changed by an act of June 3, 1926, to a fixed rate per pound. Rates for air mail were not to exceed three dollars per pound for the first thousand miles and thirty cents per pound for each additional hundred miles. Rates on other first-class mail were not to exceed sixty cents per pound for the first thousand miles and six cents for each additional hundred. During the fiscal year 1928 contractors received $4,042,777 for carrying 1,861,800 pounds of mail. As the average piece of first-class mail weighed 0.433 ounce, the receipts from postage amounted to about $3,425,712.

The transfer to private operation was completed rapidly, the last contract (the one covering the New York to Chicago division) being announced April 3, 1927, at $1.24 per pound to the National Air Transport, Inc. (N.A.T.). This company also operated the Chicago-Dallas line. These mail contracts were in the nature of a subsidy to commercial aviation, since it was intended that the private operators should develop express and passenger service along with mail service. At the end of 1928 the air-mail fliers were traveling 25,385 miles daily.

The postal rate actually charged under the act of 1925 was ten cents per half ounce. An act of May 17, 1928, reduced the minimum rate to five cents per ounce. The new schedule was announced to take effect on August 1 at five cents for the first ounce and ten cents for each additional ounce. The act also provided that mail contracts on air routes might be extended for ten years after the service had been successfully handled for two years. The effect of the new rate was reported by the Post Office Department, December 5, 1928, to have about doubled the amount of mail handled. The annual deficit was estimated at from $5,000,000 to $7,000,000.

The first step in the formulation of a general Federal policy for civil aviation was taken by Wilson in submitting to Congress (February 26, 1919) the recommendation of the National Advisory Commission for Aëronautics for legislation placing the licensing and regulation of aviation under the Department of Commerce. No action was taken on the proposal. In November, 1925, a report on civil aviation was made by a committee appointed by the Department of Commerce and the American Engineering Council. J. Walker Drake, Assistant Secretary of Commerce, was chairman. The report stated that in 1918 there were twenty-four airplane factories in the United States with a combined capital investment of $22,000,000; by 1925 these had shrunk to fourteen plants and a capital investment of $4,000,000. This decrease was laid to the government's failure after the armistice to "formulate and put into operation a continuing aviation policy." It was recommended that this deficiency should be immediately remedied. The government should license pilots and inspect planes. It should "develop, establish, or take over and maintain air routes and air navigation facilities," marking and lighting airways and emergency landing fields. The International Air Convention of 1919 should be ratified. The government should engage in no flying activities which could be "properly performed by private operation," and the use of aircraft should be extended in all practicable fields. Congress should authorize a reasonable use of army, navy, and air-mail fields for commercial aircraft. Air mail should be transferred to private operation. Government research should be conducted in aircraft design, and special types of aircraft should be purchased by the government from private builders. Competitive bidding should be abolished and provision made for "equitable compensation to the manufacturer for design and development of aircraft." The export of aircraft should be encouraged, not restricted because of fear of military use.

The Air Commerce Act of 1926 was approved by the President on May 20. The act applied to interstate and foreign air commerce and made it the duty of the Secretary of Commerce to foster air commerce: (1) to encourage the establishment of air ports, civil airways, and navigation facilities; (2) to make recommendations to the Secretary of Agriculture as to necessary meteorological service; (3) to study the possibilities for the development of air commerce, aëronautical industry, and trade in the United States and to collect and disseminate information relating thereto; (4) to advise with the Bureau of Standards and other executive agencies to promote research; (5) to investigate, record, and publish a report of accidents; (6) to exchange information with foreign governments. Regulatory powers were delegated to register aircraft at the request of the owner. To be registered as of the United States, aircraft must be owned by a citizen of the United States or by a government agency of the United States or a subdivision of the United States. Ratings were to be provided for airworthiness of craft and for airmen. Rules of air traffic and a license system were to be established by which a certificate could be refused or revoked for cause. Air-space reservations were to be set aside by executive order for military, naval, or other governmental use. Postal airways could be transferred to the Secretary of Commerce, and he could also establish civil airways. The airways were to be charted and maps were to be published. Government-owned air-navigation facilities were to be at the disposal of civil aircraft for emergency service. The Weather Bureau was to provide new service. The Secretary of War was to designate military airways. (Sections 6 and 7 applied to foreign aircraft and are discussed in another place.) A new Assistant Secretary of Commerce was provided for aviation. The act defined navigable air space as that above minimum safe altitudes prescribed by the Secretary of Commerce. The United States was declared to have exclusive sovereignty over air space above the land and waters of the United States, its territories and possessions, including the Panama Canal Zone. Under the new act William P. McCracken was appointed Assistant Secretary of Commerce in charge of civil aëronautics. On July 3, 1926, a joint resolution was approved authorizing the detailing of army and naval officers to service with the Department of Commerce for one year. In his last annual message (December 4, 1928) Coolidge reported that over seventeen thousand men and women had applied for an air-pilot's license and more than 80 per cent had applied during the current year. He reported, further, that "our national airway system exceeds 14,000 miles in length and has 7500 miles lighted for night operations. Provision has been made for lighting 4000 miles more during the current fiscal year and equipping an equal mileage with radio facilities. Three quarters of our people are now served by these routes. . . . It is noteworthy that this development has taken place without governmental subsidies. Commercial passenger flights operating on schedule have reached 13,000 miles per day."

One purpose of the transfer of the air mail to private hands was to open the way for the development of express and passenger service. The American Express Company announced a contract with the National Air Transport on November 8, 1926, service to begin on or before April 15, 1927, on two routes — New York to Chicago, and Chicago to Dallas. On July 20, 1927, contracts were announced with the Boeing Air Transport for express service from Chicago to San Francisco and with the Western Air Express from Salt Lake City to Los Angeles, service to begin September 1. It was intended to provide a thirty-one-hour service between New York and San Francisco.

A daily passenger schedule was announced August 6, 1927, by the National Air Transport, service to begin between Chicago, Kansas City, and Dallas on September 1. The fare was fixed at ten cents per mile; at this rate the Chicago–Kansas City fare was $45. The express service over this line was inaugurated with the passenger service on September 1. In this way the plans of the government for promoting commercial aviation were developed, with the air-mail contracts as the foundation for express and passenger service in private hands. On November 17, 1927, the National Air Transport announced that it had completed the first eighteen months of its existence with a perfect record — without the loss of a plane or the life of a pilot or passenger.

Secretary McCracken stated (July 7, 1927) that five large railroad companies had been in consultation with him concerning the establishment of air service to supplement their rail service. Either this would be done, or the railroads would arrange such service in conjunction with the air-transport companies already in operation.

CHAPTER XIII

ELECTRICAL COMMUNICATIONS

TELEPHONE AND TELEGRAPH

DURING the World War government control of electrical communications — telephone, telegraph, marine cables, and radio systems — was authorized by a joint resolution approved July 16, 1918. After the passing of the war necessity, Wilson presented his idea of a post-war policy in his special message of May 20, 1919. A section of his statement follows:

I can only suggest that in the case of the telegraphs and telephones, as in the case of the railways, it is clearly desirable in the public interest that some legislation should be considered which may tend to make these indispensable instrumentalities of our modern life a uniform and coördinated system which will afford those who use them as complete and certain means of communication with all parts of the country as has so long been afforded by the postal system of the government, and at rates as uniform and intelligible. . . . An exhaustive study of the whole question of electrical communications and of the means by which the central authority of the nation can be used to unify and improve it . . . would certainly result, indirectly if not directly, in a great public benefit.

During the session of 1919 the action of Congress in this case, as in many other policies, fell far short of Wilson's ideal. Government control was merely repealed by an act approved July 11, 1919, whereby such systems as were taken over by the Executive and administered by the Postmaster-General were returned to their owners at midnight, July 31, 1919. Rates in force as fixed by the Postmaster-General were to remain in effect for four months unless otherwise changed by authority of the government.

In the Transportation Act of 1920 a new policy was inaugurated for railroads and inland waterways, but electrical communications were left practically as they were before the war. Common carriers engaged in the transmission of intelligence by wire, cable, or radio were left under the jurisdiction of the Interstate Commerce Commission for purposes of rate regulation. Charges for transmission were to be just and reasonable.

With the inauguration of the Harding administration one step was made in the passage of an act approved June 10, 1921, which authorized telephone companies to apply to the Interstate Commerce Commission for a certificate to permit consolidations. In each case public hearings were to be held in which state authorities would have an opportunity to appear, and "after such public hearings, if the Commission finds that the proposed consolidation, acquisition, or control will be of advantage to the persons to whom service is to be rendered and in the public interest, it shall certify to that effect; and thereupon any act of Congress making the proposed transaction unlawful shall not apply." It was not intended that this act should place any limitation or restriction upon the then existing control and regulation of telephone companies. The measure was merely permissive, and any action under it was left to the initiative of the private corporations. This relative apathy on the part of Congress respecting domestic communications was in distinct contrast to its anxiety over external communications by cable and by radio.

RADIO

Development of the Business

"Radio" was a word to conjure with after the World War. Hertz, a German professor at Bonn University, discovered the existence of electromagnetic waves in 1887; subsequently many experimented with them for the purpose of harnessing them to communicate intelligence. Marconi was the most successful, receiving patents in England in 1896. This was a system of wireless telegraph using a code of dots and dashes. Wireless telephony soon followed; and the first musical program to be broadcast by radio was a Caruso concert at the Metropolitan Opera House in New York City during the winter of 1908–1909. The first broadcasting station was licensed in September, 1921. The four types of radio transmission were thus introduced to the world before the war. The wireless telegraph might broadcast its signals or send them from point to point; similarly, the wireless telephone might broadcast or send from point to point. In practice wireless telegraphy was usually point-to-point sending of messages; wireless telephony was primarily the broadcasting of matter of general interest.

Perfection of reception and transmission was developed by numerous experimenters. Fleming received a patent on the two-electrode, partial-vacuum tube for reception in November, 1905. De Forest invented the three-electrode tube, which was patented during 1906–1908. Both these patents were based on the principle that partial vacuum was necessary. Arnold and Langmuir, working independently, perfected a complete vacuum tube. The patent rights were unsettled. Transmission by vacuum tube was perfected by four men working independently. Armstrong was the first to be recognized, but in 1924 the court reversed previous decisions and awarded the patent to De Forest. The Alexanderson alternator was developed by the General Electric Company for tube transmission, thus producing a device which superseded the spark type of transmission.

Commercial exploitation of the patents was another but parallel story. Marconi established the parent company in England and subsidiaries in nearly all the leading countries. The Marconi Wireless Telegraph Company of America was chartered in New Jersey in 1899. Eight high-power stations were built on the Atlantic and Pacific coasts and in Hawaii. Marconi had the Fleming patent. The Federal Telegraph

Company was chartered in California in 1911 under the name of "The Wireless Development Company." It built four high-power stations on the Pacific coast. The Danish patents of Poulsen and Pederson belonged to it. The De Forest Radio Telephone and Telegraph Company was incorporated in Delaware in 1913. It held the De Forest three-electrode patent, but by court injunction was required to desist from manufacture because of infringement upon the Fleming two-electrode tube, from which it was developed. De Forest assigned his patent to the American Telephone and Telegraph Company, reserving the rights to manufacture and sell. With the expiration of the Fleming patent in 1922 he could proceed with the exploitation of his. The Langmuir patent claims were held by the General Electric Company, and the Arnold claims by the Western Electric Company. There was no basic radio patent, there were numerous patents widely held, and no one could produce the best in radio transmission or reception without combining the advantages of several or all of the leading devices. This was the situation at the end of the World War.

National-Government Promotion

War psychology, nationalism, and the overpowering demand for military security were most potent factors in explaining the policy of government promotion of internal and external communications by radio and cable. Marconi had been negotiating for the Alexanderson alternator in 1915, when Italy entered the war. Negotiations were reopened after the armistice, but the United States Navy Department intervened and on April 5, 1919, held a conference with representatives of the General Electric. They argued that the alternator was a strategic device and should be kept under American control. To sell to Marconi would in effect give Great Britain a complete monopoly of the world's wireless communication. On the contrary, it was to the interest of the United States to build up a control of radio communication in the Western Hemisphere. The answer to the navy officials was the question To whom could General Electric sell if not to Marconi? The navy's answer was to create a radio corporation to take over the patent and also the American Marconi Company with its patent rights. This would give the new organization a practically free field and would be a step in bringing essential patents together.

The Radio Corporation of America was chartered in Delaware on October 17, 1919, and began business on December 1. The plan of the Navy Department was carried out, and the contract with the Marconi Company was signed November 20. Stock in the new company was given in payment. The French station at Tuckerton was also purchased. This was a strictly United States wireless project. The charter provided that the directors and officers must be citizens. A maximum of 20 per cent of the shares were designated as foreign-share certificates which might be held and voted by foreigners.

The next step was to adjust remaining patent conflicts. The American Telephone and Telegraph Company held the De Forest three-electrode-tube patent, and the General Electric held the Langmuir vacuum patent; the Western Electric Company, owner of the Arnold claims, was controlled by the former company. In January, 1920, the United States again intervened, this time through the agency of the Bureau of Steam Engineering. A letter was addressed to each of the companies, of which the following is a part:

In the past the reasons for desiring some arrangement have been largely because of monetary considerations. Now the situation has become such that it is a public necessity that such arrangement be made without further delay, for the good of the public, for a remedy for the situation.

A system of cross-licensing agreements was accordingly worked out among fourteen different companies, the chief of which were the Radio Corporation, the American Telephone and Telegraph Company, the General Electric Company, the Westinghouse Electric Company, the Western Electric Company, and the United Fruit Company. Most of the agreements ran to 1945. Several of the companies bought stock in the Radio Corporation, the General Electric Company and the Westinghouse Electric Company holding 46.3 per cent in 1922.

Not only did the organization of the Radio Corporation solve the patent problems, but it gave the American corporation a monopoly of external communication by radio. While this radio business was being organized and developed, Congress, on the recommendation of the Navy Department, provided that government stations be opened temporarily to commercial business. A joint resolution approved June 5, 1920, opened naval radio stations for two years unless private service should be adequate before that time. In cases where service was not developed the privilege was extended until June 30, 1927.

Regulation

The first important use of radio was on ships. By acts of June 24, 1910, and July 23, 1912, steam vessels leaving United States ports and carrying fifty or more persons, including the crew, were required to be equipped with radio capable of operating day or night. The reason for this condition was obvious — the safety of passengers and crews on the high seas. The commercial use of the radio caused the inclusion in the Mann-Elkins railroad act of 1910 of a proviso giving the Interstate Commerce Commission jurisdiction over telegraph, telephone, and cable companies operating by wire or wireless in the transmission of intelligence, so far as rates and practices were concerned and only so far as such transmission took place within the United States. This grant of jurisdiction was continued after the war, but nothing was done in the case of radio. It was repeated in the Transportation Act of 1920 and the radio act of 1927.

The next step in the regulation of radio was the act of 1912, which required that every sending station must have a license. "Every such license . . . shall specify . . . particulars . . . to enable its range to be estimated . . ., shall state the wave-length or wave-lengths authorized for use by the station for the prevention of interference, and the hours for which the station is licensed to work." Licenses were revocable for cause (although the nature of the cause was not stated), and they could be issued only to stations owned by citizens or corporations of the United States or Porto Rico. In time of war the government might close stations or take them over for government use. Licenses were also required of operators. During the war the government exercised its emergency powers.

Before 1921 the radio problems had to do almost exclusively with the radio telegraph. In September, 1921, the first broadcasting station was licensed. During the next months a revolution in the field of the regulation of radio took place. The law of 1912 took on a new significance. Even without the new development the old radio policy was inadequate, and in his annual message of 1921 Harding urged new legislation; but broadcasting speedily caused new laws to become imperative.

The law of 1912 was soon tested in the case of the Intercity Radio Company *v.* Hoover. The court considered two points: the right of the Secretary of Commerce to refuse to grant a license and the right to assign a particular wave-length. On the first point the decision of the supreme court of the District of Columbia on November 23, 1921, denied the right to refuse a license. On appeal the court of appeals of the District of Columbia in February, 1923, upheld the lower court. On the second point the court held on appeal that the naming of a wave-length was mandatory, but that the naming of any particular wave-length was discretionary.

The second radio conference, held under the auspices of Secretary Hoover in March, 1923, recommended that group allocations of wave-lengths be abandoned and that each station be assigned a particular wave-length, or channel, and a time. This was in accordance with the opinion of the court in the Intercity case. From 1923 to 1926 the new method of control was worked out. Broadcasting stations were assigned wave-lengths within the range of 200 and 545 meters, or 1500 and 550 kilocycles. Since channels were spaced 10 kilocycles apart to prevent interference, there were in all a total of ninety-five channels. By agreement Canada was assigned six channels, leaving the United States eighty-nine. Broadcasting stations increased until there were 566 in 1925, 623 in 1926, and 671 in 1927. These stations must of necessity be located within the eighty-nine available channels. This meant that several stations must be assigned the same channel and divide time. The orderly development of regulation in this direction was disrupted by the Zenith case in a Federal district court April 16, 1926, when the court held that under the act of 1912 there was no power to assign particular wave-lengths and require their use. To fix such requirements would be to create conditions additional to those specified by Congress, and such procedure was not authorized by the statute. At the request of Secretary Hoover this decision was followed by a ruling from the Attorney-General (July 8, 1926) in which the opinion in the Zenith case was upheld. This overthrew the whole fabric of regulation, and confusion followed. Many of the more responsible broadcasters, however, continued on their assigned wave-lengths.

The average radio listener was interested only in low-power stations, which broadcast entertainment programs, speeches, market reports, and so on, and in consequence many important principles at stake in the formulation of radio policy were obscured if not ignored. What right had the holder of a copyright of sheet music to control its production? The copyright law protected him against a public performance of the music for profit. Was radio-broadcasting a public performance? Was a broadcasting station which did not charge its listeners operated for profit? In Witmark and Sons *v.* Bamberger and Company a district court held that the broadcasting of the music was for profit because of the advertising that the Bamberger store received in operating the station. In Jerome H. Remick *v.* The American Automobile Accessories Company another district court decided that the broadcasting of music was not a public performance. This case was appealed to the court of appeals, and the court found for the plaintiff that it was both a public performance and a performance for profit.

Could the Anglo-Saxon tradition of free speech be maintained under the conditions existing in the field of radio? This was of special importance in politics. In the presidential election of 1924 radio figured in a national political campaign for the first time. It was commonly stated after the election that the radio elected Coolidge. Whether such a statement was altogether true or not was a matter of lesser importance; what was more important was that it called attention to the tremendous political significance of the radio. The story was told in press reports that Senator Watson of Indiana had contracted with a radio station to broadcast a series of political speeches in 1926. He was asked to submit his speeches in advance for censorship. He refused and canceled the contract. Watson was chairman of the Senate committee which reported the drastic Dill bill. He was also a possible candidate against Coolidge for the Republican presidential nomination in 1928. In the campaign of 1926 the national convention of the Socialist party considered (May 3) the question of how to get on the air. They had no broadcasting station, and Hoover was refusing to license new stations. They raised a very pertinent question as to whether a political censorship could be exercised through government regulation of radio.

The question of monopoly in the radio business was one of the most widely discussed problems, and unfortunately there was little discrimination as to the nature of the problem. Monopoly in communication with foreign countries existed in practice and was justified as a matter of public policy under the conditions then prevailing. United States jurisdiction extended only to sending and receiving stations in the United States; the other end of the radio circuit was under foreign control. In foreign countries conditions of monopoly existed, and competition between independent American stations dealing with the same foreign interest was practically impossible. In the field of domestic communication and in the manufacture and sale of apparatus the problems were different and government policy was inconsistent and conflicting. The Navy Department was substantially responsible for the creation of the Radio Corporation of America, for the merging of important patent rights, and for the cross-licensing agreements. The report of the Federal Trade Commission in December, 1923, pursuant to the House resolution of March 5, 1923, was hostile to the radio combinations. On January 28, 1924, complaint was entered against eight companies for conspiring and combining "for the purpose and with the effect of restraining competition and creating a monopoly in the manufacture, purchase, and sale, in interstate commerce, of radio devices and apparatus, and other electrical devices and apparatus, and in domestic and transoceanic radio communication and broadcasting." Whatever the merits of the particular charges or policies, it should be obvious that private business could not define its practices with any degree of satisfaction to anyone when government policies and agencies were in direct conflict with each other.

On the basis of what distinction were stations to be classified? Since it was impossible for everyone to establish a station because of cost and the limitation of wave-lengths, must radio be declared a public utility and be opened to the use of everyone on equal terms like the telephone and the telegraph? Or could there be a classification according to use — some private stations and some open to the public at fixed rates? What should constitute reasonable conditions and rates for use, and what authority should exercise regulation? Should government stations be opened to private use, and if so, on what terms? Should radio advertising be labeled as such, as newspaper advertising was? Should the law of slander and libel be revised to cover the possibilities of the radio? Should manufacturers of apparatus be permitted to control the conditions of use and thus to establish a radio monopoly? Did radio stations have a prescriptive right to wave-lengths or call letters either for use or for sale? On what grounds should a license to operate a sending station be refused or revoked? What war powers of censorship and regulation should be provided? The United States was already a party to international agreements affecting radio. How far was the United States to go in post-war international agreements on radio control?

In the radio conference beginning November 9, 1925, the leading features of a policy were outlined, and by 1926 the campaign for legislation came to a crisis. The White bill in the House vested administration in the Secretary of Commerce with a commission to assign wave-lengths and make regulations, which was essentially the program Hoover had outlined to the radio conference the preceding November; this became the administration bill. The Dill and Borah bills in the Senate provided for independent commissions to exercise all powers. While these bills were pending, the Zenith decision in a Federal court held that the Secretary of Commerce did not have power to prevent the use of wave-lengths other than the one assigned. This opened the way for the pirating of wave-lengths and consequent confusion in the broadcasting field. It brought home to the radio listener the realization of the need for new legislation. It must be clearly understood that the court decision did not create the problem of radio regulation: it was merely an incident in the campaign of several years for the drafting of a new policy.

The delay in passing an adequate law was due to several factors. Probably of greatest importance was the fact that the device was new; there was little real comprehension of its political, economic, and social significance and of the possible problems which might arise from its rapid and unprecedented development. A quite practical difficulty, according to political observers, was the fact of censorship by the owners of broadcasting stations and the possible political advantage to the administration of any legislation without well-considered safeguards. Borah particularly asked for longer time for consideration, but without success. The year 1926 was a congressional-election year, and the presidential election of 1928 was throwing its shadow ahead because both Coolidge and Hoover were viewed as possible candidates. During the short session of 1926–1927 the big problem was to effect a compromise between the White and Dill bills. The report of the conference committee was submitted and was finally passed and signed by the President on February 23, 1927. It provided for a commission of five to exercise control over radio for one year; thereafter the administration was to be left to the Secretary of Commerce. Special problems might be referred to the commission for decision, or appeals might be made to it from the rulings of the Secretary of Commerce. Power was granted to classify stations, to make regulations, to issue licenses, and to assign wave-lengths. The term of licenses for broadcasting stations was three years and for other stations five years. Licenses could be revoked only by the commission. The anti-trust laws applied to both service and apparatus. If political use of a broadcasting station was granted to one candidate, it must be allowed to the other candidates for the same office, and no censorship by the owner of the station could be exercised. No station was obliged to broadcast political speeches, however. The licensing authority had no power of censorship. Advertising, whether commercial material or propaganda, must be broadcasted as such. The Interstate Commerce

Commission was left with powers over rates as assigned in the act of 1910. No license or permit to construct a station should be granted to or transferred to any alien, any government or corporation, or any corporation in which a foreigner was an officer or director or in which one fifth of the stock might be voted by aliens, nor to the representatives of any of the foregoing. The granting of permits to construct a new station and the granting of renewals or modifications of licenses should be determined by the licensing authority on the basis of "public interest, convenience, or necessity" of the service to be rendered.

This last point, the public-interest theory, deserves special treatment because it was in many respects the most important provision in the act as a foundation of public policy. There was only one case in the field of Federal regulation where discretionary authority was definitely granted to the regulating agency on the ground of "public interest, convenience, or necessity": this was that part of the Transportation Act of 1920 which related to the building of new lines or the abandonment of old lines, and the adjustment of the service rendered. The field of transportation did not present the same difficulties as radio did. Transportation of persons and property was more tangible and furnished more concrete evidence for the determination of facts. The transmission of intelligence by radio was necessarily quite intangible. The licensing authority must consider physical equipment and the efficiency of its operation, the location of the station, the service already in the field, and, last but not least, the character of the program or service rendered. It was this last point which presented the greatest prospect of difficulties in public policy. Of necessity any judgment on the relative merits of service rendered approached very near censorship, if it did not actually partake of it. This was of little importance so long as the programs were nothing but musical entertainment or the like, but it held vast possibilities in the realm of the transmission of ideas.

The origin of the principle of public interest in radio is very recent. Before 1924 broadcasting was considered strictly private, although commercial point-to-point stations were considered common carriers as early as the act of 1910, which gave the Interstate Commerce Commission jurisdiction over rates. At the Third Annual Radio Conference (October, 1924) Hoover gave the first official expression of the public-interest theory: he stated that radio had become a great public utility, and that radio problems must be solved from the standpoint of public service.

The ether is a public medium, and its use must be for the public benefit. The use of a radio channel is justified only if there is public benefit. . . . The greatest public interest must be the deciding factor. I presume that few will dissent as to the correctness of this principle . . . , but its acceptance leads to important and far-reaching practical effects . . . from which . . . there is no logical escape.

The radio conference assented to Hoover's statement of policy, but injected into it the following very important qualifying statement: "That those engaged in radio broadcasting shall not be required to devote their property to public use, and their properties are therefore not public utilities in fact or in law. . . ." This point of view was indorsed in the main by Stephen Davis, solicitor of the Department of Commerce, in his treatise on the law of radio communication (1927). There did seem to be, however, a serious defect in a policy which authorized the application of the principle of public interest, convenience, or necessity to the erection of a new station or the relicensing of existing stations and which then denied to the government the power to require that public service be rendered after the license was once granted. Just exactly what was meant by "public interest, convenience, or necessity"?

Another aspect of the question was whether the licensing authority could refuse to grant a new license even though the law specifically so provided. The Fifth Amendment to the

Constitution provided against the taking of property without due process of law. To deny a man a license to operate his radio station was equivalent to depriving him of his property. The law did not provide for compensating him in such a case. If a station had been legally erected and licensed, what recourse could be had against it so long as it did not violate the law? For stations erected under the new law there could be no question; but for stations erected and licensed under the act of 1912, when licensing was mandatory, the legality of refusing a license was open to question.

The work of the commission under the new law proved more difficult than had been anticipated, and at the end of the first year it had not completed the tasks assigned to it. After a long-drawn-out contest a bill was approved March 28, 1928, extending its period of active control a second year. At that time an amendment was added which required the allocation of wave-lengths among broadcasting stations in proportion to population. The original act had provided for equitable distribution. An act of March, 1929, extended the life of the commission again until the end of the year. The problem of a national radio policy in the broadcasting field was obviously only in its early stages of development. The legislation thus far had gone little beyond the more obvious and immediate questions of licenses and wave-lengths which had to do with the problems of interference between stations; the very important question of political uses of radio was scarcely touched.

SELECTED BIBLIOGRAPHY

JOME, H. L. Economics of the Radio Industry. A. W. Shaw Company, 1925.

DAVIS, STEPHEN. The Law of Radio Communication. McGraw-Hill Book Company, 1927.

YOUNG, OWEN D. Testimony before the Subcommittee of the Committee on Interstate Commerce respecting Senate Bill 4301, January 11, 1921.

This testimony outlines the origins of the Radio Corporation of America.

Federal Trade Commission. Report on the Radio Industry. Government Printing Office, December 1923.

CHAPTER XIV

BUSINESS ORGANIZATION

THE actual conditions under which business was conducted were probably changing with greater rapidity than at any other time in American history. If business were smaller in scope, these changes could be more easily followed; but in view of the size and complexity of the problem, no one but a specialist was in a position to hope to acquire any real grasp of the significance of the change. The application of science to manufacturing, transportation, and communication was effecting a veritable revolution in the conduct of business. Some held that industry gained tremendously by the war; others insisted that after allowances were made for post-war adjustments, business lost by the war. Whichever view was correct, there could be no question that the character of business methods and organization was profoundly modified during the war and the post-war decade.

According to a Federal Trade Commission report of 1926 the growth in national wealth was 16 per cent in terms of stable dollars (72 per cent in the actual currency) for the decade 1912–1922. During the same period the increase in population was 15 per cent. This left the increase in per capita wealth for the decade very slight — about thirty-two cents.

Control of wealth also presented some interesting facts. It was estimated that 90 per cent of the wealth was controlled by 13 per cent of the people and that 59 per cent of it was controlled by 1 per cent. A reduction in the number of large estates seemed to be indicated by figures which showed that among estates probated 52 per cent of the total value was to be found in estates of over $100,000 in 1912, whereas in 1922 only 45.9 per cent was found in estates of

that size. Employee ownership of stock was widely discussed, but it was found that only 7.5 per cent of the stock
in the concerns in which they were employed was owned
by the employees. What was even more significant, employees owned only 1.5 per cent of the common stock in
such corporations, and it was the common stock which customarily possessed a vote in corporation control.

The national income was not so closely concentrated in
the hands of a few, although the number of persons with
million-dollar incomes increased rapidly; in 1925 three fourths
of it went to persons with an income of less than $10,000
and only 4 per cent to persons with incomes of over $100,000.
The Federal Trade Commission indicated that for the same
year 207 persons reported incomes of over $1,000,000, 138
reported between $750,000 and $1,000,000, 340 reported between $500,000 and $750,000, and 8873 reported between
$100,000 and $500,000. The number of persons with incomes of over a million dollars increased from 21 in 1921 to
283 in 1928.

Prices rose to unprecedented heights during the war and
continued to rise for over a year after the armistice. Wholesale commodity prices stood at over 250 early in 1920, those
for 1914 being taken as 100. The collapse began in the spring
of 1920, reaching bottom near the end of 1921. Wholesale
commodity prices reached 125 in April, 1921. Railroad and
industrial stocks stood at about 60 per cent of normal at
the opening of the year. By 1926 normalcy was said to have
been attained. The Federal Reserve Board, reporting conditions for 1925, indicated that the economic stability of
pre-war days had been established. The situation so thoroughly satisfied the President that the White House spokesman (March 2, 1926) made the reigning prosperity the
leading topic of the regular Tuesday press conference.

American business in the generation that followed the
Civil War manifested characteristics quite different from
those of the decade that followed the World War. The

earlier period was characterized by the individualism of the "captains of industry." The title "captain" was not a misnomer, as was pointed out by W. S. Gifford, president of the American Telephone and Telegraph Company, because business was in many respects a species of warfare, and "courage, will, energy, aggressiveness, resourcefulness, even a domineering habit and a certain ruthlessness, seem to have been essential parts of their characters. They had to create their own precedents, invent their own methods, brush aside the inertia of less vigorous spirits, and drive directly to their goals." There was a strong element of luck and speculation and a cold-blooded disregard of the rights of competitors or of the public. Although the corporation was used largely as a form of business organization, it was very often little more than a trade name for some captain of industry or a group of like men, such as the Rockefellers, Vanderbilt, Gould, and Hill. The place of the corporation had not been fully defined in the economic structure of the country. The clash between the corporation and the public resulted in the antitrust movement of the latter part of the nineteenth century, the avowed purpose of which was to destroy big business.

The situation in the second quarter of the twentieth century was quite different. To use Gifford's terminology again, the director of the corporation must be a "statesman of industry." Manufacturing processes had become highly technical. Management was highly organized and complicated. Raw materials and markets were widely scattered and competition was keen. There was little or no place for luck, speculation, or guesswork, writes Gifford; "today nothing that can be foreseen is left to chance. Business is now based upon facts — statistical, technical, scientific. The American Telephone and Telegraph Company, for example, works consistently upon a twenty-year plan of future developments, with the first five years of the twenty budgeted ahead. Its experience seldom varies much from the estimates, either of needs of physical plant or of expansion of needs of capital.

And this in a business serving the whole United States, one hundred and sixteen million people, with more than sixteen million telephones, and using a permanent capital investment of nearly three billion dollars and calling for several hundred million dollars of new capital expenditures every year." Labor turnover was reduced by greater care in the selection and placing of new men to determine their abilities. Advancement was based on merit. "Business is becoming a profession." Relatively less interest was taken in acquiring personal wealth and more in accomplishment. Security of position and salary were inducements to men of high ability. In very few of the largest corporations did individuals or even a small group of individuals hold a majority interest. The management of corporations was coming more and more into the hands of men who were employees rather than owners. While the millennium had not by any means arrived in business, it was true that methods of competition and exploitation of the public had changed radically. The crude methods of the earlier generation had given way to more subtle devices and to high-pressure advertising and salesmanship, the quota system, and the like. The position of the corporation had, generally speaking, reconciled itself to a measure of regulation. The public came to recognize big business as a legitimate thing when properly conducted.

Combination and integration of industry had been going on continuously since the beginning of the Industrial Revolution. Continuation in this direction was only to be expected in an age of technical organization and processes. The small independent proprietor had an all but impossible task before him to compete with the great corporation, not only because of the corporation's greater resources in materials, capital, and economy of production, but probably even more because of its scientific and experimental resources. In the long run advance in business lay largely in science, invention, and technical progress. Every big manufacturing concern set aside a large sum each year for experimental work.

The figures as to the size of corporations were so large as to have little meaning. Of the ten billion-dollar corporations in 1925–1926, seven had to do with transportation — five of them with railroads and two with automobiles; of the remaining three, one furnished communications, one fuel, and one steel. The table below gives some figures on the subject for comparison.

TEN BILLION-DOLLAR CORPORATIONS OF THE UNITED STATES[1]

	ASSETS	NUMBER OF SHAREHOLDERS	NUMBER OF LABORERS
United States Steel . . .	$2,446,000,000	150,000	250,000
Southern Pacific Railroad .	2,147,000,000	57,000	71,000[2]
Pennsylvania Railroad . .	1,819,000,000	140,000	214,000
American Telephone and Telegraph	1,646,000,000	362,000	293,000
New York Central Railroad	1,449,000,000	64,000	163,000
Standard Oil of New York	1,369,000,000	80,000	91,000
Union Pacific Railroad . .	1,140,000,000	51,000	60,000
Atchison, Topeka and Santa Fe Railroad	1,071,000,000	63,000	60,000
General Motors	915,000,000	51,000	83,000
Ford Motor Company . .	800,000,000[2]	3	192,000

By 1928 the number of billionaires had increased to thirteen, at least, by the addition of the National City Bank, the Chase National Bank, and the Consolidated Gas Company, all of New York City.

The Standard Oil Company in its original form in 1870 was capitalized at $1,000,000; in 1873 the capital was increased to $3,500,000. It was an organization of this size, together with its accumulated assets during the last three decades of the nineteenth century, which became the chief target of the antitrust movement. This company was singled out as the outstanding example of monopoly and corporate greed and as an economic and political menace striking at the very roots of the Republic. Compare this with the Ameri-

---

[1] From a table compiled by the *New York Times*, February 13 and March 27, 1927. It will be noted that other compilations of figures differ from these.

[2] Estimated.

can Telephone and Telegraph Company, whose total assets were listed in the annual report of the company (March 2, 1927) at $3,250,000,000. The net earnings for 1926 were $204,870,000, and the increased investment for that year was $318,000,000. This company represented service to 17,574,000 telephones, 3,800,000 of which were new installments during the year. The market value of the company's securities was estimated by another source as $2,066,000,000. The 1927 report gave the assets at $4,000,000,000, the largest of any company in the world. In 1925 a summary of big business in *Forbes* stated that twelve corporations had assets of over a billion, five were capitalized at over a billion, and five had annual sales of over a billion. The size of the largest business in the years immediately after the Civil War was stated in terms of millions, and for the corresponding period after the World War it was stated in terms of billions. A billion is a thousand million. This change had occurred in approximately half a century.

Hoover pointed out, in an address before the Chamber of Commerce of the United States in May, 1926, that in 1900 there were about 13,000,000 horse power in operation in industry, and that in 1926 there were 55,000,000. "The last quarter of a century has seen the growth of larger units of production and distribution — big business. Our tools are bigger. We build a single dynamo of 100,000 horse power. This single tool would have been big business twenty-five years ago."

As business developed, it tended to take different forms, of which some achieved a stable position in the business structure and others disappeared as victims of competition. In the retail field the idea of the chain store grew slowly during the last years of the nineteenth century and the early twentieth. Chain-store operators claimed to be able to do business in groceries, for instance, at an overhead expense of from 15 per cent to 17 per cent, a figure which was about half that of the average independent grocer. Chain stores became firmly established, and in the post-war period grew at an unusual rate. In 1924 there were 384 chain systems of groceries and 327 chain systems of drug stores. In other lines much the same situation was developing. The Great Atlantic and Pacific Tea Company was an example of the rate of expansion in the grocery business. Their increase was 2366 stores in 1922, 2200 in 1923, 1100 in 1924, and 500 in 1926. This company operated 14,500 stores at the end of 1926. The leading twenty-five grocery chains at the close of 1925 included 28,752 stores, or an increase of 8 per cent for the group. Professor Paul H. Nystrom of Columbia University estimated that chain-store sales increased from 12 per cent, in 1926, to 15 per cent, in 1928, of all retail business in the United States. Professor J. L. Palmer of The University of Chicago estimated the chain sales in 1928 at over 20 per cent of the total retail sales. The average of the two would place it at approximately 18 per cent. According to Nystrom's estimate, printed in the *Chain Store Age* for January, 1929, retail sales were distributed as follows:

Type of Retail Unit	1926 (In Billions of Dollars)	1928 (In Billions of Dollars)
Department stores	6.6	6.5
Chain stores	4.8	6.2
Mail-order houses	1.6	1.4
Unit stores	25.5	25.2
All others	1.5	1.7
Total retail sales	40.0	41.0

Even the department stores, the new form of retail stores in the late nineteenth century, must, according to Mr. Filene of Boston, become chains in order to remain in business. He points out that they have already done so to a considerable extent. The interests of the chain-store form of retail organization seemed to warrant the establishment of a trade journal. This was done in 1925 in the inauguration of the *Chain Store Age*, a monthly business magazine for executives of chain stores.

In surveying business of the size found in the post-war period the question naturally arose as to where the necessary capital was to be found. The answer was diffusion of ownership of stock in small amounts among the people as a whole. The majority of the stock of the old Standard Oil Company was owned by six men. Eighty-seven per cent of the New York Central Railroad was owned at one time by W. K. Vanderbilt; in 1925 it was reported that the Vanderbilt family owned only 6 per cent of the stock and that George F. Baker, the largest stockholder, held only about 20 per cent. In all there were about 64,000 stockholders. In the case of the Standard Oil Company in 1911, when its dissolution was ordered by the court, there were 6078 stockholders; in 1926 the reports indicated some 80,000. The board of directors, including the chairman and the president (that is, the management of the concern), controlled about 20 per cent. The table on page 178 indicates the number of stockholders in the ten billion-dollar corporations. The Ford Motor Company was unique. Here the older form of personal ownership remained. General Motors was another exception. According to Ripley 60 per cent of this stock was in the hands of the Du Pont family, the remaining 40 per cent being distributed among 70,000 other stockholders. In Gifford's annual report, released on March 2, 1927, the number of stockholders in the American Telephone and Telegraph Company was given as 399,121. The average number of shares per stockholder was 26.6, and no stockholder owned as much as 1 per cent of the total outstanding stock.

In speaking to the Chamber of Commerce of the United States in May, 1926, Secretary Hoover pointed out that in 1900 there were approximately 4,500,000 stockholders; in 1926 the number had increased to 14,000,000. The extensive diffusion of ownership had taken place in three types of business: mutualized financial institutions, public utilities, and a group of certain other established manufacturing and distributing organizations. He estimated the total wealth of the nation to be approximately $340,000,000,000, of which from $90,000,000,000 to $120,000,000,000 might be classed as corporate wealth. Of this amount the three mutualized groups mentioned above held $69,000,000,000, or between 40 per cent and 50 per cent of corporate wealth.

After the war, in addition to direct investment by the people in industrial securities, there was an indirect investment through the device of investment trusts. This type of organization was British in origin, but in the United States the name applied to several types of institution. The British type of investment trust was purely an investment institution and did not attempt to control or manage any corporation in which it held securities; in fact, the amount of securities held in any one corporation was limited to a small percentage of the capital of the trust if it was properly organized. The principle of the trust was to invest in the securities of a large number of corporations engaged in diverse lines of business activity. The certificates of the trust itself were sold to the public as stabilized investments. The failure of one company in which stock was held could not seriously impair the value of the trust certificates because of the diversity of the holdings. The spread of investments in several types of business was a safeguard against depression in a particular industry. This type of organization provided expert management in choosing investments, thereby relieving the person of small income and of little or no business training of uncertainty in investing savings. Properly managed, such an institution provided the greatest possible margin of safety and insured a stable and reasonably high rate of income.

As the industrial system of the United States had developed, the number of persons working for salaries or wages had increased. This meant an increase in the demand for a means of investment of small savings. Such investments must be safe and must yield a reasonable income. The complications of the investment market made investment by the average individual a hazardous undertaking unless he confined himself to the best-established securities, where the income was low. Formerly a very large amount of such small savings was invested in land; but the closing of the frontier and the rapid increase in land prices, together with the low rate of income, had to a great extent closed this field of investment. The bond campaigns of the World War educated the public rapidly to investment in securities. The investment trust was a proposed answer to the situation.

The first investment trust of the British type was established in the United States in 1921. In November, 1927, according to the report of Attorney-General Ottinger of New York, there were 135 such organizations, with resources in excess of $600,000,000. As yet there was little or no regulation of these institutions, and early British experience stood as a warning against possible abuses. In New York and New Jersey the formulation of a legislative policy was being actively considered. An investigation of investment trusts released to the press on March 14 reported 172 in operation in the United States. Of these, 13 were Canadian. Classified according to type, 119 were of the general-management type and 32 were specialized. All of them were incorporated. There were also 21 which were set up under indenture agreements.

Diffusion of ownership presented a serious problem to corporate management. It was manifestly impossible to hold a stockholders' meeting of 399,121 stockholders. Still, it was a basic principle of corporate organization that the business was governed by its stockholders. Certain acts of the management had to be ratified, and officers had to be elected by the stockholders. Many of the problems of government of corporations were contributed by the stockholders: some through indifference, but most of them through ignorance of the technical side of organization and business problems. Most of them were also unacquainted with the management; and many stockholders were primarily small investors (in

the American Telephone and Telegraph Company 200,000
of these were women) whose intentions might be good, but
who could not contribute anything beyond the actual money
invested. The management contributed its share of difficulties by not taking the trouble to inform stockholders, or
even by withholding essential information, or by putting
questions to stockholders in such a manner as would substantially predetermine the result.

The consequences of this situation was the continued concentration of power in the hands of the executive, on the one
hand, and the disfranchisement of the stockholder, on the
other; in other words, the separation of ownership and
management was in many cases carried to the point where
the management was not responsible to the stockholders at
large. There were different methods by which this change
had come about, and the motives behind these schemes were
not necessarily the same. In some cases they might be a
matter of necessity; in others they might be the result of
a determination on the part of a financial group to wield
excessive economic power. It was not always easy to distinguish between an accidental combination of circumstances
and an arrangement resulting from a sinister desire for exploitation. One method of controlling a corporation was
through proxies for the floating stock in the hands of Wall
Street operators. Such proxies might be necessary in order
to secure a quorum of the stockholders to do business, or
they might be secured by a group to dominate a meeting
for the accomplishment of a particular design. Another
method was through the formation of a "voting trust."
This might occur in refinancing operations where the banking house involved required control of the corporation for
a definite period of time as a condition of carrying through
plans of rehabilitation. The difficulty in securing a quorum
for stockholders' meetings led to charter legislation in such
states as New Jersey and Delaware, whereby the business
of the corporation could be transacted by a majority of

those "present and voting." The newest scheme, and the one which aroused intense hostility, was the split-common-stock provisions in certain corporations. Customarily the stock of a corporation was divided into classes: preferred and common. Preferred stock provided for a fixed dividend to be paid to the holder before dividends could be paid on the common stock, but such stock did not carry voting power. The common stock was voting stock, but no fixed dividend was authorized: the dividend depended upon the earnings. The preferred stock was attractive to investors to whom fixed income was a paramount question; the common stock was attractive to those who wished to control the corporation and take the chances on dividends.

The newer development was to divide the stock further into classes A and B common; one class was voting stock, and the other was without voting power. This nonvoting common stock did not have the advantage of the fixed dividends paid on preferred stock nor the voice in the management accorded standard common stock. In this manner a very small amount of voting stock controlled the organization and was retained by the promoters, and the nonvoting stock was offered to the public or employees as an investment. This scheme was used most extensively in public utilities, but other examples were the Dodge Brothers motor deal carried through by Dillon, Reed & Company, and the proposed Van Sweringen Nickel Plate Railroad combination, which was disapproved by the Interstate Commerce Commission. The public became aware of this problem largely through the writings of Professor Ripley in the *Atlantic Monthly* during 1926 and also in other periodicals. Ripley pointed out as one example that twelve holding companies controlled light, power, gas, and water utilities representing $1,500,000,000 in 1925. Ten per cent of the stock controlled the whole.

The relation between the split common stock and the development of finance and holding companies was further illustrated by a concrete example compiled primarily from

Moody's "Manual of Corporation Securities." The Kansas Gas and Electric Company of Wichita sold 24,000 shares of stock to its customers, and was known as a customer-owned public utility. The voting stock, however, was controlled by the American Power and Light Company, which in turn was controlled by the Electric Bond and Share Company, and this, in turn, by the General Electric Company (until January 1, 1925). At that time it was transferred to the Electric Bond and Share Securities Corporation, organized January 19 to take over the General Electric holdings. Thus a few hundred thousand dollars at the top of this pyramid of corporations controlled an investment of some $25,000,000. The Federal Trade Commission (1927) gave another example where $1,000,000 at the top of a pyramid controlled several hundred million dollars of investments in underlying companies.

The owners were losing or had lost control of their property. To the management in such organizations might properly be put the question of how they would use this trusteeship. One abuse which had been complained of was the building up of high reserves or reinvesting surpluses in replacements, improvements, or extensions instead of obtaining additional capital through new issues of securities. The argument was that the earnings belong to the stockholders and should be distributed as dividends. The actual value of stock might be unknown under such plans, and the stock might be sold at a figure which later events proved to be unfair, the just returns of the investment falling into the hands of some speculator. The opportunity for abuses of inside information in unscrupulous hands was only too obvious. In the period before the World War the outstanding corporation problem was the relation between business and the public, and the government intervened to attempt an adjustment. The post-war problem emphasized an additional aspect, the relation between the corporation and its owners. This was an internal problem. How would it be met? Pro-

fessor Ripley was not an alarmist, but he put the problem
in strong language: "The prime fact confronting us as a
nation is the progressive diffusion of ownership on the one
hand and the ever-increasing concentration of managerial
power on the other." Mr. L. J. Flynn, in *Harper's Magazine*,
pointed out some suggestive conclusions respecting tendencies indicated by these newer developments in business.
First, the possible passing of private property. The corporation stood between the *man* and his *property*. Diffusion
of ownership of corporations meant the social recapture of
the tools of production. This was the ideal expressed in the
Communist Manifesto of 1840; but if it was being realized,
it was in a manner radically different from what was envisaged by the authors of that document. Secondly, the decay
of capitalism in the sense of capital lodged in the hands of a
few. The entrepreneur was being displaced by the imper-
sonal organization in the form of the corporation *publicly
owned*. The primary problem was, however, whether the
management of the corporation could be made responsible
to the owners. This problem was not materially different
from that which faced political democracy.

The trade association had come to occupy a new position
in economic life. Although it was not a new organization,
nevertheless it had not been in operation until the war period
except in a limited number of trades. During the stress of
war-time mobilization of industry its value from the standpoint of national defense was recognized, and the government
encouraged the extension of these associations throughout
the more important industries as far as possible. This policy
was continued after the war. The Chamber of Commerce
of the United States was also solidly behind the movement
from the point of view of the business men. *The Nation's
Business* said, "In these tremendous days of competition
between industries, of dependence upon research, of need for
more knowledge, the man who tries to fight alone is foolish."
The trade association included most of the firms engaged in

one line of business, and provided for research and for gathering and exchanging among members information in regard to trade practices, materials, standardization, specifications, processes, and the like which were of interest to the trade. This might have an effect similar in some respects to trust combinations as regards price-fixing and other restraints of trade. Could these practices be reconciled with the antitrust laws and with public interest so as to preserve the advantage of these organizations without permitting abuses? It was obvious that a distinct modification of the pre-war attitude of the public toward business would be involved.

A highly developed example will serve to illustrate the possible scope of such organizations. The Institute of American Meat Packers was the result of a reorganization of the American Meat Packers' Association completed September, 1919. The purposes indicated in the by-laws were as follows:

a. To secure coöperation among packers of the United States in lawful furthering and protecting the interests and general welfare of the industry.

b. To afford a means of coöperation with the Federal and state governments in all matters of general concern to the industry.

c. To promote and foster domestic and foreign trade in American meat products.

d. To promote the mutual improvement of its members and the study of the arts and sciences connected with the meat-packing industry.

e. To inform and interest the American public as to the economic worth of the meat-packing industry.

f. To encourage coöperation with live-stock producers and distributors of meat-foods products.

About two hundred and fifty companies were members of the institute in 1924, including some who were not engaged in the slaughter of live stock. The institute did not receive from its members reports of production, shipments, and stocks and redistribute the reports, and it did not report sales because the public often associated such practices with price-fixing. There were twenty committees, each assigned to different subjects; and two departments — association management and education and research. Each department was organized into bureaus. Definite machinery was created for conference between the four different groups who made up the live-stock and meat industry: producers, commission men, packers, and retailers. Here the institute had in mind much the same aim in promoting orderly marketing as had the coöperative marketing associations assisted by the division of coöperative marketing in the Department of Agriculture.

In 1922 the institute plan was adopted, which marked another step in the elaboration of the organization. A fund of $150,000 was subscribed to finance it, and changes were made in the organization. The plan contemplated making the institute (1) a trade association, (2) an industrial museum, (3) an industrial-research institute, and (4) a technical educational institution. The idea of the research institution was most fully worked out in Germany and was adopted in several industries in the United States. The research problems carried on were to be of such types as would be of general interest to the industry, and were not to conflict with the special research of individual firms. The educational plans provided for three divisions of work. First, specialized collegiate education for men who intended to enter the industry. The initial arrangements were worked out with the School of Commerce and Administration of The University of Chicago. Secondly, special training for intermediate sub-executives already in the industry. Thirdly, continuation schools for the plant employees and junior office help which would train them for more efficient service and for promotion in the industry.

Another type of association was that formed among professional men. Medical associations, bar associations, and so on had long been familiar. Somewhat the same principles were applied to various businesses. The National Association of Real Estate Boards may serve as an example. It was organized in 1908 and by 1926 had a membership of six hundred local real-estate boards. It formulated a code of ethics which it attempted to enforce on its members in the conduct of their business. In many of these local boards regular committees were established to hear and determine, without the delay and expense of legal redress, such complaints against any member as might arise out of business transactions. They also coöperated with the Bureau of Housing and Standards of the Department of Commerce in an effort to reduce costs of homes, eliminate wastes, and standardize materials. They drafted a model state real-estate law which in 1926 had been adopted in twenty-two states. In later years the features of self-government were very strongly emphasized.

The Chamber of Commerce of the United States was also a new factor in business life. The immediate suggestion for the organization was said to have arisen out of delegations of business organizations going to Washington with conflicting requests. President Taft felt that business men should work out their differences among themselves and present the recommendations resulting from such consultations for official consideration when governmental action was desired. In March, 1912, he signed a statement calling attention to this problem, and the Secretary of Commerce and Labor invited commercial organizations to meet at Washington in May. By 1913 the chamber included representation of about 50 per cent of the commercial organizations of the country, including all parts of the United States (except New Mexico), Hawaii, Porto Rico, the Philippines, and French-American and Turkish-American commercial organizations. *The Nation's Business* was established as the official organ, and in addition weekly and special bulletin service was furnished to members. Standing committees were created for foreign commerce, domestic commerce, transportation, legislation, and banking and currency. The activities included (1) mobilization of opinion of business men on questions of national interest in legislation, (2) service as a channel for supplying information to business men, and (3) coöperation for extension of foreign trade. The attitude of members was ascertained through referendum vote. Whereas the trade association sought to coördinate business within an industry or trade, the Chamber of Commerce of the United States sought, among other things, to coördinate the activities of different industries with each other and with the government.

SELECTED BIBLIOGRAPHY

Report of the Committee on Recent Economic Changes of the President's Conference on Unemployment, including the Reports of a Special Staff of the National Bureau of Economic Research. 2 vols. McGraw-Hill Book Company, 1929.

CHAPTER XV

REGULATION OF BUSINESS

Adjustments of the Newer Problems

WHILE the older problems of business — the relations between business and the public — continued, the newer problems — the relations between management and diffused ownership — were insistent. Could the corporation be democratized? As regards the former, time had given some perspective, and experience had established some precedents; as regards the latter, the full implications of the problem could not be understood. President Coolidge invited Professor Ripley to the White House for conference on these problems. The White House spokesman announced February 17, 1926, that the question of split common stock was considered by the President to be a matter of state jurisdiction. Although this view was sound so far as it went, it was still true that the Federal government did have jurisdiction in some cases. The Interstate Commerce Commission denied the Nickel Plate merger at least partly on these grounds. The states could act through their general charter regulations, and some did in the Dodge Motors deal, refusing to permit the sale of the stock within the state. Federal incorporation of interstate and foreign business would reach the problems under consideration.

On the broader question of diffused ownership of stock and corporation government Professor Ripley and others outlined some constructive adjustments. The first of these was the independent audit. The purpose of such an audit must be more than a determination of the mathematical accuracy of the accounts: it must make an examination into the business itself. This method had been used successfully in England and in Japan, but was not adaptable to the United States unless accompanied by important legislation or else linked with other devices. In England there were comprehensive laws governing auditing, and the auditor was under obligation to present the true state of affairs in a corporation. In the United States only seven of the forty-eight states had accounting laws in 1926, and in two of them the courts had declared the laws unconstitutional.

The independent audit could be combined with a permanent stockholders' committee, a body independent of the management and representative of the interests of the stockholders. The auditors could be made responsible to this body. In Germany use had been made of some such arrangement. Something of the kind was on trial in the Dennison Manufacturing Company. The idea was not new in the United States, but it would be made a regular institution. In several cases that might be cited, extraordinary committees had been organized to handle emergencies. One difficult problem which had not been satisfactorily met by those advocating this scheme was how the stockholders' committee could be made really representative and kept so.

The investment trust suggested another possible approach to an adjustment. The safety of the small investor might in this way be definitely assured. On the other hand, the experienced directors of the investment trust would be in a position to take an active and intelligent part in the affairs of each railroad or other institution in which stock was held. The weak link in this proposal was the inadequacy or absence of regulation of the investment trust.

POLITICAL REGULATION OF BUSINESS

In the last years of his administration Wilson continued his advocacy of the pre-war Democratic method of controlling corporations. In his annual message of December 3, 1919, he advocated the Federal licensing of all corporations doing an interstate business. This recommendation was repeated in his message of the next year. Congress made no response to these messages during the Wilson administration, and with the Harding-Coolidge régime a quite different policy was in vogue. There was no new legislation on regulation of corporations, but there was, nevertheless, a virtual reversal of policy. Harding's special message and his first annual message of 1921 reassured business of the assistance and coöperation of the government except where business was dishonestly or unfairly conducted. The chief center of controversy during succeeding years was associated with the activities of the Federal Trade Commission. Its duties were to administer the Federal Trade Commission Act (approved September 26, 1914), Sections 2, 3, 7, and 8 of the Clayton Anti-trust Act (approved October 15, 1914), and the Export Trade Act (approved April 10, 1919). Its members were given long terms of seven years, for the purpose of making that body as independent as possible of political changes. A commissioner might be removed by the president only "for inefficiency, neglect of duty, or malfeasance in office." In the early post-war period the majority of the commission were men of the pre-war type of liberalism representing active government regulation. The laissez faire political theory of the Harding-Coolidge administration was diametrically opposed. The first limitation on the commission came, however, from the Supreme Court in 1920. The court held that "unfair methods of competition in commerce" included only such practices as are "opposed to good morals because characterized by deception, bad faith, fraud, or oppression," or practices which are "against public policy because of their dangerous tendency unduly to hinder competition or create monopoly." From 1920 to 1925 it was charged that the commission still tried to expand its powers in the face of this decision. Of forty cases carried to the circuit court of appeals twenty-eight were reversed, and of nine carried on to the

Supreme Court seven were reversed. Such defeats tended to discredit the commission with business and with the public.

The heart of the difficulty was the rules of procedure by which the Federal Trade Commission made public the filing of complaints prior to the formal hearings held before it to determine the validity of the complaints. Business houses charged that their reputations were injured by irresponsible complaints, made by their competitors, which the commission later decided to be unfounded. Conservatives demanded the abolition of the commission. Hoover desired that the purely administrative functions be transferred to the Department of Commerce, leaving to the commission only its judicial functions. Coolidge did not advocate abolition, but in his annual message of 1923 he did recommend a change in procedure to "give more constructive purpose to this department." In his annual message of December 8, 1925, he said:

I recommended that changes in the then existing procedure be made. Since then the commission by its own action has reformed its rules, giving greater speed and economy in the disposal of its cases and full opportunity for those accused to be heard. These changes are improvements and, if necessary, provision should be made for their permanency.

This statement hardly seems adequate when examination is made into the methods by which the change in the rules was accomplished.

The controversy concerning the commission became heated in connection with the election of 1924. A report on the alleged monopoly of the Aluminum Company of America was made public by the commission during the height of the campaign. The Aluminum Company of America was known as a Mellon interest, and Andrew W. Mellon was Coolidge's Secretary of the Treasury. Coolidge was running for reëlection, and the report was used by the opposition to discredit the administration. On January 26, 1925, ex-Representative William E. Humphrey of Washington, one of Coolidge's campaign managers in the West during the election of 1924, was appointed to the Federal Trade Commission. He entered upon his duties February 25. The Humphrey appointment gave the President's faction on the commission a majority, and they proceeded to revise the rules.

It is necessary at this point to discuss in some detail the rules of procedure before the commission. The first stage was that of preliminary inquiry. An alleged violation of law was brought to the attention of the commission by a letter from some corporation or individual. The rules provided for preliminary inquiries regarding facts and an attempt to settle differences. This first stage was confidential. If the attempt to settle differences failed, the case was docketed as an application for a complaint. This was the second stage. A statement of the grievances or violation was submitted to the proposed respondent for an answer. After all the facts were assembled the chief examiner submitted the case to a board of review who, in turn, considered the matter and made recommendation to the commission. A majority vote of the commission decided whether a complaint by the commission should issue in the case. However, a stipulation (that is, an agreement between the commission and the defendant as to what constituted unfair practices) might be entered and the "cease and desist" order be issued with the consent of the defendant in lieu of the complaint and trial. The stipulation was not used until 1925, but this was the stage at which it would appear in proceedings. Thus far the matter remained secret.

The third stage was the filing of a formal complaint against the respondent with specific charges. The case became public at this point. The complaint was entered in the name of the commission as a matter of public interest. A trial was then held before the commission; and if the charges were proved, an order was issued to cease and desist from such unfair practices. If the order was contested by the defendant, it would then go to the Federal courts on appeal. This constituted the fourth stage of proceedings.

The first change in rules came on March 17, 1925. The commission stated its new position thus:

Hereafter it shall be the policy of the commission not to entertain proceedings of alleged unfair practices where the alleged violation of law is a purely private controversy redressable in the courts except where said practices substantially tend to suppress competition as affecting the public. . . .

The end and object of all proceedings of the Federal Trade Commission is to end all unfair methods of competition or other violations of the law of which it is given jurisdiction. The law provides for the issuance of a complaint and a trial as procedure for the accomplishment of this end. But it is also provided that this procedure shall be had only when it shall be deemed to be in the public interest, plainly giving the commission a judicial discretion to be exercised in a particular case.

The rule shall be that all cases shall be settled by stipulation except when the public interest demands otherwise.

In all cases before the board of review, before it shall recommend to the commission that a complaint issue, it shall give to the proposed respondent "an informal hearing."

The next change in the rules occurred April 30, 1925. At this time it was decided that no publicity be given a case until the final determination of the case. However, after the respondent had filed his answer the papers in the case might be open to inspection under regulations made by the commission. Under the old rules, publicity entered upon the filing of the complaint by the commission or at the beginning of the third stage of proceedings; under the new rule it did not enter until the end of the third stage — after the matter was settled. In regard to stipulations no changes were made, as publicity had been withheld except as to statements of the practices condemned, without publication of the names of the parties. During 1927 a member of the staff was designated to coöperate with the antitrust division of the Department of Justice in order better to coördinate the functions of the two agencies. It was argued that these changes would enable the commission to catch up with its business, would be more economical, would allow more careful preparation of cases prosecuted, and would be fair and equitable to business. The minority, Nugent and Thompson (Democrats), fought the new policy vigorously and succeeded in getting much of the story of the commission's activities before the public in spite of the new rules. Organized business was well satisfied with the new policy, but the old-type progressives, Senator George W. Norris of Nebraska and Senator Borah, demanded the abolition of the commission because of what they charged to be complete subserviance to big business.

In state as well as in national legislation this reversal of policy regarding big business had been carried out. One very conspicuous case may very appropriately be cited. During Wilson's governorship of New Jersey he secured the passage of the so-called "seven sisters" in regulation of big business. This program went a long way toward making him president in 1912. By 1927 it was heralded in the press that the last of the "seven sisters" was repealed. Important public policies were indeed ephemeral when fifteen years brought such changes; yet of such materials were the foundations of political distinction constituted.

In view of the changed policy of the Federal Trade Commission it was freely charged that the government would not follow up the prosecution of trusts. Although it was impossible to arrive at a very accurate idea of the effect of the new policy, it was clear that several important prosecutions were pushed. The annual report of 1927 summarized the work of the commission in a series of tables, from which the following conclusions are drawn. The summaries are by stages of procedure, as already indicated. The number of requests for action from the public increased rapidly until 1925, when they numbered 1623; after that date they declined, the number in 1927 being 1319. The number docketed as applications for complaint increased until 1925, when the number was 456; after 1926 the number decreased to 286, and in 1927 it increased to 293. The total number disposed of during the year increased until 1925, when the figures stood at 1671; in 1927 only 1276 cases were completed. Thus, even though the number of applications had decreased by 300 per year, the commission in 1925 carried over only 186 cases unfinished; but in 1927 the arrears in the first stage of procedure were 357.

In the second stage (applications for complaint) the figures were irregular. The high point was 1920, when 724 cases were docketed, and except for 1923 the number declined until 1927. The figures for the last three years were 340 in 1925, 273 in 1926, and 292 in 1927. In 1925 only four cases were disposed of by stipulation, but there were 102 in 1926 and 80 in 1927. The number of complaints docketed for the three years were 118, 56, and 45. The total number disposed of were 421, 344, and 255, and the number pending at the end of the year were 488, 422, and 459. The commission maintained that stipulation would permit expediting of business, but this is not perceptible in the figures. In view of the decline in the number of cases docketed, the commission was relatively farther behind in 1927 than in 1925.

In the third stage the high point in numbers of cases docketed was the year 1924, except for 1920, both presidential years. The numbers for the four years 1924–1927, inclusive, were 154, 132, 62, and 76. The number of "cease and desist" orders were 92, 73, 44, and 52. The total number of cases disposed of during the year were 128, 176, 130, and 82. The total pending at the end of the year were 264, 220, 152, and 147. Again, while there were fewer cases carried over, in view of the decline in numbers of new cases docketed, the commission was relatively farther behind in 1927 than formerly.

The fourth stage (court proceedings on appeal from the commission) showed the high points of new cases in 1921 and 1924. For the years 1924–1927, inclusive, they were 15, 6, 5, and 4. It is very difficult, if not impossible, to estimate results, as cases in the Federal courts were slow in coming to a final decision. The record in the circuit court of appeals for 1919–1925 was 18 cases won by the commission and 31 cases lost. Eleven were lost in 1921, apparently the result of the abnormal activity of 1920. Just how much post-war anti-profiteering hostility had to do with the situation cannot be answered here, nor can the question concerning the influence of the election. If allowance were made for 1921 cases, the record for appeals lost or won would be about fifty-fifty. For 1926–1927 the numbers were nine commission victories and three losses, which was clearly a better record than formerly. This analysis of the commission's activities has been presented at some length to demonstrate to the reader that the extreme claims of both parties in the commission quarrel were without foundation. Some facts seem to favor one contention; others favor the opposite. The most striking element in the record was the introduction of the practice of stipulations, and the relative effectiveness of that procedure was primarily a matter of difference in judgment as to the expediency of one or the other line of public policy. The passage of time should afford eventually both the facts and the perspective necessary for a more satisfactory evaluation.

The chain-store movement presented new problems of government regulation. As yet the problem had not come within the review of the Federal government, but not because of the absence of propaganda. Independent wholesalers and retailers and, to some extent, manufacturers joined in a demand for regulation or limitation of the new type of business organization. Both Congress and the state legislatures were asked for legislation to prevent the growth of chain stores. The Chamber of Commerce of the United States, whose slogan was "Less government in business!" indorsed the plan. Several states passed laws to limit the number of stores operated in a state, either directly or indirectly (by means of a graduated tax). In February, 1929, eleven state legislatures had bills before them for limiting chain stores, most of them bills for discriminative taxes. The status of the problem of regulation by the states was summarized in *Time* (May 21, 1928) :

North Carolina, South Carolina, and Georgia ordered special taxes on chain stores. In Maryland a law was passed forbidding anyone to own more than five stores in the county of Cumberland. Although North Carolina and Maryland courts have declared their laws unconstitutional, although South Carolina has made no attempt to enforce hers, although Georgia courts have granted a temporary injunction restraining enforcement — the passage of such laws has caused chain-store operators to stir themselves defensively.

Measures were introduced into Congress during the session of 1927–1928 directing the Federal Trade Commission to make an investigation of the chain-store business. Such a resolution was passed in May, 1928.

SELF-GOVERNMENT IN BUSINESS

The application of the laissez faire theory to post-war business contributed to experimentation in the development of organs of self-government. The Trade Association, one of the instruments for the accomplishment of this purpose, raised some serious questions. In their earlier stages the associations were designed to secure information of common interest to all members of a given line of trade, and when such information was compiled it was distributed to members. Such methods were of great advantage to individual concerns. Instead of each business incurring the expense of maintaining an organization to secure the desired information or else going without it, the common effort produced more effective results, without duplication and with much greater economy. But the temptation to use such information as to wages, specification, raw materials, processes, etc. for purposes of fixing prices throughout the trade was well-nigh irresistible. A suit was brought against the Hardwood Manufacturers' Association, and in 1922 the Supreme Court declared it to be a combination in violation of the antitrust laws. Hoover, as Secretary of Commerce, was interested in trade associations; and after conferences with the Attorney-General's office, he addressed an informal inquiry to Attorney-General Daugherty on February 3, 1922, asking for his opinion concerning eleven specific points. In the correspondence which followed, a definition of acceptable practices was evolved. The Chamber of Commerce of the United States then printed the correspondence for general distribution.

Cases were later brought against the Maple Floor Manufacturers' Association and the Cement Manufacturers' Association, and in 1925 the Supreme Court upheld those organizations. Between 1922 and 1925, however, Coolidge had made new appointments to the court which changed its point of view somewhat. The extent of the post-war reaction in legal theory was emphasized by the fact that Taft, who was generally considered as conservative, was in the minority in the two cases last named. Thus the legal status of the associations was fairly well defined. With this vindication their range of activity was much more fully developed along lines of conciliating differences within the trade without recourse to legal action, of educating the members to higher standards of competitive ethics, and of serving as channels for the exchange of information between business concerns and government.

The activities of the Chamber of Commerce of the United States as an agency of self-government may be illustrated by a few specific cases. Certain types of heavy silk were treated with synthetic rubber to give them weight. In cleaning by the gasoline process the rubber was dissolved and the fabric ruined. The manufacturers took the view that the cleaners and dyers should modify cleaning methods to suit the materials. The cleaners demanded that the manufacturers cease using the rubber process. Retailers blamed both, and the user might blame all three. Cleaners in Tennessee, Ohio, Illinois, and Washington inaugurated a black list of forty manufacturers. Agitation was started for legislation.

Some business men turned to the Chamber of Commerce of the United States. During the fall of 1926 the Chamber brought together the various trades interested. Those represented were suit and cloak makers, furriers, woolen and worsted manufacturers, dress industries, silk dyers, retail clothiers, upholstery manufacturers, laundrymen, cleaners and dyers, and retail dry-goods dealers. The meeting was not immediately successful; but a beginning was made, and agitation for restrictive legislation ceased.

Another line of activity was the adoption by the Chamber of an arbitration plan to apply to business disputes. It is said that in one line of business alone over two hundred disputes were settled without resort to the courts and at a great financial saving. Arbitration by business men through their own organizations was applied in domestic trade and also in foreign trade, where commercial disputes were often an international irritant. Was celotex lumber? This case serves well as an illustration. Celotex was made from sugar-cane pulp. The dispute between the manufacturers of the new product and the lumbermen was brought to the Chamber of Commerce of the United States, where it was settled. Another case had a different history. Could "Philippine mahogany" be used as a name for a wood which was not mahogany? The Federal Trade Commission on July 20, 1926, issued an order prohibiting its use. Here two methods were used to settle the same type of case. Which method was preferable? It was argued that if the Chamber of Commerce had been organized along these lines a few years earlier, the Federal Trade Commission would never have been created. One author stated in 1927 that "certain American business . . . is regulating itself to an extent that would have seemed preposterous to any merchant or manufacturer" in 1912.

An interesting conflict of views is presented to the investigator in Washington as to whether this rapidly increasing progress of business toward regulation of its own abuses and elimination of practices opposed to public interest will lead to eventual elimination of the

Federal Trade Commission. Some of the stanch advocates of more business in government and less government in business are predicting that gradually the chamber will supersede the commission entirely and that Congress will eventually abolish the Trade Commission. Some high official of the chamber, on the other hand, told the writer that he thought the commission would always be of value no matter how nearly the Chamber of Commerce approached a complete covering of the fields in which it is operating. The commission will always be there as a court to which any dispute which industry itself cannot adjudicate may be appealed.

Still other approaches to the problem of self-government were adopted. Professional baseball as a branch of the public-amusement business secured the services of the spectacular Kenesaw Mountain Landis, former Federal judge, as director of certain aspects of the business, as arbiter of disputes, etc. He was popularly known as the "Czar of Baseball." The moving-picture industry, likewise a branch of the public-amusement business, secured the services of Will Hays, formerly Postmaster-General in Harding's cabinet, to act in a somewhat similar capacity.

The machinery of arbitration in business disputes was originally established without government support. Gradually these functions were recognized, and eventually granted definite legal status by the United States Arbitration Act of February 12, 1925. The preamble stated that it was "an act to make valid and enforce written provisions or agreements for arbitration of disputes arising out of contracts, maritime transactions, or commerce among the several states or territories or with foreign countries." It was not to apply, however, to employment contracts of workers on railroads or to seamen or other workers engaged in interstate or foreign commerce. The act provided that written contracts to submit any controversy arising out of contracts or business transactions were valid and enforceable. Suits in such United States courts as otherwise would have jurisdiction were stayed pending settlement by arbitration. If a party to such an agreement should fail, neglect, or refuse to arbitrate, the aggrieved party might apply to the proper United States court, civil or admiralty, for an order directing that arbitration proceed in accordance with the terms of the agreement. When an arbitration award was rendered, an order of the proper Federal court should issue confirming the award; and if a court was not specified in the contract, the court otherwise having jurisdiction should issue the order.

Under the direction of Hoover the Department of Commerce inaugurated a program of coöperation with trade associations and other organized agencies of business, and during the seven and a half years that he was secretary the policy was continued. In a campaign address at St. Louis, November 2, 1928, he cited an example of the work accomplished:

In 1923, under my chairmanship, there was organized a series of committees representing the manufacturers, contractors, engineers, real-estate men, and labor in the building trades. Its purpose was to reduce the loss of time due to the seasonal character of these industries. As a result of the organization set up, the average winter unemployment in these trades has been reduced from about one hundred days to about half that number.

These coöperative activities were purely voluntary, and the department had no power of enforcement with respect to any decision arrived at. The execution of the program depended upon the self-governing machinery of business itself.

It has already been shown how trade associations contributed toward the building up of codes of ethics and trade practices in different industries. These codes in themselves had no binding effect except as the association was able to enforce them upon the membership. The importance of definite codes of fair and unfair practices had long been recognized in connection with the so-called problem of trusts. During Roosevelt's administration his critics complained of his erratic and inconsistent action in regard to regulation of big business. The antitrust law was criticized as being indefinite. Business had a grievance in the matter, as there was little to guide in determining a course of action in any but the most obvious cases. Roosevelt condemned the Northern Securities Company and approved the Tennessee Coal and Iron consolidation. The Clayton Antitrust Act and the Federal Trade Commission Act were designed to define certain kinds of cases more specifically and to provide a permanent regulating body to apply the law in a consistent fashion through its supervisory powers. Instead of prosecuting after a violation had been committed, the commission might use its powers to prevent violations, or if violations occurred it might order the offending company to cease and desist. Even this process of building up a code was slow and could not adequately include all phases of business practices. The commission resorted to a device called trade-practice conferences as a means of meeting the problems pertaining more specifically to a particular type of business. A trade-practice conference might be called when conditions which would give occasion for complaints were brought to the attention of the commission, or, on request from a trade, it might be arranged without reference to particular cases or practices. The commission called together as many as possible of the representatives of the industry in question to consult with a view to deciding upon the standing of trade practices. The commission gave the following definition: "A trade-practice conference, formerly known as a trade-practice submittal, provides a method of procedure whereby those engaged in an industry or business may formulate, under the direction or sanction of the commission, their own rules of business conduct." Here well-organized trade associations served an important function, and trade practices that were formulated were either approved or disapproved officially by the commission. Once accepted by both the commission and the trade, they became legally enforceable.

The first trade-practice conference was held in 1919; by 1925 twenty such conferences had been held. In 1926 there were applications on file from twenty-three industries or lines of business. To handle these conferences, the commission (April 19, 1926) set up a division of trade-practice conferences. In its annual report for 1927 it summed up the significance of the new procedure as follows:

The work of the division of trade-practice conferences deals with industries as units, in the matter of offering to an industry or a business an opportunity to eliminate at one and the same time any methods of competition which the industry itself considers unfair, wasteful, or bad; in other words, to permit an industry to make its own rules of business conduct, its own law merchant. . . .

The trade-practice-conference procedure is concerned solely with trade practices or methods, not with individual offenders. It regards industry as occupying a position comparable to that of "friend of the court," and not that of the accused. It wipes out on a given date all unfair methods condemned at the conference, and thus places all competitors on an equally fair competitive basis. It performs the same function as a formal complaint without bringing charges, prosecuting trials, or employing any compulsory process, but multiplies results by as many times as there are members in the industry who formerly practiced the methods condemned and voluntarily abandoned. Thus, in a single industry more than ninety separate complaints in various states of completion were pending against as many separate concerns. A trade-practice conference was held during the present fiscal year. At the time of going to print practically all of these respondents have accepted and agreed to abide by the decision of the industry to abandon all practices condemned by the conference, thus saving the expense, annoyance, and delay of individual proceedings.

The economy effected and the coöperation established by voluntary action, and the wiping out at one time from an entire industry practices which the industry considers bad, has commended this procedure to both industry and public.

The influence of this new machinery was of importance in intrastate business as well as in interstate business. In California a state law (June 5, 1923) gave legal sanction within the state to all rules of the Federal Trade Commission governing unfair trade practices in the handling of butter, cheese, or eggs. The code referred to had its origin in a trade-practice conference held in 1919.

Early attempts to regulate business were directed at the annihilation of trusts, monopolies, and the like. Later the idea of trust annihilation gave way to the policy of regulation of "big business." The mere fact that a business was large was not a reason in itself for assuming that it was contrary to the public interest: misconduct on the part of big business was the thing to be curbed. After the war the next step in economic policy was introduced, whereby the activities of the Federal Trade Commission and of economic self-government were directed toward regulation of all business without regard to size. Codes of fair trade practices as established in the several industries applied to small business as well as to big business. The public interest was affected by the character of the practice and not by the fact of the size of the offending organization. This was a quite fundamental step in the evolution of public economic policy. A few men (and Wilson was one of them) held this view before the World War.

An interpretation of the new post-war situation as viewed by William E. Humphrey of the Federal Trade Commission may serve well as a conclusion to this survey of business and of business regulation. His own words on the changed attitude toward business and on democracy in business are quoted from *The Magazine of Wall Street*, April 6, 1927.

The Federal Trade Commission has completely reversed its attitude toward the business world.

The Interstate Commerce Commission has become the bulwark instead of the oppressor of the railways.

Instead of passing obstructive laws for political purposes, Congress now satisfies its demagogic tendencies by ordering all sorts of investigations — which come to nothing.

The President, instead of scoffing at big business, does not hesitate to say that he purposes to protect the American investor wherever he may rightfully be.

The Secretary of Commerce, far from appealing to Congress for legislation regulatory of business, allies himself with the great trade associations and the powerful corporations — not to benefit them as such, but to benefit the people through them.

Through the Federal Reserve system, government and finance are harnessed together.

The chief factor in these new orientations is the investor. The people have come into business, great and little, through investment. The politician has discovered that to slap corporations is to affront voters. Behold the more radical of our great political parties urging the reduction of the rate of taxation of corporations as a popular measure. It is not that we are less democratic then we were, but more. Formerly democracy was confined to politics: now it has permeated business. Formerly the people were the government: now they are also business. The common people have become the business as well as the political world — and they will not permit one of their interests to destroy the other.

Little slips of paper — stock certificates and bonds — have been the talisman of this revolution, this wholesale fusion of political and economic life. The ballot follows the bond; the vote is the voice of business.

Laws have not greatly changed since this new conjunction became obvious. The antitrust laws are still there. The courts have not nullified them, but they are applying them from a different viewpoint. These laws, they say, were not intended to repeal economic laws. It is not that the courts flout statutory law, but that they interpret it in harmony with economic law. They are changing with the people and the times.

The people — the new sort of people — are working these changes consciously and unconsciously — the latter through the mere fact of their existence and the passive rearrangements of government to suit them, the former through the new sort of trade associations. With the enormous extension of business ownership the trade associations are coming to speak with the voice of the people. An association executive no longer conceives of himself as the agent of a few selfish corporations: he constantly envisages, directly and indirectly, millions of people as standing behind and directing him. He thinks more in terms of people than corporation magnates. There are three or four hundred trade associations represented at Washington. In the aggregate they constitute a sort of parliament of the people as business units. They maintain as against the politicians the balance between the political and economic functions of the people. As a citizen the American sovereign writes a letter to his congressman; as a business man he appeals to the executive of his association.

This statement placed the new theory of business and government in its most favorable light, but it was not for that reason to be too seriously discounted. It represented the point of view of those in power, and they were putting it into practice as rapidly as possible. It was more than a theory; it was in the process of becoming reality. It was true that the general public was not more than vaguely aware of the changed relations between business and government and did not understand their significance. Popular discussion of the so-called "trust question," therefore, tended to continue the use of the older and more familiar language and ideas of individualistic laissez faire as against government regulation, even after the new practices had become fairly well established.

CHAPTER XVI

LABOR

ORGANIZATION

AFTER the World War, organized labor suffered a decline in its membership, as indicated by the following table:

YEAR	AMERICAN FEDERATION OF LABOR MEMBERSHIP	TOTAL ORGANIZED LABOR
1920	4,078,740	5,110,800
1921	3,906,528	4,815,000
1922	3,195,635	4,059,400
1923	2,926,468	3,780,000
1924	2,865,979	3,708,000
1925	2,878,297	3,722,000
1926	2,803,966	3,649,000
1927	2,812,407	
1928	2,896,063	

The losses of the American Federation of Labor were attributed to three principal causes: First, the tendency of the leading trades to organize independently. The Amalgamated Garment Workers drew most of the membership of the United Garment Workers who had been affiliated with the federation. Secondly, changes in industry due to new machines which were abolishing old crafts, such as iron-molders and glass-blowers. Thirdly, prohibition, which eliminated one of the largest unions, that of the brewery employees. Furthermore, the death of Gompers introduced an element of uncertainty into the situation, as well as factional rivalries in the readjustment of leadership and policy.

The policy of organized labor underwent material changes at some points. President William Green of the American Federation of Labor voiced a modified spirit in discussing the relations of capital and labor before the Harvard Union in 1925:

Both are essential in industry and each is dependent upon the other. Between them there is an interdependence so fixed and irrevocable as to make complete success attainable only through understanding and coöperation.

It is to these problems of industrial coöperation and understanding that modern trade unionism is addressing itself. During the formative period organized labor relied almost solely upon its economic strength, while today it places immeasurable value upon the convincing power of logic, facts, and the righteousness of its cause. More and more organized labor is coming to believe that its best interests are promoted through concord rather than conflict. It prefers the conference table to the strike field.

The field of labor activities also expanded. In several instances unions undertook the management of capitalistic enterprises. Under the leadership of Warren S. Stone, president of the Brotherhood of Locomotive Engineers, the first labor bank in the United States was opened October 28, 1920. After that beginning nearly forty labor banks were established. In New York the clothing workers undertook the building of coöperative apartment houses.

To the Socialist party as an organization of the workers the World War brought little less than disaster. Many of the more conservative socialists renounced their economic theories. Many of the more radical went over to communism. As a party, during and immediately after the war the socialists were pro-German, opposed the war, sympathized with the Bolsheviki in Russia and with the International, and opposed the League of Nations. Such a program inevitably brought them into general disrepute. The decline in party strength and fluctuations in general support are reflected in the following table:

YEAR	VOTE	PAID MEMBERSHIP
1912	897,011	118,045
1916	590,294	83,284
1920	915,302	26,766
1928	267,835	

War between socialism and communism began in 1919. Serious losses to socialism resulted. Again, in 1921, a secession of radicals occurred, leaving the membership much below the figures given above. After the death of Eugene V. Debs in 1926 Victor Berger was recognized as the head of the party, but his policies followed closely the socialist traditions.

The Detroit convention of socialists in 1921 made a new departure politically. Instead of the traditional policy of independence, the executive was instructed to make a survey of other organizations with a view to possible political federation with organizations of similar views. This, if it materialized, would be similar to the British Labor party. In 1924 the party decided to support La Follette for president.

The group who were in control of the party offered little beyond the old program. *The New Leader* (New York), a socialist weekly, published a series of articles in 1926–1927 on the problem of socialism. The view of W. J. Ghent represented an opposite angle to that of the traditional school. He pointed out that all scholars agreed that the French Revolution occurred during a period of prosperity and diffusion of wealth. Fourierism in the United States came during the period of recovery after the panic of 1837. These facts should be applied to the post-war conditions.

Any hope of a revival based upon an impending disaster to industry and an impoverishment of the workers is a delusive hope. Everything we know makes against such an outcome, and the stars in their courses fight against it. Trade-unionism, social legislation, welfare work, diffusion of stock ownership, the Federal Reserve system, the International Labor Office, industrial Locarnos, the League of Nations, and a hundred other instances of improving social mechanism throughout what is called the civilized world give promise of better times for labor. Even where labor is determined to wreck itself (as a part of it seems bent upon doing in England), it finds many obstacles in the way. The socialist argument and the socialist tactics of the future must be based upon a realization of the generally improving condition of the masses. If socialism has nothing to offer in the face of that condition it had best shut up shop and throw the key in the ocean.

There were two phases of Ghent's program, one negative and the other positive. The negative phase was that the party must dissociate itself from the policies which had brought it ruin — pacifism, communism, and exploitation of their war record — and must repudiate its old leaders such as Berger, who had learned nothing and had forgotten nothing, but still followed long-exploded economic theories. The positive side was summed up by three terms: "Americanization," "resocialization," and "laborization." By "Americanization" he meant that socialism had largely been alien in character and under alien leadership. To secure the confidence of Americans, it must recognize nationalism and adopt American leadership and an American program. Under "resocialization" he pointed out that most socialist speakers were engaged in exploiting exploded economic theories, platitudes, and stereotyped phrases which had no relation to the facts of life. Leadership in social democracy had been furnished by other agencies than the Socialist party. If socialism was to realize its ideal, it should be producing leaders and programs. "Laborization," the third element of the program, emphasized the desirability of working with and through labor unions instead of against them. Which type of program would be supported by American socialism, or would socialism as an organized movement disappear?

Extreme radicalism, in the form of the Industrial Workers of the World, communism, or otherwise, received little support within the United States, either with the public at large or with labor. The American Federation of Labor denounced it. President Green said (August 10, 1925): "The Communists have no place with us. In so far as my influence can be brought to bear they shall be driven from our ranks. There is no room in our platform for those who preach a destructive philosophy." In New York City a series of meetings among trade-union leaders during November and December, 1926, resulted in a "call to action," summoning all the unions of the city to join in a movement to "eliminate speedily and effectively all traces of the Communists' disruptive activities within the labor movement." In several of the states such organizations as the I. W. W. were placed under the ban.

INDUSTRIAL DEMOCRACY

In his special-session message of May 20, 1919, Wilson declared that antagonism between capital and labor had gone too far, that another way must be found.

It must lead not merely to accommodation but also to a genuine coöperation and partnership based upon a real community of interest and participation in control. . . . The object of all reform in this essential matter must be the genuine democratization of industry, based upon a full recognition of the right of those who work, in whatever rank, to participate in some organic way in every decision which directly affects their welfare or the part they are to play in industry.

The ideal of industrial democracy was one of the newer aspects of the relation between employer and employee which had become conspicuous after the war. According to W. J. Lauck industrial democracy meant equality of opportunity and its guaranties in industrial life. Political democracy, evolving out of the eighteenth and nineteenth centuries, established guaranties of civil and political liberty. The task of the twentieth century is to establish economic equality and equivalent guaranties in industrial life. Much that was done was experimental. The chief lines along which the newer ideas developed were (1) coöperation and participation of labor in profits, (2) employee ownership of stock and control of business, (3) employee representation on boards of directors, (4) customer and employee provision of new capital. The precedents came largely from Europe, and particularly from England, where the Whitley plan was inaugurated in 1916. This consisted of committees made up of employers and employees from local unions, with a National Joint Council for each industry made up of representatives of the employer associations and labor unions. Experiments were carried out in the United States along one or more of the different lines indicated in a number of concerns, but in few of these cases did the experiments meet the ideal combination of principles.

The profit-sharing movement after half a century or more had made little headway. In its generally accepted form it was not a success. In 1920 only ninety-one plans were in use, and forty-two of these were merely bonus schemes. Employee representation in management was particularly popular just after the war, and by 1924 was said to have numbered 814 workers' councils, covering 1,117,037 workers. Employee ownership of stock was hailed by Professor T. N. Carver of Harvard University as "a deeper revolution than . . . the Industrial Revolution." Such cases were cited as the Standard Oil Company of New Jersey, the Philadelphia Rapid Transit Company, the New York Central Railroad, and the Armour Packing Company. This point of view was answered, however, by another writer, who pointed out that less than one tenth of one per cent of the corporations sold stock to employees. In the case of the New York Central Railroad, employee ownership of stock diminished radically with post-war wage reductions. In the case of some corporations that sold stock to their employees limitations were attached which provided for the surrender of the stock under certain conditions, usually such as would result from a strike. In labor circles it was held that individual ownership of stock was a delusion and could not bring control, and it was obvious that ownership of nonvoting stock, in public utilities for instance, was useless from that standpoint. Employee control of business could be effected only through joint or group ownership of stock. There were only five cases cited where the aim of employee ownership of stock was to realize complete democracy. Employee representation on boards of directors was rare, but it was in operation in a slowly increasing number of establishments. Customer and employee provision of new capital was also limited in its

application. The point of greatest significance in this connection would be the elimination of the investment banker,
with his profits and sometimes control through refinancing
operations. The essentials of industrial democracy (again
following Lauck's analysis) were (1) labor unions as a basis
of procedure, (2) participation in revenue by labor and
management on a fixed ratio, (3) collective purchases of
common stock, (4) new capital from reinvestment of profits
and from employee and customer purchases of stock from
their savings, and (5) interests of the workers as consumers.
The company that probably carried out this program most
fully was the Philadelphia Rapid Transit Company.

The favorable attitude of labor toward schemes of so-
called industrial democracy was essential to its success.
During the war and for some time after, the American Federation of Labor supported the shop-committee plan, but later
serious questioning arose as to the purpose of management
in introducing these devices. The Whitley plan in England
was based upon the national unions, and it was assumed that
such would be the case in the United States. The Transportation Act of 1920 provided for boards of adjustment. The
labor unions insisted upon national organization. The railroad executives insisted upon limiting them to local boards
or to the individual railroad system. The question of agreements concerning conditions of labor met with the same
difference in point of view. The shopmen's strike of 1922
practically decided the issue in favor of the executives. Company unions were formed in many cases, and local agreements were worked out. The open-shop movement, indorsed
by the Chamber of Commerce of the United States and the
American Bankers' Association, also was hostile to organized
labor. It is not to be wondered at that labor came to look
upon the shop committee, the company union, wage bonuses,
employee ownership of stock, and the like as industrial paternalism the purpose of which was to break up the labor-union
movement and render the employee more and more de-

pendent upon the employer. Labor was inclined to make a sharp distinction between this industrial paternalism on the one hand and true industrial democracy on the other.

GOVERNMENT POLICIES

Harding's first annual message of December, 1921, reflected the political ideas of the pre-war period regarding labor policy. He said, "The right of labor to organize is just as fundamental and necessary as is the right of capital to organize," and urged that as in the case of the corporation so in the case of the labor organization the public must be protected. This means that both the corporation and the labor organization must submit to public regulation, and he insisted that since the spirit of the time demands that political disputes between nations be settled without resort to war, similar principles should apply to differences between organized capital and labor. He added, "It should be possible to set up judicial or quasi-judicial tribunals for the consideration and determination of all disputes which menace the public welfare."

By 1925 Coolidge had come to favor the idea represented in the Watson-Parker railroad labor act — a policy of agreement between capital and labor through conciliation and arbitration machinery worked out between themselves. In his annual message of 1925 he held up the railroad scheme as a model to other industries. He reported :

No progress appears to have been made within large areas of the bituminous-coal industry toward creation of voluntary machinery by which greater assurance can be given to the public of peaceful adjustment of wage difficulties such as has been accomplished in the anthracite industry. The bituminous industry is one of primary necessity and bears a great responsibility to the nation for continuity of supplies. As the wage agreements in the unionized section of the industry expire on April 1 next, and as conflicts may result which may imperil public interest, and have for many years often called for action of the executive in protection of the public, I again recommend the passage of such legislation as will assist the executive in dealing with such emergencies through a special temporary board of conciliation and mediation and through administrative agencies for the purpose of distribution of coal and protection of the consumers of coal from profiteering. At present the executive is not only without authority to act but is actually prohibited by law from making any expenditure to meet the emergency of a coal famine.

It was evident that the President's idea was that self-government should be the regular method of adjustment, with the Federal government in the background to step in and handle such emergencies as could not be met by the regular machinery.

LEGAL STATUS OF LABOR ORGANIZATIONS

In spite of the Clayton act of 1914 the legal status of labor organizations was still very precarious. This act was supposed to exempt labor organizations from the operation of the antitrust acts. In the United Mine Workers *v.* the Coronado Coal Company the opinion was expressed that labor unions were liable to suit under the trust acts and for damages arising out of restraint of interstate commerce.

Other principles which were generally recognized were the right to organize, the right to strike, the right to picket, and the right to boycott. Morris Hillquit, in the *New Leader* for December 4, 1926, summed up the matter pointedly:

Theoretically this is the recognized code of conduct in industrial disputes. . . . In practice the rules have been hedged in by so many exceptions and weakened by so many modifications and departures that they have been reduced to the status of an abstract social philosophy rather than a statement of positive law.

The use of the injunction also presented problems of vital importance. Chancellor Kent in 1819 condemned what is now called the "blanket injunction." By 1894 the opposite view was recognized by the courts and was elaborated from time to time until its climax in the Daugherty injunction of 1922, and this in the face of what had been intended as a restriction of its use by the Clayton act. The preliminary injunction was usually issued upon application of the plaintiff without notice to the defendant and without hearing, and was usually followed by an order to the defendant to show cause why the injunction should not be made permanent. At such hearing, sooner or later, each side presented its case; that is, affidavits were presented and arguments of counsel were heard. It was not until the trial that witnesses were heard and examined. This might mean a lapse of two or three months. In a labor controversy this delay would very frequently if not usually decide the strike. Hillquit suggested a remedy which would be a distinct advance over the Clayton act:

> The hope of needed reform in this branch of law now seems to lie mainly in procedural remedy; that is, in laws which will provide that no injunction should issue in a labor dispute without notice to the defendant and without proof of the charges by oral testimony of witnesses, subject to examination and cross-examination.

Various other methods of limiting injunctions were proposed, and organized labor insisted that a remedy be found. William Green, president of the American Federation of Labor, announced on August 10, 1925, that "so far as I can make my influence felt, the five million workers of the nation will never sit still until they curb the judiciary of the state and nation and bring back freedom to American citizens." This declaration was later repeated on numerous occasions.

SELECTED BIBLIOGRAPHY

LAUCK, W. J. Political and Industrial Democracy. Funk & Wagnalls Company, 1926.

The American Labor Yearbooks. New York, Rand School of Social Science, 1921–19 .

The American Federationist. Official magazine of the American Federation of Labor.

Report of the Committee on Recent Economic Changes of the President's Conference on Unemployment, including the Reports of a Special Staff of the National Bureau of Economic Research. 2 vols. McGraw-Hill Book Company, 1929.

CHAPTER XVII

IMMIGRATION

THE question of restriction was not a new one in American history. It was an issue in politics after the middle of the nineteenth century. In the early stages of the agitation practically all the arguments for and against restriction were formulated; later they were restated from time to time in terms of changing circumstances. Nevertheless each generation tended to view each recurrence of intense agitation as new and unique. There were two important differences in the later periods that must be taken into account. During the eighteen eighties there began a substantial amount of immigration from southern and eastern Europe and Asia. These immigrants differed widely from the predominating population in the United States and from the predominating type of immigrant in race, religion, economic and cultural background, education, and political experience. This southern and eastern immigration was designated in the literature of the subject as the "new immigration" as distinguished from the "old immigration" from northwestern Europe. The new immigration grew rapidly until in 1895 it became the majority. At the same time that these changes were taking place the American frontier was passing. A large part of the old immigration went into the West as agricultural pioneers; the new immigration tended to congregate in the industrial centers. These factors greatly complicated the problems which arise inevitably when peoples of different types must live together.

In discussing the immigration question one must always bear in mind that it is impossible to distinguish between qualities in immigrants which are inherent in the racial stock, and those which are due to environment. The propagandist, who was the most important element in immigration agitation, was not accustomed to make careful distinctions. To him differences from himself were often evidences of inferiority. The stock arguments against the new immigrants were that they contribute largely to illiteracy, crime, pauperism, problems of disease and sanitation, labor difficulties, low wages, corruption and inefficiency in government, and radical political, economic, and social theories, and that they are not readily assimilated or Americanized. On the other side equally strong arguments based on equally sound statistics were advanced to prove the contrary, but their advocates were in the minority.

The determination to apply some form of general restriction on immigration was crystallized before the World War. This fact is more important historically than the problem of the validity of the arguments. The real problem was to agree upon a method of restriction. The leading method then advocated was the literacy test. Bills were passed by Congress and vetoed (1897, 1913, and 1915) by three different presidents. A measure was passed again during the session of 1916–1917, was vetoed again, and was passed over the veto February 5, 1917.

The restrictions were first a head tax of eight dollars except on children under sixteen years of age accompanying a parent. The basic restriction was a literacy test which excluded all persons over sixteen years of age "physically capable of reading, who cannot read the English language or some other language or dialect, including Hebrew or Yiddish." To prevent undue hardship certain persons were exempt from the test: an immigrant's father or grandfather over fifty-five years of age, or his wife, mother, grandmother, or widowed or unmarried daughter; also persons fleeing from religious or political persecution, and skilled laborers, actors, and professional men.

Certain other persons were excluded altogether. These may be grouped into six classes: mental defectives (idiots, imbeciles, the feeble-minded, and the insane), physical defectives (persons afflicted with dangerous or contagious diseases, including tuberculosis), moral defectives (criminals, polygamists, and prostitutes), economic irregulars (inebriates, paupers, beggars, and persons liable to become a charge upon the public, and contract laborers), the politically unorthodox (anarchists and persons who believed in the overthrow of government by violence), and the racially different (Asiatics, except Japanese). It was further provided that any of the excluded classes who entered illegally should be deported, and that an immigrant was subject to deportation within five years after entrance if he should come within the limits of those classes which would be excluded from entering.

The European war situation helped to carry the act of 1917 over the presidential veto. After the war every aspect of the problem of immigration was intensified. "Hundred per cent Americanism" was pitted against "hyphenated Americanism" in the public mind. All types of unorthodox political ideas were branded as "red." The deportation act of October 16, 1918, was the basis of the deportation raids of 1919 and 1920. It was reported that millions of Europeans were awaiting the opportunity of coming to the United States. Organized propaganda under the auspices of such organizations as the American Federation of Labor, the American Legion, and the Ku-Klux Klan demanded suspension of immigration or else more drastic restriction. The literacy test was very generally condemned as inadequate to meet the situation. The country as a whole was overwhelmingly agreed on further restriction. The difference of opinion was primarily on the method of restriction, the manner of its application as respects the old immigration and the new, and the extent of restriction. The right of a nation to restrict immigration was unquestioned in international law; the aspect of the question that aroused international complications was unequal application of restriction as it affects different foreign states and races.

The quota system became the favorite device to substitute for the literacy test. The first suggestion of the method dates from the report of the immigration commission of 1911, often referred to as the Dillingham report. This method was popularized by the National Committee for Constructive Immigration Legislation. It was included in the Dillingham bill in Congress. Such a bill, restricting immigration, until June 30, 1922, to 3 per cent of the number of each nationality in the United States according to the census of 1910, was passed in 1921 and was pocket-vetoed by Wilson.

One of the "emergency" tasks of the special session of 1921 under the Harding administration was to pass an emergency immigration act. The Dillingham bill was approved by the President on May 19 and was to remain in force until June 30, 1922, with practically the same provisions as the preceding bill vetoed by Wilson. It even denied privilege of asylum from political and religious persecution. The avowed purpose of the act was to limit the new immigration in favor of the old. The total quota for northwestern Europe was 197,555 for 1923, whereas for southern and eastern Europe, including Asiatic Turkey and other Asia, it was 159,646. The permanent law was not agreed upon by 1922; hence the emergency measure was extended to June 30, 1924, by joint resolution of May 11, 1922.

In his annual message of December 6, 1923, Coolidge presented his views on the question — views which reflected very accurately the reactions of the average American.

American institutions rest solely on good citizenship. They were created by the people who had a background of self-government. New arrivals should be limited to our capacity to absorb them into the ranks of good citizenship. America must be kept American. For this purpose it is necessary to continue a policy of restricted immigration. It would be well to make such immigration of a selective nature with some inspection at the source, and based either on a prior census or upon the record of naturalization. Either method would insure the admission of those with the largest capacity and best intention of becoming citizens. I am convinced that our present economic and social conditions warrant a limitation of those to be admitted.

We should find additional safety in a law requiring the immediate registration of all aliens. Those who do not want to be partakers of the American spirit ought not to settle in America.

Congress meanwhile was working on a new measure. The House bill was amended by the Senate and received the President's approval on May 26, 1924. By this act the basic act of 1917 was amended to provide for restriction by numerical quota calculated on the basis of the census of 1890 instead of that of 1910. The percentage was reduced from 3 per cent, as provided in the emergency act of 1921, to 2 per cent, with a minimum quota of 100 for any one country. Immigration offices were provided in foreign countries to examine emigrants at the country of origin rather than to leave all inspection until arrival in the United States. The classes exempted were reduced. The burden of proof that an immigrant was eligible was placed upon the immigrant. Those not eligible for naturalization were excluded. The exempt classes were officials, travelers, seamen, and merchants. The quota system, however, did not apply to the Western Hemisphere.

This numerical-quota scheme was to remain in effect only until July 1, 1927; at that time the national-origins method was to be applied. The maximum immigration for each year was fixed at 150,000, which was to be apportioned among the national groups in the United States as determined by the census of 1920.

Under this act the quotas for 1924–1925 were announced by proclamation and totaled 164,667; the quotas for the preceding year under the emergency law were 357,803. In this way not only was the total immigration reduced to less than half, but quotas based on the census of 1890 drastically restricted the new immigration in favor of the old. Northern Europe was reduced from 197,630 to 141,099, or 29 per cent; and southeastern Europe, with Asiatic Turkey, Siberia, and Armenia, was reduced from 158,540 to 20,447, or 87 per cent.

The national-origins proposal, which was not to become operative until 1927, aroused great hostility and presented so many difficulties that by joint resolution of March 4, 1927, the date of its going into effect was postponed one year. The actual differences in application between the two proposals (the numerical quota of 2 per cent and the national-origins quota) were very small as respects the old immigration and the new, but there were radical differences in respect to nationalities. The English, Dutch, Italians, and Russians would be radically increased by the national-origins method, whereas the Germans, Norwegians, Swedes, Danes, Swiss, French, Irish, and Bohemians would be reduced. The objections of the racial groups were again effective in the face of a presidential election, and by an act approved April 2, 1928, another year's postponement was ordered. The proclamation applying the national-origins method was issued, although reluctantly as a mandatory duty, March 22, 1929, to be effective July 1.

The law of naturalization was for the most part left as it was. The act of 1870 authorized naturalization of white persons and persons of African descent. An act of May 9, 1918, provided that men honorably discharged from the military or naval service of the United States might be admitted to citizenship without meeting the residence requirement of five years. An act of September 22, 1922, provided that the marriage of an alien woman to a citizen of the United States did not naturalize her; to become an American citizen she must go through the same process as any other alien.

SELECTED BIBLIOGRAPHY

ABBOTT, EDITH. Historical Aspects of the Immigration Problem. The University of Chicago Press, 1926.

ABBOTT, EDITH. Immigration: Select Documents and Case Records. The University of Chicago Press, 1924.

GARIS, R. L. Immigration Restriction. The Macmillan Company, 1927.

STEPHENSON, G. M. History of American Immigration. Ginn and Company, 1926.

CHAPTER XVIII

THE AGRICULTURAL CODE

THE CONDITION OF AGRICULTURE

TWO general causes underlay the post-war farm depression: the retardation of agriculture and the abnormal conditions produced by the war. The disparity between the development of the city and the country had been due to the application of steam to industry more than to any other single cause. Steam could not be applied to agriculture. In 1850 rural wealth and urban wealth were about equal, but by 1890 urban wealth was three times rural wealth. Population was concentrated in the cities. Political power followed the shift of wealth and population. Legislation did not discriminate against the farmer; but public policies were framed by the power in control, and that was for the most part city-minded during the last part of the nineteenth century and after.

There were many differences also in the character of production in the two groups. City business was incorporated; the farm was individual. The quantity and quality of manufactures could be controlled, but the weather largely determined these for the farmer. The farmers were a large number of small producers selling to a small number of purchasers; with the manufacturers the situation was the reverse.

Closely associated with these problems was the fact of the closing of the American frontier and the resulting change of the American farmer from extensive to intensive agriculture. Cheap production was no longer possible. The value of the land did not increase as rapidly in the more stabilized civilization as it had under frontier conditions. The farmer's profits must be made out of the product of the land rather than out of the increment in value due to the development of the community. The more successful farmer was obliged to give more attention to scientific methods and management. The simple process of acquiring a home through the stages of hired man, renter, and then owner became difficult or impossible without assistance. In the struggle for existence a greater and greater number failed to reach the stage of land ownership and remained renters or else moved to town.

The war period and the following years brought about what resembled an agricultural revolution. The internal-combustion engine had been brought to a high state of perfection, and the automobile, the truck, and the tractor gave to the farmer for the first time a convenient and adequate form of power. What steam did for urban industry, the gas motor seemed to be doing for the farmer. The new device also brought its difficulties, because it resulted in a decreased demand for farm products: horses, mules, and hay, corn, and other feeds. What made the transition more difficult was that it came at the time of a great world-wide economic depression.

The World War demand for food caused an expansion of agriculture far beyond the limits of profitable production in normal times. It also stimulated the one-crop system, especially in the Middle West, where wheat was the grain crop, and in stock-raising sections which produced cattle and hogs. This expansion did not stop with the end of the war, and the year 1919 became a year of speculation in land at unheard-of prices. Similar speculation occurred in urban industry. There was a general delusion that the world was suffering from underproduction. The collapse came in the spring and summer of 1920.

The price paid to the farmers for corn fell from $1.56 per bushel in 1919 to 57 cents in 1921, wheat fell from $2.14 per bushel to $1.19, cotton from 29.6 cents per pound to 12.3

cents, cattle from 9.72 cents per pound to 5.53 cents, and hogs from 16.23 cents per pound to 7.84 cents. The average price of land decreased from $108 per acre in 1920 to $76 in 1926. The total value of farm land fell from $79,000,000,000 in 1919–1920 to $58,000,000,000 in 1927. During the same period the capital invested in corporations increased from $99,000,000,000 to $134,000,000,000. Under these conditions rural taxation became ruinous. Warren and Pearson placed it at one third of the farm income in 1921.

EVOLUTION OF AGRICULTURAL POLICIES

There was general agreement that something should be done for agriculture, but no one knew just what should be done. It took several years to work out policies. Congress established a joint committee of agricultural inquiry (June 7, 1921). Its report exonerated the Federal Reserve system of the charge that rural credits had been curtailed in favor of city credits as the result of a conference (May 18, 1920), the so-called "crime of 1920." It recommended that a new system of rural credits should be provided in order to adjust the credit system to the period of agricultural turnover, six months to three years.

The farm bloc, composed of members of both parties in both Houses who were willing to coöperate to secure agricultural relief, was organized in Congress May 9, 1921. Senator William S. Kenyon of Iowa was chosen chairman in the Senate, but after his appointment to the judiciary he was succeeded by Arthur Capper of Kansas. J. L. Dickinson of Iowa was leader in the House. Outside of Congress the farm bloc was supported by the leading agricultural organizations,— the Farm Bureau Federation, the Farmers' Union, the National Grange, and so on,— although they did not necessarily all agree on all measures brought forward. Laws sponsored by the bloc included amendments to the farm-loan system, the futures trading act, the packers control act, the extension of the War Finance Corporation's activities to include agricultural credits for emergency purposes, the emergency tariff, the joint commission on agricultural inquiry, and tax-reduction bills.

Harding called together a National Agricultural Conference in January, 1922, to advise regarding an agricultural program. Its views were similar in many respects to those of the farm bloc, and it indorsed the action of that group. During the campaign of 1924 Coolidge promised another commission. It sat during 1925. It recommended longer live-stock credits, better utilization of public lands for grazing, revision of the freight-rate structure, increased appropriations for agricultural research, revision of the banking system, tariff on agricultural products, development of coöperatives, and reorganization of departmental administration.

In 1926 the National Industrial Conference Board committee reported on farm relief, and during the same year it joined with the Chamber of Commerce of the United States in another investigation. This joint committee made its report in April, 1927. It recommended efforts to equalize the tariff as between agriculture and manufactures, but condemned the McNary-Haugen bill. Among other recommendations in the report were the following: Markets should be extended and a farm board should be established to aid in stabilizing prices and production. The cost of production should be reduced. Farmers' coöperatives should be encouraged and assisted in reducing production and marketing costs. A carefully planned land-utilization program should be formulated by a national board. Economy in government was stressed. Reform should be made in state and local taxation systems. Agricultural credits should be developed further. Railroad rates should be revised and waterways systems extended.

The world-wide character of agricultural difficulties was emphasized by the report of the international economic conference at Geneva in the summer of 1927. The recommendations of the agricultural commission of this conference were similar in many respects to those discussed above for American agriculture. To a certain extent American conditions were affected by the international depression, and to that extent national remedies could not reach the causes.

The proposals named were selected from outside official circles. The policy of the Federal administration paralleled this development in many respects. Wilson urged greater production and better marketing and improvement in farm management, sanitation, and medical service. This was in the annual message of December 2, 1919, and reflected the prevailing point of view about stimulation of production. Harding's first annual message proposed tariff, marketing reform, and reduction of railroad rates. The following year he suggested particularly agricultural credits. By the time Coolidge sent his first annual message of December 6, 1923, the surplus question was acute, and he recommended the additional remedy of controlled production. There should be no government price-fixing. While Secretary Wallace was in the cabinet there seems to have been some disagreement within the administration in regard to the proper farm relief, but the appointment of William M. Jardine, president of the Kansas State Agricultural College, to the cabinet in 1925 appeared to produce more harmony.

The reading of Coolidge's annual messages gives the impression that he did not take the farm question very seriously until 1926. In his annual message of that year the question was treated in detail. The first part of the section devoted to the subject reviewed what had already been done: the packers and stockyards act, the establishment of intermediate credit banks, the agricultural research act, the coöperative marketing acts, the warehouse act, extension of farm loans, tariff on agricultural products, promotion of waterways and highways, and the reduction of Federal taxes. He then outlined additional legislation which would further the purpose of relief: readjustment of the freight-rate structure, the consolidation of railroads, the continuation of waterway development, provision of an adequate supply of cheap fertilizer, better use of public lands for grazing, the strengthening of coöperatives, the prevention of forest fires, and the eradication of animal and plant diseases. In his next message he indorsed the idea of a farm board to assist the coöperatives in handling the surplus problem through more orderly marketing and controlled production.

The economic theory which underlay much of the agricultural agitation is of interest to the student of history. Secretary Wallace expressed one point of view, and the one which was probably most widely held, in the following language:

> During the next twenty years, either consciously or unconsciously, the United States will adopt fairly definite policies as to industry and agriculture. We are approaching that period which comes in the life of every nation when we must determine whether we shall strive for a well-rounded, self-sustaining national life in which there shall be a fair balance between industry and agriculture, or whether, as have so many nations in the past, we shall sacrifice our agriculture for the building of cities.

This idea of a balanced empire was strictly in keeping with the spirit of the times and the development of neomercantilist economic theories. Another view also widely held, but for the most part in the agricultural sections, was stated by Senator Capper of Kansas as follows: "The soil is the foundation of all real wealth and only through fostering production from the soil can national growth be assured." This was physiocratic economic theory handed down from the eighteenth century, just as the other sprang from a modification of the ideas of the sixteenth and seventeenth centuries. The McNary-Haugen faction were quite realistic in their theories as well as in their practices. Their argument was that manufacturers received protection for their interests through the tariff. Railroads were protected by the rule for rate-making incorporated in the Transportation Act of 1920.

Labor was organized and was protected by the Railroad Labor Board, as well as by restriction of immigration. Agriculture should therefore be granted the same measure of government assistance and protection.

LEGISLATIVE POLICIES: EMERGENCY ADJUSTMENTS

Three classes of remedies were brought forward: emergency reliefs, transitional measures, and permanent policies. Among the emergency reliefs were sales of nitrates from the War Department for fertilizer, advance of seed in areas where crops had failed, and postponement of payments for water rights on irrigation projects and of payments for grazing rights on the public domain. The second group of measures were the emergency tariff, reductions on railroad rates on agricultural products, and extension of special credits by the War Finance Corporation. These measures provided some relief, but not enough to satisfy the farmers. The measures of the second group were mere stop-gaps to give time for fuller study of the questions involved and the formulation of more permanent policies.

PERMANENT POLICIES: TARIFF

The emergency tariff had committed the agricultural group to high protection by placing high duties on agricultural products. This could do little toward farm relief, since the manufacturer needed protection against importation and the farmer was for the most part an exporter. The high rates on wheat, rye, corn, beef, lamb, fruits, etc. were continued under the permanent act. In the case of butter there was some real protection. Wool and sugar rates were raised, but here most of the product consumed in the United States was imported, and the effect was to raise the cost of living. Under the flexible clause the President raised the duty on wheat and on butter. The general ineffectiveness of the tariff finally became an important factor in the development of the McNary-Haugen movement after 1924. Finally, in January, 1927, the McMaster resolution was passed by the Senate demanding either reduction of tariff on manufactures or else an equivalent protection to agriculture by some other means.

REDUCTION OF RAILROAD RATES

The general readjustment of railroad rates centered around the Hoch-Smith resolution of January 30, 1925. It instructed the Interstate Commerce Commission to adjust the rate structure as between sections and industries, and in fixing agricultural rates to take into consideration the general condition of the industry. Hearings were held, but by 1928 they were not completed. In the meantime some individual commodities were granted relief.

STANDARDS

One of the most important aspects of farm legislation, if not the most important, centered around the marketing question. The fixing of standard grades for agricultural products in interstate commerce began in 1908. An act of 1914 made the use of standard grades obligatory in cotton sales when made by grade. This act was amended in 1923. Grain standards were similarly fixed in 1908 and were required after 1916. Butter and milk were defined in acts of 1923. The use of live-stock and hay standards were not required, but were used to some extent. The standard-container act of 1916 fixed the sizes of fruit containers used in interstate commerce.

CENTRAL MARKETING MACHINERY

Warehouses were brought under the control of the Secretary of Agriculture by an act of 1916 for the storage of cotton, grains, wool, tobacco, and flaxseed. An act of 1923 extended the system to other storable products. Warehouse receipts were issued indicating the grade of the product as fixed by Federal inspectors. The cotton futures act of 1914 regulated all markets which were authorized to sell cotton for future delivery. This was to prevent manipulation of the markets. Similarly, the grain markets were placed under control by acts of 1916 and 1921. The responsibility for proper management of these "contract markets" was placed on the members of the market. If they did not meet their responsibilities the Secretary of Agriculture might intervene or the privilege of the market might be revoked. Coöperative associations were given the right of membership in these markets. The packers and stockyards act extended similar regulation in that field in 1921. The markets for perishable products were placed under supervision by an act of 1927.

COÖPERATIVE MARKETING

The ideal of a good marketing program was to insure an economical and orderly flow of products to market. Coöperation among producers offered the best promise for eliminating the long-standing evils. This movement was fairly well established in a small way before the World War, but under the antitrust acts there was a question whether coöperatives were not combinations in restraint of trade. The Clayton Anti-trust Act of 1914 legalized them when they were formed without capital stock and for legitimate purposes. This did not go far enough; and the agricultural producers associations act of 1922 authorized them to handle their own products and a limited amount of the products of others, whether organized with or without capital stock. The supervision of the system was vested in the Secretary of Agriculture. An inclusive definition of interstate commerce in agricultural products was enacted in 1927. It included essentially all transactions from the producer to the distributor of the finished products. This seemed necessary in order to reach all phases of the marketing problem. This Federal action was supplemented in most states by local coöperative legislation designed to facilitate organization.

During the period of acute depression the coöperative movement grew too fast and too much was expected of it, so that in later years there came a period of readjustment and stabilization. By 1926 coöperatives were operating in the following fields: grain, dairy, live stock, fruit and vegetables, cotton, wool, poultry and products, and tobacco. Forty-six per cent of them were located in the north-central states. Coöperatives might operate in three different stages of the handling of products: as producers' shipping associations, as commission associations at the terminal markets, or as packing houses. There were numerous examples of each class, but the greatest success was attained by the shipping organizations. Coöperative purchase of farmers' supplies was also the subject of much experimental activity, but did not develop very rapidly. The most successful examples seem to have been limited to the Eastern states.

AGRICULTURAL CREDIT

There were some important differences between the requirements of agriculture and of urban business in the way of credit facilities. Commercial credit for short-time transactions did not exceed ninety days. Long-time credits were always available through the medium of bond sales. Agricultural credit fell into three general classes: short-time credits under six months, intermediate credits from six months to three years, and long-time credits for periods above three years. The commercial bank provided short-time credits of not to exceed three months. This meant that if the farmer secured adequate credit accommodations he must plan to renew his notes one or more times and take the chance that renewal would be permitted. The farmers' crops for the most part were produced once a year, and live stock often required longer. Before 1913 no regular means of providing this credit were provided. National banks were prohibited from making loans on real-estate security. The beginning of the recognition of this problem was inaugurated in the Federal Reserve Act of 1913.

LAND CREDIT

For the most part long-time credits in agriculture meant land credit; that is, credit for the purchase of a farm or for more land or for permanent improvements on the land. Of the three the purchase of a farm presented the more serious problem. It meant a larger relative outlay, longer time, and more favorable interest rates. The fact that free or cheap land was gone was making this problem more and more acute.

The Federal Reserve Act provided that national banks might lend money on farm land to the extent of 50 per cent of its value and for a maximum of five years. This made the land-credit system an adjunct of the commercial-credit system and was the conservative solution. The more radical element insisted upon the establishment of a separate system on a more liberal plan. The Federal Farm Loan Act of July 17, 1916, represented substantially this view. A board of five members was created to administer the system, one member being the Secretary of the Treasury. The country was divided into twelve districts, in each of which a Farm Loan Bank was to be established. The banks made loans to the farmers through the medium of three possible agencies: national farm-loan associations made up of farmers wanting loans, banks or other credit institutions designated by the bank, or joint-stock land banks, which were a new type of private institution. Capital was provided in the first instance by the Federal government, but additional funds were to come from stock subscriptions of the local borrowing institutions and from the sale of debenture bonds secured by farm mortgages. The national farm-loan associations came nearest to meeting the requirements of the home-purchaser, but the coöperative nature of these institutions and the obligations assumed made progress slow among the individualistic American farmers. The other two agencies were better adapted to serve the farm-owner who was adding to his holdings or improving his land. For example, the borrower from a joint-stock land bank was not required to cultivate the land being purchased, whereas the borrower from a national association must cultivate.

There were no material legislative changes in the system during the post-war decade; there were, however, amendments of minor character to adjust details of operation. The credit stringency of 1920–1921 caused the capital of the twelve land banks to be increased to an aggregate of $50,000,000. This act was approved July 1, 1921. Certain aspects of administrative policy caused controversy. The Treasury wished to dominate the Federal Farm Loan Board and treat it much as a bureau in the department; the majority of the board members held the view that the board was an independent organization. A similar fight had been carried on in the Federal Reserve Bank system, and for the most part the board had won. In the farm-loan system the results tended in the other direction. The President opposed the principle of independent boards. During 1927 and 1928 the Farm Loan Board was reorganized by the appointment of men reputed to hold the views of the administration.

SHORT-TIME CREDITS

The first step in the adjustment of short-time credits to meet the requirements of farms was also incorporated in the Federal Reserve Act. The credit time allowed on paper made for agricultural or live-stock financing was extended from the customary ninety days to a maximum of six months, and this paper was made discountable with the Federal Reserve Banks. During the war no new legislation was enacted, but the agricultural requirements were favored by rulings of the Federal Reserve Board regarding classification of agricultural paper for various banking purposes. In the post-war period the demand for both short-time and intermediate credits was insistent. Conservatives insisted that all legitimate demands could be met by adjustment of existing machinery; the more radical elements insisted upon a new intermediate-credits system. The result of the contest was an extension of the short-time-credits machinery into the border zone between the two fields. The intermediate-credits act of March 4, 1923, liberalized the provisions for the use of short-time agricultural paper within the Federal Reserve system, and in addition extended the maximum time of maturity for certain classes of it to nine months. The McFadden banking act of February 25, 1927, extended the maximum to ten months. The security on which this paper was based was warehouse receipts or shipping documents.

INTERMEDIATE CREDITS

The credit collapse of 1920–1921 was not brought on by the discount policy of the Federal Reserve system or by a conspiracy to curtail agricultural credit, as was often charged: the most important factors were cessation in buying both at home and abroad and the precipitate decline in prices, especially farm prices. The collapse in prices sharply reduced the value of security for loans, and consequently it was necessary to reduce loans somewhat in proportion in order to maintain a safe margin between the loans and the security.

The remedies brought out three points of view: first, the enactment of purely emergency legislation; secondly, amendment of the Federal Reserve system; thirdly, the establishment of a new intermediate-credits system. In the long run all were tried. Before any legislation could be enacted private assistance was extended, at the suggestion of the Secretary of the Treasury, through the Stock Growers' Finance Corporation sponsored by bankers in June, 1921. The War Finance

Corporation was revived in January, 1921, to assist in financing the exportation of agricultural products. Its scope was enlarged by an act of August 24, 1921, to include emergency agricultural credits. It continued until 1924, when the new intermediate-credits system was put into operation.

It was March 4, 1923, before the intermediate-credits act became law, and then the measure contained three schemes sandwiched together. This seemed the only way in which enough votes could be mustered to pass any bill. It was hoped that in this manner some part or parts of the combination would help agriculture, and the enactment of some measure was necessary to help the political situation because the farmer was becoming impatient.

The Federal Farm Loan Board was increased from five members to seven and was given jurisdiction over the new intermediate-credits system. Twelve Federal intermediate-credit banks were to be organized, one in each Federal Reserve Bank district. These banks were authorized to make loans to coöperative producing and marketing associations. The security should be warehouse receipts, shipping documents, or live-stock mortgages. The maturity of the loans was from six months to three years. The capital of the banks was subscribed by the Treasury; they might issue collateral trust debentures for periods not to exceed five years secured by cash or agricultural paper. This was scheme number one.

National agricultural-credits corporations could be formed by five or more persons for agricultural or live-stock purposes under authority of the Comptroller of the Currency. The corporations were authorized to discount or buy and sell agricultural paper and to lend money for agricultural and live-stock purposes. They might issue debentures. The security for both loans and debentures was similar to that required under the intermediate-credit bank system. This was scheme number two.

The third scheme provided for the amendment of the Federal Reserve system (see page 239).

It is very important to the understanding of the new agricultural code to see how completely all the previous farm legislation was tied together in the short-time and intermediate credits systems. The establishment of standards for farm products under Federal inspection, the control of terminal markets, the control of warehouses which issued warehouse receipts, and the legalization and promotion of coöperatives were all essential to the sound functioning of the principle of basing agricultural credit upon farm products as security. Just how much assistance the new institutions gave to agriculture was a question of controversy, except that the national agricultural-credits corporations section scarcely functioned at all. The system was drafted during an abnormal period and was organized under the most adverse conditions. It had to be built from the ground up, and almost without American precedents except where it was tied up to the Federal Reserve system. In this respect the success of the agricultural-credits system cannot fairly be compared with the Federal Reserve system, which was drafted after six years of intensive study of normal times and was put into operation in 1914, before there was any serious financial disturbance. Furthermore, the Federal Reserve system was built upon the national bank system, which had been in operation for fifty years.

The principle of using agricultural products as the basis of a system for solving the farmer's financial problems was not new in the United States. The Farmers' Alliance subtreasury plan adopted by the Populist party in 1892 provided for the issue of paper money on the security of farm products stored in warehouses. They also proposed a land-credit scheme. The farmers of that period did business with money rather than with credit. In 1916 and 1923 agricultural financing was assisted if not solved by the creation of credit institutions which utilized the same security — land and agricultural products. In the latter period business was done with credit rather than with money. The Populist scheme was considered too radical to receive serious consideration from sound financiers; the later schemes were pronounced conservative and sound when they were established.

THE PROBLEM OF THE SURPLUS

After enacting the credit legislation the Federal government faced another issue which was to dominate the discussion of farm relief for over five years, the question of the surplus. The leading measure advocated as a solution of this question was the McNary-Haugen bill, introduced into Congress during the session of 1923–1924. The radical farm group took the aggressive part in formulating the program, and no administration measure was presented until late in the contest. Inasmuch as each successive McNary-Haugen bill was different in details from its predecessors, only the general principle of the equalization fee is discussed here. It started with the assumption that tariff did not really protect agriculture, but that an equivalent could be provided by fixing the domestic price at a point which would insure a profit. The surplus of each year's crop over domestic needs could be sold in the world's markets for what it would bring. The loss would be assessed, in the form of an equalization fee, against every unit of the product sold by the producer. The net price to the producer would be the fixed price minus the fee. The larger the surplus the greater the loss and consequently the fee, which would leave the net price low and discourage production. Where the surplus was very small there would be no need for the system. By applying these tests to agricultural crops in normal years it was clear that only two crops, wheat and hogs, would be seriously concerned. Producers of cotton and tobacco sold too great a proportion of their crop abroad to be interested; other producers usually did not have enough to sell abroad to interest them. The McNary-Haugen bills were therefore Middle West measures.

On April 12, 1926, Jardine, Secretary of Agriculture, presented the administration bill through Senator Capper. It approached the question from the standpoint of controlled production and improved marketing conditions. Policies already inaugurated were to be continued, especially the coöperatives and agricultural research. A Federal farm board was to be created which could assist the Secretary of Agriculture and the coöperatives in maintaining an adjustment of production and in finding market outlets. In emergency cases it could administer a revolving fund to assist in holding crops for the purpose of allowing orderly marketing.

During the next session the McNary-Haugen group secured the support of the cotton and tobacco sections of the South and passed their bill. Coolidge vetoed it February 25, 1927. The veto message declared that the bill was a grant of special favors to particular crops and to particular sections. It was price-fixing; it was an abuse of the taxing power; it would increase prices to the consumer and would increase the cost of production. Other industries would ask for similar protection. The plan was contrary to policies of preventing combinations in restraint of trade; it would put the government into business; it would encourage speculation. Under such a plan sale of United States products in the world's markets would be treated as dumping and would cause discrimination against American goods. The plan would be difficult if not impossible to administer and would build up bureaucracy. The method of appointment was an unconstitutional invasion of the president's appointing power.

Nearly all these objections would be equally valid against a high protective tariff. As a matter of fact, most of them had been frequently used in earlier years by the exponents of low tariff. Why should they have been used by an advocate of high protection? It was the very heart of the whole McNary-Haugen bill to grant to the farmer the same measure of protection that the manufacturer was already enjoying. The last group of objections were more easily defended.

The country seemed, on the whole, to indorse the wisdom of the veto without necessarily approving all the reasons.

During the winter of 1927–1928 a revamped McNary-Haugen bill was pushed through Congress. It contained the equalization-fee plan, and it was almost certain of a veto. The presidential campaign was well under way, and the McNary-Haugen group expected either to force the acceptance of the measure or to take it into the campaign. It went to the President on May 18 and was vetoed May 23. The McNary-Haugen group had lost in Congress, so they prepared to fight the issue out before the political party conventions in June.

THE JARDINE-COOLIDGE PROGRAM, 1925–1928

The further development of agricultural research was provided by an act of February 24, 1925, which allowed additional grants of money to experiment stations — $20,000 for 1926 and an increase of $10,000 each year until 1930, when the annual appropriations would reach $60,000. The plans for the creation of a division of coöperative marketing in the Department of Agriculture were proposed in 1925 but were not enacted into law until July 2, 1926. This act was to create a Federal agency to foster the growth of the coöperatives and to provide them with adequate information and service to enable them to function fully. Jardine's ideal was controlled production at low cost and orderly marketing. His plan was to build the foundation on farmer-controlled coöperatives and then to create farmer-controlled central stabilization agencies to coördinate the thousands of coöperatives on a national scale. Each major crop would have its own organization. A Federal farm board would serve as the national instrument through which these central bodies would be created and coördinated. As a law creating the farm board was not enacted the question became an issue in the campaign of 1928.

In the meantime agriculture had made a practically complete recovery in some localities and crops, a partial recovery in others; but depression still persisted in many places. The most serious period had been 1920–1923. By 1924 more favorable conditions were clearly perceptible. A good price for wheat in that year gave relief to the wheat areas. In 1926–1927 the cotton situation was substantially improved. By 1927 live stock had recovered for the most part, and real-estate sales were reported in many communities at advances in price. Jardine reported in 1927 that the farmer had regained three fourths of his buying power.

The restoration of agriculture to approximately the pre-war level was looked upon by many as the solution of the agricultural question. From this point of view only emergency measures had been required, consequently by 1928 little real need existed for further action. During the pre-war period, however, agriculture was far behind urban industry in application of power machinery, utilization of existing scientific knowledge, organization for controlled production, orderly marketing, economical financing, elimination of waste, etc. The purpose of a sound agricultural policy should be to place the industry upon a stabilized basis and redress the balance between urban and rural economic and social systems. There was a third view also, — that of extremists, — which had as its purpose to place agriculture upon a specially favored basis through a form of price-fixing or government subsidy. Either of the two latter policies called for further Federal action.

FARM POLICY IN THE ELECTION OF 1928

With the veto of the McNary-Haugen bill the farm leaders called for a march of the farmers on Kansas City to force the adoption of a plank in the Republican platform indorsing the equalization fee. In spite of their efforts the Republican convention refused to submit; it adopted the administration policy instead. When the nominations of candidates were being made, Lowden, who favored the equalization fee, withdrew his name on the ground that the party had not met the farm issue. The convention nominated Herbert Hoover by an overwhelming majority. Hoover was known to advocate the administration program and was considered by some as the originator of the farm board plan.

Having been defeated all around at Kansas City, the corn-belt leaders (that is, the most radical of them) raised the rallying cry "On to Houston." They went, and were heard. The Democratic platform, however, did not indorse the McNary-Haugen bill itself: the indorsement was of the principle that the cost of marketing surplus crops should be assessed against the crop benefited. This was the principle of the equalization fee. Alfred E. Smith, the Democratic candidate, accepted the plank as written.

The proposed agricultural policies of the two candidates, as defined in the platforms and expounded in campaign speeches, were identical on most points: inland waterways, highways, coöperatives, credits, and so on. Smith criticized the Republican tariff policy, but in the last analysis there was little apparent difference between them even on that subject. The primary difference between the programs centered about the Democratic equalization fee and the Republican farm board. In neither case did the party or the candidate present a concrete description of the machinery required to put the program into effect. The Democratic plan emphasized Federal regulation; the Republican proposal stressed Federal assistance associated with economic self-government. Smith promised to appoint a commission immediately after election to frame the mechanics of his scheme. Hoover promised that if Congress did not enact legislation in the winter session after election he would call a special session to provide the legislation. The farmers' revolt did not materialize. McNary indorsed Hoover immediately; McMullen of Nebraska, who made the call for the farmers to march on Kansas City, indorsed him later in the campaign. Others followed their example.

It is impossible to make any conclusive evaluation of the effect of government policy during the years under review. Part of the restoration came through natural causes and general post-war adjustment. There can be no doubt that government policy contributed substantial assistance. The fact of greatest importance was that between 1913 and 1929 a body of legislation was enacted which may very appropriately be called an Agricultural Code. Such legislation was essentially new in American history. Prior to 1913 United States agricultural policy was focused upon the problems of production. In that year a new departure was inaugurated which for the first time placed systematic emphasis upon the problems of marketing. The practical application of the combined program was carried to the farmer through the coöperative extension service established under an act of 1914 (utilizing the state agricultural colleges, the county agents, and the farm bureaus), and the marketing news service developed through the bureau of marketing and rural organization created in 1913. The ideal of the Code, of which the departure of 1913 was only the beginning, was to provide the facilities for maintaining a stabilized agriculture and rural life. Using these as a foundation, agriculture was in process of transformation. Partisan politics had little to do with the achievement. The Wilson, Harding, and Coolidge administrations each contributed a share. A large part of the new program did not come from administrative initiative. Some measures were forced upon the administration by the bipartisan farm bloc. In much of the administration policy, support in Congress was drawn from both parties. It was difficult for either party to make political capital out of agricultural policy.

SELECTED BIBLIOGRAPHY

WARREN, G. E., and PEARSON, F. A. The Agricultural Situation. John Wiley & Sons, Inc., New York, 1924.

CAPPER, ARTHUR. The Agricultural Bloc. Harcourt, Brace and Company, 1922.

National Industrial Conference Board. The Agricultural Problem in the United States. National Industrial Conference Board, New York, 1926.

Committee of the National Industrial Conference Board and of the Chamber of Commerce of the United States. The Condition of Agriculture in the United States and Measures for its Improvement. New York and Washington, 1927.

ELY, R. T., and MOREHOUSE, E. W. Elements of Land Economics. The Macmillan Company, 1924.

CLYDE L. KING (Editor). "Farm Relief," *Annals of the American Academy of Political and Social Science*, Vol. CXLII, No. 231.

SELIGMAN, EDWIN R. A. The Economics of Farm Relief. Columbia University Press, 1929.

> This book was prepared for the Democratic National Committee in connection with the presidential campaign of 1928, but was not published until afterwards.

NOURSE, E. G. American Agriculture and the European Market. McGraw-Hill Book Company, 1924.

CLEMEN, R. A. The American Livestock and Meat Industry. The Ronald Press Company, 1923.

Institute of American Meat Packers. The Packing Industry. The University of Chicago Press, 1924.

PUTNAM, G. E. The Land Credit Problem. University of Kansas Humanistic Studies, Vol. II, No. 2. Lawrence, 1916.

BENNER, C. L. The Federal Intermediate Credit System. The Macmillan Company, 1926.

NOYES, A. D. The War Period of American Finance. G. P. Putnam's Sons, 1926.

Report of the Committee on Recent Economic Changes of the President's Conference on Unemployment, including the Reports of a Special Staff of the National Bureau of Economic Research. 2 vols. McGraw-Hill Book Company, 1929.

Special attention is also called to the publications of the United States government, particularly those of the Department of Agriculture and those of the Census Bureau entitled "Census Monographs."

CHAPTER XIX

PUBLIC LAND AND NATURAL RESOURCES

PUBLIC land played one of the leading rôles in American history. It is a factor which ranks with transportation in importance. Public-land policy passed through three stages: at first revenue was a primary objective; next, rapid development and settlement became the leading factor (1841–1890); finally, conservation and reclamation seemed to have become imperative with the passing of the frontier and the appropriation of natural resources by private individuals. This last stage appeared first in the termination of the practice of granting lands to railroads, and took definite constructive form in 1888 and 1891 in the conservation of reservoir sites and forest resources and the revision of the public-land code.

During the period 1891–1916 nearly all other aspects of conservation and reclamation were formulated. Reclamation of arid lands by private initiative was the subject of legislation in 1877, the Carey act (1894) turned certain public lands to the states for reclamation, and the act of 1902 inaugurated Federal reclamation. The basic forest reserve act was passed in 1891. A positive policy about dams began in 1906 and was extended in 1910. Conservation of mineral resources and separation of ownership of the surface from the subsoil were provided in 1910. The utilization of resources for social purposes appeared first in the establishment of Yellowstone Park in 1872 and by 1916 developed into the National Park Service. The preservation of wild life for both economic and social purposes is found in restrictions on seal-hunting and salmon-fishing, the preservation of migratory birds, the establishment of game reserves, and the work of the Fish Commission.

HOMESTEAD POLICY

An act of February 19, 1909, provided for enlarged homesteads of 320 acres instead of the usual 160, because of the diminished productiveness of available lands. An act of July 3, 1916, extended the system by making it possible for an entryman of 160 acres, before his patent was issued, to enter additional noncontiguous land within twenty miles to make a total of 320 acres. The new entry was to be cultivated, but the residence on the first entry applied on the second. An act of February 20, 1917, went further in providing that a person receiving title to a homestead of less than 160 acres might enter enough new land so that when half was added to his original holding the total should not exceed 160 acres.

Stock-raising homesteads were created by an act of December 29, 1916. Lands chiefly valuable for grazing and forage crops and not susceptible of irrigation might be designated by the Secretary of the Interior as stock-raising lands, and stock-raising homesteads of 160 acres might be entered by eligible homesteaders. To entrymen who held this type of land additional entries were permitted, contiguous if possible, otherwise within twenty miles of the first entry, to make a total of 640 acres. Instead of the requirement of cultivation improvements equal to $1.25 per acre were required, one half of which must be completed within three years. In the case of additional entries residence on the original entry was credited to the second, but the improvements must be made. The homesteader was permitted to surrender his original entry and make a new one on a 640-acre grazing tract instead. However, the government reserved coal and mineral rights, water holes or other bodies of water needed for public purposes, and land for driveways for cattle. A separate act (August 21, 1916) was passed to promote the discovery, development, and protection of streams, springs, and water holes in the desert and arid public lands and to render these more readily accessible, and to establish and maintain signboards and monuments to mark them. An act of March 4, 1923, extended both the enlarged-homestead provisions and the stock-raising-homestead provisions to homesteaders within national forests.

The Desert Land Act of 1877 was coördinated with the new features by the act of February 29, 1917. An enlarged-homestead entryman was privileged to enter desert lands, provided the enlarged homestead plus the desert entry did not exceed 480 acres. A post-war act of January 6, 1921, extended the Desert Land Act to Colorado and provided that an entryman must be a resident citizen of the state in which the entry was made, except in Nevada.

RECLAMATION POLICY

Wilson's reclamation policy for the reconstruction period was ambitious. He outlined it in his annual message of December 2, 1918, recommending the reclaiming of arid, swamp, and cut-over lands in coöperation with the states. A total of more than 300,000,000 acres was held to be redeemable for cultivation: Western arid lands, 15,000,000 acres; denuded forest lands, 230,000,000 acres; and swamp land, 80,000,000 acres. These could be used for homes for thousands of returned soldiers and would also open the way for a great rural and agricultural development.

The lease of water on irrigation projects for other purposes than irrigation was authorized by an act of February 25, 1920, on condition of the consent of the water-users, when there was no other practicable source and when it would not be detrimental to the reclamation project. Lands no longer needed under the reclamation act of 1902 were to be sold under the provisions of an act of May 20, 1920.

The encouragement of the reclamation of arid lands in Nevada was to be promoted by an act of October 22, 1919. Permits were authorized for prospecting for water supply on tracts of 2560 acres. No more than one permit was to be granted for each forty square miles of arid lands. The permittee, on discovery of underground waters for irrigation and the development of 20 acres of irrigated land in two years, should receive a patent for one fourth of the 2560-acre tract; the remainder was to be open to entry under the Homestead Act. Three years later an extension of time for two years was authorized at the discretion of the Secretary of the Interior to complete such development projects.

An act of August 11, 1916, provided that when public lands were within the limits of state reclamation projects and constituted less than half the district, they should be treated as private lands for the purpose of the development of the project. All such state projects, however, must first have been approved by the Secretary of the Interior. By an act of January 6, 1921, authority was granted to restore to the public domain such lands under the Carey act as had not been developed. The utilization of Federal irrigation facilities to assist state reclamation was the subject of an act of May 15, 1922. Legally organized irrigation districts might make contracts for water rights from Federal works. By a later act (May 20, 1926) a commissioner of reclamation was created to administer the Bureau of Reclamation.

During the agricultural deflation after 1920 new aspects of policy presented themselves. Coolidge's first annual message of December 6, 1923, asked for authority "to suspend, readjust, and reassess all charges against water-users." Relief measures were granted by Congress, but difficulties became serious at some points. During 1926 violence threatened at Scottsbluff, Nebraska, among the farmers on the North Platte valley irrigation project. Commissioner Elwood Mead and Secretary Hubert Work ordered water shut off because of nonpayment of past charges. They were both hanged in effigy on May 27. Another dispute on the Verde River project in Arizona had a similar outcome. The action of the government only aroused ill will.

In his third annual message of December 8, 1925, Coolidge reported that "about one third of the projects are in good financial condition, another third can probably be made profitable, while the other third is under unfavorable conditions." He insisted that new methods of financing should be formulated and that "the states should be required to exert some effort and assume some responsibility, especially in the intimate, detailed, and difficult work of securing settlers and developing farms which directly profit them, but only indirectly and remotely can reimburse the nation." He recommended further that the Federal government should continue planning and constructing these projects. In 1926 conditions on reclamation projects were reported as satisfactory.

Secretary Work, however, did not take so optimistic a view. In an interview published September 28, 1925, he said:

If the reclamation department had taken time to test a single experiment to its conclusion before starting on a big program, many millions might have been saved. But our enterprising Westerners would not have been satisfied.

Today we have more than six thousand farms with no farmers on them. The government has invested about $200,000,000 in reclamation projects, of which $27,000,000 probably will never be collected. We have, worst of all, a disposition on the part of some delinquent settlers to repudiate their debts regardless of their ability to pay.

At the same time that the agricultural depression was at its worst and the surplus of products of the farms was glutting the markets, the reclamation projects were bringing additional acreage into cultivation. It was often pointed out that while the Department of Agriculture was attempting to solve the surplus question the Department of the Interior was adding to the difficulties. A delegation of the Farmers' National Grain Dealers Association was received by President Coolidge on October 19, 1926. The object of their mission was to ask that no further reclamation projects be opened in the near future.

FOREST POLICY

Wilson's annual message of December 2, 1919, called attention to the desirability of further action on the part of the states and the Federal government to preserve and develop forests on private lands as well as on public lands. Coolidge's first annual message of December, 1923, referred especially to reforestation and to the special committee which was investigating the problem with a view to formulating a constructive policy.

An act of March 20, 1922, authorized the exchange of lands held by private individuals within the bounds of national forests for other lands if in the opinion of the Secretary of Agriculture such exchange was considered as contributing to the public interest in consolidating national forests. An act of June 7, 1924, outlined a comprehensive policy of coöperation of the Federal government with the states or other agencies in systems of fire prevention to protect "forest and water resources and the continuous production of timber." Money used by the Federal government should not be in excess of the amount expended by the state or private agency under state direction. "In the coöperation extended to the several states due consideration shall be given to the protection of watersheds of navigable streams. . . ." The Secretary of Agriculture was further directed to examine and recommend to the National Forest Reservation Commission the purchase of forest, denuded, or cut-over lands for the regulation of the flow of streams. This last provision was in continuation of activities under the act of 1911 (usually called the Appalachian Forest Reserve Act), and the protection of the watersheds of navigable streams was the constitutional peg on which was hung the legal right of the Federal government to buy up private lands for national forests, primarily in the Eastern states. The secretary was also authorized to accept donations of land to become parts of the national forests. He was instructed to examine public lands to determine whether they were valuable for control of stream flow or for forest production or for irrigation, and to report the fact to Congress.

Another related line of activity that was authorized was the coöperation of the secretary with the states for the distribution of forest-tree seeds and plants, the secretary to pay half the expense. An appropriation of $250,000 a year was authorized. He was to coöperate with the states also in assisting farmers to establish timber belts, shelter belts, and windbreaks and to grow useful timber crops.

Coöperation with the states was extended by an act of March 3, 1925, giving forest protection to watersheds for domestic water supply or for irrigation. Federal expenditure again should not exceed state expenditure and due consideration should be given to the protection of the watersheds of navigable streams.

A forest experiment station was established in California by an act of March 3, 1925, the Federal government coöperating with California and surrounding states for the purpose of determining the best methods of conservation, management of forests and forest lands, and the protection of timber and other forest products. The Secretary of Agriculture was further authorized to undertake, independently or in coöperation with states, universities, individuals, etc., investigations and experiments relating to forestry. An act of July 3, 1926, provided for a station similar to the one in California to be established in the Ohio and Mississippi valleys. A forest research act approved May 23, 1928, authorized a ten-year program with expenditure starting at $1,000,000 and increasing to $3,500,000.

Policy regarding Nonmetallic Minerals

The legislative basis of the conservation of subsoil resources on public lands began with the Taft administration. By an act of June 25, 1910, public lands might be reserved from sale or entry for purposes of power sites, irrigation, classification, and other public purposes. The work of classification was particularly important in the light of the remainder of the act. Mining rights for coal, oil, gas, and phosphates were reserved, thus separating the surface from the subsoil resources. Having reserved these products of the subsoil, the next step was the formulation of a general policy of regulated and economic exploitation of the reserves. By an act of October 2, 1917, two-year permits might be granted to citizens or to American corporations on tracts not in excess of 2560 acres to prospect for chlorides, sulphates, carbonates, borates, silicates, or nitrates of potassium. On discovery of such deposits the prospector should receive a patent on not to exceed one fourth of the land included in the permit, and he was eligible to lease the remaining land subject to general provisions. Leases could be granted through competitive bidding, advertisement, or some other method adopted by general regulation. Tracts so leased should not exceed 2560 acres. Royalties were not to exceed 2 per cent of the product, and rentals were fixed at twenty-five cents an acre for the first year, fifty cents for the second to fifth years (inclusive), and one dollar a year thereafter, the rentals to be credited to each year's royalties. The known deposits of the Searles Lake region in California and of Sweetwater County in Wyoming should be leased under similar terms. Royalties and rents were to be paid into the reclamation fund, and after they were once used and returned, one half should be paid to the states to be used for schools or roads. The prices of minerals extracted and sold from the leases might be fixed by the president, and, furthermore, the minerals must be used within the limits of the United States.

A scheme similar to that outlined above was adopted in the general leasing act of February 25, 1920, applying to "deposits of coal, phosphates, sodium, oil, oil shale, or gas, and lands containing such deposits owned by the United

States." Exploitation was limited to citizens of the United States and to American corporations, except that citizens and corporations of countries granting reciprocal treatment should not be excluded. The right of extracting helium from all natural gas from such public lands was reserved. The military argument and the international struggle for raw materials dictated these latter terms. Each of the different deposits was dealt with separately in the general act, since each required a different treatment of details. The last sections related to general matters and contained one extraneous subject. Hours of labor underground were restricted to eight, employment of women and of children under sixteen was prohibited, and wages must be paid every two weeks. The distribution of royalties and rentals was slightly different from the act of 1917: 10 per cent should be covered into the Treasury as miscellaneous receipts, $52\frac{1}{2}$ per cent should be credited to the reclamation fund, and $37\frac{1}{2}$ per cent should be paid to the states in which the deposits were located to be expended for education or roads as the state legislatures should direct. Royalty oil, gas, coal, phosphates, and sodium were to be sold by sealed competitive bids and at not less than market price.

Steps were taken to develop potash-mining on private lands by an act of June 25, 1926. An appropriation of $100,000 was provided for the fiscal year 1927, and a similar amount was authorized for each of the four succeeding years to be spent by the Secretary of the Interior and the Secretary of Commerce jointly in determining the location, extent, and mode of occurrence of potash deposits in the United States and in conducting laboratory experiments. They were authorized to make agreements to coöperate with individuals, associations, corporations, states, municipalities, educational institutions, or other bodies for the purpose of this act. Contracts might be entered into with owners or lessees of land for mineral rights, the costs of exploratory operations to be a preferred claim against the deposits discovered. To prevent profiteering, the secretaries should act as referees to fix maximum prices of potash rights within one mile of the discovery, and owners of potash deposits should be required to enter into contracts not to sell potash above the maximum price fixed by the joint action of the secretaries. Amendments of detail were made to these acts during 1926 and 1927, leaving the principles as established in the three basic acts here reviewed.

Two deposits, lignite coal and sulphur, were the subject of separate legislation. An act of February 25, 1919, directed experiments to be made in lignite coal and peat to determine the commercial and economic practicability of their utilization in producing fuel oil, gasoline substitutes, tar, solid fuels, gas for power and other uses. An appropriation of $100,000 was provided. An act of April 17, 1926, promoted the production of sulphur on public lands. Permits for two years for prospecting for sulphur on tracts of 640 acres were authorized. On discovery of sulphur deposits, leases might be granted on the tract with a 5 per cent royalty. Oil and gas permittees, on discovery of sulphur, were extended the same leasing privileges. On known sulphur lands leases were to be let only on competitive bidding or other method fixed by general regulation. The general leasing act of 1920 was amended to include sulphur as one of the list of minerals.

WATER-POWER POLICY

Industrial power in the form of electrical current became an outstanding factor in post-war economic programs. The generative force for such power was derived from coal, oil, gas, and water. Coal was the principal foundation of the development of power in the industrial Northeast. With this aspect of the question the Federal government could have little direct control, since the coal deposits of the region were in private hands. Much the same was true of oil and gas. Therefore Federal policy in the matter of power centered about the utilization of water. These great sources of electrical energy would supplement each other. Giant-power or super-power schemes were advanced to interconnect the power-producing units throughout the nation, pooling these resources for the benefit of the country as a whole. Thus excess power in one region could be utilized by another, and power supply and power demands of distant areas might be coördinated. Gifford Pinchot, governor of Pennsylvania, was one of the most conspicuous advocates of giant power.

The controversy over Federal water-power policy was continuous during and after the Roosevelt administrations. There were three groups of conflicting factors: conservation against free private exploitation, government operation against private operation, and Federal control against state control. The result was all but hopeless confusion. The first act on dams was approved June 25, 1906. It provided that all plans and specifications for dams on navigable streams must be approved by the War Department. The licenses were indeterminate in duration but were revocable for violations of the conditions imposed. The second law, approved in June, 1910, added some important points. Charges could be collected where government improvements were of benefit to the licensee. The duration of the license was fixed at fifty years. If the project was taken over by the government for public use, a reasonable value was to be paid. The campaign for a more comprehensive act on power continued through the remainder of the Taft administration and through the Wilson administration. The conservationists and the power companies were the chief contending groups. The campaign centered chiefly on three items: the right of the government to impose charges for the use of waters on public lands and navigable streams, recapture provisions at the end of the lease period, and the definition of navigable streams to include such sites as Muscle Shoals. The Federal power act finally received Wilson's signature on June 10, 1920. A Federal water-power commission was created, composed of the Secretary of War, the Secretary of the Interior, and the Secretary of Agriculture, with an executive secretary in direct charge. The act applied to public lands of the United States, excluding reservations, and to navigable streams, including any falls, shallows, or rapids which interrupt navigation, and any parts of streams which it should at any time be planned to make navigable by Federal improvement. The full administration of the act was vested in the commission, including the issuance of licenses for the construction and operation of facilities for improving navigation and developing and utilizing power. Licenses were limited to fifty years. Preference was to be given to state and municipal applicants and to the applicant whose plans seemed best adapted to public interest. If in the opinion of the commission the United States government itself ought to undertake a project, licenses might be refused and plans for the development submitted to Congress. Licenses were not to be transferred without the consent of the commission. Charges were due the government for the cost of administering the act, for the use of government land, and for excess profits, and if the licensee was benefited by the work of another or of the government. Combinations in restraint of trade were prohibited. Upon expiration of the lease, the government reserved the right to take over and operate facilities on two years' notice, the government to pay the licensee the net investment and damages resulting from severing the project from other property. If the government did not take over the project, a new license was to be issued to the original licensee. Public-service licenses were to be regulated by the states, and power rates in interstate commerce should be reasonable. The act was, generally speaking, a victory for the conservationist group, but it was not a complete victory. A very serious administrative defect was the inadequacy of the personnel placed at the disposal of the executive secretary for proper examination of projects for which licenses were requested.

The Federal water-power act was passed on the eve of the conservative revolution, and almost immediately it was challenged in the greatest power projects within the jurisdiction of the government. The disposition of Muscle Shoals was the most conspicuous case in point. The National Defense Act of June 3, 1916, authorized the president to construct, maintain, and operate power and navigation facilities for the production of nitrates for munitions and for fertilizers and other useful products. Under this authority Wilson, in a letter dated February 23, 1918, directed the construction of a dam and facilities at Muscle Shoals.

Muscle Shoals comprised a thirty-five-mile section of the Tennessee River running from east to west in northern Alabama, with a fall of one hundred and thirty-four feet. Except for the Hales Bar development, granted to the city of Chattanooga in 1904, it had not been utilized for power production. Two dams were planned called No. 2 and No. 3. No. 2, called the Wilson Dam, was completed; No. 3 was not begun. Nitrate plants Nos. 2 and 1 were constructed southwest of the Wilson Dam. No. 1 was unsuccessful and was not operated; after the war No. 2 was operated for power under lease to the Alabama Power Company. The Waco limestone quarry twenty miles to the southwest was planned to furnish stone, and the Gorgas-Warrior steam-power plant eighty-eight miles to the southeast furnished power to nitrate plant No. 2. The total expenditure was about $135,000,000.

The Ford plan, presented July 8, 1921, provided for [a $10,000,000 corporation to buy the two nitrate plants and the quarry, and guaranteed 40,000 tons of fixed nitrogen a year for fertilizer. It included also a hundred-year lease on Muscle Shoals, provided the government would complete both dams. The rental was to be at the rate of 4 per cent on the cost of construction exclusive of $17,000,000 expended on the Wilson Dam before May 31, 1922. The nitrate plants would be kept in readiness to produce explosives in case of war. A board of nine men would fix a fair price for fertilizers. It would be appointed by farmers' organizations, the government, and the Ford corporation. This plan was accepted by the House of Representatives on March 10, 1924, by a vote of 227 to 143. Whatever the merits of the plan, it ignored completely the power act of 1920.

The leading competitive plan, that of the Associated Power Companies of the South, was presented January 8, 1924. It was based upon the power act of 1920 and provided for the lease of one nitrate plant. It guaranteed the production of 50,000,000 tons of nitrates a year, pledged $1,000,000 for research in fertilizer production, and promised a rental of $3,000,000 a year.

Both the plans outlined above were based on the principle of private lease or purchase and private operation. Senator Norris reported from the committee on agriculture and forestry a third plan based on the principle of government operation. The Federal government was to complete the dams. A Federal power corporation was to be created to operate Muscle Shoals and to produce explosives, fertilizers, and power. The corporation was to be managed by a board of three appointed by the president with the consent of the Senate, and was to be removable only by concurrent resolution of both Houses of Congress. Surplus power might be leased to public or private corporations. A plan similar to this was adopted by the Senate on March 13, 1928, by a vote of 48 to 25.

President Coolidge, in accordance with his general policy in such matters, recommended in each annual message, beginning with 1923, that the property be sold to the highest bidder, to be operated by private management. Ten years after the war Congress was still unable to agree to do anything, and the issue was carried into the campaign of 1928. Hoover, the Republican candidate, tended to the principle of private ownership and management of water power, but evaded specific pledges on projects or details. Smith, the

Democratic candidate, indorsed the principle of government ownership and operation but was indefinite with respect to how it might be applied in particular cases.

The second great project for flood control, irrigation, and power was Boulder Dam on the Colorado River. An act of August 19, 1921, authorized the states of Arizona, California, Colorado, Nevada, New Mexico, Utah, and Wyoming to enter into a compact respecting the disposition and apportionment of the waters of the Colorado River. The compact was signed November 24, 1922, at Santa Fe, but was not approved by Congress for several years. The leading points in controversy were government or private ownership, operation, and distribution of power, and the jealousy of certain states, particularly Arizona and California. One of the greatest lobbies in history was said to have been maintained by the power interests to defeat government ownership and operation. In the meantime Congress prohibited the issuance of all power permits on the Colorado River system until action could be taken upon the compact and a plan of construction agreed upon.

The full report of the Department of the Interior, together with plans, was submitted in 1922. The Johnson-Swing bill, based on this report, was introduced into both the House and the Senate. It provided for approving the compact and for authorizing construction of the project. The contest lasted till December 21, 1928, when President Coolidge finally approved it in a somewhat modified form. The Boulder Canyon Project Act provided for three units which had to be taken together: first, to construct, operate, and maintain a dam at Black or Boulder Canyon adequate for the storage of twenty million acre-feet of water; second, to construct or cause to be constructed a main canal to connect Laguna Dam or some other diversion dam with the Imperial Valley and the Coachella valley in California, such canal to be wholly within the United States; third, to construct, equip, operate, and maintain, or cause to be constructed, a complete power plant for the development of electrical energy. The construction of the dam and the canal were to be carried out by the United States. The power plant might be built by the government or it might be leased to private enterprise. The operation of power plants might be by government enterprise or by private enterprise: the discretion lay with the Secretary of the Interior. All leases must be made subject to the terms of the Federal power act of 1920. The financing plan was designed to repay to the government all expenses of construction, operation, and maintenance. The canal was to be financed under the terms of the reclamation service. The dam and the power plant, if government-built, were to be financed on a fifty-year amortization plan. A Colorado River dam fund of $165,000,000 was authorized, from which advances were to be made by Congress from time to time. Of this sum $25,000,000 was allocated to flood control and was to be repaid out of $62\frac{1}{2}$ per cent of all revenues in excess of amortization payments. The remaining $37\frac{1}{2}$ per cent was to be divided between the states of Arizona and Nevada to equalize benefits to the three lower basin states. The allocation of water provided that of the 7,500,000 acre-feet assigned to the lower basin, 4,400,000 should go to California, 2,800,000 to Arizona, and 300,000 to Nevada. This arrangement was to be the subject of an agreement among these states. Surplus water was divided, half to California and one fourth to each of the two others. The Gila River was reserved to Arizona. The Colorado River compact was approved and was to go into effect as soon as approved by the legislatures of the seven states or of six states including California. The act was not to go into effect until the compact became effective. Surveys were authorized to provide plans for further development of the Colorado River in other states. The Boulder Canyon project was by far the largest project for reclamation and power ever undertaken by the government.

Other great projects pending were on the Columbia River and on the St. Lawrence River. Congress authorized a state compact between the states of Washington, Idaho, Oregon, and Montana by an act of March 4, 1925, and the Secretary of the Interior was authorized to coöperate by an act of April 13, 1926. The St. Lawrence plans were being worked out in coöperation with Canada not only for power but also for the ship canal from the Great Lakes to the Atlantic.

Public utilities, and especially the development of electrical-power companies, became one of the great problems of the period. Problems of financing, monopoly, and rates for service from interstate systems presented new or aggravated difficulties. In no other field was the pyramiding of companies through the disfranchisement of the stockholder carried to greater lengths than in public utilities. The leading combinations, which controlled about 77.5 per cent of the power of the United States in 1924, when the Federal Trade Commission investigation was made, were General Electric, Insull, North American, and Stone and Webster. Independents and municipalities controlled the remaining 22.5 per cent. The commission held that the problem called for congressional legislation. In 1928 Senator Walsh of Montana presented a resolution calling for a Senate committee to investigate the power situation. It was amended February 15 to refer the investigation to the Federal Trade Commission. The vote on this proposition was considered one of the most significant Senate votes in years. The issue was conservative against progressive. The conservatives favored the commission and won. The parties were split wide open. The Republicans were divided twenty-eight conservatives to twelve progressives; the Democrats, eighteen conservatives to nineteen progressives. The progressives were anxious to force the power issue into the presidential campaign, and had the Democrats as a whole joined them they could have carried their point. Many Southern Democrats, however, took the conservative view, as they feared that extended agitation by a Senate committee might retard power and industrial developments in their section.

SOCIAL USES OF PUBLIC LANDS

The practice of establishing game preserves was begun before the war and was continued. An act of June 7, 1924, provided for a bird refuge on the upper Mississippi River, and acts of February 2 and March 4, 1925, provided game refuges in South Dakota and on the upper Mississippi River. The reorganization of the administration of national parks was carried out by the act creating the national park service (August 25, 1916). During 1926 and 1927 acts were passed authorizing the use of public lands for recreational purposes by the states, counties, or municipalities under certain conditions. In addition to the salmon and seal controls, the Northern Pacific Halibut Act was approved June 7, 1924. Acts of July 1, 1922, and June 7, 1924, prohibited the pollution of inland and territorial waters with oil by oil-carrying or oil-burning steamers.

SELECTED BIBLIOGRAPHY

HIBBARD, B. H. A History of the Public Land Policies. The Macmillan Company, 1924.

ISE, JOHN. United States Forest Policy. Yale University Press, 1920.

ISE, JOHN. United States Oil Policy. Yale University Press, 1927.

KERWIN, J. G. Federal Water-Power Legislation. Columbia University Press, 1926.

"Great Inland Waterway Projects." *Annals of the American Academy of Political and Social Science* (January, 1928), Vol. CXXXV.

CHAPTER XX

SOCIAL POLICIES

THE remarkable mobilization of physical, moral, and emotional resources for war effort seemed for a time to mark the culmination of the development of comprehensive social policies of the Federal government. This spirit carried over for a short time into the post-war period, but not long enough to permit the realization of the program. In Great Britain and in France departments of public health were created to meet the social demands of post-war reconstruction. During the campaign of 1920 such a department was discussed in the United States. In his special message of April 12, 1921, Harding recommended its creation. The scheme as outlined in the press provided for four divisions: education, public health, social service, and service to veterans. It was soon obvious that Congress was not interested. In his first annual message of December, 1923, Coolidge urged the assumption of larger social and humanitarian activities by the Federal government, but he did not definitely indorse a new department.

In the field of pure-food regulation no new legislation was enacted. The Department of Agriculture inaugurated an experimental service in grading and stamping choice and prime beef at Chicago, New York, Philadelphia, Boston, Kansas City, St. Joseph, and Omaha. The aim was to emphasize meat of high quality and to enable the consumer to know the grade of meat purchased. The service was also expected to react to the benefit of the farmer in placing a premium price on the best grades of live stock. An important step was taken in the regulation of drugs by an act of March 4, 1927, safeguarding the distribution and sale of

caustic poisons, corrosive acids, alkalies, and the like in interstate and foreign commerce. A narcotic-drug act approved
May 26, 1922, amended the act of 1909 prohibiting the importation and exportation of narcotic drugs.

A maternity and infancy act, approved November 23,
1921, provided for an appropriation of $480,000 to be divided
equally among the states, and authorized an appropriation of
$240,000 each year thereafter for five years. Additional sums
of $1,000,000 for the current year and for each year there-
after were also provided, to be divided on a different basis:
$5000 was to be apportioned to each state, and the remainder
was to be divided according to population, provided an equal
sum was contributed by the state. A board of maternity
and infant hygiene was created, composed of the chief of
the Children's Bureau, the Surgeon-General of the Public
Health Service, and the Commissioner of Education. The
administration was to be in the Children's Bureau of the
Department of Labor. State plans for use of funds must be
approved by the board. After a bitter fight this act was renewed by an act (January 22, 1927) which extended the
service two years.

The child-labor movement of pre-war days resulted in two
acts designed to deny to products of child labor the privileges
of interstate commerce. Both were declared unconstitutional.
Under these conditions it seemed impossible to prohibit child
labor by Federal enactment except by constitutional amendment. A joint resolution for that purpose was passed and
approved June 4, 1924. Its provisions were as follows:

SECTION 1. The Congress shall have power to limit, regulate, and
prohibit the labor of persons under eighteen years of age.

SECTION 2. The power of the several states is unimpaired by this
article except that the operation of state laws shall be suspended to the
extent necessary to give effect to legislation enacted by the Congress.

This amendment was declaratory, leaving Congress to
provide such legislation as was considered necessary. The
child-labor legislation referred to above had been directed

at child labor in factories, but the amendment was general. This turned the agricultural sections almost solidly against it. The states' rights argument also served the opposition. The crusading spirit of pre-war days in the interest of social justice had passed, along with other aspects of progressivism. The amendment was rejected by the states.

Before the war national participation in education in a direct manner was limited to vocational education. The Smith-Lever Act of 1914 opened a new era. Agricultural-extension work was to be carried on by coöperation of the national government and the states. Allotment of funds to the states would be made contingent upon the provision of like amounts by the states. The plans must be approved by the Secretary of Agriculture. This was the first use of the so-called fifty-fifty plan, which later was applied to roads, maternity, and other matters. The requirement that all plans be approved by the Federal government meant that the Federal agency not only controlled Federal money but also state money. In 1917 the same scheme was applied to vocational education in the secondary schools and in the training of vocational teachers. Previously all government grants for education had been to institutions of college grade. A Federal Board of Vocational Education was created to administer the act. On June 2, 1920, the industrial reha-bilitation act was approved; it provided for "promotion of vocational rehabilitation of persons disabled in industry or otherwise and their return to civil employment." This fol-lowed the same plan of financing and was administered by the Federal Board of Vocational Education.

The capstone of the system was to be the creation of a department of education with a secretary in the president's cabinet, and Federal aid to the states, on the fifty-fifty plan, in promoting elementary education. The original bill was introduced by Senator Hoke Smith of Georgia in 1918. At-tempts to create a department of education were not new: it was the particular plan and purpose that were relatively new. The origins lay largely in the war situation. The examinations of men drafted for military service had shown an astonishing amount of illiteracy and of physical deficiency. The war sympathies of emigrant stocks gave encouragement to programs of Americanization to be carried out through the schools. In this way military and nationalistic aims played a large part in the campaign for a national educational system. Similar measures were before Congress later, but were not passed. Harding planned to include education in the new Department of Public Welfare. In his first annual message of December 6, 1923, Coolidge advocated a separate department of education and returned to the subject in the annual message of December 6, 1927.

Prohibition

The prohibition policies of the Federal government fall into three periods. Before the war the policy was negative. The Wilson act of 1890 and the Webb-Kenyon act of 1913 merely released Federal control over intoxicating liquor in interstate commerce to the states. In this manner it was possible for each state to follow such policy as it saw fit in dealing with the question. In the Penal Code of 1909, Sections 238–240, the only positive action by the Federal government restricted the methods of delivery by common carriers, but this was done in the spirit of giving assistance to the prohibition states in enforcing their legislation. At the very end of the period, or rather in the transition to the war period, the Reed "bone-dry" amendment was attached to the Postal Appropriations Act of March 3, 1917. It provided that "whoever shall order, purchase, or cause intoxicating liquors to be transported in interstate commerce, except for scientific, sacramental, medicinal, and mechanical purposes, into any state or territory the laws of which state or territory prohibit the manufacture or sale therein of intoxicating liquors for beverage purposes, shall be punished. . . ." Traffic in liquor was thus made an offense under Federal law, for which a penalty was imposed.

The period of the World War marked the development of national prohibition. A combination of elements worked to this end, and the one which served as a peg to hang it on was the urgent demand for conservation of food supplies to win the war. This was emergency war-time prohibition, the second stage. In the Food and Fuel Control Act (August 10, 1917) a prohibition was placed on the use of food products for the manufacture of distilled beverages, and the president was granted power to restrict the manufacture of beer and wines from foodstuffs. Under this latter provision beer with not more than 2.75 per cent of alcohol was permitted. The prohibition movement went farther; and a rider was attached to the agricultural appropriations act (November 21, 1918), passed after the armistice, providing that between June 30, 1919, and the end of the war and demobilization no distilled liquors should be sold, and no intoxicating liquors except for export. After May 1, 1919, and to the end of the war and demobilization, no food products should be used in making intoxicating liquor. The importation of liquor was also prohibited. Wilson was not in sympathy with this extreme measure, and in his message of May 20, 1919, recommended that it be repealed or modified so far as it applied to wines and beer.

The third phase of national liquor policy was national prohibition as a permanent policy. This movement began in the early part of the war and paralleled the emergency policies. The joint resolution proposing the Eighteenth Amendment was passed by the House on December 17, 1917, and by the Senate on December 18. The campaign for ratification by the states was carried on in the atmosphere of war hysteria. On January 16, 1919, the requisite number of states had ratified, and the amendment was proclaimed on January 29. The two pertinent sections were as follows:

SECTION 1. After one year from the ratification of this article the manufacture, sale, or transportation of intoxicating liquors within, the importation thereof into, or the exportation thereof from the United States and all territory subject to the jurisdiction thereof for beverage purposes is hereby prohibited.

SECTION 2. The Congress and the several states shall have concurrent power to enforce this article by appropriate legislation.

It should be noticed that the language of the amendment was declaratory and did not provide the means or method of enforcement. The national prohibition act was first passed by Congress in October, 1919, and was vetoed by Wilson on October 27. His objections were based on the combination of two objects in one bill : the continuation of war-time prohibition and the legislation for putting the new amendment into operation. Since he had already asked Congress to repeal or modify the war-time prohibition act, he could not approve this extension. The two measures should be separated and each considered on its own merits. On October 28 Congress passed the bill over the veto. Intoxicating liquor was defined as any liquor containing more than one half of one per cent of alcohol. The administration of the law was vested in the Bureau of Internal Revenue under the immediate direction of a commissioner of prohibition. The definition of what constituted intoxicating liquor was derived from a decision of the Bureau of Internal Revenue in 1902, when the standard of one half of one per cent was fixed as the minimum for purposes of taxation. The same standard was applied by the bureau to war-time prohibition and was now taken over by Congress for the purpose of national prohibition. Several states had also taken over this definition for purposes of state prohibition before the national act. The constitutionality of both the amendment and the prohibition act were tested and upheld in full by the Supreme Court. A supplementary act was approved November 23, 1921, limiting the amount of liquor which might be prescribed on physicians' permits and also the number of permits per physician. The searching of dwellings in enforcement of the act was declared illegal without search warrants.

The attitude of the states was an important aspect of enforcement. At the time of the adoption of the national amendment every state had some restrictive liquor legislation and thirty-two had adopted prohibition; 88 per cent of the area, representing 61 per cent of the population, was dry by a vote of the people. After the amendment was passed, all the states but one (Maryland) provided legislation for assisting in enforcement, although in New York the enforcement law was repealed in 1923.

The post-war reaction against prohibition was fully as marked as the reaction in other policies. The administration stood for law enforcement, which naturally included prohibition laws as well as others. As the liquor question entered politics public officials and politicians became more and more careful not to take too positive a stand either for or against prohibition on its merits. They all stood for "law enforcement" in its general sense, a phrase which became the standard formula for evasion of the real issue.

The most important change in enforcement administration was made by the prohibition reorganization act of March 4, 1927, which came as a result of a long-fought campaign. The original method had been to operate a dual force: one directed from the central authority and one by state directors. In 1925 a radical change was made when the country was divided into districts following the lines of judicial districts. In each a director was made fully responsible for his district, and an assistant secretary was created in the Treasury Department, although there was no statutory authority for this. This proved more efficient, and the statute referred to above gave the reorganization legislative sanction and carried it farther. The prohibition unit was established as a separate organization in the Treasury, directed by a prohibition commissioner under the assistant secretary. Civil-service reform was extended to the prohibition unit. The first examinations were given late in 1927. Some 13,500 persons (including enforcement agents then in the service) took the examinations. In round numbers all but 5000 failed, and this included 1500 agents in the service. It meant one of two things: either the examinations were unreasonable or, as many people suspected, the prohibition agents were unusually deficient. Commissioner Doran insisted that the examinations were reasonable and practical. All this seemed to confirm the charges that party-spoils politics had overloaded the prohibition unit with inefficient political henchmen.

The prohibition issue was carried into the campaign of 1928. The Republican party and candidate indorsed enforcement, Hoover going farther than his party. The Democratic party evaded the issue completely, but Smith, in accepting the nomination, injected the issue into the contest in spite of efforts at party compromise. In his speech of acceptance he pledged enforcement, but he stated clearly that he would use his influence to secure a modification which would place the question primarily in the hands of the states. He absolutely opposed the return of the saloon. The election did not turn on this issue, so the result was not necessarily an indorsement of the Volstead Act or the Eighteenth Amendment. The administration set about more effective enforcement. Congress passed an act (approved March 2, 1929) which increased penalties for violation of the prohibition act to a maximum of five years' imprisonment and $10,000 fine. One of the important purposes was to make the violation of the act a felony in order to enable the government to deport alien offenders.

The enforcement of prohibition early involved the United States in difficulties of international character. It was held that liquor on board a ship entering an American port was subject to the prohibition act. There was also great difficulty in preventing the landing of liquor cargo from ships outside the three-mile limit. Through agreement with Great Britain it was agreed that British vessels might carry liquor into American territorial waters "when such cargoes are listed as sea stores or cargo destined for a port foreign to the United States, and are kept under seal continuously while the vessel on which they are carried remains within said territorial waters." In return the United States was to be permitted to seize vessels suspected of smuggling liquor into the United States within a distance of approximately twelve miles. This treaty was ratified May, 1924. Similar treaties were made with some other countries.

‹ PART THREE ›

United States Foreign Policies after the World War

CHAPTER XXI

INTRODUCTION TO FOREIGN POLICIES

THERE has been a tradition in American history that the United States has had no foreign policy, or, stated in less extreme form, that there has been no continuity in foreign policy. Historians have persisted in writing American history from the standpoint of isolated and unrelated episodes rather than from the standpoint of development of ideas, policies, and movements. It is true that in most phases of its foreign relations the United States has placed relatively less emphasis upon basic principles of policy than some European powers; but the difference is primarily a matter of relative stress rather than an absence of policy. Even this distinction applies only to some phases of foreign relations, since few nations held more tenaciously to a line of policy than did the United States to the principles embodied in the so-called Monroe Doctrine or persisted with less deviation from a primary objective over an equal period of time.

Sustained public interest in public questions seems impossible in democracies. Each question as it impinges upon public consciousness tends to be registered as a relatively new or wholly new experience. With responsible public officials this is less true than is popularly supposed. In dealing with domestic questions it is possible to reverse public policy or to make a radical change in direction; it is much more difficult in foreign affairs, and frequently impossible. It is a basic principle in international law that obligations assumed by one administration or government are binding upon its successors until such obligations are honorably dissolved. Every incoming administration finds itself bound to a considerable degree by its predecessors. This is especially true on all routine matters and on questions of continued national interest. As new developments arise they must be dealt with in accordance with existing precedents, obligations, and commitments. Another determining consideration is the matter of prevailing interest: economic, military, and political. These national interests change slowly, and policies derived from them necessarily show only gradual modifications. No matter what personal or party opinions may be expressed before election, the incoming administration must conform to the existing conditions. Numerous examples appear in this book, none of which is more important to contemporary politics than the attempt of the Harding administration to ignore the League of Nations. The explanation of that failure lies in the fact that the League was the outgrowth of years of development in which the United States had actively participated. Coöperation in League activities represented continuity of policy. The short-lived refusal of Harding and the Senate to coöperate represented a change in direction which could not withstand the driving force of continuity of interest and policy.

In speaking of American foreign policy (November 30, 1923) Secretary of State Hughes opened his address with the following statement:

Foreign policies are not built upon abstractions. They are the result of practical conceptions of national interest arising from some immediate exigency or standing out vividly in historical perspective. When long maintained they express the hopes and fears, the aims of security or aggrandizement, which have become dominant in the national consciousness and thus transcend party divisions and make negligible such opposition as may come from particular groups. . . . Statesmen who carry the burden of empire do not for a moment lose sight of their imperial purposes and requirements. . . . When we have a clear sense of our interests we are as inflexible as others.

The influence of misconceptions concerning continuity in foreign policy is vicious in contemporary politics. The public is prone to assume that as questions arise the attitude of the government is determined by the facts alone, or by ideals of abstract right and justice, or possibly by corrupt and selfish interests of officials. It is quite probable, however, that a careful examination of the problem as a whole in relation to its background will reveal that an important and possibly a deciding element in determining action arises out of a basic policy of long standing. The real problem is how to meet the particular situation in such a manner as to carry out most effectively the underlying line of policy. The approach to foreign relations from the standpoint of policy is usually an illuminating experience to the student of American history. A word of caution, however, is not out of order. The extremes to which the factual and episodical historians have gone should stand as a warning not to go to the opposite extreme when adopting a different method.

Another important criticism of the traditional approach to American diplomatic history is the dominance given to the political aspect of foreign relations, even to the exclusion of foreign economic and military policy. When the economic and military rivalries of the modern industrial states are generally recognized as determining elements in world history (and the United States has been for some three quarters of a century one of the world's half dozen most important industrial states), it is obvious that there is something lacking in American history when diplomacy is written in terms of political relations alone. In the last analysis political policy has no meaning except as it is the political expression of the varied interests of the state. Certainly two of the most important of the varied international interests are economic opportunity and national security, and these must find their place in diplomatic history.

The United States is the only major nation in the modern world whose history has been written almost exclusively by its nationals. This tends to explain many of the defects of American historiography, both in domestic history and in foreign relations. There have been a lack of objectivity and perspective, a strongly nationalistic tone, and a refusal (or at least a failure) to accept certain obvious facts candidly. For instance, why should certain policies be labeled imperialism when practiced by European nations, and the same or similar policies of the United States be presented in all standard histories as the reluctant assumption of the duties of civilization in the interests of an unselfish and enlightened idealism? This justification deceives no one — except Americans.

The history of the other major nations has been written and rewritten by the ablest historians of various nations and from many points of view. At present there is hardly a European historian who has established a reputation for scholarship in the field of the history of the United States. Few Europeans know enough of American history to criticize the United States and its policies intelligently. Almost as few Americans know enough of their own history to recognize its inadequacies or to appreciate the appropriateness of intelligent foreign criticism. After the World War European universities began for the first time to establish courses and lectureships in American history. It was only a beginning, though, even ten years after the war. The growing interest of Europe in American history is one of the most important new developments in American historiography, and when it becomes productive it will certainly tend to check the dry rot which permeates so great a portion of the field. Americans must face a greater and greater amount of unpalatable analysis.

The rapidity of change in the contemporary world has been so extraordinary as to challenge the historian to rebuild his historical methods and his historical structure in order to meet adequately the new demands of acquainting the public with the significance of the revolutionary changes which were precipitated upon the world after the World War.

Without neglecting earlier history, a new emphasis is being placed upon very recent history, especially upon foreign affairs and their influence on domestic problems.

It is essential to keep in the foreground the relation of different lines of public policy to each other. One important problem is the relationship of the forces which are at work in foreign affairs. The policies of isolation, nationalism, imperialism, militarism, high protective tariff, and economic discrimination represent one side of the question; they are old conservative traditions which have been in operation for generations. The policies of coöperation, arbitration, international peace, equality of economic opportunity, military and economic disarmament, and international regulation of certain economic and social questions represent newer principles; they must be classified as liberal or progressive foreign policies.

A second general problem is the relationship between domestic policies and foreign policies. There have been notable examples in public life of men who were classed as conservatives in domestic policies. Such were Taft and Root, who took a leading part in contributing to liberal foreign policies. On the other hand, there have been many outstanding liberals in domestic policy who followed conservative or even reactionary foreign policies. When the conservative in domestic policy supports liberal foreign policy, the logical reaction of that conduct is to force a revision of his domestic policies. Thus, one of the most illogical lines of conduct is to support high protective tariff and at the same time indorse equality of economic opportunity and the removal of economic barriers to international trade. When the liberal in domestic policy indorses exaggerated nationalism and opposes international coöperation and economic and military disarmament, he imposes upon the country those domestic policies which he professes to oppose, such as high protection, militarism, imperialism, and international economic warfare. It was in just such mental confusion that, on the one hand, the United States rejected the League of Nations and the World Court, placed upon the statute books the tariff act of 1922 and the Merchant Marine act of 1920, and fell into the tariff controversy with France, and, on the other hand, ratified the German commercial treaty of 1925, the agreement to limit armament, and the treaty to renounce war. In practical politics can one of these lines of policy be followed logically, or is it necessary to compromise on inconsistency and contradiction?

CHAPTER XXII

ECONOMIC BASIS OF FOREIGN POLICIES

FOREIGN TRADE

THE foreign trade of the United States went through a series of readjustments to post-war conditions which makes generalizations difficult. Fluctuations were frequent and sometimes radical. For that reason five-year averages are probably more indicative of conditions. If we use 1911–1915 as a base of 100, the annual average for 1921–1925 shows an increase of 84 per cent in the value of exports. By 1925 the increase was 107 per cent, but a slight decrease placed it at 105 per cent in 1927. For imports the annual average for 1921–1925 shows an increase of 101 per cent. The increase by 1925 was 147 per cent, and at this level it remained in 1927. The annual average of per capita exports for 1911–1915 was $23.98; for 1921–1925 it was $37.97. By 1925 it was $41.14, but in 1927 it declined to $39.52. The annual average of per capita imports for 1911–1915 was $17.46, and for 1921–1925 it was $30.15. By 1925 it was $35.66, but in 1927 it declined to $34.57. The twelve leading exports in order of importance in 1927 were as follows, with the position in 1913 indicated in parenthesis: first, cotton (1); second, petroleum (3); third, machinery (2); fourth, automobiles (15); fifth, wheat and flour (5); sixth, iron and steel (6); seventh, copper and its products (4); eighth, tobacco (12); ninth, cotton manufactures (11); tenth, fruits and nuts (14); eleventh, animal fats and oils (7); twelfth, coal and coke (9). The twelve leading imports were first, crude rubber (4); second, raw silk (5); third, coffee (1); fourth, sugar (3); fifth, paper (19); sixth, furs (15); seventh, petroleum (20); eighth, hides and skins (2);

ninth, tin (8); tenth, wood pulp (17); eleventh, copper and ore (7); twelfth, fruits and nuts (10).

Among exports crude materials decreased in relative importance from 30.48 per cent of the total in 1913 to 29.51 per cent in 1925 and to 25 per cent in 1927. Food products, raw and manufactured, declined from 20.72 per cent in 1913 to 18.50 per cent in 1925 and remained at that point in 1927. Semimanufactures also declined from 16.83 per cent in 1913 to 13.82 per cent in 1925, but recovered slightly to 14.7 per cent in 1927. Manufactured products formed the only group that increased in relative importance, being 31.97 per cent in 1913, 38.26 per cent in 1925, and 41.64 per cent in 1927. Among imports this situation was practically reversed. Crude materials increased from 35.82 per cent in 1913 to 41.26 per cent in 1925, but declined to 38.25 per cent in 1927. Crude and manufactured food products were practically stationary at 22 per cent. Semimanufactures decreased from 19.27 per cent to 17.87 per cent between 1913 and 1925 and remained at this level in 1927. Manufactures decreased from 22.51 per cent to 18.83 per cent between 1913 and 1925, but recovered to 21 per cent by 1927. The tariff and the growth of the industrial system placed a premium on imports of raw materials and exports of manufactures. The United States was rapidly becoming a converting nation: it was manufacturing goods from the world's raw materials, not to be consumed at home but to supply a large part of the world with finished products.

The position of the leading powers in world trade in 1913 was, first, Great Britain with one seventh of the total; second, Germany with one ninth; third, the United States with one tenth; fourth, France with one thirteenth. In 1925 the ranking was Great Britain, United States, Germany, and France. In export trade the order was the United States, Great Britain, Germany, and France. American exports increased from 13 per cent of the world total in 1913 to 18 per cent in 1925.

The distribution of exports is shown in the following table : [1]

ANNUAL AVERAGE	NORTHERN NORTH AMERICA	SOUTHERN NORTH AMERICA	SOUTH AMERICA	EUROPE	ASIA	OCEANIA	AFRICA
	Per Cent	Per Cent	Per Cent	Per Cent	Per Cent	Per Cent	Per Cent
1911–1915	14.2	7.7	5.2	64.0	5.6	2.2	1.1
1915–1920	12.0	7.7	5.5	63.2	8.6	1.7	1.3
1921–1925	14.3	10.1	6.8	52.7	11.3	3.2	1.6
1919 . .	9.5	6.9	5.6	65.5	9.7	1.6	1.2
1920 . .	12.0	11.5	7.6	54.3	10.6	2.1	2.0
1921 . .	13.4	11.8	6.1	52.7	11.9	2.5	1.6
1922 . .	15.2	8.7	5.9	54.4	11.7	2.7	1.5
1923 . .	15.8	10.2	6.5	50.2	12.3	3.5	1.5
1924 . .	13.8	9.9	6.8	53.3	11.2	3.4	1.5
1925 . .	13.4	9.8	8.2	53.0	9.9	3.9	1.8
1926 . .	15.5	8.9	9.2	48.0	11.7	4.4	2.1
1927 . .	17.3	8.4	9.0	47.6	11.5	4.0	2.2

The distribution of imports is shown in the table below : [1]

ANNUAL AVERAGE	NORTHERN NORTH AMERICA	SOUTHERN NORTH AMERICA	SOUTH AMERICA	EUROPE	ASIA	OCEANIA	AFRICA
	Per Cent	Per Cent	Per Cent	Per Cent	Per Cent	Per Cent	Per Cent
1911–1915	7.7	14.5	12.8	46.6	15.8	1.1	1.4
1915–1920	12.7	17.5	17.6	20.3	27.1	2.1	2.7
1921–1925	11.5	14.9	12.2	30.4	27.3	1.6	2.1
1919 . .	12.8	16.8	17.6	19.2	28.4	2.3	2.9
1920 . .	11.6	19.9	14.4	23.3	26.5	1.5	2.8
1921 . .	13.5	16.6	11.8	30.5	24.6	1.4	1.6
1922 . .	11.8	14.6	11.5	31.8	26.6	1.6	2.1
1923 . .	11.0	15.4	12.3	30.5	26.9	1.6	2.3
1924 . .	11.1	16.4	12.9	30.4	25.8	1.4	2.0
1925 . .	10.9	12.3	12.3	29.3	31.2	1.8	2.2
1926 . .	11.0	11.9	12.8	29.0	31.6	1.5	2.2
1927 . .	11.6	12.0	12.4	30.5	30.0	1.3	2.2

PROBLEMS OF THE EXPORT TRADE

During the war the United States expanded its foreign trade to an extent which would have seemed impossible a few years before. This expansion continued for some time

[1] United States Statistical Abstract for 1928.

after the peace, and then in 1920 came the world-wide collapse. The period of recovery was necessarily a time of uncertainty. Would the United States be able to hold its lead? Or would Europe, with its lower standard of living, its cheap currency, and its cheap capital, be able quickly to regain its lost markets? A study of the preceding tables will throw some light on the general situation, and a few examples will illustrate the experience in some individual products.

Of over four million automobiles manufactured in the United States in 1925, about 7 to 8 per cent were exported. During the year 1927 there was an increase of 20 per cent. In Canada the tariff was reduced, but in Great Britain the duty was $33\frac{1}{3}$ per cent, and there was an annual tax of one pound sterling for each horse power. The slogan adopted was "Buy British cars and be proud of it." In 1922 British factories supplied only 49 per cent of the market; in 1927 they supplied 86 per cent. In Australia the United States supplied 65 per cent of the cars, whereas Great Britain sold only 22 per cent during 1925. In Italy motor-car manufacturers appealed to Mussolini in February, 1928, to consider steps to be taken to meet American competition. He replied that customs barriers could not meet the situation, and suggested that the question be considered at the coming meeting of European motor-car manufacturers at Paris. In 1924 Canada and Australia made a tariff agreement on dried fruit which permitted free entrance of Australian fruit into Canada. This was directed particularly at United States fruit. Australian fruit-canners were granted a subsidy in 1928 on export to Great Britain in order to meet American competition. The moving-picture industry was restricted in Spain, Sweden, Germany, Hungary, Austria, Italy, Russia, England, Canada, and France. It was reported, however, that in 1926 the United States supplied 83 per cent of the world's films.

RAW MATERIALS

During the last quarter of the nineteenth century there was a renewal of imperialism throughout the world. Accompanying this movement, the mercantile theories of economics of the sixteenth and seventeenth centuries were revived in modified form, usually referred to as neomercantilism. The dominating idea was to create self-supporting empires, both in war and in peace, through control of all essential raw materials and adequate market outlets. The protection of these empires entailed the maintenance of powerful military establishments. The United States had followed the drift of events during the same period along with the other industrial nations. However, instead of this imperialism's creating independent and self-sufficing empires, the nations became more and more interdependent. The industrial demands for raw materials drew upon every portion of the globe without regard to the political boundaries drawn by governments.

Since steel is one of the basic industries of the modern economic system, it serves admirably to illustrate this fact of interdependence, not only for the United States but for all nations. In 1921 the president of the United States Steel Corporation compiled a list of materials used in the steel industry which it was necessary to import. This list covered fourteen and a half typed pages and included forty commodities from fifty-seven different countries. Copper was imported from Chile, Portuguese Africa, Mexico, Canada, and Peru in considerable quantities. Americans had investments in Chile, Peru, Mexico, and Canada. Lead was imported from Chile, Peru, Mexico, and Canada. Iron ore came from Sweden, Chile, Cuba, and North Africa. Manganese was used as an alloy metal in such high-duty products as steel rails and structural steel. From 1 to 3 per cent of the manganese consumed in the United States was of domestic production. The chief sources of this metal were Brazil, India, and Russia. In June, 1925, it was reported that Americans had secured a concession in Russian Georgia to operate manganese mines. Chromium, another alloy metal of vital importance, was used in armor plates, rifles, and machine guns, in various kinds of high-speed tools for industrial purposes, in all kinds of engines, in cutlery; in fact, anywhere that steel of the highest quality was needed. It was also important outside the steel industry; for example, in tanning and printing. Domestic production was negligible. The chief sources of the metal were Rhodesia, New Caledonia, Asia Minor, Russia, and Brazil. Americans controlled mines in New Caledonia. Tin was not produced in the United States. The United States used half the world's output and was the largest producer of tin plates. The world's supply of tin came from the Malay Peninsula and the East Indies, although recently deposits in the Bolivian Andes had been worked, producing about one fourth of the supply. The Bolivian fields were under control of Americans. This ratio of one fourth was being steadily increased. Palm oil was essential for making tin plates and was produced in British West Africa and the Belgian Congo. Nickel was not produced in the United States, but was another essential alloy metal, being used in armor plates, ordnance, bridges, steel rails, and heavy-duty machinery. A list of the alloys of nickel covered five printed pages. Canada was the source of this product, and American capital controlled a large portion of the mines. Tungsten was essential for both peace and war purposes, from 90 to 95 per cent of it being used in tool steel (it was also essential in electric-light elements). The United States produced little of the metal. During the pressure of the World War, production ran as high as from 12 to 25 per cent of consumption, but none was produced in 1921 and 1922. China was the chief source of this ore, but Bolivia, Portugal, and Spain produced small quantities. Vanadium was one of the newest alloy metals, and was produced in the Andes of Peru. The Vanadium Company of America, a United States corporation, operated the mines, carrying the ore to Pittsburgh for smelting. Since the United States was the largest user of these alloy metals, which were indispensable in both peace and war, it was only to be expected that American interest was directed toward the sources of their production. What was true of the steel industry was also true of other industries — leather, paints, cordage and jute, vegetable oils, rubber, and so on.

Great publicity was given after 1922 to the fact that nine essential raw materials were controlled abroad by combinations of foreign-producing organizations, in some of which governments participated. The list usually given was sisal by Mexico, nitrates by Chile, iodine by Great Britain, potash by Germany, rubber by Great Britain and the Netherlands, quinine by the Netherlands, tin by Great Britain, mercury by Spain and Austria, coffee by Brazil, and quebracho by Argentina and Paraguay. Long-staple cotton, produced under the encouragement and assistance of the British government, was also sometimes included. Besides these "controlled" raw materials, there were many others on which the United States was absolutely dependent and which were produced abroad. Raw silk and camphor were practically monopolies of the Japanese. The air service and the artillery would be severely handicapped without silk. Wood oil, a Chinese monopoly, was the base of most waterproof varnishes. The United States used four fifths of the supply. Political disorder in China seriously interfered with production. Shellac and jute were monopolies of British India and were of such importance that to be without them was almost inconceivable. A large part of American cocoa came from Ecuador, and after 1918 the crop was financed by American interests.

The Department of Commerce reported (March 13, 1926) that foreign nations levied a toll of $300,000,000 against American consumers in 1925 through indefensible official restrictions on trade. These warnings of a trade war against the United States became commonplace, not only from the Department of Commerce but from other official and private sources.

FOREIGN INVESTMENTS

At the outbreak of the World War the United States was a debtor nation. Foreign investments in the United States were estimated at $4,500,000,000, and United States investments abroad at about $2,500,000,000. As a result of the war the financial center of the world shifted from London to New York. By 1924 the United States held four and a half billion dollars' worth of gold, or about half the world's supply. Loans, exclusive of government loans, floated in the United States between 1914 and 1925 aggregated nearly $9,000,000,000, whereas the London market for the same period absorbed only $3,000,000,000. In January, 1928, the Department of Commerce estimates of United States investments abroad were $13,000,000,000, exclusive of the $10,000,000,000 of government war loans. The new investments for the year 1927 were estimated at $1,574,960,575 and for the year 1928 at $1,426,487,580. This was the sixth year that the annual totals exceeded a billion dollars, the others being 1916, 1924, 1925, 1926, and 1928. The year 1924 marked the approximate recovery of most parts of the world from the post-war deflation. The figures of Dr. Max Winkler prepared for the Foreign Policy Association, announced in February, 1928, were higher, since he included estimates not considered in this account. Exclusive of the debts owed the United States government on account of the war, he placed United States investments at $14,500,000,000, or a grand total of nearly $25,000,000,000. While American investments increased, foreign investments in the United States decreased, amounting in 1925 to about $3,000,000,000. This was an unprecedented revolution in the world's financial structure and entailed a realignment of the credit channels of foreign countries as well as the investment habits of the United States.

The distribution of investments in 1913 were estimated by Fisk, in his "Inter-Ally Debts," as follows:

COUNTRY		AMOUNT (IN MILLIONS)
Canada	$750	$750
Caribbean		
Porto Rico	30	
Cuba	100	
Mexico	1050	
Central America	50	1230
South America	100	100
Europe	350	350
Asia		
China and Japan	100	
Philippine Islands	75	175
Total		$2605

At the end of 1927 Dr. Winkler's figures were as follows:

COUNTRY	AMOUNT
Canada	$3,922,000,000
Central America	2,914,600,000
South America	2,246,500,000
Europe	4,327,000,000
Far East	726,500,000
Miscellaneous	383,400,000
	$14,520,000,000

The purposes of foreign investments may be classified under four general heads: government loans, exploitation of raw materials, manufacturing, and construction and operation of public utilities. The reasons for American entrance into different countries vary with conditions. In Canada the reasons were to establish factories inside the tariff barriers instead of exporting from the United States, to enable manufacturers to secure more favorable export privileges in British dominions offering preferential treatment, to gain access to such raw materials as wood pulp and nickel, or to comply with patent laws, which required that a patented article must be produced in order to hold the patent.

A brief summary of the character of United States investments in a selected group of countries is compiled from the detailed study of the subject by R. W. Dunn in "American Foreign Investments." In Canada copper and brass, drugs and chemicals, patent medicines, automobiles, paint and varnishes, and artificial abrasives were controlled by United States capital. In most lines of manufactures United States capital exceeded British capital. In Mexico the leading United States investments were in oil, mining, railroads, public utilities, manufacturing, and lands. In Nicaragua capital was invested in fruit, mining, railroads, and lumber. In Colombia investments were in oil, in gold-mining and platinum-mining, in food industries such as the fruit, coffee, and meat trades, and in public utilities and railways. In Venezuela the interests were in oil, coal, magnesite-mining, and public utilities. In Cuba the two basic industries, sugar and tobacco, were under American control. In Santo Domingo United States investments controlled about one third of the sugar as well as a large part of fruits, flour, and dyes. The National City Bank largely dominated the financial life of the island republic.

In Argentine the leading American interests were in meat, oil, and cement. In Brazil they were in manganese-mining, meat-packing, and public utilities. On the west coast of South America Chile, Bolivia, and Peru were of chief interest. United States capital was interested in copper, iron, and nitrates. In Bolivia the interests were in oil, tin-mining, railways, and public utilities. In Peru the mining of copper and vanadium was under the control of United States capital. Peru furnished 92 per cent of the world's supply of vanadium. Other interests were in oil and public utilities.

American interests in various parts of Asia were too complicated to summarize here, but included practically all fields: exploitation of raw materials, manufactures, communications, transportation, and banking. In connection with the disturbances in Shanghai in 1927, a magazine published a list of twenty-seven American firms engaged in manufacturing at that place.

In the field of investments, as in foreign trade, there was discrimination. At the British Empire Exhibition at Wembley the slogan was "Keep your money in your empire." It was also an accepted principle that in construction contracts and the purchase of raw materials preference should be given to British firms. What was true of the British was also more or less true of the others. The British were more conspicuous because their interests were broader, and because they were financially able to take an aggressive part. In regard to oil development it was reported "that France and the French colonies are more completely closed to development by American companies than any other part of the world." Exploitation could be carried on only by a French company in which at least two thirds of the directors were French citizens.

After the war, and for the first time in American history, the people in large numbers became investors in foreign securities of all kinds. When the number of holders of foreign securities was added to the number of Americans interested in productive enterprises abroad and to the number interested in foreign commerce, it was natural that a substantial number of Americans should be interested in foreign affairs and that this wider interest should be definitely reflected in public policy.

SELECTED BIBLIOGRAPHY

Government publications of particular interest are those of the Department of Commerce such as the Yearbook, the Statistical Abstract, and the Commerce Reports, and the reports of the Federal Trade Commission.

REDFIELD, W. C. Dependent America. Houghton Mifflin Company, 1926.

MILLER, E. M., and others. Some Great Commodities. Doubleday, Doran and Company, Inc., 1922.

CULBERTSON, W. S. Commercial Policy in War Time and After. D. Appleton and Company, 1919.

CULBERTSON, W. S. International Economic Policies. D. Appleton and Company, 1925.

    This book is particularly important.

WILLIAMS, B. H. Economic Foreign Policy of the United States. McGraw-Hill Book Company, 1929.

This book is the best work in print on the subject.

KLEIN, JULIUS. Frontiers of Trade. The Century Co., 1929.

The author is director of the Bureau of Foreign and Domestic Commerce of the Department of Commerce.

Report of the Committee on Recent Economic Changes of the President's Conference on Unemployment, including the Reports of a Special Staff of the National Bureau of Economic Research. 2 vols. McGraw-Hill Book Company, 1929.

DUNN, R. W. American Foreign Investments. The Viking Press, 1926.

FISK, H. E. Inter-Ally Debts. Bankers Trust Company, 1924.

Foreign Policy Association publications and pamphlets of the International Conciliation Series of the Carnegie Endowment for International Peace.

CHAPTER XXIII

ECONOMIC POLICIES: OFFICIAL AGENCIES OF TRADE PROMOTION

THE FOREIGN SERVICE OF THE UNITED STATES

THE campaign for the reorganization of the diplomatic and consular services was carried on for more than a generation but without making radical changes. An act of February 5, 1915, provided that appointments of consuls and consuls-general should be made by commission to rank, but not to a particular post. The assignments to post would be made by executive order, and the appointees might be shifted as needed or serve for a time in the Department of State. An act of 1919 established three vice consuls of career to be chosen by promotion or upon examination. The next year the rank of economist consuls was created, with provision for twenty-five places. The most important measure after the war was the Rogers Act of May 24, 1924. The distinction between the two services, diplomatic and consular, was dropped, and the reorganized service was named the Foreign Service of the United States. All officers below the rank of minister were designated foreign-service officers and might be assigned to either field of activity or transferred from one to the other. Appointments were to be made upon examination, and appointees were to be assigned to the Foreign Service School for one year. Promotions were to be made on the basis of merit under the direction of a personnel board. Salaries were raised to range from $3000 to $9000. The offices of second and third assistant secretaries of state were changed to assistant secretaries, and a new assistant secretary was created to replace the director of the consular service. Such a thoroughgoing reorganization was quite in keeping with the opening of a new era in American relations with the world and the larger political and commercial interests of the country. A further step, an act of May 7, 1926, brought nearer the attainment of another goal: Congress authorized the acquisition of buildings and grounds in foreign countries for the use of the United States government.

THE FOREIGN COMMERCE SERVICE

The Department of Commerce largely superseded the consular service of the Department of State as an agency for promoting trade abroad. The activities of this department were carried on by the Bureau of Foreign and Domestic Commerce, created in 1912. Within the bureau were four types of divisions: administrative, technical, commodity, and regional.

The work of the bureau abroad was carried on by three groups of officers: consular officers, trade commissioners, and commercial attachés. Trade commissioners were first created in 1905 under the name "commercial agents"; commercial attachés were created in 1914. The latter were accredited to American embassies through the Department of State. An executive order of April 4, 1924, directed that American representatives stationed in the same foreign city should meet every two weeks for consultation in order to prevent excessive duplication of the work of the Department of State and the Department of Commerce. An act of March 3, 1927, established the Foreign Commerce Service of the Bureau of Foreign and Domestic Commerce. Officers of the service on foreign duty were to be attached to the diplomatic missions by the Department of State, but should not have the character of public ministers. The Secretary of State might reject any person who in his judgment would be prejudicial to the interests of the United States. This act opened the way for an extensive reorganization of the bureau's activities.

Within the United States the information gathered by the Foreign Commerce Service was disseminated through various publications: the weekly magazine *Commerce Reports*, the *Monthly Summary of Foreign Commerce*, and three annuals — *Foreign Commerce and Navigation*, the *Statistical Abstract of the United States*, and the *Commerce Yearbook*. Supplementing these were various special reports, including mimeographed reports sent to the exporters on the bureau's mailing list. To bring the work of the department more directly into touch with domestic needs, the country was divided into districts, and a branch of the bureau was established in the leading commercial city of each district.

COMMERCIAL TREATIES

The commercial privileges of the merchants of one country in another are determined primarily by commercial treaties. The American type of commercial treaty contained the conditional most-favored-nation clause, by which a concession granted to one state was not extended to a second state except on condition that the second could or would grant an equal or equivalent concession in return. This policy was the inheritance from the early days of the Republic, when the rest of the world maintained the closed door or discrimination. The purpose was to secure equal trade privileges for Americans. In the course of the nineteenth century Europe came to adopt the open door in commercial relations and, with it, the unconditional most-favored-nation clause. This type of clause meant that when a concession was granted to one state it automatically extended equally to all states with most-favored-nation treaties. Under these conditions the effect of the American policy of special concessions or reciprocity based on the conditional most-favored-nation treatment tended to develop a discriminative commercial warfare for special trade concessions instead of the open door and equality of treatment. In other words, the same policy on the part of the United States operated in the opposite direction at the end of the nineteenth century from what it did in the beginning of the century. American reciprocity tariffs after 1890 were based on the principle of special favors. The United States was out of harmony with the world tendencies toward equality of treatment.

After the World War there was a general reaction throughout the world toward conditional most-favored treaties and discriminatory treatment of foreign commerce on the basis of reciprocity. France led in 1918 by denouncing her most-favored-nation treaties. This action was followed by the law of July 29, 1919, which provided for greater flexibility of tariff arrangements. Here the term "flexibility" meant variation from equality of treatment. The French interpretation of the term "equitable treatment" in the League of Nations covenant was not equal treatment, but rather discriminatory treatment which would vary among different countries according to conditions on the reciprocity basis. Spain and Italy tended to follow the French lead. In the United States many of the nationalists stood for the same thing, and to a certain extent wrote their point of view into the Merchant Marine Act of 1920. By 1924 the Spanish and French commercial treaties negotiated with Germany showed a tendency to return to the pre-war standards of equality of treatment. In dealing with the United States, France held in 1927 that so long as the United States retained the high protective system, France was justified in maintaining the system of "equitable treatment" and reciprocity. The whole problem of tariffs, import and export restrictions, and prohibitions, however, still remained a source of international irritation.

Under the direction of Secretary of State Hughes a change in the commercial policy of the United States was inaugurated in 1923 with respect to commercial treaties. The new commercial treaty with Germany marked the new departure. It was signed December 8, 1923, but was not ratified until

February 10, 1925, after a hard fight with the extreme nationalists, who insisted upon the right of discrimination.
The treaty contained the European type of the unconditional most-favored-nation clause. The administration in
recommending the treaty for ratification made this new form
an issue and an occasion for the formal declaration that
future commercial treaties were to be made upon this plan.
Most American commercial treaties were old and needed
general revision, a process which was carried out as rapidly
as possible. For the first time in recent history this squared
the United States on this point with the prevailing commercial tendencies of the world.

THE TARIFF

Americans were accustomed to look upon the tariff as a
purely domestic policy. This view was emphasized especially in connection with the League of Nations debates,
and at that time it was made clear that no interference with
the tariff as a domestic policy would be approved by the
United States. From the standpoint of the economic relations of states with each other tariff policies were clearly
foreign economic policies and, as such, were of international
concern. Wilson's message vetoing the emergency tariff
(March 3, 1921), which is quoted at some length in Chapter VII, presented the matter in the light of both domestic
and foreign policy. The tariff act of 1922 set up excessively
high duties on many classes of manufactured articles, some
of them even prohibitive. According to Taussig's analysis
the duties on all but the finest-grade cotton and woolen
goods were prohibitive. This particularly affected the British. Most duties on manufactured silk were prohibitive.
These affected France, Japan, and China. The duty on
toys was made prohibitive in order to close the door to
Japanese toys and to prevent the recovery of the toy
market by the Germans. The duty on cotton gloves was

designed to shut out German goods. The duties on certain varieties of cutlery amounted to 75 per cent to 400 per cent ad valorem and had the same purpose. Chemicals and dyes received radical protection in the emergency revenue act of 1916; the schedules were reorganized in 1922, and very high duties were imposed to prevent Germany from regaining preëminence in the American market. The special justification here was the close relation between chemicals and dyes and the manufacture of explosives for war purposes. The militant nationalistic sentiment demanded American independence and self-sufficiency in that industry.

The average rate of duty under the tariff of 1913, on the basis of total imports, was 7.4 per cent ad valorem for the period it was in force; the average under the act of 1922 for the first three years was 14.5 per cent. The average rate of duties, on the basis of dutiable imports alone, was 21.9 per cent and 35.4 per cent respectively. Under the former act 66 per cent of the imports were free, whereas under the latter only 60 per cent were free. According to economic classes the following table[1] indicates the percentages of free imports:

YEAR	CRUDE MATERIALS	CRUDE FOOD AND ANIMAL PRODUCTS	MANUFACTURED FOOD	SEMIMANUFACTURES	MANUFACTURES	TOTAL
	Per Cent	*Per Cent*	*Per Cent*	*Per Cent*	*Per Cent*	*Per Cent*
1910–1914 .	80.2	81.0	8.9	52.2	22.2	53.6
1910 . . .	76.8	78.5	5.2	43.2	17.7	48.5
1914 . . .	86.2	81.4	16.3	62.9	28.4	59.5
1915–1920 .	88.7	85.7	13.4	73.9	44.6	67.3
1921–1925 .	80.3	79.0	12.6	67.6	35.2	59.7
1923 . . .	77.6	76.9	9.8	65.5	31.3	56.3
1925 . . .	80.1	79.4	16.7	68.5	33.8	62.7
1927 . . .	82.2	77.9	16.8	70.3	35.4	62.7

This tabulation indicates the extent to which crude products and semimanufactures for use in finished goods were placed upon the free list, while at the same time manufactures were dutiable in about the same proportion.

[1] United States Statistical Abstract for 1928.

The bargaining features of the act of 1922 were of the greatest importance to foreign trade. The flexible provision embodied an authorization for the president to raise or lower duties as much as 50 per cent in order to maintain the protective wall against changing cost of production. The findings of the tariff commission provided the figures on which action was taken. By December, 1927, there were sixteen increases and five decreases. The countries against which the increases were made were Germany, Canada, Norway, Switzerland, Denmark, Italy, and British India. Countervailing duties were authorized on certain goods coming from a country which imposed a duty or a higher duty on the importation of a similar article. The amount of the duty to be imposed was to be equal to the duty charged on the American goods in case the article was imported free into the United States, or equal to the difference in duty on dutiable goods. Similar countervailing duties were provided to offset bounties and export taxes. Except in the case of bounties, these countervailing duties raised serious questions in international policy. So long as American goods were charged equally with those of other foreign countries, countervailing duties were scarcely defensible. Other nations had the same rights as the United States to set up a tariff wall against any particular class of goods. Equal treatment was the most that could be asked. Retaliatory duties or even prohibition of imports were authorized against dumping and discrimination against American goods, unfair trade practices, violation of patent and trade-mark rights, and so on. Such duties were defensible, even necessary, in order to secure equal and fair treatment in the world's markets. Certain classes of goods might be restricted or even prohibited in the interest of public health or morals or to prevent fraud. The United States exercised practically no control over exports, except liquor, narcotics, munitions, and inspection of animals, meats, and the like for the protection of public health.

The application of the flexible tariff raised difficulties, because it was necessary in some cases to conduct investigations in foreign countries. In the case of Argentina there was strong resentment against the United States tariff barriers; and when the tariff commission took steps toward sending agents on a mission of inquiry into the cost of producing grain, the Argentine ambassador, Pueyrredon, protested. Under these conditions it became necessary to abandon the mission, and its abandonment was announced on September 14, 1927.

Retaliation against high American rates occurred in the new schedule of rates imposed by France, September 6, 1927. The rates were reported to be, in some cases, from four to six times higher than any previous ones. Germany and England received more favorable treatment, and American competition with them in France was difficult if not impossible in the goods affected. Articles specially mentioned in the press reports were magnetos, electric machinery, small hardware, pumps, razor blades, prepared and worked leather, and enamel ware. Steel furniture, which enjoyed a large market in France, was faced with an increase in duty from one franc fifty centimes to eight francs eighty centimes, or about 50 per cent ad valorem. The duty on fountain pens, formerly five francs, or 20 per cent ad valorem, was increased to twenty francs, or 80 per cent. The United States immediately protested against the new duties, and on September 12 transmitted a draft of a new commercial treaty to France urging that the new rates be suspended pending the completion of negotiations. To this request France refused to agree. She was reported to have indicated her unwillingness to negotiate except on the basis of complete reciprocity. The United States in turn refused to negotiate except on the basis of most-favored-nation treatment. Meanwhile there was talk of an international trade war and the invoking of the penalties of Article 317 of the American tariff of 1922 against the French. In October the penalty duty was ordered. A truce was not arranged until the middle of November, when most of the old rates were restored pending the completion of a commercial treaty. Since the tariff commission was engaged in an investigation of French silks and perfumes, the final treaty was not expected until 1929. Late in November, 1927, the French caused another disturbance by increasing duties on wheat from 18.20 francs per 200 pounds to 35 francs and by shifting frozen meats from the free list and imposing a duty of 85 francs per 200 pounds. These new rates were general, but they were of particular importance to exporters of agricultural products in restricting the markets for American surpluses.

Barriers to international trade were the subject of a report of international bankers, including six Americans, issued October 19, 1926. It contained these words:

> There can be no recovery in Europe until politicians in all territories, old and new, realize that trade is not war, but a process of exchange; that in time of peace our neighbors are our customers, and that their prosperity is a condition of our own well-being. If we check their dealings their power to pay their debts diminishes, and their power to purchase our goods is reduced. Dependent as we all are on imports and exports, and on the processes of international exchange, we cannot view without grave concern a policy which means the impoverishment of Europe.

The reaction to the statement was varied in the United States. Coolidge thought that it did not apply to the United States. Mellon made a formal statement (October 24) in which he gave his unqualified support to the suggestion that drastic reductions must be made in European tariff barriers, but he was equally emphatic that the high protective tariff of the United States was essential to the prosperity not only of the United States but of Europe as well. Senator Borah, chairman of the Senate Committee on Foreign Relations, protested against the bankers' statement vigorously. He was an extreme nationalist and declared that the League, the abandonment of the Monroe Doctrine, the cancellation of European debts, and the repeal of the tariff were all a part of the same plan: "Our foreign policy, our industries, and our money are to be sacrificed in this general scheme of readjusting our relationship with the world."

The resentment against the United States on account of the tariff was not confined to Europe. Probably the most direct attack on the system came from Argentina. On May 4, 1927, Luis Duhan, president of the Argentine Rural Society, made an attack on United States tariff policies and advocated the creation of a commission of business men to study commercial difficulties between North and South American countries. The question was to come up for discussion at the third Pan-American conference.

At the meeting of the Pan-American Union at Havana on January–February, 1928, Dr. Honorio Pueyrredon, Argentine ambassador to the United States and head of the Argentine delegation at Havana, led the movement, which demanded that the Pan-American Union be empowered to study means to lower or abolish the excessive tariff walls and other barriers in inter-American commerce. The United States refused to permit the Pan-American Union to become a political organization or to be invested with any such powers. Dr. Pueyrredon refused to sign any convention which did not include this question, and eventually he was deposed by his government in order to prevent a complete deadlock.

There were a few outstanding advocates of the liberal point of view among American political leaders, but only a few. William S. Culbertson, member of the tariff commission and one of the ablest advocates of liberal economic policies among the Republicans, withdrew from the tariff controversy. Cordell Hull, Democratic member of Congress from Tennessee, in November and December, 1925, urged a program of tariff reduction and the establishment of a permanent international-trade organization or congress. As a member of the minority he was not able to secure any action and apparently did not even receive much encouragement from some members of his own party. A conspicuous factor (aside from traditional nationalistic sentiments) standing in the way of the alignment of the Democratic party in support of such a program as Hull advocated was the industrial revolution taking place in the South. The North was not alone in fostering high tariff sentiment. Both the holders of Southern capital and of Northern capital invested in the South were fairly well united, regardless of party allegiance, in maintaining many of the important tariff schedules. If any considerable body of revisionist sentiment developed in the nation there seemed to be little immediate possibility of the Democratic party's serving as the agency to give it cohesion.

COLONIAL POLICY

Colonial policy was closely linked with raw materials, because raw materials and markets for manufactures were the primary reasons for the existence of colonies. Generally speaking, only three of the great imperial powers stood for the open door in the colonies; that is, equal treatment for nationals and foreigners in their colonial trade. These were Great Britain, the Netherlands, and pre-war Germany. This does not mean that these powers did not make exceptions. Italy, Portugal, and Spain customarily gave preferential treatment to their nationals. The third group, which followed the narrowest nationalistic policy of either assimilating their colonies for economic purposes or giving preferential treatment to nationals, were France, Japan, and the United States. In each of the three, however, there were some colonies in which the door was open. The United States maintained the open door only in Samoa and the Canal Zone. Preferential treatment to nationals was given in the Philippines, the Virgin Islands, and Guam. The policy of economic assimilation was applied to Alaska, Hawaii, the Virgin Islands, and Porto Rico through the establishment of free trade between the mother country and the colony and through the inclusion of the colony within the coasting system of the mother country, which excluded foreign ships. The Merchant Marine Act of 1920 authorized the extension of the coasting system to the Philippines under certain conditions, but the presidents declined to act. The scheme of closing the door in the Philippines more completely, as the statute proposed to do, was diametrically opposed to the American policy of the open door in the Far East. Such policies were embarassingly inconsistent; and, furthermore, the Philippines belonged geographically to the Asiatic economic system, not to the American. Their enforced connection with the United States through legislative action was an artificial, an unnatural relation.

SELECTED BIBLIOGRAPHY

LAY, T. H. The Foreign Service of the United States. Prentice-Hall, Inc., 1925.

FISK, G. M., and PIERCE, P. S. International Commercial Policies. The Macmillan Company, 1923.

CULBERTSON, W. S. International Economic Policies. D. Appleton and Company, 1925.

WILLIAMS, B. H. Economic Foreign Policy of the United States. McGraw-Hill Book Company, 1929.

KLEIN, JULIUS. Frontiers of Trade. The Century Co., 1929.

CHAPTER XXIV

ECONOMIC POLICIES: THE REGULATION AND ORGANIZATION OF FOREIGN TRADE

CONTROL OF FOREIGN TRADE

IN REORGANIZING control over domestic industry in 1914 the scope of regulatory policy was broadened by the Federal Trade Commission Act to include foreign trade. Section 6h directed the commission to investigate "trade conditions in and with foreign countries where associations, combinations, or practices of manufacturers, merchants, or traders, or other conditions may affect the foreign trade of the United States."

The work of the commission in this field was handled by the export-trade division; but on July 1, 1927, it was transferred to the legal division, and an export-trade section of that division was created. Complaints by foreign business men were received and investigated, and when possible adjusted, in order to preserve the good will of the foreign business world and protect the good name of Americans.

In 1926 an interdepartmental liaison committee, composed of members of all offices and departments of the United States government concerned in the foreign trade, was established at Washington for information, discussion, coöperation, and prevention of duplication in foreign-trade activities.

EXPORT ASSOCIATIONS

The organization required for the export trade was quite different from that for domestic marketing. The capital investment in facilities, agents, warehouses, and advertising were unusually heavy, and returns were not immediate.

The habits and tastes of each country had to be studied, and in some cases merchandise had to be modified in the process of manufacture to suit different local conditions. Only business organizations with large capital could expect to establish themselves in foreign trade. In most lines of trade and in most localities foreign exporters had already gained a foothold, and the American competitor had to make a place for his products. One of the most important factors in the development of European exportation was the export combination, or cartel.

The campaign for legislation to legalize combinations of exporters in the United States developed during the pre-war period. In its annual report for 1916 the Federal Trade Commission recommended that "declaratory and permissive legislation be enacted by Congress to make it clear that such organizations are lawful." It was not until the war gave the added stimulus to trade promotion that Congress responded. The Exports Associations Act (Webb-Pomerene), approved April 10, 1918, supplied the desired authority. Exemption from the antitrust laws was granted to associations or combinations "entered into for the sole purpose of engaging in export trade and actually engaged solely in such export trade." It amended Sections 1, 2, and 3 of the Sherman Act of 1890, Section 7 of the Clayton Act of 1914, and the Federal Trade Commission Act. The law prohibited restraint of export trade among domestic competitors by such an association, or any act which substantially or intentionally enhanced or depressed prices within the United States of commodities exported by such associations, or which substantially lessened competition within the United States or otherwise restrained trade therein. The Federal Trade Commission was granted supervisory and regulatory powers over these associations in the administration of the act and could enforce laws against unfair competition on the part of such organizations, even though the acts were committed outside the territorial jurisdiction of the United States.

The first year that the act was in operation 92 associations filed papers, representing nearly 840 business organizations. Owing to a misunderstanding of the act many were not qualified, and the year ending June 30, 1919, was the last of the post-war boom period. The report for 1920 listed only 43 associations with 732 members. There were 48 associations in 1921, 56 in 1922, 55 in 1923, 50 in 1924, 50 in 1925, 51 in 1926, 55 in 1927, and 56 in 1928. The fifty associations of 1925 represented 506 member firms, and the fifty-five associations of 1927 represented nearly 1000. The stabilization of the new organizations was not accomplished until 1924.

The volume of exports handled by export associations during the last four years for which statistics were available were $140,000,000 in 1924, $165,000,000 in 1925, $200,000,000 in 1926, and $371,500,000 in 1927. The scope of business represented was illustrated by the figures for different groups of products in 1926: lumber and wood, $35,700,000; metals and products, $56,000,000; chemicals, $3,100,000; raw materials, $14,300,000; miscellaneous manufactures, such as abrasives, paper, cotton, rubber, etc., $55,900,000; foodstuffs, $35,000,000.

Americans, both private individuals and public officials, frequently charged Europeans with permitting combinations and cartels in the export trade to engage in trade practices which were deemed unfair by the United States. Europeans answered these charges by pointing out various policies of the United States, among them the tariff and the export associations. The point made against export associations was that such combinations, if formed in the domestic trade of the United States, would be contrary to the antitrust laws. The United States permitted its business men to do things abroad which they could not do at home. It was difficult to arrive at any dependable conclusions on the merits of the controversy, except that appeals to national prejudices and international recrimination through the public prints could not lead to a fair adjustment.

The importance of China as foreign-trade territory was especially recognized by the China Trade Act of September 19, 1922, which authorized the creation of corporations, chartered in the District of Columbia, to engage in business in China, including Manchuria, Tibet, Mongolia, the leased territories, Hong Kong, and Macao. The certificates of incorporation were issued by the Secretary of Commerce. The corporations must include five persons a majority of whom were citizens of the United States. The majority of the directors and the president, secretary, and treasurer must be citizens of the United States resident in China. The corporations were prohibited from engaging in banking or insurance business. The purpose of the measure was, in the language of the act, to "aid in developing markets in China for goods produced in the United States." An act of February 26, 1925, amended the original law; it reduced the number of incorporators to three, defined the prohibited lines of business more carefully (including the operation of ships unless the controlling interest was American within the meaning of the shipping act of 1916), and required as an agent a legal resident of the District of Columbia.

RAW MATERIALS

The policies of governments which directly or indirectly controlled access to raw materials, or which contributed to or permitted restriction of production or unfair manipulation of markets, aroused heated discussion after the World War. The first international scramble was for oil. Before the war a large part of the ships of modern navies were oil-burners, and all new construction called for oil fuel. The motorization of armies and the development of air service depended upon oil. Before the end of the war the desire for control of the oil reserves of the world became a mania. Great Britain was first in the contest. Two lines of policy were possible: (1) to build up oil storage for emergencies so as to insure

control of the seas and insure access to oil supplies, and
(2) to undertake oil production under government auspices
and to secure control of oil resources for itself or its nationals
or both. The British government apparently led in developing the second policy, but the others followed closely. The
oil of the dismembered Turkish Empire was the richest
single item of booty to be divided among the victorious
Allies, but the scramble extended to Persia, Asia, the East
Indies, and Latin America.

In the United States the fear of the exhaustion of oil
reserves was widely exploited, even in government reports.
The United States was producing about 68 per cent of the
world's oil and controlled about 12 per cent more in Mexico.
This represented the present, but what about the future?
Of reserves to be developed in the future it was held that the
United States controlled only about 8 per cent, and that the
remainder was largely under British control. The Wilson
administration inaugurated an active raw-materials policy,
especially with respect to oil in the Near East. The Minerals
Leasing Act of 1920 provided that United States mineral
reserves could be exploited only by citizens, provided,
however, that citizens of foreign nations which granted exploitation privileges to Americans might be admitted on a reciprocity basis. The Democratic platform of 1920 demanded
equal privileges for Americans to develop oil and minerals
abroad. The extent to which oil dominated domestic politics
and directed American diplomacy cannot be stated as yet
with definiteness, but the outlines of certain episodes are
known. Harding said at Oklahoma City (October 9, 1920)
that "after an excursion of some eight years into the realm
of lofty and no doubt ennobling idealism," the country must
return to the practical fact of oil; that while the American
government was "attempting to organize a model state of
society," other governments had been securing oil. Americans faced "the danger of being barred out of a chance for
fair participation in future developments," and he proposed

to make a change. Just what changes were made it was difficult to determine, but the Harding administration continued the Wilson oil policy in the Near East, and eventually Americans received a 21.5 per cent interest in the Turkish Petroleum Company.

In the Dutch East Indies the American oil companies complained against what they considered exclusion from the richest oil fields, which were assigned to Anglo-Dutch interests. The support of the government was given to solving the question. On September 12, 1922, Albert B. Fall, Secretary of the Interior, refused the Shell Company, an Anglo-Dutch oil corporation, a lease to public lands under the terms of the Leasing Act of 1920. The controversy was prolonged until 1928, when the United States and the Netherlands reached an agreement on reciprocity treatment in oil exploitation, the announcement being made September 17.

The American government blocked an oil concession to the Lord Cowdray interests from Colombia during 1913. In the meantime negotiations, which had been pending almost continuously after 1909 for the adjustment of differences with Colombia arising out of the Panama revolution of 1903, were resumed by the Wilson administration. A treaty was signed in 1914 and was blocked by the Republicans in the Senate for seven years. Immediately after Harding's inauguration the treaty was ratified. One of the major considerations which dictated this consummation was the desire for access to Colombian oil.

Among the nine controlled raw materials of importance to the United States, later controversies centered especially about rubber and coffee. Restrictions on the sale of rubber from the British East Indies were inaugurated in 1921, after the collapse in the rubber market. The price rose to $1.21 per pound by July, 1925, instead of being maintained at the 36-cent level which was the original aim as a fair price. It was stated that in 1921 the manufacturers of rubber in the United States were offered five-year contracts at low prices in order to stabilize conditions, but they refused, hoping for further declines in price. The restrictions were the last resort, and then speculation began, which forced the excessive prices. Since the United States consumed about 75 per cent of the world's annual rubber supply and was absolutely dependent upon foreign sources, the effect of the rise in price was severe.

As a matter of general policy Hoover warned against trade wars supported by governments, but nevertheless an active campaign against monopolies of rubber and coffee was inaugurated under his leadership and continued through 1924 and 1925. The main features of the program were (1) disapproval of loans to support monopolies, (2) reduction of consumption, (3) development of new sources of supply, and (4) legalization of buyers' pools or import associations. The restrictions on loans to Brazil were ineffective because the desired coffee credits were secured in Europe. Reduction of consumption in coffee was about one fifth and in rubber about one fourth. New sources of production could not yield new supplies for several years, but new rubber plantations were planned in the Philippines and in Liberia and South America. Government loans, however, were refused for the establishment of new sources of production. No legislation was enacted relative to buyers' pools. The price of both coffee and rubber fell early in 1926 to more moderate figures. To what extent the fall in prices was due to American policies was open to question; but American influence had some effect. Between 1922 and 1925 the British share of the world's production of rubber fell from 72 per cent to 58 per cent. The chief gain was enjoyed by the Dutch East Indies.

In the later stages of the controversy a buyers' pool was in operation. It was formed in December, 1926, when a credit of $40,000,000 was provided by manufacturers of tires and motors. By 1928 surpluses of rubber had accumulated and prices were below the fixed minimum. The British government decided to abandon the policy of restriction, and announced in April that it would end in November, 1928.

It was in the rubber controversy that the buyers' pool became conspicuous, but it was important as a matter of general policy. Export associations had been legalized, but there was no mention of import associations. Legislation was introduced into Congress, and in a letter to Senator Capper (March 6, 1924) Secretary Hoover outlined his policy in support of the principle. They should be authorized to operate in raw materials without profit to themselves, and under such restrictions as would safeguard the public against abuses. Bills were before Congress more or less continuously, but without success. During the winter of 1927–1928 Secretary Jardine also urged buyers' combinations in order to secure better prices in the purchase of potash and sisal.

The grievances of the United States against foreigners are only one side of the story. At the height of Hoover's rubber war in December, 1925, a controversy developed over wheat. The London *Morning Post* charged that the United States government had sought to restrict wheat production in time of world need. Hoover answered that the United States Grain Corporation had bought wheat after the war when there was a surplus in order to maintain the government's fixed minimum price and that these surpluses had been sold to starving Europe, part in actual charity and part on credit. He said:

The American government has never passed any legislation restricting production. This story probably originates from the fact the Department of Agriculture, a year after the armistice and after the world famine was passed, did warn the American farmer there was overproduction of wheat in the world and they should get back to normal.

The net result of the argument was that Hoover admitted that the price of wheat in the United States had been maintained at an artificially high figure after the armistice, and that the Department of Agriculture had advised reduction of acreage to prevent surpluses which would depress prices. The ideal of orderly marketing, which was the goal of government agricultural policy, involved a degree of restriction of production. From the standpoint of international trade the question at issue was what degree of reduction of acreage could be urged in the interest of orderly marketing without overstepping the limits which would create shortage and result in abnormally high prices. This was exactly the issue in the British rubber control also.

Hoover's answer did not satisfy British critics, and British explanations of the control of rubber did not satisfy Hoover. He made a comparison of rubber and wheat prices and made the statement that in proportion to the price of rubber the price of wheat should be $8 per bushel. Under this stimulus wheat advanced seven cents on December 29, 1925, setting a high record for the season of $1.89 for December wheat and $1.85½ for May wheat.

In July, 1926, the London *Daily Mail* was quoted as declaring that the British-American meat war was an attempt on the part of American packers to capture the world market. The war had to do with the importation of Argentine meat into England. This fight to control the London market was thought to be a preliminary to a manipulation of other markets, which meant that "the interests of the whole British Empire may be at stake."

The Americans, represented by the Swifts, Armours, and the Wilsons, have attempted to drive British firms out of the market by sending Argentine chilled beef to Great Britain regardless of the known requirements, thereby forcing down prices and causing Argentine meat to be sold below the cost of importation. They, of course, lost severely on British trading, but their control of the American home supply enabled them to force up prices in the United States so as to cover their losses here.

In December, 1926, *The Westminster Gazette* said, "The United States imitates the British rubber scheme." This was a comment on Coolidge's annual message in which he reported that sufficient pledges had been secured to finance the storage of four million bales of cotton. The *Gazette* continued, "Remembering Secretary Hoover's indignation over the rubber restrictions, London will chuckle over the President's recommendation." Relative to the President's recommendation that the acreage be reduced one third, a member of the Federation of Master Cotton Spinners was quoted in the press as saying that it was received with great concern in Manchester, since it would mean higher prices and would have a bad effect generally on the world situation.

Helium, one of the most essential gases for dirigible aircraft, was produced only in certain parts of the world. The United States was one of the largest producers of this raw material. The act of March 3, 1925, prohibited the export of helium except on permission of the president on joint recommendation of the Secretary of War, the Secretary of the Navy, and the Secretary of the Interior.

At the time that the United States was demanding equal privileges in oil development in Persia, Mesopotamia, and the East Indies, the British and the Dutch pointed out that the Philippine oil reserves were closed to exploitation by foreigners. Later (December 1, 1926) General Wood as governor-general signed a bill passed by the Philippine legislature prohibiting the export of abaca seeds (hemp plant) in order to maintain a monopoly on that raw material. At an earlier time Mexico, Java, and other countries had experimented with the planting of abaca seed, but with little success. The occasion for legislation at this time was that attempts to establish the abaca industry were being renewed by several tropical countries.

In the preceding pages some of the leading charges made against the United States by foreigners have been presented as they affect the problem of raw materials in world trade, also some examples of restriction in regard to access to such materials. The charges by both sides were *ex parte*, and what degree of merit there was in them is sometimes difficult to determine. The most unfortunate element in the situation was that regardless of facts each nation had a tendency to assume that the other was wrong. It should be evident, however, from these controversies that access to raw materials and stabilization of prices were world problems of the first order, and that they could not be successfully adjusted by international recrimination. International coöperation promised greater possibilities of success and of preservation of good will.

SELECTED BIBLIOGRAPHY

Reports of the Federal Trade Commission.
WILLIAMS, B. H. Economic Foreign Policy of the United States. McGraw-Hill Book Company, 1929.
KLEIN, JULIUS. Frontiers of Trade. The Century Co., 1929.

CHAPTER XXV

ECONOMIC POLICIES: FINANCIAL

FOREIGN BANKING AND CREDIT

THE central aim of most foreign economic policies is promotion of trade. The national banking system had been designed and evolved during a time when the primary interest of the country was focused on internal development. The defects of the system became more and more apparent with the growth of foreign trade in terms of exports of manufactured products. It was then that the exporter began to appreciate the significance of foreign banking facilities and machinery for effective financing of foreign business operations through short-time and long-time credits.

In 1914 there were twenty-six American foreign branch banks. Six of these were branches of institutions engaged in both domestic and foreign business; the remaining twenty were branches of banks engaged exclusively in foreign business. All of them were chartered under state laws. The International Banking Corporation with sixteen branches was of greatest importance. Few states, however, permitted branch banking. A national bank was required by Section 5190 of the Revised Statutes to transact its business "at an office or banking house located in the place specified in its organization certificate." In the foreign trade bank acceptances had become an important means of financing exports where short-time credits were needed. The great acceptance markets had been developed in European financial centers, but not in the United States. There were important reasons for this state of affairs. New York money rates were higher, credit customs once established were hard to break, and national banks were not permitted to accept commercial paper. Private banks and state-chartered trust companies were not restricted regarding acceptances. Long-time credit institutions had not been developed, since United States investments abroad were relatively small and the public at large had not become purchasers of foreign securities. The English type of investment trust had been developed during the nineteenth century in England as a means of stabilizing foreign securities in order to make them attractive to the small investor. This was still to be done in the United States.

The Federal Reserve Act of December 23, 1913, and its amendments included provisions for remedying these defects. On the subject of foreign banking it provided that national banks with a capital and surplus of $1,000,000 or over might establish branches in foreign countries or in the possessions of the United States, they might own subsidiary foreign-banking corporations which could establish branches, or two or more smaller banks might join in the establishment of foreign-banking corporations to establish branches. The state banking law of New York was amended April 16, 1914, along similar lines. On the subject of acceptances it authorized national banks to accept drafts upon them for six months or less arising out of import or export of merchandise or domestic shipments of goods when warehouse receipts or shipping documents were attached. Drafts to create dollar exchange might be drawn under limitations fixed by the Federal Reserve Board. Federal Reserve Banks were authorized to discount drafts and acceptances running not longer than ninety days when offered by member banks, and were furthermore authorized to buy bankers' acceptances and bills of exchange of similar character in the open market. New York and Connecticut state banking laws were remodeled to conform to these new practices. The Federal Reserve Act did not include the third point, foreign-investment banking.

During the World War unusual strain was placed upon export credit because of the enormous volume of exports on account of the war. To supplement the credit extended by regular banking institutions during the war and reconstruction, the War Finance Corporation was created by an act of April 5, 1918. For a period of five years it was authorized to furnish long-time credits to assist in the export of goods. On account of post-war deflation the life of the organization was subsequently extended to January 1, 1925.

After the armistice it was feared that the United States would lose much of the business gained during the war. Appeals were made for further government assistance in promoting trade through additional financial facilities. The Edge amendment to the Federal Reserve Act, approved December 24, 1919, provided for Federal incorporation of foreign financial institutions. Prior to this act all foreign-banking corporations were state-chartered. It was thought that the national institutions would be more effective in holding and expanding post-war foreign trade. They were authorized to engage in both commercial banking (short-time credits by means of acceptances) and investment banking (long-time credits by means of debentures based on securities of foreign corporations). While the law contemplated the possibility that one corporation might handle both types of business, in practice the Federal Reserve Board limited them to one or the other field exclusively. The foreign-investment banks were of the debenture type, following English precedents fairly closely. Since it was difficult to sell securities of foreign business institutions directly to the investor, the investment trust solved this difficulty by selling its own debentures.

The expansion of foreign banking was rapid until the deflation of 1920. Inasmuch as this type of business was relatively new for American bankers, much of it was experimental. During the depression trade decreased about 50 per cent, and with it foreign banking had to be readjusted and stabilized. In 1920 there were 181 bank branches in foreign countries and possessions, and 38 branches of the American Express Company, which did some banking business. On June 30, 1926, there were 107 bank branches and 47 branches of the American Express Company. Of the bank branches, 72 were branches of banks engaged in domestic business also, and 35 were branches of subsidiaries of two of these banks, which were engaged only in foreign-banking business. The Equitable Trust Company had branches in London, Paris, and Mexico City and owned the Equitable Eastern Banking Corporation with branches in Shanghai and Hong Kong. The Guaranty Trust Company had branches in London and Paris and for a time owned the Asia Banking Corporation, which was liquidated in 1924. The Farmers' Loan and Trust Company owned a branch in London, but sold its Paris branch to the National City Bank. The Empire Trust Company had a London branch. The National City Bank had 51 direct branches throughout the world, 35 of which were in the Caribbean (24 in Cuba and 7 in Santo Domingo). It also owned, after 1915, the International Banking Corporation, which had branches in Asia (China, Japan, and India) and in Spain (Madrid and Barcelona). The First National Bank of Boston owned branches at Buenos Aires and Havana. The Bankers' Trust Company owned branches in London and Paris. The Chase National Bank held branches in Havana (Cuba), Panama City, and Cristobal (Panama), which were originally established by the American Foreign Banking Corporation.

Most large banks developed an acceptance business; but it took some time after the passage of the Federal Reserve Act to break the old credit habits and build up new ones. So long as European credits were cheaper than American it was impossible to make much headway, and even after the shift in the money market to New York the customary channels were followed. The Guaranty Trust Company was a pioneer in the field. Paul M. Warburg organized the International Acceptance Bank to do acceptance business. Several such institutions were formed later. Acceptance banks organized under the Edge Act developed even more slowly. In the field of the investment trusts under the Edge Act the first foreign-banking institution of the debenture type was organized in 1926.

The legal status of American banks in England was for the most part the same as for domestic banks. In France, after 1882, American banks were on an equality with French banks; however, taxation was based on the total capital of the bank, a circumstance which discouraged foreign branches in France. This was avoided by establishing an American-owned subsidiary incorporated in France, as was done by the National City Bank, or by establishing foreign-banking corporations with a small capital. The Italian laws of 1919 were based on the principle that foreign banks would be given the same treatment in Italy that Italian banks were granted in foreign countries. In practice American banks were not discriminated against. The Spanish laws of 1917 and 1920 were designed to give protection to native industry, and included a proviso for retaliation against any state discriminating against Spanish banks. Argentina and Brazil applied the reciprocity principle, and Canada prohibited the establishment of branches of foreign banks.

The legal status of foreign banks in the United States varied with the laws of the forty-eight states; but there was a similarity of historical background in all the Eastern states, which were of greatest financial importance. Early in the nineteenth century discrimination against banks from outside the state was adopted as a protection of depositors against unsound banking and as a protective measure to build up infant industries. Foreign banks, when allowed to do business in the state at all, were as a rule not permitted to accept deposits. The New York law of 1914 excluded branches of banks of other states and of foreign countries. Agencies of foreign banks could be established, but could not accept deposits, issue notes, or engage in savings and loan-association business or trust business, and real-estate holdings were limited to five years except in the case of institutions from other states or from Canada and Mexico when the reciprocity principle was applied. An annual agency license with a fee of $250 was also required. These laws could be evaded partly by the establishment of local subsidiaries. After the war attempts were made to repeal these restrictions, but in 1920 the bill was vetoed, and in 1923 it was defeated by the Senate. In California similar legislation was in force. These restrictions, it was agreed, were a hindrance to New York in competing with London as a money market, and foreign retaliation was threatened. The International Chamber of Commerce at its first meeting in London in 1921 adopted a resolution which was in part as follows:

> The congress demands urgently of all countries in which the present legislation contains restrictive measures or special treatments to take the initiative to abolish these laws, if not in every case, at least for the benefit of those foreign countries which accord reciprocity.

This resolution was drafted and passed, with the United States in mind as one of the chief offending countries, if not the principal one.

The Government and Foreign Loans

The fact that the United States was a creditor nation in a large way and was, for the time being at least, the world's financial center gives a very particular significance to the question of how this unique position was used. It was a position of tremendous potential economic and political power. In pre-war days there were isolated occasions when the government had approved or disapproved particular foreign loans, but it was not customary to exercise a general supervision over such transactions. On May 25, 1921, an informal announcement was made to bankers asking that the Department of State be kept informed concerning loan plans. This policy was made more definite March 3, 1922, by the issuance of a formal public statement of foreign-loan policy:

The flotation of foreign-bond issues in the American market is assuming an increasing importance, and on account of the bearing of such operations upon the proper conduct of affairs it is hoped that American concerns that contemplate making foreign loans will inform the Department of State in due time of the essential facts and of subsequent developments of importance. . . .

The Department of State cannot, of course, require American bankers to consult it. It will not pass upon the merits of foreign loans as business propositions, nor assume any responsibility whatever in connection with loan transactions. Offers for foreign loans should not, therefore, state or imply that they are contingent upon an expression from the Department of State regarding them, nor should any prospectus or contract refer to the attitude of this government. The Department believes that in view of the possible national interests involved it should have the opportunity of saying to the underwriters concerned, should it appear advisable to do so, that there is or is not objection to any particular issue.

Somewhat later (August 26, 1924) A. N. Young, economic adviser of the Department of State, made a fuller exposition of the policy:

The purposes to which foreign loans may be put are a matter of concern to the Department of State. It is obviously desirable that American capital going abroad should only be utilized for productive purposes. . . . The government of the United States could not but object to the utilization of American capital for militaristic ends. In short, the Department of State could not be expected to view with favor the utilization of American capital abroad in such a manner as to prevent or make difficult the carrying out of essential American policies, nor to promote the carrying out abroad of policies inimical to the proper interests of the United States. The Department obviously could not view with favor proposed arrangements involving provisions that might redound to the injury of relations between the United States and the borrowing country.

These were statements of general policy; they left the government free to vary procedure in special cases to suit its own particular purposes and the circumstances, a discretion which was freely exercised.

The problem of the interallied debts was an important occasion for applying the capital blockade as a coercive influence. The Italian settlement was made during November, 1925. Loans were also pending, but at the instance of the Department of State they were not concluded by American bankers until after the settlement of the debts. It was then understood that the loan of $100,000,000 received the approval of the United States government.

In the settlement of the French debt more drastic methods were used. Loans to France were disapproved during 1925; and then, on account of efforts made to restore the franc, a rumor was started that the ban was lifted. The administration then restated the policy that the government would not stand in the way of private loans to any country which had funded its war debt to the Treasury, provided that such loans were of a reasonable nature and were to be devoted to the improvement of the borrower's general economic condition. It was reported in February, 1927, that France had finally been able to secure loans through Dutch and Swiss bankers, and in that way had circumvented the capital blockade of Washington and London. Again, in the fall of 1927, France proposed to refund an 8 per cent bond issue at 5 per cent. According to press reports Senator Borah wrote Secretary Kellogg asking that approval be withheld. It was announced, however, that the French loan was approved. Two points were significant in this incident: (1) the loan was not an addition to French indebtedness, but a refunding operation at lower rates, which would strengthen French finances; (2) it was pointed out by observers that the tariff controversy of September and October had a bearing on effecting a compromise in which this was the American concession. In January, 1928, it was reported that disapproval had been withdrawn from the floating of loans to be applied to the development of French industry.

In the stabilization of the German financial situation American money played a large part. In an address on October 24, 1924, Coolidge expressed gratification "that American capital has been able to facilitate the carrying into effect of the Dawes plan," but declared that these "loans are made without commitments on the part of this government." During 1927 the Department of State emphasized that loans to Germany must be of such a character as not to interfere with German reparation payments.

In the Caribbean area United States loan policy developed along somewhat different lines. In 1922 a Cuban loan of $20,000,000 was approved in accordance with the principles of the Platt amendment. During the military occupation of Santo Domingo by the United States loans were made in the name of the Dominican government. The first loan (in 1921) announced that the military government would not be withdrawn until a treaty was made validating the loan. The second loan was offered to the public March 5, 1922, with the following statement:

The issue of these bonds has received the approval of the United States government required by the terms of the American-Dominican Convention of 1907, and the Secretary of State consents to the inclusion in the bonds of the following statement:

The acceptance and validation of this bond issue by any government of the Dominican Republic as a legal, binding, and irrevocable obligation of the Dominican Republic is hereby guaranteed by the military government of Santo Domingo. . . .

A loan to the Republic of Salvador was offered to the public in October, 1923, and in the advertisements in the press the following statement was included:

The United States of America and El Salvador entered into an exchange of formal diplomatic notes with reference to this loan, by which Salvador on its part assures the United States that it will coöperate in every respect with the government of the United States and the bankers in carrying out the terms of the loan contract, and the United States on its part takes cognizance of the terms of the loan, contract and states that the Secretary of State of the United States is prepared to carry out the stipulations with reference to him in Articles IX, XIX, and XXIII of the loan contract should it be necessary to do so.

The security pledged was a first lien on 70 per cent of the customs revenue collected by a representative of the Metropolitan Trust Company in San Salvador. The safety of the loan as an investment was emphasized in italics in these words:

The history of government bonds secured by customs revenues collected by agents of the bondholders or by representatives of foreign governments is without a record of default.

These examples are sufficient to illustrate clearly and concretely the use the government of the United States made of foreign loans in furtherance of its political policy in the Caribbean area.

In the economic warfare among nations for raw materials foreign-loan policy played a part. In 1925 Brazilian authorities sought loans from American bankers and were refused at the instance of the government. Hoover issued a statement November 12:

The administration does not believe the New York banking houses will wish to provide loans which might be diverted to support the coffee speculation which has been in progress for the past year at the hands of the coffee combination in São Paulo, Brazil. Such support would simply bolster up the extravagant prices to the American consumer.

The loans were then secured in London. In connection with Hoover's rubber war during 1925 and 1926 it was widely understood that if the states interested in rubber should apply for loans they would receive the same treatment from the American government.

The loan policy as it affected Russia was a still different problem. The United States refused recognition to the existing government, yet Americans were doing business with

Russians and with the government. Loans to finance exports from Germany to Russia were disapproved in 1926. In 1928 an issue of Russian railroad bonds was being offered privately to American investors, and three American financial institutions were acting as agents for payment of interest and retirement charges. American holders of pre-war Russian bonds protested to the Department of State. An investigation was made, and the bonds were disapproved, February 1, 1928, since they were secured by the same railroads as the Czarist bonds which the Soviet government had repudiated. The American banks then withdrew from the arrangement. The announcement of the Department of State went farther than this particular issue. It stated that "the department does not view with favor financial arrangements designed to facilitate in any way the sale of Soviet bonds in the United States."

The French-loan episode was the occasion of a formal attack on the loan policy of the government by Senator Glass of Virginia, formerly Secretary of the Treasury. His statement (October 14, 1927) held that the practice of scrutinizing loans was without constitutional or statutory authority and, besides, was an improper exercise of powers which might lead to national scandal. Senator Borah was quoted as saying that while he did not wish to criticize the Department of State he thought it was a practice which should be terminated. The attack had no appreciable effect on the President, who, on the same day, indicated that there would be no change in the practice.

SELECTED BIBLIOGRAPHY

PHELPS, C. W. The Foreign Expansion of American Banks. The Ronald Press Company, 1927.
SPEAKER, L. M. The Investment Trust. A. W. Shaw Company, 1924.
FOWLER, JOHN F. American Investment Trusts. Harper & Brothers, 1928.
DUNN, R. W. American Foreign Investments. The Viking Press, 1926.
WILLIAMS, B. H. Economic Foreign Policy of the United States. McGraw-Hill Book Company, 1929.

CHAPTER XXVI

ECONOMIC POLICIES: TRANSPORTATION AND COMMUNICATION

THE MERCHANT MARINE

THE program for the promotion of trade in the post-war period entailed the active development of an international transportation and communication system under government encouragement. The merchant marine received the most definite consideration. The Shipping Act of 1916 outlined a policy under the stress of war conditions. Its preamble stated the purpose of "encouraging, developing, and creating a naval auxiliary and naval reserve and a merchant marine to meet the requirements of the commerce of the United States with its territories and possessions and with foreign countries. . . ." American ownership was a prerequisite to American registry; and a ship to be American-owned must be owned by a citizen or by a corporation in which the controlling interest was American, in which the president and managing directors were American, and which was incorporated under American laws. The administration of the merchant marine was vested in a Shipping Board of five commissioners with terms of six years. Authority was granted, with the approval of the president, to construct ships in American shipyards or to purchase, lease, or charter vessels to meet commercial demands or for use as military or naval auxiliaries, provided that such vessels as were already in American service should not be acquired by the Shipping Board unless it was necessary to retain them in operation. Vessels in the possession of the board could be sold, leased, or chartered to citizens of the United States, and any vessel acquired from the board was entitled to United States registry and might engage in the coastwise trade. Such vessels could not be sold, leased, or chartered without the consent of the board, and in time of emergency no vessel under United States registry could be transferred to anyone not a citizen or to a foreign flag without the board's approval.

A shipping corporation to operate ships was authorized if it was considered desirable by the board during the war and for five years thereafter, but only in case citizens could not be found to undertake operation. Investigations were to be carried out by the board to determine the cost of building ships in the United States or abroad and of operating ships, and to inquire into rules of operation, marine insurance, navigation laws, mortgage laws, and marine loans. Unreasonable rates, discrimination, and unfair practices of competition were prohibited, except that rate agreements might be entered into with the consent of the board and, when approved, would not be subject to the antitrust laws. The board was directed to investigate unequal treatment given United States vessels by foreign governments, and if the president could not secure adjustments through diplomatic channels a report should be made to Congress.

An act of October 6 opened the coastwise trade to foreign ships, except trade with Alaska. This was purely a temporary emergency measure. An act of July 15, 1918, made considerable amendment to the Shipping Act of 1916. It defined more rigidly citizenship of a corporation and aimed to prevent the transfer of ships from the United States to foreign registry. This was an emergency measure, but with slight exceptions it became a part of permanent policy.

The Merchant Marine Act of 1920, approved by Wilson on June 5, 1920, made the following declaration:

It is necessary for the national defense and for the proper growth of its foreign and domestic commerce that the United States shall have a merchant marine of the best equipped and most suitable types of vessels sufficient to carry the greater portion of its commerce and serve as a naval or military auxiliary in time of war or national emergency, ultimately to be owned and operated privately by citizens of the United States; and it is hereby declared to be the policy of the United States to do whatever may be necessary to develop and encourage the maintenance of such a merchant marine.

Emergency war legislation was repealed, including the sections on construction in the act of 1916, and practically the whole merchant-marine code was revised. In some points the revision was confined to details; in others new features of policy were added. The Shipping Board was reorganized and was to consist of seven members. Ships were to be sold to citizens as soon as possible. Sales to aliens were authorized on two definite conditions: (1) that the ships were not needed to promote the purpose of this act and (2) that the board was unable to sell to citizens, and a full statement of reasons must be made a matter of record.

In the promotion of shipping lines the board was directed to investigate the establishment of lines for the purpose of advancing trade and mail service. The size, character, and number of vessels needed in each proposed service were to be determined and the necessary vessels were to be sold or chartered to private operators. In case private capital would not undertake the project the board should operate the ships in that service until the business should become established. Mail contracts with these lines were also authorized. In the sale of ships preference should be given to those already in the service in which the lines were established or in service to ports related to these lines. Such lines should be continued in operation unless the board approved of discontinuance because the service was unnecessary or uneconomical. When government service competed with private service the rates must not be less than cost including depreciation.

The board was directed to coöperate with the Secretary of War in the investigation of the coördination of water and rail transportation facilities, and if rail rates were found to be detrimental to certain ports the finding was to be referred to the Interstate Commerce Commission. An insurance fund was authorized, and a construction-loan fund was to be made up out of the proceeds of sales and operations. The board was authorized to make necessary rules for carrying the act into effect, and, if a ruling of some other department interfered with shipping, to request that it be suspended, except public-health regulations, consular service, or steamboat inspection. No new rules affecting shipping in foreign trade were to be made without the approval of the board or until final action was taken in the matter by the president.

Section 21 provided that the coastwise laws be extended to the remaining island possessions on February 1, 1922, and the board was directed to establish service until private service could be established. It was further provided that if service to the island possessions could not be established within the specified time the president might suspend this section until service was supplied. In the case of the Philippines the coastwise provision was not to be effective until adequate service was established and announced by presidential proclamation. The act of October 6, 1917, admitting foreign ships to the coasting trade, was repealed.

Encouragement to private operation was further provided by exemption of earnings of vessels in the foreign trade from war and excess-profits taxes for ten years, provided amounts equal to the exemption were devoted to the building of ships in American shipyards. However, at least two thirds of the cost of such ships must be out of ordinary funds of the owner. Operators were also exempt from all income taxes on proceeds of sales of vessels built before 1914, provided these proceeds were invested on new building in American shipyards. All mails were required to be carried on United States vessels where practicable. Section 28 was unusual in providing preferential rail charges on goods or persons transported from a foreign country to the United States in United States ships, but if service of such ships was inadequate the provision might be suspended on any particular commerce. Marine-insurance associations were exempt from the antitrust laws. A Merchant Ship Mortgage Act was made a part of the Shipping Act, and some revisions were made respecting seamen, wages, and injuries. Another unusual provision was Section 34 directing that all treaties restricting discrimination in customs and tonnage dues in favor of goods imported in United States ships be terminated in ninety days. The definition of citizenship of a corporation was again revised to insure the complete exclusion of foreign control, direct or indirect, of American ships.

A program of encouragement might include government ownership and operation, government ownership and private operation, mail subsidies or outright subsidies, discrimination in favor of national shipping, construction loans, tax exemptions, or revision of navigation laws. All these methods were incorporated in the shipping laws except the direct subsidy. Mail contracts were awarded which amounted to a subsidy in disguise. The rates on letters and other articles under the Universal Postal Union rates were 35 cents and $4\frac{1}{2}$ cents a pound, respectively, but the government paid 80 cents and 8 cents per pound. Outright subsidies were advocated for a time by the Harding administration, but legislation failed. Coolidge opposed money subsidies as contrary to his program of economy. The difference between cost of operation and receipts on government ships was paid by the government — a sum of from $30,000,000 to $50,000,000 annually in earlier years, but reduced to $19,000,000 in 1926 and to $16,000,000 in 1927. This was also a form of indirect subsidy, although it was intended to be temporary. The provision for construction loans was amended three times after the act of 1920. The original clause set aside $25,000,000 annually for five years for construction loans. The act of June 6, 1924, extended the use of these loans to reconditioning ships with engines of the most economical type. Ships so reconditioned must remain under United States laws for five years. No loan should run for more than fifteen years, and interest should not be less than $5\frac{1}{4}$ per cent when the vessel was engaged in the coasting trade and $4\frac{1}{4}$ per cent when engaged in the foreign trade, and no loan should exceed half the cost of the vessel. The reconditioning of vessels with the most economical type of engines was defined to include internal-combustion engines, and such vessels must serve part time at least in the foreign trade. Reconditioning was not to be undertaken until a contract for sale, lease, or charter of the vessel was made. The act of March 4, 1927, made slight changes except in granting a larger discretion in the purposes of loans for construction. The loan fund was doubled by an act of May 23, 1928.

The most significant contribution of the extreme nationalist group was embodied in the Merchant Marine Act of 1920 providing for a system of tariff discrimination against goods carried in foreign ships. Article 34 directed the president to denounce all treaties with foreign countries granting national treatment of foreign ships with reference to customs duties and tonnage dues. Article 28 provided that goods imported or exported in foreign ships should pay domestic railroad rates and that those shipped on American vessels should receive preferential rates. Wilson, Harding, and Coolidge refused to execute Article 34, since it would mean the termination of treaties with twenty odd states, and this would leave merchants without any rights in foreign commerce with those states. Furthermore, under the discriminative conditions imposed foreign governments would not negotiate new treaties as favorable as the existing ones. Under Article 28 the Shipping Board advised the Interstate Commerce Commission that adequate national shipping facilities did not exist, and the preferential rates were not put in force; in February, 1924, they certified that adequate facilities did exist, and preferential rates were ordered. Before the rates went into effect, however, both boards decided that the discriminative policy was unwise and countermanded the preferential orders. In this way the congressional merchant-marine policy was defeated, although it still remained on the statute books and might be invoked at any time.

Advocates of discrimination argued that it was this policy which placed the United States in the high position it occupied in the carrying trade in the early part of the nineteenth century, and that a revival of the policy would restore the merchant marine. These advocates used only such portions of history as were convenient for their purpose. In the early nineteenth century all nations were still dominated by mercantilist theories of trade regulation and monopoly. The United States as a new nation had to establish itself against the system. Discrimination was the method employed against foreign discrimination, but the object in view was equal treatment, not special favors. To what extent American discrimination caused the abandonment of the European system of discrimination is a debated question. Mercantilism was giving way to new theories of economics which emphasized free trade. Probably both elements, American policy and the new economic theories, entered into the European change of policy. When merchant-marine agitation was revived in the last quarter of the nineteenth century under the influence of imperialistic ideas and neomercantilism, the policy of discrimination was revived with it. American discrimination under prevailing open-door conditions, while ostensibly a mere revival of old policies, was in effect a reversal of those policies. What the United States wanted in the earlier period was equal treatment; what was asked for in the later period was special favors. Another important effect of the adoption of the discriminative policy would be the revival of customs duties on what were then free goods, when they were imported into the United States in foreign ships. This would have been a serious hindrance to trade, since from 55 per cent to 70 per cent of American foreign commerce was carried in foreign vessels. Although Coolidge disapproved the discriminative aspects of the act of 1920 as a government policy, yet he criticized business men for not discriminating in favor of American ships. In his annual message of December, 1926, he said, "Our merchants are altogether too indifferent about using American ships for the transportation of goods which they send abroad or bring home." An importer testified before a House committee in 1924 that he refused to accept a shipment, and let it "rot" in a warehouse because it had been shipped to the United States in a foreign vessel. Joseph E. Sheedy of the government Fleet Corporation is quoted as exclaiming that he felt like "jumping up and kissing him" for his "loyal American action."

The policy of discrimination in customs and tonnage dues in favor of nationals was repudiated, at least temporarily, by the new German commercial treaty of 1925. The Senate, however, added a reservation that after one year this section might be terminated on ninety days' notice. The new policy was in line with the open-door and equal-treatment policies of both Wilson (the Fourteen Points and the League covenant) and Hughes, who negotiated the new treaty.

The sale of ships by the Shipping Board directed by the Shipping Act was the source of prolonged controversy. In practically every case where a sale was under consideration the board was divided, and there was conflict of jurisdiction between it and the head of the Emergency Fleet Corporation. Coolidge wished to concentrate authority in the hands of the president of the Fleet Corporation to negotiate the sales; the board intervened and deposed Palmer, the head. Legislation was contemplated during 1925 to reorganize the shipping administration. This difficulty was under consideration at the same time as the tariff-commission and Federal Trade Commission controversies. The President was quoted as considering the abolition of all these independent commissions and the vesting of their functions in the cabinet departments. Curtis, the leader of the majority in the Senate, said the Shipping Board should be abolished and the ships be transferred to the Department of Commerce to be sold. In March, 1926, Hoover recommended that the Shipping Board be deprived of its jurisdiction over the Fleet Corporation. The deadlock was finally broken by the President's requesting the resignation of B. E. Haney, Democrat. This resignation was presented in February, to become effective on March 1, 1926. The new appointment gave the President's party a majority, and on July 8 the head of the Fleet Corporation was summarily deposed and an administration man was put in his place.

The sale of shipping lines in the Pacific was completed February 16, 1928, when the last ships in those waters were sold. The Dollar Lines, owned by R. Stanley Dollar, became the largest single owner in the Pacific. The readjustments also marked the passing, on November 24, 1925, of one of the oldest American shipping lines in the Pacific trade — the Pacific Mail Steamship Company. Its first ship had entered San Francisco Bay seventy years before. In the Atlantic the United States Lines operated the *Leviathan*, the *George Washington*, the *Republic*, the *President Harding*, and the *President Roosevelt*. In 1927 there was a profit on operation for the first time, but in 1928 there was again a loss. This line was finally sold to the P. W. Chapman Company along with the American Merchant Lines, the sale being announced on February 6, 1929.

What was the result of United States policy thus far in shipbuilding and in operation of ships? The historic shipbuilding firm of William Cramp and Sons withdrew from the shipbuilding business in April, 1927. The announcement stated that "this decision is due to the general curtailment of the naval-construction program and the continued depression in merchant shipbuilding." Lloyd's register reported that for 1925 Great Britain and Ireland had built 885,013 tons, Italy 309,578 tons, Germany 234,145 tons, and the United States 105,211 tons. The report of the Shipping Board for 1927 said that for every first-class merchant ship built in the United States after 1921, Great Britain had built 41 ships, Germany 12, Italy 5, and France and Japan 4 each. The trend of foreign building was for speed, which meant that the United States was being outclassed not only in tonnage but in the character of the service to be rendered. The best cargoes went to the best ships.

The operation of American ships declined relatively after the war. In 1920 American ships carried 39 per cent of United States imports and 45.2 per cent of exports; by 1927 these proportions had fallen to an average of 32 per cent of United States trade carried in American ships. According to the Shipping Board's report for 1927, of the $600,000,000 paid annually for freight by American shippers, $480,000,000 went to operators of foreign ships. Secretary Wilbur attributed the high cost of operation of United States ships to two primary sources: (1) the navigation laws, including the Seaman's Act; (2) the high cost of building, which he placed at from 20 per cent to 30 per cent higher than in foreign countries. He placed operating expenses under American registry at from 8 per cent to 10 per cent higher than under foreign registry. The ranking of merchant fleets in 1928, however, placed the United States second, the first six being Great Britain, the United States, Japan, Italy, Germany, and France.

The remedy for the United States shipping situation was outlined by the Shipping Board in recommendations to Congress in January, 1928. Government ships should be transferred immediately to private ownership; and since there was no prospect of a direct subsidy system, the indirect aids should be extended. The provisions for mail contracts and the system of loans for construction should be liberalized. Tax exemption for ships operated in the foreign trade should be extended. Business handled by navy and army transports and by the Panama Steamship Line should be turned over to privately operated ships. Pay in the merchant-marine reserve should be increased. Such amendments to the marine-insurance system should be made as would place American ships on an equality with foreign ships in regard to insurance.

Congress responded partly to the recommendations and passed a bill which was approved by the President on May 23, 1928. It provided that sales should require the vote of five members of the board, that repair and reconditioning should include remodeling, and that it was essential to plan replacement programs and estimates which should be presented to Congress from time to time. Loan privileges were extended to remodeling or improving vessels already built. The maximum time for loans was extended from fifteen to twenty years, with repayment in installments. The interest rates on loans for vessels engaged in the foreign trade should be the same as the lowest rate on any outstanding government obligations except postal-savings bonds. The amount of a loan was increased from two thirds to three fourths of the cost of construction, reconditioning, or remodeling. The amount of the loan fund was increased by appropriation from $125,000,000 to $250,000,000.

A complete change was made in the law on ocean mail. The Ocean Mail Act of 1891 and other laws on the subject were repealed. The Postmaster-General was directed to present to the Shipping Board plans for mail routes. The board would then make estimates of the ships required. When the routes were approved, the Postmaster-General would be authorized to make contracts after advertisement and public bidding, the contracts to run not longer than ten years. The performance of the contract must begin within three years. Ships must be built in the United States, must be of United States registry of not later than February 1, 1928, or under construction at that date, and must remain under United States registry during the life of the contract. All licensed officers were required to be citizens, as well as half the crew for the first four years and two thirds after 1932. Ships were divided into seven regular classes, and compensation was fixed accordingly. In particular cases where speed was considered essential, discretionary authority might be exercised to vary from the maximum compensation quoted of twelve dollars. The estimated cost of the compensation was fixed at $14,000,000 by competent authorities. A final provision of the act amended the insurance law.

OCEAN MAIL RATES UNDER ACT OF 1928

MAXIMUM RATE PER NAUTICAL MILE	CLASS	SPEED IN KNOTS	GROSS TONNAGE
$1.50	7	10	2,500
2.50	6	10	4,000
4.00	5	13	8,000
6.00	4	16	10,000
8.00	3	18	12,000
10.00	2	20	16,000
12.00	1	24	20,000

In the coasting trade foreign-owned ships were excluded altogether. Here the extreme nationalists scored again. The trade of Porto Rico, Hawaii, and Alaska had for years been included within the coasting system. The Merchant Marine Act of 1920 provided for extending the coasting system to the remaining island possessions — Samoa, Guam, the Virgin Islands, and the Philippines. The extension to the Virgin Islands was postponed until September 30, 1926. In the case of the Philippines it was conditioned by the existence of adequate shipping facilities, so that the execution of this part of the act was postponed. The nations using the open door in colonial shipping were Great Britain, the Netherlands, Belgium, Italy, and Germany before the war; those using preferential policies were France, Canada, Australia, and the British West Indies; those limiting colonial trade to national bottoms in strict mercantilist fashion were the United States, Spain, Portugal (in part), and Japan (in part). In the last group the colonies in question were located close to the mother country and were geographically in the same economic system, excepting the United States, which extended the system to distant outlying possessions.

LAND TRANSPORTATION

The project of Pan-American railroad connections by which rail service would be available from Canada to Argentina and Chile was considered in Pan-American conferences in 1919 and after. Many links in such a system were built, but the expense of building and operation was a formidable objection in view of the development of water and air service. The rapid progress of automobile transportation suggested also a rival mode of land service. The United States was interested in motor highways at home, and this interest was extended to the southward. Coolidge discussed the question in his fifth annual message of December 6, 1927. He said that Canadian and United States connections were already made; that in regard to the countries south of the Rio Grande the United States had supplied advisers for naval and military purposes, but it was even more important to assist them, at their request, with engineering advisers to assist in the construction of roads and bridges. He recommended that "private interests should look with favor on all reasonable loans sought by these countries to open such main lines of travel," and since a Pan-American highway congress was to convene in Rio de Janeiro in July, 1928, Congress should provide for sending delegates. At a conference of the American Road Builders Association at Cleveland in January, 1928, a possible trunk highway was outlined from Montreal, Canada, through Detroit to Laredo, Texas, thence to Mexico City and southward to Valparaiso, Chile. It was stated that the links in such a system would be completed from Montreal to Guatemala in time to be open to summer tourists in 1929.

AIR TRANSPORTATION

The problems of aviation as a foreign policy of the United States were very different from those of European countries. In Europe the boundaries separating the great powers were imaginary lines, whereas the eastern boundary of the United States was the Atlantic and its western boundary the Pacific. Until the air carrier conquered these great bodies of water in a practical manner, air policy with respect to the great centers of population and business of Europe and Asia was of small importance. The spanning of the Atlantic by Lindbergh and Byrd in airplanes in 1927 and by Eckener in a dirigible in 1928 showed that the day of transatlantic service was closer than was generally realized.

The case of the Western Hemisphere was different. In his annual message of December 6, 1927, Coolidge said that it was understood that the sister countries would be willing to coöperate in the development of aviation:

The Post Office Department should be granted power to make liberal long-term contracts for carrying our mail, and authority should be given to the army and the navy to detail aviators and planes to coöperate with private enterprise in establishing such mail service with the consent of the countries concerned. A committee of the cabinet later will present a report on the subject.

It is possible that French interest in South American aviation was a factor in hastening American policy. A long-discussed French air-mail line was put in operation from Paris by way of Senegal, Africa, to Brazil and Argentina on February 29, 1928. During January and February, 1928, Lindbergh made a good-will flight in which he circled the Caribbean area from Mexico around to Cuba. This definitely blazed the way for future developments. It was reported in January, 1928, that negotiations were under way with Mexico, and by March 8 Congress had passed a bill authorizing ten-year air-mail contracts for transportation to foreign countries and to possessions of the United States.

Foreign air-mail service was inaugurated on October 1, 1928. Two lines were put into operation: one from Albany to Montreal, Canada, and the other from Laredo, Texas, to Mexico City. These lines connected with the internal-airways system. The postal rates were 20 cents an ounce. On January 28, 1929, a reduction was announced to 5 cents for the first ounce and 10 cents for each additional ounce. Plans for additional lines were rapidly formulated. On December 4, 1928, the Pan-American Airways, Incorporated, announced three lines. The first would begin operations between Miami, Florida, and Nassau, Bahama Islands, on January 2, 1929, and would carry mail and passengers. The second would begin on January 9 and would operate between Miami and the Dominican Republic by way of Havana. This would connect with another line to Trinidad. The third was from Miami to Cristobal (Panama Canal Zone) by way of Havana, Honduras, Nicaragua, and Costa Rica. Eventually it would be extended down the west coast of South America to Santiago, Chile. This would reduce the time of the trip from Santiago to New York from three weeks to five days. Lindbergh piloted the first plane on this route from Miami to the Panama Canal Zone, leaving February 4. This accomplished what Coolidge planned in his sixth annual message of December 4, 1928, when he said, "This will give us a circle around the Caribbean under our own control."

Because of its military significance aviation was sponsored by governments directly or indirectly. The French gave the largest direct subsidies. The British subsidies began in 1921. The United States did not give direct subsidies. The Air Commerce Act of May 20, 1926, outlined in Sections 6 and 7 the first statement of general air policy as it affected service with foreign nations. The United States asserted exclusive sovereignty over air space above the land and territorial waters of the United States, including the Canal Zone. Foreign military aircraft were excluded from American air space, including the Canal Zone, except on permission of the Secretary of State. Other aircraft were forbidden to navigate in the United States except on authorization of the Secretary of Commerce, and the secretary was permitted to grant privilege of navigation to the aircraft of countries which granted similar privileges to United States aircraft. Foreign aircraft were prohibited from engaging in interstate or intrastate commerce. Existing laws relating to foreign commerce were expressly applied to air commerce, except such navigation and shipping laws as are not applicable to aircraft. The Secretary of the Treasury was authorized to designate ports of entry and to provide customs and public-health administration, regulation of entry, and clearance of ships. The Secretary of Labor was directed to designate ports of entry for aliens carried in foreign air commerce and provide the necessary administration. The development of the air mail and passenger service made it necessary to name seven airports of entry in February, 1929.

ELECTRICAL COMMUNICATIONS

Cables

Communications were of vital importance both from the standpoint of trade promotion and of military policy. During the war the British controlled most of the world's cables. In 1917, according to the New York *Nation*, the British War Trade Intelligence Department made a twenty-eight-page report on German interests in the American metal trade. It contained a full analysis of the foreign-trade relations of certain American metal companies gleaned from intercepted messages. Similar control by France and Japan over cable messages was charged. To what extent this policy was followed after the war is uncertain; but the war demonstrated that these governments had the means of acquiring and using such information. The laying of American-owned and American-controlled cables was held to be as vital to American interests — military, commercial, and news — as a merchant marine. Capital did not seek this form of investment to any great extent, however, because of its precarious nature. The Allied appropriation of cables during the war had set bad precedents and created a suspicion which post-war assurances could not allay. Of the world's cables in 1923 the British owned 136,000 miles and the Americans 73,500 miles out of a total of 318,158 miles. Only one Atlantic cable was laid after 1910. This was owned by the Western Union. Foreign cables received government subsidies; and the British were building an interimperial system with which to bind the empire together more closely. The chief problems to be solved were secrecy of messages, rebates, preferential service, monopoly of materials (gutta-percha), and monopoly of landing rights. The cable-landing policy of the United States was outlined for the new era in an act approved May 24, 1921. A license, issued by the president, was required for any cable connecting the United States or its possessions directly or indirectly with a foreign country. Such a license could be withheld or revoked in order to enable the president to secure landing rights in foreign countries, to maintain the rights or interests of the United States or its citizens abroad, or to promote the security of the United States. The terms of the license should insure just and reasonable rates and service, should not grant exclusive rights, and should not limit the jurisdiction of the Interstate Commerce Commission.

Radio

At the close of the war the cable service of the world was disrupted just at the time when there was an abnormal amount of service required. The cable companies were far behind in their business in Europe and in transatlantic and transpacific service. By a joint resolution approved June 5, 1920, naval radio stations were opened to the public for transmission of press reports and private messages. Rates were not to be less than private stations and were subject to review by the Interstate Commerce Commission. This privilege was to be terminated in two years, or sooner if private service became adequate. Subsequently the privilege, with certain modifications, was extended from time to time until June 30, 1927.

The only legislation affecting the radio as a national foreign policy was the act of February 23, 1927. Licenses for commercial use between the United States and foreign countries were made subject to the license rules found in Section 2 of the cable act of May 24, 1921. The control of all radio stations was limited to United States citizens and corporations in which not more than 20 per cent of the voting power was foreign.

The major interest in the external radio communications of the United States lies in the history of the Radio Corporation of America. This organization had a monopoly in external commercial point-to-point business, except for the allied United Fruit Company's low-power stations in the Caribbean. In the transatlantic service traffic agreements were in operation with European systems for relaying and delivering messages. In the United States agreements were in effect with the Western Union for delivering messages but not for receiving them, because such agreements would compete with its cable facilities. The Postal Telegraph handled radiograms both ways. In 1923 radio service forced a reduction in cable rates from 25 to 20 cents, which was the radio rate. In 1924 the Radio Corporation handled 30 per cent of Atlantic traffic; in 1927 it handled only 20 per cent.

In the South American field the Radio Corporation and Marconi interests worked out a joint project in 1920 which gave American interests control. The French and German stations invaded the field in 1921 and were admitted into the combination at a conference held in Paris on October 14, 1921. The agreement provided for a board of trustees of nine members, and to this board the four companies assigned all concessions for communications between South America and external points until 1945. The right to use patents was exchanged, but not the right to manufacture and sell under them. The board of trustees was made up of two members appointed by each party; a ninth member (an American not connected with the Radio Corporation but nominated by them) was designated as chairman. The chairman, when appealed to by the minority, was granted a veto power on any action taken by a majority if in his judgment an injustice would be done to the minority interest. Later Central America and the Caribbean (except European possessions) were included in the agreement. For a time a joint selling agency was established to distribute apparatus, but it was abandoned, and each of the four companies competed in that field. The South American Radio Corporation, controlled by the Radio Corporation of America, has developed internal communication in South America.

In China the British, the Americans, the Danish, and the Japanese held concessions, and the Radio Corporation of America suggested a trustee agreement similar to that in South America; but the radio question in regard to the Pacific was avoided at the Washington Conference. In 1921 the Federal Telegraph Company of California contracted with the Chinese government for five high-power stations to be built within ten years in conjunction with the Chinese government. The Radio Corporation of America was asked by the Federal Telegraph Company to assist. The Federal Telegraph Company of Delaware was created in 1922 to take over the contract. Transpacific communications were in the hands of the Radio Corporation of America, which took over the Marconi stations and the Federal Telegraph Company, which was allied with it. In 1924 the Radio Corporation was credited with 50 per cent of the transpacific traffic, and in 1927 with 60 per cent. Cables carried the remainder.

CHAPTER XXVII

MILITARY POLICY

THE opposition to militarism reached its highest point in the United States before the World War. Like the progressive movement in politics, it clearly dominated the country. The World War brought about a reversal of sentiment. After the war militarism was stronger than ever before in the history of the Republic. Such was the outcome, for the time being at least, of the war to end war. Opposition to war was found among so-called radicals, such as socialists, or among some college groups or in some religious groups. Such groups were suppressed in some places by so-called patriotic organizations. When the Federal Council of Churches made a recommendation against the Reserve Officers' Training Corps in schools and colleges in June, 1926, it aroused serious criticism and protests that the recommendation was made without authority. At least six state universities in the Middle West figured conspicuously in the newspapers, because it was charged that opponents of war were refused opportunities to speak or because propaganda in opposition to military training in educational institutions was suppressed.

The extreme militarist propaganda was conspicuous in patriotic organizations, in organizations for national defense, and among many army and navy officers. The administration was consistently moderate in plans for defense, and on the whole was supported by public opinion. But what was the nature of even the moderate program in comparison with the prewar program? One study of the situation held that between 1912 and 1927 there was an increase of 400 per cent in the number of men under military training in the United States.

Army Policy

The basic legislation which furnishes the point of departure for a study of post-war military policy is the National Defense Act of June 3, 1916. The army of the United States was to consist of the regular army, the volunteer army, the officers' reserve corps, the enlisted reserve corps, and the National Guard when in the service of the United States. The maximum enlisted force was fixed at 175,000 men. Increases in the commissioned and enlisted personnel were to be made in five annual installments, provided that in an emergency the entire force might be raised immediately. Enlistments in the regular army were fixed at seven years — three in active service and four in reserve service. An officers' reserve corps was provided, the commissions running five years. Reserve officers' training corps were created to be established in educational institutions. An enlisted reserve corps was to consist of reservists in noncombatant services. The militia was composed of all male citizens and declarants between the ages of eighteen and forty-five and was of three classes: the National Guard, naval militia, and unorganized militia. Enlistments in the National Guard were for six years — three in active service and three in reserve service. In 1915 the force was estimated at 125,000, which was to be increased in five years to a total of 425,000.

A board on the mobilization of industries essential to military preparedness was created, and arms and munition plants and plants capable of conversion were to be listed. Contracts were to be made with private manufacturers when necessary; but if they refused, their plants could be seized and operated by the ordnance department. A board was also authorized to investigate and report on the question of government manufacture of arms. The Secretary of War was to prepare gauges, dies, jigs, and so forth necessary for the manufacture of arms, together with specifications and drawings, so that arms, ammunition, and special equipment necessary to arm the land forces of the United States could at once be made either by the government or by private manufacturers. The president was authorized to investigate the question of nitrate supply and to determine the best means of production for military purposes and fertilizers. He was also authorized to designate hydroelectric sites for government use and to construct and operate plants.

The act of 1916, by far the most comprehensive defense act ever passed by Congress as a matter of permanent policy, could not have been enacted but for the war in Europe. With the entrance of the United States into the conflict, emergency legislation of temporary character was enacted; but some of these laws left their influence on permanent policy. The Selective-Service Act, commonly referred to as the draft law, was passed May 18, 1917. The Council of National Defense was provided for in the Army Appropriation Act of March 29, 1916, and from this grew the war-time institution, the War Industries Board, reorganized by an act of March 4, 1918. The World War demonstrated fully that modern warfare was not conducted by means of battles between armies, but by a mobilization of the whole of the resources of the belligerent nations which were thrown into the conflict. The measures indicated above provided the machinery for the mobilization and coördination of national resources (both man power and material) in war time, and as a result the principle was carried over into post-war and peace-time programs for national defense.

The Wadsworth compulsory-training bill was made an issue during the winter of 1919–1920. As the campaign approached, the attitude of the political parties became a matter of concern. The Democratic position was defined in February, 1920. The prevailing opinion seemed to be that the party should make a decisive statement against compulsory training in time of peace. Wilson interposed with a letter addressed to Secretary Baker (February 7, 1920) in which he advised against a sweeping statement on the subject because the future of international relations was too uncertain. The House caucus, by a vote of 106 to 17, condemned the passage of a universal compulsory-training bill by the existing Congress. As the political situation developed, public opinion was such that the compulsory-training question was not made an issue. Congress did succeed, however, in carrying through an act (approved June 4, 1920) for reorganizing the general army.

The new act amended the National Defense Act of 1916 and added some new material. The United States army was to consist of the regular army, the National Guard while in the service of the United States, the organized reserves, the officers' reserve corps, and the enlisted reserve corps. Two new branches of the service were provided: the air service and the chemical-warfare service. The maximum enlisted strength was fixed at 280,000 men. The general-staff corps was to consist of the chief of staff, the general staff of the War Department, and the general staff with troops. The duties of the general staff of the War Department included the preparation of plans for national defense and the use of military forces, the mobilization of the "manhood of the nation and its material resources in an emergency," and an investigation and report on the preparation and efficiency of the army. The Assistant Secretary of War was charged with the supervision and procurement of military supplies and the assurance of adequate provisions for the mobilization of material and industrial organizations essential to war-time needs. The policy was clearly stated that supplies should be manufactured at government arsenals and factories so far as they could be produced economically. A war council was created to consider policies; it consisted of the Secretary of War, the assistant secretary, the general of the army, and the chief of staff. The reserve officers' training corps in educational institutions were continued.

The drafting of industry for war purposes presented one of the most difficult of military problems. It was customary from time immemorial for men to be called upon for military service; but the drafting of property was a different question. The criticism of opponents of war, as well as the bitter hostility aroused by war profiteering and war fortunes, forced the issue into the foreground. The Defense Act called for the mobilization of industry, but it did not provide for drafting; it was assumed that in the event of war men would be drafted as a matter of course. Harding met the issue in his inaugural address (March 4, 1921) by a declaration for drafting all resources of the nation, human and material, and he restated this position in his second and last annual message of December 8, 1922. Coolidge, in his third annual message of December 8, 1925, again revived the question, and on the occasion of the dedication of the Kansas City war memorial on Armistice Day (1926) he gave special emphasis to the problem. During this period, however, the policy was not carried beyond a mere public indorsement of the principle. The Capper conscription bill in Congress in 1926 did not make much headway. Senator Reed of Missouri issued a statement (November 13, 1926) commenting on the President's Armistice Day address. He declared that such conscription would abrogate the right of life, liberty, and property guaranteed under the Constitution. "The astonishing thing," he said, "is that a president should so far forget the principles underlying our form of government." There were few, however, who took the matter so seriously. The policy was received, for the most part, with a vague general approval or with silence. The *New Leader* (Socialist) said: "Senator Reed throws a fit without justification. Business will not be paralyzed. It will thrive and wax fat as it did in the last war."

Plans for the mobilization of industry, not for conscription, were worked out in detail. On March 2, 1925, for instance, a conference of some four hundred railroad men was called in Washington, where the plan of the War Department for coördinating transportation for national defense was presented and discussed. In November of the same year Secretary Davis summarized the status of these plans for national defense as follows:

We are now prepared to equip any military force up to four million men more rapidly, completely, and economically than a new army of that size has ever been equipped before. That is because we have a systematic plan for the mobilization of industry in case of war.

It is the first time in our history that we have had such a plan, or a plan for the mobilization of man power which is worthy of the name. Consequently the country today is in a better state of preparedness for national defense than ever before in its history in time of peace. This condition will continue as long as we maintain our war reserves of ready equipment — which are now endangered — and replace experienced veterans of the World War with younger men and properly trained leaders.

A year later (November 12, 1926) Colonel H. B. Ferguson of the War Department stated before the War Industries Board Association that "if this nation again were called into war the industries would be put on a war-time basis within four months. The last time it took fourteen months. We learned our lesson then, and since 1918 we have devoted our efforts to preparing these plants for conversion."

In the years following the war the standing army was reduced until 1923. In his annual message of December 6, 1923, Coolidge warned that further reduction in the army and navy should cease. This marks a turning point in the preparedness program. The national debt was being reduced to a point where funds could in the future be more easily available for current military needs. By 1926 the upward turn began. The replacement of ammunition reserves and the inauguration of a new housing program were emphasized in 1925–1926; but Coolidge was very cautious about expansion. In his annual message of 1926 he pointed out that the regular army stood at about 115,000 and, with the land and sea reserves, totaled about 610,000 men. It was the greatest force for defense ever maintained by the

United States in time of peace. He still emphasized the war debt as the weakest point in national defense. The budget estimates in December, 1926, were designed to provide for a standing army of 115,000 men, but the House Appropriation Committee demanded the maintenance of the previous level of 118,500. The Secretary of War then presented (January 18, 1927) a ten-year program of army expansion from 118,500 men to 165,000 men, but for reasons of economy he did not recommend the immediate inauguration of the program. In December, 1927, Secretary Davis presented another program outlining what he considered a grave situation regarding reserve munitions and the means of expansion in case of war. Davis asked for a board of nine men to evolve a systematic program for placing the land forces in a state of preparedness. The survey on which the report was based was prepared by Assistant Secretary MacNider, who stated that ammunition on hand would not last an army of one million men one hour and that reserve arms were provided for only two of the six field armies called for by army-mobilization plans. He also emphasized artillery and tank shortages. The National Defense Act of 1916 directed the preparation of jigs, dies, gauges, and other tools necessary for the production of arms and ammunition in time of war, which could be furnished to manufacturers. In this way the private manufacturer could most quickly convert his plant to the production of government munitions. The Army Reorganization Act of 1920 emphasized the policy of government manufacture of munitions. MacNider's new plan of December, 1927, for matériel reserve proposed a change in policy. It was based on a system of "educational orders" for munitions to be placed with a large number of private manufacturers at regular intervals. The purpose in view was to make it possible for each manufacturer to build up and maintain a nucleus of trained employees which could be made the basis of war expansion. The government, as provided in the act of 1916, would provide the jigs, dies, gauges, etc. to such private manufacturers as were included in the new "educational orders" plan.

The annual report of the chief of staff, made public November 27, 1928, announced a new plan for the mobilization of man power. A possible total force of three and a half million men was contemplated, to be divided into six field armies. The nation was divided into nine corps areas. In each area the corps commander of the area would be responsible for mobilization of men called for at any particular time.

An attempt was made to establish a National Defense Day on which all the forces of the country should be mobilized each year as a defense test. There were some protests, but the first Defense Day was celebrated September 12, 1924. The next year military authorities planned to choose November 11, Armistice Day, as the permanent annual defense day. It was reported that Coolidge objected, and July 4 was chosen instead. After 1925 the policy was not continued.

NAVAL POLICY

In naval policy the United States resumed work on the three-year program which had been suspended or retarded during the war. Potentially American naval power was the greatest in the world. In the Washington Conference on limitation of armament in 1922 equality was established with the British navy for capital ships and airplane carriers, and a ratio of 5 : 5 : 3 : 1.75 : 1.75 to the navies of Japan, France, and Italy was agreed upon among the powers. Many authorities have minimized this seeming sacrifice of strength in capital ships, on the argument that new branches of the service, the submarine and the airplane, were the decisive elements in future sea power. Light cruisers were also limited in size to ten thousand tons with eight-inch guns. Poison gas was outlawed, and submarine warfare was put under the same regulations as the use of cruisers.

Naval policy went through the same cycle as army policy. Until 1923 steady reductions were made; but in that year Coolidge stood for maintaining the *status quo*, and soon afterwards came the upward turn. The demand for naval building was stronger than for army expansion. In airplane carriers and cruisers the United States was deficient; hence building was continued within the limits set even after the Washington Conference. On December 8, 1924, eight cruisers were authorized. Appropriations were provided for five. In 1927 an issue was made by the big navy group of appropriating money for the remaining three cruisers as well as authorizing ten additional ones. An appropriation of $450,000 was finally accepted, and the bill was signed by Coolidge on March 2, 1927. An appropriation was also made for the elevation of guns on battleships. A similar appropriation had been made earlier, but was not used. In the naval controversy the Republican party was badly divided. Speaker Longworth, a presidential possibility, openly opposed the administration.

The act of December 18, 1924, also authorized the modernization of six battleships. This called for additional protection against submarines, protection of the deck against air attack, and conversion to oil-burning engines. Two ships were to be equipped with new fire-control systems. By an act of May 27, 1926, further alterations in battleships were authorized.

During the winter of 1926–1927 the preparatory negotiations for a general disarmament conference were being held in Geneva, and during the midsummer the three-power naval conference (United States, Great Britain, and Japan) was held at the same place. The failure of the conference was of unusual importance in naval history. The President had used the possibility of further limitations of armament as a means of opposing the big navy agitation. The conference was held, and failed. It seemed to be the signal for dominance of the big navy group. Between September, 1927, and January, 1928, the program of the Navy Department was formulated and presented: a twenty-year building program which would not fall far short of $3,000,000,000. Rumors of this program were mentioned in the press as early as September 3, but the plans were not announced by Secretary Wilbur to the House Committee until January 12, 1928. For immediate prosecution, however, the Secretary presented (January 11, 1928) a $750,000,000 building program to be carried out in about five years, although no definite time limit was set. This called for twenty-five cruisers in addition to the eighteen built and building, or a total of forty-three. The President was reported to be solidly behind the new program. An increase in navy personnel had already been asked for (December 10) which would permit an increase of enlisted men from 82,932 at that time in service to the full strength previously planned of 86,000 men.

In his sixth annual message of December 4, 1928, Coolidge said: "The cost of national defense is stupendous. It has increased $118,000,000 in the past four years. The estimated expenditure for 1930 is $668,000,000." New cruisers, however, should be built to replace old ones. "We have ten comparatively new vessels, twenty-two that are old, and eight to be built." "The bill before the Senate, with the elimination of the time clause, should be passed." The bill referred to provided for fifteen 10,000-ton cruisers to be armed with 8-inch guns at an estimated cost of $274,000,000. Five ships were to be begun each of the three fiscal years 1929, 1930, and 1931. Another aircraft carrier was to be begun before 1931. Congress refused to eliminate the time limit for the ships, and Coolidge signed the bill on February 13, 1929. A rider was attached to the bill by Borah's calling for an international agreement establishing the rights of neutrals at sea in time of war. An appropriation bill carrying an item of $12,000,000 toward the first five cruisers was passed and signed by the President on March 2.

The close relation between the navy and the merchant marine should not be overlooked. The Merchant Marine Act, it will be remembered, stated that one purpose of its promotion was national defense. Ships would serve as troop transports and as carriers of supplies for military operations. Sailors trained in merchant shipping were important as naval reserves. The merchant marine reserve was authorized by law, but money was not provided. Nevertheless orders were issued August 5, 1927, for putting the new scheme into operation. This serves again to illustrate, what has often been revealed, that there is no clear line of demarcation between private business and public military establishments.

The celebration of Navy Day was inaugurated October 27, 1921. It was designed to keep alive an active interest in the support of naval armament. The choice of the particular day served also another purpose. It was the anniversary of the birth of Theodore Roosevelt and was selected by his admirers among naval propagandists as a means of paying tribute to the vigorous assistance he had given to the building of the greater United States navy.

MILITARY AIR POLICY

The status of aviation was a matter of much doubt and of bitter controversy among military authorities. Extensive experiments were carried out to try to determine the effectiveness of air warfare against battleships. The results were inconclusive. To such men as Colonel Mitchell they were decisive in proving the superiority of aircraft. One idea he stood for was the reorganization of all air units into a new department. After investigation Coolidge decided against any radical changes and so reported in his annual message for 1925. Legislation for 1926 provided that army and navy air units were to be strengthened, and an assistant secretary for air service was provided in each department. A five-year program of naval air building was adopted on June 24, 1926, authorizing an expenditure of $85,000,000 for 1614 planes and 333 planes annually thereafter in order to maintain an effective total of 1000 planes in service after 1932. Two dirigibles were authorized. These were to be larger than the ill-fated *Shenandoah*, which was wrecked in 1925. Although Coolidge opposed the appropriation for the dirigibles, the bill was passed along with the cruiser appropriations of March 2, 1927. In his annual report, presented December 10, 1927, Secretary Wilbur reported that on July 1, 1926, there had been on hand 351 planes, and that the total on July 1, 1928, would be 718 planes.

The Army Air Act (July 2, 1926) authorized the equipment and maintenance of 1800 serviceable planes and replacement at not to exceed 400 planes per year. For further encouragement of military air preparedness the "air cabinet," composed of four officials (the Postmaster-General, the Assistant Secretary of War, the Assistant Secretary of the Navy, and the Assistant Secretary of Commerce), was reported on July 4, 1927, to be developing a broad commercial air policy which had as a supplementary purpose military defense. One immediate objective was the creation of a corps of at least 10,000 trained commercial fliers. Such a body of trained men would form the nucleus around which to build a great flying corps with the least possible delay in case of war. This again emphasizes the difficulty of separating what may on the surface appear purely domestic peace policies from the international armament problem.

Military Supplies

The increased importance of oil for naval use, motor transports, and air service led to an aggressive policy of international competition for oil reserves throughout the world and, at home, to the setting aside of naval oil reserves. The exploitation of these reserves and the plans for oil storage in Hawaii gave occasion for the Fall-Doheny-Sinclair oil scandals of 1922.

The manufacture of munitions gave rise to the special protection of chemicals and dyestuffs in the Emergency

Revenue Act of 1916. After the war both Wilson and Harding urgently recommended the fostering of these industries. The Muscle Shoals power project was also associated with the production of munitions through the manufacture of nitrates for explosives in war and for fertilizers in time of peace.

Helium is a noninflammable gas used in balloons and dirigible airships, and was of special importance in military service. The known world supply was very small, and for that reason military policy dictated a positive policy respecting its production. The General Leasing Act of 1920 provided that the government might extract helium from all gas taken from the public reserves. An act of March 3, 1925, authorized the government "to acquire land or interest in land by purchase, lease, or condemnation, where necessary, when helium could not be purchased from private parties at less cost, to explore for, procure, or conserve helium-bearing gas; to drill or otherwise test such lands; and to construct plants, pipe lines, facilities, and accessories for the production, storage, and purification of helium. . . ." The operations of the government were to be carried out by the Bureau of Mines. It was provided further "that any surplus helium produced might, until needed for government use, be leased to American citizens or American corporations under regulations approved by the president." No export of helium was permitted except upon application to the Secretary of the Interior approved by the president on joint recommendation of the war, navy, and interior secretaries.

Traffic in Arms

The question of private manufacture and commerce in arms and ammunition was an important phase of the international armament problem. So long as private business of this character was permitted, there must be some control of such commerce. For many years the president had exercised, under authority granted by Congress, the power of regulating traffic in arms in certain emergencies. The last enactment on the subject was an act of January 31, 1922. It provided that in case of domestic violence in any American country or in any country where the United States exercised extraterritorial jurisdiction, the president might prohibit export of arms and munitions of war when such violence was found to be promoted by arms and munitions from the United States.

CONCLUSION

The first and primary purpose of a military establishment was national defense. This was not its sole use, however. It was used in promoting domestic engineering enterprises of a public nature. It was also used by an imperial power, such as the United States, in colonial administration or in governing weak and backward peoples. To strengthen the military power of neighboring states, an act of 1921 authorized the president to detail officers of the United States navy to assist the governments of the republics of South America in naval matters. By an act of May 19, 1926, this power was expanded to include details of officers and enlisted men of either the army or the navy to assist such states. Furthermore, on different occasions in relations with Mexico and Nicaragua the United States government sold arms and munitions in order to strengthen the recognized governments in maintaining order. On still other occasions troops were landed to protect United States citizens and interests abroad. "National defense" was an elastic term which had more than a military significance in the minds of public men. It is evident that Coolidge, in his third annual message of December 8, 1925, had definitely in mind these broader uses of the military establishment because at that time he said of the army and the navy, "they are the instruments by which we undertake to promote good will and support stability among all peoples."

CHAPTER XXVIII

POLITICAL POLICIES: THE PACIFIC

WHEN one refers to political policies of government the phrase is customarily understood to be limited literally to the generally accepted concept of the term "political." It should be obvious to the reader that the instrumentalities of political action are far wider in scope and character than this narrow interpretation of the term: they embrace the economic and military policies which have been outlined — sometimes rather indirectly and sometimes very directly. Trade-promotion agencies, commercial treaties, tariff, colonies, export and import organizations, banking, loans, transportation and communication, the army and navy, naval bases, all fit somewhere and somehow into the intricate fabric of foreign political relations. The Coolidge doctrine respecting the protection of the interests of the United States was clearly enunciated in an address before the United Press Association in New York on April 25, 1927. It was asserted that "the person and property of a citizen are a part of the general domain of the nation, even when abroad."

PACIFIC-AREA POLICIES

The origins of the broader aspects of United States policies in the Pacific date from the middle of the nineteenth century. The primary policies were equal economic opportunities for all Western powers in the Far East, and the territorial integrity and the administrative integrity of the Far Eastern powers. On these points there was little essential variation. There was much difference of both opinion and practice, however, in regard to the methods for the realization of these policies. One extreme in method was full coöperation with the Western powers in the Far East. This is illustrated by Seward's course of action. The opposite extreme was independent action on the part of the United States regardless of what other powers were doing or even in opposition to them. This point of view is illustrated by Cleveland's administration. Between these two extremes were all degrees of variation; but the more usual method after 1899 was a form of coördinated action in which the powers might consult as to common aims and principles but each retain independence of action in determining its own course within the limits more or less fixed by common agreement. In the beginning the principles of the open door and integrity were applied generally to all parts of the Far East; but with the imperialistic encroachments of Western powers in the Pacific, and the rise of Japan from a position of helplessness to that of a world power, the scope of their application came to be limited to China. Japan, on the other hand, came to be included with the group of Western powers in the pledge to maintain the principles of the open door and the integrity of China. At the same time Japan was developing for eastern Asia a body of policies of her own by which she was assuming approximately the same relationship to that area as the United States had assumed for the Western Hemisphere under the Monroe Doctrine. How far Japanese policy would go and to what extent the Western powers should combine to restrain her ambitions and maintain their historic position were questions which were at the foundation of the whole problem of the Pacific after the World War.

Hughes summarized United States policies in the Pacific after the World War in an address on November 30, 1923. There he said: "In relation to the Pacific Ocean and the Far East we have developed the policies of (1) the open door, (2) the maintenance of the integrity of China, (3) coöperation with other powers in the declaration of common principles, (4) coöperation with other powers by conference and consultation in the interests of peace, (5) limitation of naval armament, (6) the limitation of fortification and naval bases." Except for the fifth and sixth points there was nothing new in this policy but the method of meeting the other interested powers in a general conference, the Washington Conference, and the creation of some permanent machinery of coöperation. The idea of a general conference was attempted by certain European powers at least as early as 1899, but the United States objected. The Root-Takahira agreement of November 30, 1908, provided for consultation on Pacific questions. Similar agreements were made by Japan with some other powers. Thus the Washington Conference is seen as the logical outcome of a quarter-century of development.

The machinery set up by the Washington Conference was one of the most unusual aspects of its work from the standpoint of United States policies. Five commissions were provided: first, a board of reference for Far Eastern questions to decide whether specific doubtful acts or cases accord with the open-door principle; secondly, an international tariff-revision commission to adjust the Chinese tariff to an effective 5 per cent level; thirdly, a conference on the tariff and the abolition of the likin charges; fourthly, a commission on extraterritoriality to study the judicial systems of China and make reports; fifthly, a commission to investigate issues raised by the presence of foreign troops in China. In participating in these commissions (the treaties with which these bodies were associated were ratified by the Senate) the United States was doing in the Far East what it declined to do in Europe and other places under the auspices of the League.

UNITED STATES POSSESSIONS

In the Pacific the principal American possessions were Alaska, the Hawaiian Islands, the Samoan Islands, Guam, and the Philippine Islands. With respect to these the economic policy of the United States was to bind them closer

to the empire by economic ties, to include within the coastwise shipping system those not already incorporated, and
to promote the development of their resources. Politically
no very definite general policies were in evidence. Each
possession presented a different problem.

ALASKA

Transportation was one of the great handicaps to development in Alaska. A railroad into the interior was authorized
in 1912. The route was definitely chosen from Seward and
Anchorage to Fairbanks in 1915, and the road was opened to
travel in 1922. The newer industries of the territory — agriculture, reindeer-raising, and mining — were fostered. The
Homestead Act was extended to Alaska in 1903; after the war
it was amended to make its operation more liberal. The
public-land policy of the United States was extended for the
most part to the public domain of Alaska. The subsoil deposits and the forests were reserved for public benefit. An
act of March 4, 1927, provided for the establishment of a
system of grazing live stock on the public lands. The grazing
districts were to be fixed by the Secretary of the Interior.
They might be leased for twenty years or less, subject to the
general principles of policy outlined in the act.

It is hereby declared to be the policy of Congress in promoting the
conservation of the natural resources of Alaska to provide for the
protection and development of forage plants and for the beneficial
utilization thereof for grazing by live stock under such regulations
as may be considered necessary and consistent with the purposes
and provisions of this act. In effectuating this policy the use of
these lands for grazing shall be subordinated (1) to the development
of their mineral resources, (2) to the protection, development, and
utilization of their forests, (3) to the protection, development, and
utilization of such other resources as may be of greater benefit to
the public.

Agricultural experiment stations were established before
the war in different districts to determine the possibilities

of the different sections. In 1923 an agricultural college was opened. A definite reindeer policy was worked out to foster reindeer-raising by the natives in a kind of government partnership. The attempts to open up mining of coal and oil did not produce the results anticipated. Whatever the future economic possibilities might be, it must be admitted that there was little success in these policies. The fur-seal and salmon industries had been under government control for many years. The former was fairly successful, but the latter was the subject of much controversy after the war. Coolidge asked for further legislation in order to save the fisheries from destruction.

The problem of government in Alaska defied satisfactory adjustment—the area was so large, the resident population so small, the geographical diversities so extreme, and the distance from Washington so great. The Taft administration favored a commission similar to that of the Philippines; but in 1912 a territorial form of government was established. It provided local autonomy in certain features of administration; but a great deal of departmental control from Washington in matters of national interest was retained. Coolidge, in his annual message of December, 1925, was dissatisfied with the "very large amount of money . . . being expended for administration." "It appears so far out of proportion to the number of inhabitants and the amount of production as to indicate cause for thorough investigation."

An act of February 10, 1927, provided commissioners for Alaska. Each of the three major departments interested (Interior, Agriculture, and Commerce) was directed to designate an official to represent the department in all business and to reside in Alaska and supervise all employees of the department in the territory. The Secretary of the Interior was directed to investigate and report on the feasibility and propriety of consolidating the police and law-enforcement agencies into a single force.

HAWAII

Hawaii presented little that was unusual in its post-war history. Its government was of the territorial form, and its citizens were citizens of the United States. A point of irritation that remained until 1926 was the privilege of citizens of Oriental origin of traveling freely in the United States; but the administrative rules on this matter were revised. As a naval base Hawaii was conspicuous after the World War. During the early months of the Harding administration active steps were taken to develop Pearl Harbor and San Francisco Harbor. The Pearl Harbor development included the building of storage facilities for naval oil, a project which became involved in the Doheny-Fall oil-lease scandal. The Washington Conference did not include Hawaii in the limitations placed upon Pacific naval bases.

THE PHILIPPINE ISLANDS

In the Philippines centered the most prolonged controversy of all. Since the United States held no other possessions in the Orient and no leased ports on the Asiatic coast, the Philippines stood as the outpost of American power in the Far East. Their political, military, economic, and sentimental significance could not be ignored. For years before the United States occupation the people of the Philippines had looked forward to an independent national existence, and it was the avowed policy of the United States to hold the islands in trust until their people should be ready for self-government; in practical politics, however, the American imperial point of view was balanced against the Philippine ambition.

It was the policy of the Wilson administration to prepare as rapidly as possible for Philippine independence. The Jones act of 1916 provided for a native legislature of two houses, with an American as governor. With the return of the Republicans under Harding during a time of general conservative reaction and exaggerated nationalism, the direction of policy was suddenly reversed. In his last annual message of December 7, 1920, Wilson said:

Allow me to call your attention to the fact that the people of the Philippine Islands have succeeded in maintaining a stable government since the last action of the Congress in their behalf, and have thus fulfilled a condition set by the Congress as precedent to a consideration of granting independence to the Islands. I respectfully submit that this condition precedent having been fulfilled, it is now our liberty and our duty to keep our promise to the people of those Islands by granting them the independence which they so honorably covet.

President Harding on taking office seemed to doubt the judgment of Wilson and his advisers, and determined to send a special commission headed by General Leonard Wood and W. Cameron Forbes, former governor-general (1909–1913), to investigate and report. They arrived in Manila on May 4, 1921. Their report is dated October 8, 1921. The Filipinization policy of the Wilson administration was condemned on most points. In 1913, 72 per cent of the government service was Filipino; by 1921, 96 per cent. The report held that this change was too rapid to maintain efficiency. Before 1913 the service was highly efficient; but the subsequent inefficiency was not so much due to the incompetence of the Filipinos as to the Americans.

This is due in part to bad example, to incompetent direction, to political infection of the services, and, above all, to lack of competent supervision and inspection. This has been brought about by surrendering, or failing to employ, the executive authority of the governor-general, and has resulted in undue interference and tacit usurpation by the political leaders of the general supervision and control of departments and bureaus of the government vested by law in the governor-general. . . . All these defects can and — unless we fail to understand the spirit of the legislature and the leaders — will be corrected in the Islands.

Different branches of administration — education, judiciary, health service, finances, public works, etc. — received severe criticism. The entrance of the government into business — banking, railroads, and coal — was particularly condemned. The conclusion and recommendations were as follows:

We are convinced that it would be a betrayal of the Philippine people, a misfortune to the American people, a distinct step backward in the path of progress, and a discreditable neglect of our national duty were we to withdraw from the Islands and terminate our relationship there without giving the Filipinos the best chance possible to have an orderly and permanent stable government.

1. We recommend that the present general status of the Philippine Islands continue until the people have had time to absorb and thoroughly master the powers already in their hands.

2. We recommend that the responsible representative of the United States, the governor-general, have authority commensurate with the responsibilities of his position. In case of failure to secure the necessary corrective action by the Philippine legislature, we recommend that Congress declare null and void legislation which has been enacted diminishing, limiting or dividing the authority granted the governor-general under . . . the Jones bill.

3. We recommend that in case of a deadlock between the governor-general and the Philippine Senate in the confirmation of appointments, the president of the United States be authorized to make and render the final decision.

4. We recommend that under no circumstances should the American government permit to be established in the Philippine Islands a situation which would leave the United States in a position of responsibility without authority.

This report was clearly partisan and could be evaluated only in the light of the personal and political elements in its origin. The Wilson administration had refused both Roosevelt and Wood army commands in Europe during the war. There had been disagreement on most questions associated with the war period, and the bitterness engendered was most intense. Forbes was the governor who had preceded the Wilson régime, and Wilson's policy of Filipinization was directly contrary to Forbes's policy. It was almost more than could be expected of human frailty for these men to view the situation in any other light. They frankly characterized the Republican régime as constructive and efficient, especially from 1907 to 1913; the Democratic régime was stigmatized, either in so many words or by implication, as destructive and inefficient. There was no attempt to evaluate the degree to which war conditions and post-war deflation, both economic and moral, had affected the public service. A comparison with the bankruptcies, embezzlements, graft, and corruption in the United States during the post-war deflation period would have been of value in placing conditions on a comparable basis.

General Wood took office as governor-general of the Philippines on October 15, 1921. Within two years he had come to an open break with the Philippine legislative leaders, and the deadlock continued until his death in 1927. The situation was so serious that Coolidge decided to send Carmi A. Thompson to make an investigation. Thompson spent the time from July 9 to October 4, 1926, in the Islands. He was a man personally and politically friendly to General Wood. They were both of the same political party. For these reasons the adverse prejudice so conspicuous in the report of 1921 was absent in his; but the report was not altogether favorable to the administration.

Thompson reported that the political and economic aspects of the situation "are inextricably bound together"; that "business in the Islands is practically at a standstill." In his opinion the key to the situation was a solution of the political problem, which had two phases: the independence movement, and the deadlock between the governor-general and the legislature. Immediate Philippine independence, he thought, was impossible because of a lack of financial resources, lack of common language, bitter religious differences, lack of a controlling public opinion, and the need of the United States for the Philippines as a commercial base in the

Far East. He pointed out also that the abandonment of the Islands might complicate the international situation in the Orient, and independence would deprive them of their free markets and would bring economic ruin.

The deadlock between the governor-general and the legislature could not be solved, he thought, by enlargement of the powers of the former by congressional action, as such a course would seem only to aggravate the situation. The responsibility lay with both parties. The military atmosphere was particularly unfortunate. He said:

These officers have excellent military records, but evidently lack training and experience in the duties of civil government and in dealing with legislative bodies and civilian officials. . . . My observations lead me to believe the people would be more contented and less inclined toward unrest under a more purely civil administration. In the past there has been no coördination between the government of the Philippines and that of our other overseas possessions. . . . Besides the principal items now raised, such as rice, tobacco, sugar, copra, and hemp, the Philippines, within a comparatively short time, should be able to supply the United States with a large part of its requirements of rubber, coffee, camphor, pineapples, lumbang, hardwood lumber, and many other tropical commodities. . . . I have the honor to recommend

First, that such steps be taken as may be required to reëstablish coöperation between the executive and legislative branches of the Philippine government.

Second, that the granting of absolute independence to the Philippines be postponed for some time to come, that this matter be considered at some future date when the islands are sufficiently developed to maintain an independent government, and that in the meantime there be granted such further autonomy in the management of internal affairs as conditions may from time to time warrant.

Third, that the United States government establish an independent department for the administration of the Philippine Islands and other overseas territory.

Fourth, that the governor-general be provided with the necessary civil advisers in order to relieve him of the present necessity of selecting such advisers from the United States army.

Fifth, that Mindanao and Sulu should not be separated from the rest of the Islands, but that American control be strengthened in the Moro country.

Sixth, that the Federal Reserve system should be extended to the Philippine Islands.

Seventh, that one or more Federal land banks should be established in the Philippines to provide loans at reasonable interest rates for the farmers, who now pay from 12 to 30 per cent interest.

Eighth, that the United States Department of Agriculture establish a sufficient number of experiment stations in the Philippine Islands to properly develop the agricultural resources of the islands.

Ninth, that the fundamental law governing the Philippines, known as the Jones Act, be not amended or changed at this time.

Tenth, that the Philippine legislature should amend the Philippine land laws (with proper safeguards) so as to bring about such conditions as will attract capital and business experience for the development of the production of rubber, coffee, and other tropical products, some of which are now controlled by monopolies.

Eleventh, that no amendments be made at this time to the Philippine land laws by the American Congress.

Twelfth, that the Philippine government withdraw from private business at the earliest possible date.

The fundamental problems in the Philippines concern the government of the Islands and their future relations with the United States. Upon the proper solution of these problems depends the political, social, and economic welfare of the Filipinos.

Coolidge's annual message of December, 1926, emphasized the desirability of placing the Islands under a civil department. In this particular he indorsed a point of view similar to that of the Thompson report. Some other things he did not approve, but his letter transmitting the report (December 22, 1926) did not state just which these others were. The death of Wood on August 7, 1927, opened the way for a different policy. Henry L. Stimson, former Secretary of War in the Taft cabinet, was appointed governor-general and assumed his duties at Manila on March 1, 1928. The ideas which were emphasized at his inauguration were coöperation with the local leaders and the economic development of the Islands.

The economic relations between the Islands and the United States changed little after 1909, when free trade between the two was established, except for certain limitations on particular articles. The tariff of 1913 established free trade without the limitations, and the tariff of 1922 did not change the policy. By this means the Philippines were made economically dependent to a great degree upon the United States for markets for their products and for such products as they are required to import. About two thirds of their trade after the World War was with the United States. This was an example of the closed door in the East, and became an argument against Philippine independence, since the sudden closing of these markets would disrupt the economic stability of the Islands. Culbertson, a liberal Republican critic, has summarized this situation as follows:

In developing their closed-door policy in the Philippines the American people have maintained an attitude both naïve and uncritical. At the same time that they have urged the open door in China, they have enacted discriminatory legislation in the Philippines. Only occasionally a voice has been raised against the inconsistency of such a position. Genuinely liberal forces have at times even sanctioned it on the grounds of justice to the Filipinos and fairness to America. Our policy, however, appears less broad when compared with that of the French in Indo-China and the Italian in Eretria, or when viewed not from the purely nationalistic standpoint but from that of world policy.

Among the products of the Philippines hemp and copra were of most importance to the United States. Ex-Secretary of Commerce Redfield pointed out in connection with the copra supply that if the Philippines fell into instable hands it would be serious, but if they should fall into hostile hands it would be disastrous. With the possible development of rubber and oil, the economic importance of the Islands would be enhanced immeasurably, and the uncertainty with regard to their eventual independence would almost inevitably be decided in the negative. That Coolidge recognized this situation to a certain extent in respect to rubber was shown in his annual message of December 7, 1922:

No one contemplates any time in the future either under the present or a more independent form of government when we should not assume some responsibility for their defense. For their economic advantage, for the employment of their people, and as a contribution to our power of defense, which could not be carried on without rubber, I believe this industry should be encouraged.

CHINA

At the Washington Conference of 1921–1922 three treaties respecting China were drafted and an important group of resolutions on the subject of China were signed. The nine-power treaty relating to China was signed by the United States, Belgium, the British Empire, China, France, Italy, Japan, the Netherlands, and Portugal. This treaty was put in force on August 5, 1925. The first article sums up the basic principles of the agreement.

The Contracting Powers, other than China, agree:

1. To respect the sovereignty, the independence, and the territorial and administrative integrity of China;

2. To provide the fullest and most unembarrassed opportunity to China to develop and maintain for herself an effective and stable government;

3. To use their influence for the purpose of effectually establishing and maintaining the principle of equal opportunity for the commerce and industry of all nations throughout the territory of China;

4. To refrain from taking advantage of conditions in China in order to seek special rights or privileges which would abridge the rights of subjects or citizens of friendly States, and from countenancing action inimical to the security of such States.

Article VII provided the method of future adjustment:

The Contracting Powers agree that, whenever a situation arises which in the opinion of any one of them involves the application of the stipulations of the present Treaty, and renders desirable discussion of such application, there shall be full and frank communication between the Contracting Powers concerned.

The second treaty was between the same nine powers and dealt with the Chinese customs tariff. It provided that a Tariff Revision Commission should revise the tariff as fixed in 1918 to an effective 5 per cent ad valorem basis, and that regular periodic revisions should be made thereafter. This treaty was put in force August 5, 1925.

The resolutions accompanying the treaties provided a board of reference for Far Eastern questions and a commission on possible relinquishment of extraterritorial rights, indorsed the principle of relinquishment of post offices in China, provided for the adjustment of difficulties respecting armed forces of the powers in China and for the regulation of radio stations in China, indorsed the principle of unification of Chinese railroads under the Chinese government, and provided for the compiling of all commitments with and concerning China.

The third treaty to be considered was not, strictly speaking, a part of the other group, but was negotiated as a result of the conference and is therefore connected with it. The treaty between China and Japan respecting Shantung provided that Japan should restore to China the German-leased territory of Kiaochow within six months. All Japanese troops were to be withdrawn. This agreement was in accordance with the representations made to Wilson at the conference at Paris in 1919, when the Peace Conference assigned the German rights to Japan.

The future of China had not for many years looked so bright as in 1922. The great question of the future lay with China rather than with the powers. Could China meet her obligations and carry out her responsibilities? Internal strife soon removed all semblance of a central government in China capable of dealing in a responsible fashion with the outside world. The questions which occupied foreign governments were how to protect their rights in China and how best to contribute to the stability and unification of China. The Chinese Nationalist movement, whose power centered in southern China, was determined to terminate the unequal treaties and foreign interference and control. The campaign against foreigners created an acute situation during 1926. The British concession at Hankow was overrun and the international settlement at Shanghai was threatened. The powers, including the United States, sent troops. On March 24, 1927, occurred attacks upon foreigners in Nanking. They gathered for defense on Socony Hill. British and American gunboats opened fire to protect their escape.

What was the basis of American interest in China, and why should the United States have taken an active part in Chinese affairs? In actual numbers there were relatively few Americans there, and most of these were missionaries. American investments were relatively small, and the majority were in mission property. United States trade with China was relatively small compared with that of other powers interested there. It was also relatively small compared with the total of United States foreign trade. Statistics did not tell the story. Ever since the first ships went out to China after the American Revolution, China has had a romantic hold upon the American mind. At the time of the Spanish War the trade with China was small; but the future possibilities of that vast empire both as a source of raw materials and as a market for manufactures were the determining factors. This was one of the primary reasons for annexing the Philippines — to establish an adequate commercial base in the Orient. At the time of the World War the situation was much the same. Foreign banking houses were established in order to finance trade. The China Trade Act was passed by Congress to promote trade. These anticipations of future commerce, and the idealistic conceptions clustering around the missionary idea, were intangible factors, but possibly for that reason more powerful factors than the concrete realities.

In spite of internal disorder American business had prospered in China after the World War, and business men were in several cases aggressive in demanding government protection. The American Chamber of Commerce in Shanghai was particularly active. In June, 1923, a request was made to the Department of State for joint intervention with Great Britain. Again, after the Nanking incident a very positive appeal was addressed to the department for united action of the powers to restore order, property, and responsible government.

After the Washington Conference the powers interested in China undertook to fulfill their pledges. The treaties went into effect on August 6, 1925. Negotiations were begun, but by 1927 the conclusion of any definite arrangements was impossible because of the dissolution of the Chinese government. On January 27, 1927, Secretary of State Kellogg issued a statement reviewing what had been done and restating United States policy for the future. The closing paragraphs of his statement were as follows:

The government of the United States was ready then and is ready now to continue the negotiations on the entire subject of the tariff and extraterritoriality or to take up negotiations on behalf of the United States alone. The only question is with whom it shall negotiate. As I have said heretofore, if China can agree upon the appointment of delegates representing the authorities or the people of the country, we are prepared to negotiate such a treaty. However, existing treaties which were ratified by the Senate of the United States cannot be abrogated by the president but must be superseded by new treaties negotiated with somebody representing China and subsequently ratified by the Senate of the United States.

The government of the United States has watched with sympathetic interest the nationalistic awakening of China and welcomes every advance made by the Chinese people toward reorganizing their system of government.

During the difficult years since the establishment of the new régime in 1912, the government of the United States has endeavored in every way to maintain an attitude of the most careful and strict neutrality as among the several factions that have disputed with one another for control in China. The government of the United States expects, however, that the people of China and their leaders will recognize the right of American citizens in China to protection for life and property during the period of conflict for which they are not responsible. In the event that the Chinese authorities are unable to afford such protection, it is of course the fundamental duty of the United States to protect the lives and property of its citizens. It is with the possible necessity for this in view that American naval forces are now in Chinese waters. This government wishes to deal with China in a most liberal spirit. It holds no concessions in China and has never manifested any imperialistic attitude toward that country. It desires, however, that its citizens be given equal opportunity with the citizens of the other powers to reside in China and to pursue their legitimate occupations without special privileges, monopolies, or spheres of special interest or influence.

The Kellogg note indicated a willingness to depart from the policy of coöperation with the other powers, and in the diplomacy of 1928 the United States did so. It must be noted, however, that the objectives of this independent diplomacy were closely coördinated with the principles already enunciated in the preceding joint negotiations. The British and Japanese stood so firmly on the Nanking settlements, the abrogation of treaties, and the autonomous tariff that there seemed to be little hope of securing immediate results from joint negotiations. The settlement of the Nanking incident, so far as it affected the United States, was secured March 30, 1928, by an exchange of notes. The Nationalist government assumed responsibility even though the outbreak had been incited by the communists, expressed profound regret, and agreed to the fixing of damages to persons and property by a mixed commission. The Chinese government suggested negotiations for treaty revisions, but the matter was delayed. The international situation was again complicated by a conflict between the Japanese and Chinese at Tsinan, in Shantung, between May 4 and May 11, which added another difficulty to Chino-Japanese harmony.

The Nationalist government in June took over Peking (now called Peiping (bay′ping)), and established the permanent capital of the near-united China at Nanking. A Chinese note of July 11 requested negotiations with the United States for new treaties. Secretary Kellogg's note in answer (July 24) expressed the willingness of the United States to negotiate a tariff treaty on the basis of equality and autonomy. This was in accordance with the resolution adopted at the tariff conferences at Peking in 1925–1926 recognizing the right of China to tariff autonomy January 1, 1929, except that it was not joint action. The treaty was signed July 25, 1928. It provided that all previous treaties regarding tariff should be annulled, that complete national tariff autonomy should apply, and that the United States should be granted most-favored-nation treatment. The treaty was to take effect on January 1, 1929, or four months after the exchange of ratifications. The Senate ratified it on February 11, 1929. The effect of the signature of the treaty was to grant official recognition to the new Chinese government. Simultaneously with the opening of negotiations (July 24) the first contingent of marines was withdrawn from Tientsin. On October 9–11 the Chinese celebrated the seventeenth anniversary of the republic by promulgating a new constitution and installing Chiang Kai-shek as "President of the Republic." Settlements of the Nanking incident were reached with Great Britain on August 9 and with Italy and France in October. Japan alone had not reached a settlement on this question, as well as on the question of the tariff.

The New Year statement of the Chinese government summarized what had been accomplished during the last six months of 1928. Twelve states had signed autonomous tariff treaties, and five had signed treaties relinquishing extraterritoriality. The new criminal code and the new code of criminal procedure had been promulgated September 1, 1928, and the new commercial code would be promulgated January 1, 1930. An act was promulgated prohibiting the production and use of opium except for medicinal purposes after March 1, 1929. The new tariff schedules were promulgated December 10, 1928, and went into effect on February 1, 1929. The Japanese government did not accept the new schedules until January 31, and then only with such conditions attached as had to be settled in the permanent treaties still to be negotiated.

JAPAN

At the Peace Conference of 1919 at Paris, Japan appeared in an aggressively nationalistic spirit. She had been promised in the secret treaties the German colonies north of the equator, and she intended to exact execution of the promise in full. She sought a clear recognition of the principle of equality among the nations. During the war and the years immediately after it she was aggressive in Far Eastern policy, particularly in encroachments upon China and in Siberia. These policies were contrary to the American interpretation of the open door and the integrity of the Far East. Japan seemed to be in the process of creating for herself an Asiatic Monroe Doctrine. In the United States the antiforeign agitation was particularly severe on the Japanese, especially on the Pacific coast, and gave Japan just grounds for grievance. The Japanese were declared by these agitators to be unassimilable and were denounced for not becoming Americanized and for retaining their loyalty to Japan. Nothing else, of course, was to be expected when the United States refused them citizenship. Of necessity they were obliged to retain their Japanese nationality. On the question of assimilability there could be no adequate ground for positive judgments, as the Japanese had not been in the United States long enough to warrant conclusions on such a question. Probably the most basic grievance was the economic efficiency of the Japanese. The result of these differences was a dangerous amount of talk, on both sides of the Pacific, of war between the United States and Japan. Extremists wrote books and numerous magazine articles on the subject. Inevitably this only increased the tension. Japan could no more afford to permit this growing hostility to come to a crisis than could the United States. The Chinese boycott of Japanese goods had crippled trade. Commerce with the United States was too vital an interest to sacrifice. Raw silk and camphor made up the bulk of Japan's foreign trade, and the United States took about 90 per cent of the silk. These were some of the most tangible and obvious facts of the Japanese situation.

The Washington Conference marked a sharp modification of Japanese policies. The limitation of naval armament and the limitation of naval bases in the Pacific removed what seemed to be threats on both sides. The settlement of the Chinese question cleared the atmosphere in Far East politics. Japan adopted a policy of conciliation in China. The Lansing-Ishii agreement was terminated in 1923. The question of United States rights in the island of Yap was settled by a treaty between the United States and Japan. The United States was to have the same rights in establishing electrical communication as Japan had. The question of Japanese immigration into the United States and of treatment of Japanese within the United States seemed about to be settled by the Morris-Shidehara treaty of 1921. This agreement provided that Japan would restrict absolutely the emigration of laborers to the United States, and that the Japanese in the United States should enjoy most-favored-nation treatment except with respect to naturalization. The effect of this latter provision would be to nullify the discriminative California legislation and that of other states. Johnson of California protested the treaty, and it was dropped by the administration.

This period of increasing good will was interrupted by the immigration act of 1924, which provided for limitation of immigrants to the United States to 2 per cent of the number of each nationality recorded in the census of 1890. This would have allowed the Japanese, with the basic 100, a total of 146 immigrants per year. The extremists were not satisfied, and included in the bill a special section excluding all "aliens not eligible to citizenship." There could be no doubt that this was aimed at the Japanese.

On April 10, 1924, the Japanese ambassador, Hanihara, addressed a note to Secretary Hughes concerning the Japanese-exclusion legislation which was then pending. He restated the terms of the "Gentlemen's Agreement" and insisted that his government had enforced it in absolute good faith. The net number of Japanese entering the United States from 1908 to 1923, according to American figures, was 8681, or an annual average of 578. These figures included all classes of Japanese, such as merchants, students, tourists, officials, and so on. He expressed his personal belief that his government would be willing to modify the agreement to make it still more strict. The communication closed with the following paragraph:

Relying upon the confidence you have been good enough to show me at all times, I have stated or rather repeated all this to you very candidly and in a most friendly spirit, for I realize, as I believe you do, the grave consequences which the enactment of the measure retaining that particular provision would inevitably bring upon the otherwise happy and mutually advantageous relations between our two countries.

Secretary Hughes acknowledged the receipt of the note in a cordial reply and stated that he was forwarding copies of it to the chairman of the appropriate committees of both houses of Congress. His reason was that the "note is directed toward clearing away any possible misapprehension as to the nature and purpose of the 'Gentlemen's Agreement.'" The effect was very different, however, from anything anticipated by either of them. In the Senate the note created unusual excitement, some senators declaring that the phrase "grave consequences" in the Hanihara note was a "veiled threat" to the United States. The Japanese ambassador on April 17 disavowed any such meaning. Hughes replied that he had understood the phrase in the sense in which the ambassador had explained it. The incident changed a few votes, but there is no evidence that it affected enough votes to change the result. The bill passed both houses and was approved by Coolidge on May 26, 1924.

A memorandum of protest was then formally presented by the Japanese government against the discriminative features of the law. It was definitely stated that Japan would have been willing to negotiate a more drastic agreement had this law not been enacted. The law went into operation on July 1, 1924, and the Japanese observed the event as a day of national humiliation. Intense hostility was shown toward the United States by a large portion of the Japanese public. In 1925 great naval maneuvers in Hawaiian waters increased irritation. Although the popular hostility subsided in later years, and cordial relations were apparently restored, yet the grievance remained and might easily be revived. No one — least of all the Japanese government — questioned the right of the United States to regulate immigration: it was the method of exclusion by statute, as a discrimination against the Japanese, that was resented.

SELECTED BIBLIOGRAPHY

General

BLAKESLEE, G. H. The Recent Foreign Policy of the United States. The Abingdon Press, 1925.
> The book is rather too favorable to the work of Hughes.

LATANÉ, J. H. A History of American Foreign Policy. Doubleday, Doran and Company, Inc., 1927.
> The last chapters give the best available short treatment of major political policies.

HUGHES, CHARLES E. The Pathway of Peace. Harper & Brothers, 1925.
> Selected addresses delivered by Hughes while he was Secretary of State.

Alaska

NICHOLS, JEANNETTE P. Alaska. The Arthur H. Clark Company, 1924.
> This is the only history of the internal problems of Alaska. It furnishes the background. There is no single reliable work on the territory after the World War.

Hawaii

KUYKENDALL, R. S. History of Hawaii. The Macmillan Company, 1926.

This is a school history, but is practically the only book available.

LITTLER, ROBERT. The Governance of Hawaii. Stanford University Press, 1929.

The Philippine Islands

FORBES, W. CAMERON. The Philippine Islands. 2 vols. Houghton Mifflin Company, 1929.

The author is a Republican in politics and a former governor-general of the Islands.

REYES, JOSÉ S. Legislative History of America's Economic Policy toward the Philippines. Columbia University Press, 1923.

ROOSEVELT, NICHOLAS. The Philippines: a Treasure and a Problem. J. H. Sears and Company, 1926.

CHAPTER XXIX

POLITICAL POLICIES: THE WESTERN HEMISPHERE

INTRODUCTION

IN THE Western Hemisphere the Monroe Doctrine was the most conspicuous factor in foreign policy. Because of criticisms of indefiniteness, Secretary of State Hughes used the occasion of the celebration of the centenary of the doctrine to redefine it. His address of August 30, 1923, is summarized in these words: "The Monroe Doctrine is opposed (1) to any non-American action encroaching upon the political independence of American states under any guise and (2) to the acquisition in any manner of the control of additional territory in this hemisphere by non-American power." It is a policy of self-defense, not aggression, and is interpreted and enforced by the United States alone. Thus far the statement of the doctrine is negative and refers to the relations of the European powers to the Western Hemisphere. The relations of the United States to the sister states of the Western Hemisphere were not defined in the original doctrine; consequently a body of positive policies — corollaries of the Monroe Doctrine — were formulated from time to time to meet changing needs. There were three of these positive policies or groups of positive policies: Pan-Americanism, international coöperation, and Caribbean policies. It was the policy of the United States not to encroach upon the independence and sovereignty of American states.

Before the World War the Monroe Doctrine was severely criticized in the United States, and many argued that it should be abandoned; after the war there was a strong nationalistic reaction, and very few advocated any modification of the Doctrine and its corollaries unless it were an extension of their scope. Formerly there was no serious objection to having European states sit on boards of arbitration for the settlement of American questions, and there are numerous instances of the kind. After the war it is doubtful whether public opinion would have permitted the submission of any case to such settlement.

Pan-Americanism and international coöperation in the Western Hemisphere were closely associated after 1889, but they were not fully accepted throughout Latin America because of the feeling in some quarters that they were policies participated in by the United States primarily for facilitating its own economic penetration to the southward. Opposition movements which stressed Latin-American solidarity were fostered in these southern states to oppose the influence of the United States and to emphasize the cultural, institutional, religious, and historical connections between Latin America and Latin Europe.

Caribbean policy was more restricted geographically, and its main principles were worked out definitely between the Spanish War and the World War. They were designed to give the United States a sort of guardianship over the area in the interest of American security and the protection of American interests. These principles may be grouped as follows: (1) Transportation was promoted across the Isthmus. (2) Naval bases were acquired in Cuba, Porto Rico, and the Virgin Islands; the Panama Canal was fortified; and such control was established over Haiti and Santo Domingo as would prevent these strategic positions from falling into the hands of an enemy for military purposes. (3) Financial administration was established in varying degrees over Cuba, Santo Domingo, Haiti, Nicaragua, and Salvador. (4) Sanitary supervision was maintained in Cuba, Panama, Haiti, and Santo Domingo. (5) Orderly government was maintained through supervision of elections in Cuba, Santo Domingo, Nicaragua, Panama, and Haiti, and through policing in Cuba, Nicaragua, Santo Domingo, and Haiti; embargoes were placed on the shipping of arms to insurrectionary movements in Mexico; and recognition was refused to revolutionary movements in Cuba, Nicaragua, and Mexico. (6) Revolution was promoted to facilitate the overthrow of a government disapproved by the United States through authorizing export of arms to Mexico under Huerta, through recognition of revolutionary movements in Panama, Nicaragua, and Mexico, and through the prohibition of military movements by Colombia to suppress the rebellion of 1903.

After the World War a few details were added to these, though no essential changes were made in general policies. Caribbean policy, however, was employed more widely than formerly, and the public became more definitely conscious that these activities did constitute a definite body of policy. Hughes called attention to Caribbean policy as such in his addresses on foreign policy in 1923, and Coolidge again restated it on April 25, 1927, at an Associated Press dinner where he discussed the Nicaraguan situation. In that connection he said:

> Toward the governments of the countries which we have recognized this side of the Panama Canal we feel a moral responsibility that does not attach to other nations. ... Revolutions will be discouraged in these countries. For that purpose the United States has taken a hand in Nicaragua. ... We are not making war on Nicaragua any more than a policeman on the street is making war on a passer-by.

Many newspaper editorials hailed this as a new doctrine; but it was clearly not a formulation of new ideas, — it was rather a restatement of existing facts and principles of recognized standing.

CARIBBEAN POLICIES

Mexico

The revolutionary movement of 1910 in Mexico was primarily an economic and social movement. The first direct step toward carrying out land reforms was the provisional agrarian decree of January 6, 1915, issued by Carranza, which provided for either restoring village communal lands or providing such lands, and established a commission to administer the decree. The constitution of 1917 elaborated the economic and social program. Article XXVII provided more fully for carrying out the agrarian reforms; it nationalized subsoil deposits, limited the acquisition of property in Mexico by foreigners, and laid the foundation for religious and educational reforms.

The laws for enforcing the agrarian decrees were enacted between 1920 and 1922, and large amounts of land were expropriated from the great estates, with compensation, in order to provide communal lands for the people. Certain irregularities in the proceedings were made grounds for objections by Americans in Mexico, but there was nothing which could not be explained by the exigencies of the situation and adjusted accordingly.

The nationalization of subsoil deposits proved a more difficult question. Before 1884 all subsoil deposits were nationalized, but between 1884 and 1909 these rights passed to the owner of the surface. The constitution of 1917 was an effort to restore the policy which had obtained up to 1884. The Harding administration defined its position clearly in a proposed treaty of amity and commerce (May 27, 1921). It would have provided for national treatment of citizens on a reciprocity basis, for a guaranty that land laws should not be applied retroactively or property be taken without compensation, and for freedom of worship. The United States made this treaty the condition of the recognition of the new Obregón government. But the Mexican president refused to purchase recognition by accepting such a treaty. His program was to settle claims by commissions, and required that recognition must not be made the subject of any conditions. In the meantime the Mexican government had reached an agreement, known as the Lamont–De la Huerta agreement, with the international committee of bankers on Mexico. This removed an important American grievance against Mexico and tended to establish Obregón more firmly in control of the Mexican situation.

During 1923 a new procedure was followed, with better results for all concerned. A commission was appointed which met in Mexico City to arrive at an agreement on the agrarian loans and on the subsoil question. Associated with these discussions was the drafting of two claims conventions: one for revolutionary claims against Mexico arising out of the period 1910–1920, and the other to comprehend all claims arising since 1868 which might be presented. Obregón was recognized by the United States, and the claims conventions were signed in September.

During 1925 the Mexican question was reopened by the enactment of two laws: the alien land law and the petroleum law. The constitution had prohibited foreigners or foreign corporations from acquiring lands or waters or concessions to develop mines, waters, or minerals unless they agreed to be considered as Mexican in respect to such property; and near the border or shores even these privileges of foreigners were denied. The new law (approved on December 31, 1925) was enacted in accordance with this constitutional provision. Foreign corporations owning over 50 per cent of the stock in Mexican agricultural corporations before May 1, 1917, must dispose of the stock in excess of 50 per cent within ten years. A petroleum law, approved December 26, 1925, provided for a fifty-year confirmation of rights to lands acquired before May 1, 1917, provided some positive act had been performed for the purpose of exploiting the petroleum resources. Such confirmation of rights must be applied for within one year or the rights would lapse.

The question immediately arose whether the application of these laws would be retroactive. If so, it would be in conflict with the agreement reached in 1923. The diplomatic correspondence during the winter of 1925–1926 analyzed various aspects of the application of the laws. In the case of the petroleum laws, for example, the United States maintained that the exchange of fifty-year titles for permanent titles was a retroactive application of the law. It also maintained that the requirement that a citizen must renounce the protection of his government could not be accepted. These matters were not fully cleared up until early in 1928.

Both laws went into effect in January, 1926. The year allowed for meeting conditions expired in January, 1927. At that time legal proceedings were instituted under the petroleum law. Conditions were complicated by the Nicaraguan crisis in January, 1927, when Coolidge charged the Mexican government with aiding the revolutionaries, and Kellogg published his charges that Mexico was engaged in Bolshevist propaganda. Later in the month the question of arbitration of the interpretations of the alien land law and the petroleum law was proposed in the Senate. Kellogg was asked for his opinion. On January 18 he was reported in the press as approving the pending Senate resolution. The Mexican foreign minister also approved (January 20). On January 21 Coolidge was quoted as saying that the question was whether American property legally owned was to be confiscated, and this could not be arbitrated. It was obvious that the President and the Secretary of State had been misquoted or else that they were not in agreement on the Mexican policy. The Senate proceeded on January 25 to pass a resolution approving arbitration by a vote of 79 to 0.

The case of the Mexican Petroleum Company was decided by the Mexican supreme court on November 18, 1927. It held that Sections 14 and 15 of the petroleum law, which were the subject of controversy, were unconstitutional. The Mexican government then prepared amendments to the law in conformity with the court decision. The amending statute was passed by the Mexican congress in December and became effective on January 11, 1928: "Oil rights acquired by owners of the surface lands [before 1917] will be confirmed without time limit. Rights acquired by contracts with owners of surface lands will be confirmed for the period of those contracts." Rights not confirmed within one year would be forfeited. This law closed the petroleum controversy.

The religious and educational provisions of the constitution of 1917 were not put into effect until February, 1927. The constitution provided that religious institutions should not hold property and that all church property should become the property of the nation. Primary instruction was declared to be free, nonsectarian, and subject to government supervision. "No religious corporation nor minister of any religious creed shall be permitted to establish or direct schools of primary instruction." Every person should be at liberty to practice the religion of his choice. A minister of any religious creed must be a Mexican by birth. It should be emphasized that these provisions applied equally to all religious groups, although they affected the Catholic Church more widely because the overwhelming mass of Mexicans were Catholic.

Deportations of foreign-born clericals began immediately. Religious schools were closed. Americans of different religious denominations made protest to Washington, and on March 9 the United States asked that care be taken that Americans should not suffer unduly in the application of these provisions. On March 12 the orders against offenders were revoked on condition that they conform in the future to the provisions of the law. Although the religious question remained a center of public and private agitation, it did not become a matter of official American action which would create a political crisis.

The intensity of American interest in Mexico may be more accurately appreciated after a summary of the amounts of United States investments. In 1912 several observers estimated the holdings of Americans in Mexico at about $1,000,000,000. At the same time the total value of Mexican wealth was estimated at $2,500,000,000; in other words,

Americans owned between two fifths and a half of the whole. In 1924 the Department of Commerce estimated the holdings again at $1,000,000,000, and the next year Dunn's estimates were $1,280,000,000.

Central America

The republics of Central America lie between Mexico and Panama. They are Guatemala, Salvador, Honduras, Nicaragua, and Costa Rica. The topography is such that there is no geographical unity to the area as a whole or to the individual countries. With the exception of Salvador they front on both the Pacific and the Caribbean. Mountain ranges cut them into at least three general regions. The east coast is for the most part a low, broad, tropical jungle; the west coast is narrow; the interior is high, partly mountains, partly plains. Nicaragua was of greatest importance because it possessed the best route for an Isthmian canal which would supplement the Panama Canal. It is for this reason that political interest centered for years in Nicaragua rather than in her sister republics. On the east coast the economic interests were bananas and timber. The population was mostly Indian. The economic and political center of the country was in the plains surrounding the lake country and on the western coast. There was no railroad connection between the east and the west; the only line ran from Granada to the coast. Coffee was the chief agricultural interest of this area.

Political parties did not exist in the sense in which they were known in the United States. In Nicaragua the conservative party centered about the city of Granada, under the domination of the leading families of that place; the liberal party similarly centered around the city of León. There seemed to be no distinctive political program associated with either party. The conservative party governed from about 1863 to 1893; the liberal party, from 1893 to 1909; after that time the conservative party again. Regular elections

were held from time to time, but they were habitually controlled by the party in power. The only way in which a
change in party control came about *normally* was by *revolution*. What is true of Nicaragua in this respect is largely true
of the other republics of the Caribbean area.

There were three possible approaches to the Central American problem: The United States might use its influence to
bring about a loose organization for international coöperation,
among the several republics, based on multilateral treaties.
This was used in 1907 in coöperation with Mexico. In 1909
the second policy was followed: dealing with each country
separately. The Taft and Wilson administrations brought
about a financial supervision of Nicaragua and the negotiation of the Bryan-Chamorro Treaty (concluded in 1914).
This provided for a payment by the United States of
$3,000,000 for the option on the Isthmian canal, a naval
base on the Gulf of Fonseca, and a lease of ninety-nine years
on Great Corn Island and Little Corn Island. Another article was proposed by the United States, but was dropped
because of objection by the Senate. This provided that
Nicaragua should not declare war nor enter into any treaty
which would impair its independence or territorial integrity,
and that the United States should have the right of intervention to maintain order. Costa Rica, Salvador, and Honduras protested against the treaty as a violation of their
rights — Costa Rica because of joint interest in the proposed
canal, and the other two because of joint interest in the Gulf
of Fonseca. The United States Senate ratified the treaty in
1916 with a declaration that nothing in the treaty should
affect the rights of the three protesting countries. Costa
Rica and Salvador brought suit in the Central American
Court of Justice. Nicaragua and the United States ignored
the action. The court rendered a decision against Nicaragua
on September 30, 1916, in the Costa Rica case and on
March 2, 1917, in the case of Salvador. The United States
and Nicaragua both ignored the decisions. This episode put

an end to the Central American Court of Justice. On March 9, 1917, Nicaragua gave notice of withdrawal.

The third line of Central American policy came to the front just after the World War. Since 1921 was the centenary of independence, many thought it appropriate to celebrate the event by reviving the old project of a union of the five republics. This action was an attempt to solve their problems independently of the United States and was aimed at checking United States influence. The conference met at San José, Costa Rica, on December 4, 1920. The principal obstacle to agreement was the relations between Nicaragua and the United States. Nicaragua demanded that the Bryan-Chamorro Treaty be recognized; the other states refused. The agreement was finally signed on January 19, 1921, without Nicaragua, although the door was left open. Honduras, Guatemala, and Salvador promptly ratified; Costa Rica delayed. The first three proceeded to draft a constitution, which was promulgated on September 9, and the new government was inaugurated on October 1. A revolution in Guatemala in December precipitated a crisis concerning the recognition of the new government, and the union broke up February 4, 1922. The three phases of the policy had thus run their course, and a second cycle began.

Revolutionary activities were in progress during 1922 against Chamorro, the conservative president in Nicaragua, and disorder prevailed in Honduras and Salvador. As a result of a proposal from Chamorro the United States offered the *Tacoma*, in the Gulf of Fonseca, as a meeting-place (August 20, 1922). Among other things a second conference was proposed to include the other two Central American powers. Later the United States invited the five republics to Washington. All accepted, and the conference began on December 4, 1922. Their work was finished on February 7. The treaties provided a general treaty of neutrality similar to the treaty of 1907, a Central American tribunal, international commissions of inquiry which included the United

States, and limitation of armament. Other conventions included finance, communications, labor, agriculture, and other activities. Only a part of the treaties and conventions were ratified. In 1924 a revolution in Honduras was adjusted through action of the United States followed by a conference of the five republics. This was repeated in 1925. In 1926 the external debt of Honduras was refunded.

In Salvador the chief point of interest was the loan contract granted to Minor C. Keith on June 24, 1922, calling for $16,500,000. The republic agreed to appoint a fiscal agent designated by Keith. The service of the loan was created a charge upon 70 per cent of the customs revenues, both import and export, and was to be collected by the fiscal agent so long as the bonds were outstanding. The customs collected for this purpose were to be paid in United States gold coin directly to the representative of the fiscal agent. In case of disagreement between the parties to the contract the difference was to be submitted to the Chief Justice of the Supreme Court of the United States through the Secretary of State. No change should be made in the customs which would reduce the receipts. The bonds were to be issued in three series, the final date of maturity being 1956. In case the republic should default any of its obligations for thirty days, the fiscal agent should require the creation of a customs administration and appoint a collector-general who should administer the customs revenues. The appointment should be made through the nomination of two persons, with the concurrence of the Secretary of State of the United States, one of whom should be chosen by the republic. The collector-general might be removed on request of the fiscal agent either directly or else through the Department of State. The republic might request the removal of a collector-general because of either incompetence or political interference with its affairs. This contract was written in both English and Spanish, but the English version was to govern. The contract was to "be construed in accordance with the laws of the State of New York, United States of America."

After 1923, Central American affairs again centered in Nicaragua. Internal difficulties developed in 1923 with the death of the president, Diego Chamorro. The vice president, Martínez, was a conservative of a different faction and controlled the election machinery. The conservatives and liberals both split, and a coalition was formed between the Martínez faction of the conservatives and the majority faction of the liberals. The candidates agreed upon were Solorzano, a conservative, for president and Sacasa, a liberal, for vice president. The election was carried out under a new election law drafted by H. W. Dodds of the United States. The United States government refused to approve or disapprove any candidates. The coalition ticket was elected. The United States legation guard was withdrawn in 1925 for the first time since 1912. Emiliano Chamorro soon acquired control of the military forces and forced a reorganization of the government. Eighteen members of the congress were unseated. Sacasa fled, his office was declared vacant, and he was banished for two years. Solorzano presented his resignation, which was refused by the congress, but he was granted a vacation. Chamorro, who had been elected by the congress as *designado*, took possession of the presidency in January, 1926. The United States refused recognition, and eventually he retired in favor of Uriza, the second *designado*. Sacasa appealed to the United States; he was put off and, in discouragement, turned to Mexico. In the meantime the United States looked with favor on the calling of a congress by Uriza in which the expelled members were restored. Adolfo Díaz, a conservative, was elected president and was recognized by the United States; Mexico recognized Sacasa as the legal president. The United States and Mexico thus seemed pitted against each other in Nicaragua. Fighting in Nicaragua commenced, marines were landed, and neutral zones were established to protect foreigners. The British and Italian governments called attention to the danger to their nationals. This resulted in more drastic action by the United States.

Criticism of the administration policy was freely expressed in the United States and in Latin America. Coolidge addressed a special message to Congress on January 10, 1927, in defense of his action. The message recounted the principal facts of the Nicaraguan situation, beginning with 1924, and pointed out Mexico's policy in assisting the liberals. Díaz had repeatedly appealed for assistance, and foreign governments expected protection for their nationals. The President defended the constitutionality of the Díaz régime. In closing, however, he came to the real heart of the whole matter:

Manifestly the relation of this government to the Nicaraguan situation, and its policy in the existing emergency, are determined by the facts which I have described. The proprietary rights of the United States in the Nicaraguan canal route, with the necessary implications growing out of it affecting the Panama Canal, together with the obligations flowing from the investments of all classes of our citizens in Nicaragua, place us in a position of peculiar responsibility. I am sure it is not the desire of the United States to intervene in the internal affairs of Nicaragua or of any other Central American republic. Nevertheless it must be said that we have a very definite and special interest in the maintenance of order and good government in Nicaragua at the present time, and that the stability, prosperity, and independence of all Central American countries can never be a matter of indifference to us. The United States cannot, therefore, fail to view with deep concern any serious threat to stability and constitutional government in Nicaragua tending toward anarchy and jeopardizing American interests, especially if such state of affairs is contributed to or brought about by outside influences or by any foreign power. It has always been and remains the policy of the United States in such circumstances to take the steps that may be necessary for the preservation and protection of the lives, the property, and the interests of its citizens and of this government itself. In this respect I propose to follow the path of my predecessors.

This broader view of the Nicaraguan question escaped most critics of the administration policy. There were a few notable exceptions; for example, an editorial in the *Kansas City Star* of January 17, 1927, entitled "Nicaragua as an Incident":

The Nicaraguan affair has brought to the front the broad question of the relations of the United States with Latin America. Few persons realize that such a question exists. They think of the dispute over Nicaragua as a mere matter of the relation of this government to a single Central American state. . . .

The problem of Nicaragua can be considered intelligently only in connection with the general and permanent policy of the United States toward its southern defenses, especially the Panama Canal.

Nicaragua is a country occupying a position strategic to the United States such as Gibraltar and Suez occupy toward Britain; Morocco, Algeria, and Tunis toward France; Tripoli toward Italy; and Constantinople toward Russia.

Such regions must be controlled either because they are regarded as essential to the protection of the controlling powers, or because these powers fear they may fall into unfriendly hands.

After reviewing the growth of the United States power in the Caribbean area as a whole, the editorial sums up the logical conclusion in the following paragraph:

Nicaragua, then, is only an incident in the working out of a great policy of national defense. The debate in the Senate on that country's right to determine its own destiny can be only academic. The inexorable march of events forces us to accept responsibilities in Nicaragua and through the American tropics. We cannot escape them, try as we will.

This editorial, as well as the President's message, was sound, logical, imperialistic doctrine, but the editorial states the case more clearly. It strikes at the essential weakness of the critics of the Senate and especially throws into relief the position of Borah, chairman of the Committee on Foreign Relations. On January 13 Borah attacked the administration policy, but admitted that the immediate withdrawal of the marines was impossible; in effect he himself admitted that his arguments against the government policy were merely academic.

Whatever effect the President's message might have had in clarifying the situation was offset by Secretary Kellogg's publication (January 12) of a memorandum, previously submitted to the Committee on Foreign Relations, in which he charged that Mexico was the center of Bolshevist propaganda against the United States and was plotting to stir up revolutions between the United States and the Panama Canal. Public opinion reacted against these charges. Examination of Kellogg's evidence made the charges appear doubtful.

Criticism of the administration's policy, both at home and abroad, continued. The situation in Nicaragua became more serious. The President then called upon Henry L. Stimson, formerly Secretary of War under Taft, to undertake a special mission to Nicaragua to investigate and, if opportunity presented itself, to settle difficulties. Stimson left New York on April 9, 1927, and during the latter part of April and the first part of May conferred with both parties. A peace settlement was arrived at, and Stimson departed on May 16. The agreement was that the liberals deliver their arms at ten dollars apiece and that the United States guarantee a free and fair election in 1928. In the meantime Díaz should serve as president, and liberals should be admitted to a share in the government. The program was accepted under pressure, but all except a handful of liberals submitted. Sandino was the chief one to refuse, and the marines undertook to subdue him. When it came time to pass the legislation necessary to legalize the United States supervision of elections in Nicaragua, the bill was defeated in the Nicaraguan congress, supposedly through the influence of Chamorro. The United States was in a dilemma. It had given to the liberals a pledge which was the basis for their surrendering their arms, and the conservatives now refused the legal authority to carry out the pledge, to which they had previously agreed. The American government announced its intention of carrying out the pledge whatever the circumstances. President Díaz appointed General Frank R. McCoy president of the election board. A peaceful election followed, and resulted in the choice of General Moncada, a former leader in the Sacasa liberal forces.

The economic consequences of the policy of the United States were of the greatest significance in the realization of the government aims. In 1911 the Dawson agreement had provided a collector-general of the customs, who remained in office through all changes in political control. The Bryan-Chamorro Treaty provided that both governments should have a voice in determining the disposition of the canal money. This led to the appointment of a body later known as the High Commission — one member selected by the United States, although technically appointed by the president of Nicaragua, and one appointed by Nicaragua. The High Commission controlled internal finances and budgets and supervised the debt and relations with foreign creditors. The arrangement was worked out by executive agreement, and the United States Congress was not consulted.

The financial administration asserted that it had reduced the debt from $32,000,000 to about $8,000,000 between 1911 and 1927. Technically this is true, but the claim was misleading without explanations. Claims against the government amounting to nearly $14,000,000 were adjusted and scaled down to a little less than $2,000,000. This should be subtracted from the $32,000,000. The American claimants received about 7 per cent of their claims, the average being about 14 per cent. In addition the government was enabled to buy back the National Bank and the National Railroad. Undoubtedly this was a great contribution to stability so far as the relations of Nicaragua to her creditors were concerned.

The economic interests of the United States in Central America, except Nicaragua, are summarized as follows from Dunn's estimates. Investments in Guatemala increased from $15,000,000 to $50,000,000 between 1920 and 1925. A large part of this was the International railways and the United

Fruit Company. The investment of the latter in 1923 was about $4,000,000. Investments in Honduras increased from $18,000,000 to $40,000,000, of which the United Fruit Company held $24,000,000. Investments in Nicaragua, according to an Associated Press dispatch, were $12,000,000 in January, 1928. The so-called Wall Street interest in that amount was $185,000, which was scheduled to be paid within three months. By 1928 both the National Bank and the National Railroad were owned by the Nicaraguan government. The United Fruit interest was estimated at $200,000. There were some lumber, gold, silver, and coffee investments. The only oil interest listed was the West India Oil Company, which was purely a selling agency. The British interest totaled $2,500,000. Investments in Salvador were predominantly American. The public debt that was outstanding in 1925 was $6,000,000. Data were not available on other investments. Investments in Costa Rica were from $20,000,000 to $30,000,000 in 1925. The total American investment in Central America was therefore somewhere near $125,000,000.

Colombia

Relations with Colombia centered about the settlement of the differences arising out of the Panama revolution of 1903. Attempts to settle these questions date from the last year of the Roosevelt administration. They were continued by the Taft administration. Colombia's position was settlement by arbitration. This the United States persistently refused. United States offers had to do chiefly with indirect money payments. These Colombia refused. The Wilson administration was willing to approach the matter in a different spirit. The Colombian terms were (1) moral reparation, (2) preferential use of the canal, (3) determination of the boundary, and (4) money indemnity. This is essentially what was incorporated in the treaty signed at Bogotá on April 6, 1914. In the preamble it was stated that the purpose of the treaty was to remove all misunderstandings growing out of the political events in Panama in November, 1903. By the treaty the United States expressed sincere regrets that anything had occurred to mar the friendship between the two countries. Colombia was granted preferential rights in the use of the canal. The United States was to pay $25,000,000 to Colombia. Colombia recognized the independence of Panama and agreed to a boundary. The treaty was submitted to the Senate on June 16, and then the storm broke. In the Senate the friends of Roosevelt attacked the treaty, because they interpreted it as an admission that Roosevelt stole Panama. Roosevelt himself attacked the treaty and demanded a hearing, which was granted on February 23, 1915. Business interests joined with the Democrats in urging immediate action. As long as the quarrel continued, Americans found a cool reception in Colombia. Since the Colombian government had ratified the treaty promptly, it was impatient at the delay. During 1915, however, the treaty was practically dropped. In 1917 it was revived with amendments expressing mutual regrets. Colombia refused to accept the changes, and another postponement occurred. In 1919 the treaty was revived again with three important amendments: the regrets clause was to be struck out, the preferential rights to be granted to Colombia in the use of the canal were to be reduced, and the payments were to be made in five annual installments instead of in a lump sum. Lodge claimed that these changes had been worked out by himself, Knox, Root, and Lansing in 1917 after the previous failure of the treaty. In August, 1919, Lodge asked for postponement of the treaty because of a subsoil-nationalization decree which threatened oil rights in Colombia. These matters were adjusted by the petroleum law of December 29, 1919, together with a decision of the supreme court of Colombia. With this difficulty removed, it seems that the treaty should have been revived, but it was not reported favorably until early in June, 1920. Even then there were further delays.

Action on the treaty came promptly with the inauguration of the Harding administration. On March 9, five days after his inauguration, Harding sent a special message to the Senate urging prompt ratification. The debate on the treaty was in public executive session. Lodge led the campaign for ratification just as in years past he had led the fight against it. He reviewed Roosevelt's policy and argued that the amendments proposed in 1919 and then before the Senate changed the character of the treaty. The money payment was excessive, but as a matter of expediency he would accept it. He argued the importance of the Panama Canal and of stability and security in that area, and of South American commerce. More particularly there was an understanding that this treaty would be followed by a favorable commercial treaty; and then there was the international scramble for oil. In this connection he introduced letters of Albert B. Fall, Secretary of the Interior, who also had reversed his position on the treaty after 1917. Fall's letters stated that oil interests were in favor of the treaty. Business men recognized that there was a crisis at hand in the struggle for control of the world's oil for commercial and naval use. The British controlled the Venezuelan fields; Americans had the strongest hold on the Colombian fields, and United States support was needed and was proper. There were a few, such as Borah, who were irreconcilables. They considered the treaty a reflection on Roosevelt. Most of the Democrats supported the treaty to right the wrong done by the United States in the Panama revolution of 1903. The treaty was ratified, with the amendments of 1919, on April 20, 1921, by a vote of 69 to 19. The affirmative vote included 40 Republicans and 29 Democrats; the negative vote included 15 Republicans and 4 Democrats. Eight senators did not vote. It is clear that the treaty was ratified only with the support of the Republicans after seven years of delay; by whatever line of reasoning they arrived at the decision to vote for it, the lubricant that made the wheels go round was oil.

The aftermath of the Colombian settlement was full of interest. One illustration will suffice. In 1912 the United States investments in Colombia were estimated at $2,000,000. Comparatively little capital went in before 1921. By 1925 the Department of Commerce estimates placed the investment figures at $70,000,000. Venezuela investments may be presented here for comparison. In 1912 they were $3,000,000, by 1920 they were $40,000,000, and by 1924 they were $75,000,000. About half this last amount was in oil.

Panama

The survey of relations with Central America and Colombia on both sides of the Panama Canal very properly introduces the question of relations with Panama. The original statement of these relations was contained in the treaty of November 18, 1903, signed immediately after the Panama revolution. Article I read, "The United States guarantees and will maintain the independence of the Republic of Panama." The major portion of the treaty dealt directly with the proposed canal. Panama granted "in perpetuity the use, occupation, and control of a zone of land" ten miles wide "for the construction, maintenance, operation, sanitation, and protection of said canal," and under like terms "any other lands and waters outside of the zone above described which may be necessary and convenient" for these purposes, and also all islands within the zone limits, together with the four islands in the Bay of Panama named Perico, Naos, Culebra, and Flamenco. All these lands and waters were granted with "all rights, power and authority . . . which the United States would possess and exercise if it were the sovereign of the territory . . . to the entire exclusion of the exercise by the Republic of Panama of any such sovereign rights, power or authority." Subsidiary to these grants there was a further grant of the rights to use the rivers, streams, lakes, and other bodies of water as were convenient or necessary. When private property was taken, damages were to be assessed by a joint commission. The United States was granted a monopoly on transportation across the Isthmus by canal or railroad. Within the cities of Panama and Colon and in their vicinity, rights were granted to acquire property by right of eminent domain and to construct works for water supply, sewerage, and sanitation for a period of fifty years, after which they should revert to the republic. Sanitary ordinances prescribed by the United States were to be enforced by these cities; and if Panama failed, the United States was authorized to enforce them. Order was to be maintained in these cities and adjacent territories and waters or the United States would maintain such order. Mutual facilities were pledged for extradition of persons charged with crimes etc. Article XXIII provided that "if it should become necessary at any time to employ armed forces for the safety or protection of the canal, or of the ships that make use of the same, or the railways and auxiliary works, the United States shall have the right, at all times and in its discretion, to use its police and its land and naval forces or to establish fortifications for these purposes." Article XXIV stated that "no change either in the government or in the laws and treaties of the Republic of Panama shall, without the consent of the United States, affect any right of the United States under the present convention, or under any treaty stipulation between the two countries that now exists or may hereafter exist touching the subject matter of this convention." The last article authorized the sale or lease of naval or coaling stations on both the Pacific and Caribbean coasts of Panama for the protection of the canal.

It must be noted that the form of these provisions was unilateral, not bilateral. This meant that in their application the United States interpretation was binding. The conditions of the Panama revolution made it necessary for the embryo republic to accept any terms it could get as the price of recognition and protection. Possibly Panama leaders did not realize the extent of the concessions. Disagreements in interpretation were almost continuous.

In the execution of the treaty there were numerous problems which were worked out between the two governments. The execution of certain of these was effected by executive orders. The Panama Canal Act of August 24, 1912, "ratified and confirmed" them. The orders of particular importance here were dated December 3, December 6, and December 28, 1904, January 7, 1905, and January 5, 1911. Article VIII of the treaty had provided for free importation of goods for use in canal-construction operations. The order of December 3 prescribed, among other things, that no goods should be entered at Ancon and Cristobal except as agreed in the treaty, provided the new import duties were reduced from 15 per cent to 10 per cent in Class 2 of the schedule and remained the same in the other schedules, provided merchandise entered at Panama and Colon was not subject to any other direct or indirect taxes, and provided the consular fees were reduced 60 per cent. This agreement should not go into effect unless a gold standard of value was adopted in Panama.

The operation of this executive order and its enforcement by officials of the United States on the one hand, or a compliance with and performance of the conditions of its operation by the Republic of Panama and its officials on the other, shall not be taken as a delimitation, definition, restriction, or restrictive construction of the rights of either party under the treaty between the United States and the Republic of Panama.

The question of commissaries touched upon in the order of January 7 later became a serious problem of controversy. It provided that goods entitled to free entry at Ancon and Cristobal should be such as were necessary and convenient for the construction of the canal and for the use of officers and employees of the United States stationed in the Canal Zone and must be certified by a member of the commission. Persons normally excluded from these benefits were employees and workmen, natives of the tropics, who could secure goods to which they were accustomed at the regular business establishments of Panama. However, if merchants charged excessive prices, the commissaries might sell to all employees or workmen of the United States or its contractors. These summaries indicate the nature of these orders and need not be given in full.

After the World War the United States was decidedly active in matters relating to the defense of Panama. In 1919 the island of Taboga was ceded to the United States. In 1921 the government intervened in the boundary war which threatened with Costa Rica. Chief Justice White in 1914 had decided the dispute in favor of Costa Rica, but Panama had not accepted the award. At this time marines were sent to the point of threatened hostilities, and Panama was required to acquiesce.

The United States was not satisfied with the status of relations existing with Panama, and Congress took action by a joint resolution (approved February 12, 1922) to abrogate the executive orders as a step toward a new permanent agreement. Notice was given Panama, and the President's proclamation was dated May 28, 1924, setting June 1, 1924, as the date of termination. Negotiations in the meantime were instituted, but the new treaty was not signed until July 28, 1926. An official synopsis was issued by Panama and confirmed by the United States July 29 and July 31. The text was withheld. Though it was published in Cuba, copies of the papers were suppressed in Panama. It was also published in Europe. Kellogg and Borah did not consent to publication in the United States until late in December, 1926. These men were not nearly so eager for publicity as when the official synopsis of the Treaty of Versailles was published, but not the text.

Article I worked out details regarding expropriation of private property in Panama by the United States for canal purposes. The next article redefined the boundaries in the harbor of Colon as desired by the United States and granted all cable rights to the United States. A uniform highway agreement was included, giving both governments mutual use of roads in the republic and the Zone. The United States was permitted to build telephone and telegraph lines in the republic for official use. The commissary question was restated, to terminate the long-standing difficulties. United States commissaries should sell only to those connected with the canal and its protection. Both entrances to the canal were declared free ports except for tolls and for goods destined for Panama's consumption, which must pay duties. Alcoholic liquors could be passed through the Zone under seal. Sanitary powers were enlarged, the United States being authorized in emergencies to take over control throughout the republic. Radio apparatus could be installed in Panama only with a license from the republic, except that the United States might object in particular cases. United States inspection was authorized, and the United States might request the closing of any station. United States stations could be installed wherever necessary in the republic. Commercial aviation centers were to be subject to a joint license under the Geneva regulations of 1919. The United States gold dollar was made legal tender in Panama, and the Panama silver currency was not acceptable for canal tolls.

Probably the most important single section of the treaty was the article given below:

The Republic of Panama agrees to coöperate in all possible ways with the United States in the protection and defense of the Panama Canal. Consequently the Republic of Panama will consider herself in a state of war in case of any war in which the United States should be a belligerent, and in order to render more effective the defense of the canal will, if necessary in the opinion of the United States government, turn over to the United States in all the territory of the Republic of Panama, during the period of actual or threatened hostilities, the control and operation of wireless and radio communication, aircraft, aviation centers, and aërial navigation.

The civil and military authorities of the Republic of Panama shall impose and enforce all ordinances and decrees required for the maintenance of public order and for the safety and defense of the territory of the Republic of Panama during such actual disorder or threatened hostilities, and the United States shall have the direction and control of all military operations in any part of the territory of the Republic of Panama.

For the purpose of the efficient protection of the canal, the Republic of Panama also agrees that in time of peace the armed forces of the United States shall have free transit throughout the Republic for maneuvers or other military purposes, provided, however, that due notice will be given to the government of the Republic of Panama every time armed troops should enter.

The treaty was submitted to the United States Senate on December 9, 1926. In Panama it received a hostile reception. On January 26 the Panama Assembly requested the president to reopen negotiations.

Many detailed questions were raised by the treaty, such as the question of the sovereignty of Panama over the Canal Zone. It should be noticed that the treaty of 1903 did not cede the territory: it granted the *use* in perpetuity, and the United States might exercise all the rights of sovereignty. One of the larger questions was the relations of Panama with the League of Nations, of which it is a member. As a member of the League it was pledged to submit disputes to peaceful settlement and not to engage in war until all peaceful methods had failed. It was also pledged to abrogate all agreements contrary to this obligation. The proposed treaty obliged it to consider itself in a state of war automatically when the United States went to war. This seemed to repudiate its League obligation. However, in Article XIV of the treaty of 1903 it was stated that Panama should not enter into any agreement which would modify its relations with the United States under this treaty or any subsequent treaty. Here was plainly a conflict of obligations. But there was one important loophole — the article of the Covenant recognizing the Monroe Doctrine.

Cuba

The relations between the United States and Cuba were based upon two important agreements: the Platt Amendment treaty, proclaimed in 1904, and the commercial treaty proclaimed in 1903. The Platt Amendment treaty provided that Cuba should never enter into any agreement which would impair its independence or permit foreign control of any of its territory, that Cuba should not contract any debt which could not be served from its ordinary revenues, that the United States might intervene to maintain its independence or maintain order, that sanitary measures and control of epidemic diseases should be continued and extended, and that naval stations should be sold or leased to the United States. The commercial treaty provided that products of the soil and industry of Cuba admitted to the United States should be given preferential treatment over all like imports from other countries, and that sugar should be admitted at a reduction of 20 per cent. It was also agreed that products of the soil and industry of the United States should be given preferential treatment over those of any other country, the schedule ranging from 20 per cent to 40 per cent below normal rates. Geographical location plus these treaties made Cuba politically and economically tributary to the United States.

The World War placed special emphasis upon the production of essential war materials; and sugar, the primary product of Cuba, was stimulated in a most abnormal manner. By decidedly drastic methods Cuba was induced to make an agreement for the marketing of sugar in return for essential food supplies and manufactures from the United States. In the United States the Sugar Equalization Board was authorized to purchase Cuban sugar at a fixed price profitable to sugar production. This control was abandoned in 1919. Speculation in sugar then drove the price up from about 6 cents to 22 cents in May, 1920; by December, 1920, it had collapsed to $3\frac{3}{4}$ cents. Sugar mills and plantations, and banks which had extended abnormal credits to these, failed in large numbers, among them the Banco Nacional, which served as fiscal agent of the government. As has already been indicated, this speculative mania and the deflation of 1920 was world-wide, so that what happened in Cuba is not necessarily a reflection on Cubans.

During prosperity, as was always particularly true of Cuba, politics was quiescent. Economic depression and, in many cases, ruin brought a sudden revival of political discontent and agitation, and unfortunately this came in a presidential-election year. General Enoch Crowder had been sent to Cuba in March, 1919, to assist in the revision of election machinery. On August 30, 1920, as the election approached, the United States issued a definite warning in regard to the election. The economic strain was coming to a crisis at the same time. On October 11 President Menocal proclaimed a moratorium. United States observers were present, but nevertheless violence occurred on November 1, election day. During the winter of 1920–1921 the government was burdened with election disputes and financial difficulties.

The United States again felt the necessity of extending a guiding hand to prevent the breaking down of government on the expiration of the president's term in May. On January 2, 1921, the Department of State announced that General Crowder was being sent to Cuba again "to confer with President Menocal with respect to the political and financial condition of Cuba." Crowder indorsed the financial measures then before Congress for raising the moratorium and for a bank-liquidation commission. Further advice was prepared for extended reforms during 1921 and 1922, but the enactment of a suggested program was delayed by the Cuban congress. A crisis occurred during 1922. There was the widest divergence of statements as to the part played in it by the United States. One eminent publicist of the United States wrote that in the fall of 1922 the Cuban government requested approval under the Platt Amendment of an issue

of $50,000,000 in bonds to carry out financial and adminis-
trative reforms. The assent of the United States was given.
Another account of the crisis, which appeared in the press
in August, 1922, said that General Crowder presented to the
Cuban government a ten-day ultimatum in which he demanded, with the approval of Secretary Hughes, that a
particular legislative program be enacted. The program consisted of five laws prepared under Crowder's direction providing for a reform of the government accounting system,
suspension of the civil-service law in part, judicial reforms,
the adjustment of current indebtedness, and the flotation of
a $50,000,000 foreign loan. This pressure resulted in the
desired arrangements. The formal application for the loan
was dated October 18, and the consent of the United States
was given November 2. The full and authentic details were
not obtainable, since the Department of State was very ret-
icent in regard to the exact methods of conducting United
States diplomacy. The fiction of the voluntary request from
the Cuban government deceived no one acquainted with the
Caribbean diplomacy of the United States; in fact, it is exceedingly doubtful if any Caribbean republics had "voluntarily" requested the intervention of the United States in
their affairs, the Department of State to the contrary not-
withstanding. Enough official documents came to light to
disprove positively certain alleged "voluntary" requests
(dating from Roosevelt down), to throw doubt on the whole
practice, and to render the official disclaimers practically
worthless. In regard to this particular Cuban episode all
the available facts of the Crowder era seem to confirm the
approximate truth of the ultimatum story. General Crowder
remained in the island until January, 1923, as resident adviser to the government. The status as adviser in Cuba was
not radically different from the similar missions of advisers
of European countries, such as the British in Egypt. Crowder
returned to Cuba shortly on the altogether different basis of
ambassador. This mission continued from 1923 to 1927. The

extent of Crowder's supervision during this period was some-what uncertain. The cry of "nationalism" was raised in 1923, and for the next two years was in strong evidence. The presidential election in the United States may have contributed to a less urgent policy in the Caribbean. The most obvious fact in the situation was that the economic recovery of the island removed the excuse or necessity for drastic interference as in the earlier years.

With the recovery of sugar prices the economic recovery of Cuba was rapid, but its economic status was radically changed. Before the war United States capital had been largely interested in sugar and some other investments; after the war and deflation it was dominant in the most im-portant lines of industry. In 1911 United States capital was credited with control of 35 per cent of sugar production, by 1920 with 48 per cent, and by 1926 with 79 per cent. In public utilities little money was invested until the war and post-war periods, when American capital controlled the field. Of Cuban railroads United States capital controlled one of the two great systems. The iron resources were among the great fields of the world, but were scarcely worked. The Bethlehem Steel Corporation and the United States Steel Corporation were among the leading owners. These resources were almost all under American control. Of the banking resources 75 per cent were controlled by the United States. The total United States investments in Cuba were estimated by the Department of Commerce in 1924 at $1,250,000,000. In 1909 reliable estimates were $141,000,000. Most of the capital was exported during the war or was derived from war and post-war profits. The amount of money represented in Cuba dwarfed into insignificance the investments in a Cen-tral American country like Nicaragua. One estimate of in-vestments in Nicaragua in 1928 was $12,000,000. Estimates of relative distribution of United States investments to the southward in 1923 assigned 27 per cent to Cuba and 17 per cent to Mexico.

Haiti

The formal entrance of the United States into Haiti occurred in 1915. The immediate pretext was to maintain order when the mob raided the French Legation, and seized the fugitive president of the republic and killed him. Another reason, of longer standing, was the desire on the part of the United States to restore and administer Haitian finances. This leads still farther back to the determination to protect investments. The National Railway was in difficulties with the Haitian government and, in order to prevent foreclosure, appealed to the United States. Diplomatic intervention in September, 1914, stayed proceedings. The National Bank of Haiti was also in difficulties over the handling of public funds and, according to the United States minister, forced the issue in order to secure intervention and an American financial adviser of Haitian finances. Marines were landed in December, 1914, and seized $500,000 of gold for the bank-owners. In the contracts of both these institutions with the Haitian government the recipients had waived the right of diplomatic recourse. In this case the United States government, as in later years in the Mexican oil-land controversy, refused to sanction the right of a citizen to renounce national protection. The National City Bank of New York was the chief American interest involved. The United States was interested in teaching the Haitian government a lesson in the sanctity of contracts. Critics, however, insisted that contracts tainted with fraud were not binding. The final argument for intervention was presented by Lansing in a statement to the McCormick committee (May 6, 1922) to the effect that there was danger in 1915 that either Germany or France would seize a foothold in the republic. The Mole St. Nicholas as a naval base on the Windward Passage was the particular point of danger should it fall into foreign hands. No conclusive evidence in support of Lansing's contention was made public.

Shortly after the landing of marines a treaty was presented which was to constitute the basis of future relations between the republics. It was similar in many respects to the Platt Amendment treaty imposed upon Cuba, but went much farther. It was stated as the purpose of the treaty that the United States shall, "by its good offices, aid the Haitian government in the proper and efficient development of its agricultural, mineral, and commercial resources and in the establishment of the finances of Haiti on a firm and solid basis." A receiver of the customs was provided, as well as a financial adviser who was to supervise budgets, expenditures, accounts, revenues, and the service of the public debt. Haiti was not to increase her debt or reduce taxation without the consent of the United States. A constabulary was to be created under American officers. Haiti was to pledge not to alienate any territory to any foreign power. Advice was to be furnished for the development of natural resources and improvement of sanitation. The term of the treaty was to be ten years, but if for any reason either party considered that its purpose had not been attained in that time it should be extended. The extension to 1936 was later required by the United States.

An election of a new president was held under United States supervision on August 12, 1915. The candidates were informed that they must accept the provisions of the treaty beforehand. Dartiguenave was approved and elected. The treaty was then formally presented to the government on August 14. Five days later the seizure of the customs was ordered from Washington. The president was to be asked to request it, but the orders were "whether president requests or not, proceed." The government was then deprived of current funds in order to bring sufficient pressure to secure ratification of the treaty. Finally, military pressure was applied also before compliance was forthcoming. The treaty was ratified by the United States Senate and approved by the President on March 3, 1916.

The next step was the drafting and ratification of a new constitution. After two attempts, procedure by a constituent assembly composed of the congress was abandoned. The constitution was drafted by Franklin D. Roosevelt, Assistant Secretary of the Navy, in 1917. The second constituent assembly had not accepted it because of the provision permitting alien ownership of land. A plebiscite was then held (June 11, 1918) under the direction of the marines; and the electorate, the overwhelming majority of whom could neither read nor write, approved the new constitution by a reputed vote of 98,294 to 769. The voting was by white ballots for affirmative and blue ballots for negative.

The constitution provided for a president and a two-house congress. The president was to be elected by the congress. However, it was possible under certain contingencies not to call an election of congressmen, in which case the legislative power was vested in a council of state. This arrangement tended to produce stability of government, since the members of the council of state were appointed and removed by the president, and they in turn elected the president at four-year intervals. Before 1925 two regiments of marines, and afterwards one, were quartered behind the president's palace under the direction of the American high commissioner. In this manner the Haitian executive was protected and furnished with constructive advice. By an agreement of August, 1918, all proposed laws relating to treaty subjects had to be submitted to the American high commissioner for approval before they were enacted. This was later extended by interpretation to include all laws. Under these conditions there could be no doubt that the Haitian government could do nothing that was definitely disapproved by the United States. Furthermore, United States action under the treaty and constitution of 1918 was carried out with the strictest regard to the forms of law. In the technical sense there was no question of legality; in the moral sense the forcible procedure may offer a different problem.

Under the American occupation, roads were built by forced labor and at a great sacrifice of life. Revolutions were subdued and bandits eradicated. In all, some two thousand to three thousand natives were killed in the process. The misconduct and atrocities of some of the marines were a disgrace to the American occupation. The whole question was brought to public attention during 1921 and 1922, when the Senate committee, under the chairmanship of McCormick, investigated both Haiti and Santo Domingo. The financial administration was used to reward American politicians until 1923. A loan of $40,000,000 was authorized, and a claims commission was set up by a protocol of 1919 to refund indebtedness and stabilize finances. The terms of the bonds required United States control of finances until 1953. The railway and bank questions were for the most part settled in favor of the security-holders. The mixed-claims commission considered claims amounting to a total of $40,000,000, but awarded about 8.7 per cent as valid. From the standpoint of the foreigner there is little question of the good that was accomplished; from the standpoint of the native there is a radical difference of opinion. One of the weakest points in the American case in Haiti was the neglect to educate the Haitians in the highly technical problems of government introduced into the island. Elementary education was neglected, and higher education did not exist.

Santo Domingo

The republic of Santo Domingo occupied the eastern two thirds of the island of the same name; Haiti occupied the western third. The populations of both were predominantly Negro, especially of Haiti. Santo Domingo was Spanish in colonial tradition; Haiti was French. United States control in Santo Domingo began in 1905 and was legalized in 1907. A collector of customs was established, with the Egyptian precedent definitely in mind. In 1915, after several years of difficulties, a new plan was presented on November 19. It was similar to the treaty just presented to Haiti. Instead of a mere collector of customs, a financial adviser was to be appointed. The army and guard were to be replaced by a constabulary officered by Americans. The financial system was to be revised. The scheme was positively opposed. The government gradually dissolved. On May 4, 1916, military occupation of the island began. The treasury was seized on June 16. There were still attempts to reorganize the civil government. These were partly successful on July 25, when a new president was elected. The president refused to issue decrees putting the American reforms into effect. All money for current expenses was withheld after August 18 in order to coerce the government, but without success. Finally, on November 29, military government was proclaimed. The American military government became "supreme legislator, supreme judge, supreme executive" of Santo Domingo.

The military government lasted from November, 1916, to the fall of 1922. The population was disarmed, and order was maintained by drastic martial law. The atrocities of the marines were as bad or worse than in Haiti. In a few cases officers or enlisted men were punished. Financial reports of the occupation show very favorable results, although analysis dissolves much of these good appearances. The tariff of 1919 was particularly favorable to the products used by foreign business interests and, in conjunction with internal taxation, bore particularly heavily on the natives. The favorable trade balances due to very large exports went almost exclusively to foreign investors in the form of interest, dividends, and services. The revision of the land law failed to meet the necessities of the situation, but it did open the way to acquisition by foreign interests of large tracts of land often accompanied by the greatest hardships to the helpless evicted natives. Freedom of speech and of the press was drastically limited by censorship. It became an offense punishable by fine and imprisonment to criticize the military government. The case of Fabio Fiallo, the famous poet, was used as the rallying cry for the hatred of Latin America directed against the United States. To carry out the expensive operations and adjust claims and debts against the native government, loans were resorted to. Dominicans protested that these loans made by a foreign military government were not valid against the republic. It was under these circumstances that the United States provided a guaranty that the future Dominican government would recognize the obligations.

Plans for the withdrawal of the military government from Santo Domingo were first announced in December, 1920, by the Wilson administration. Again in June, 1921, the Harding administration presented a plan, and again the Dominicans refused to coöperate in carrying out the conditions imposed. Finally "the Memorandum of the Agreement of Evacuation" was accepted by representatives of the various political groups under the date of June 30, 1922. The provisional government was inaugurated later in the year. Elections for congress occurred nearly a year later, and elections for president in the spring of 1924. A new constitution was framed and proclaimed on June 13, 1924. The president was inaugurated in July, and the agreement of evacuation was ratified by the permanent government. With the consummation of these events the marines were withdrawn, but the customs supervision was continued. The native government immediately refused to make a $25,000,000 loan which would extend the time of supervision, and imposed a tax on the use, sale, or consumption of foreign goods. This last measure was to offset the tariff of 1919 in order to require foreign interests to pay what was considered a fair share of the taxes.

Porto Rico

Porto Rico and the Virgin Islands were the only possessions of the United States in the West Indies. The government of Porto Rico was originally established during the

American period by the Foraker act of 1900. The governor and the commission were appointed by the president. The lower house was elected by the Porto Ricans, and this house, together with the commission, constituted the legislative body. Before 1913 the commission had an American majority. In this way there were three vetoes possible on anything the native legislature might do: the senate, the governor, and Washington. In 1913 Wilson appointed the majority of the commission 'from Porto Rico. The Porto Rico government bill was approved on March 2, 1917. It was similar to the Jones bill for the Philippines. The governor was appointed by the president, and a two-house legislature was to be elected by the people. Porto Ricans were made citizens of the United States. A resident commissioner was to represent the island in Congress, but have no vote.

Porto Rico's nationalistic spirit, which dates from Spanish rule, had not disappeared with American annexation. Many Porto Ricans looked upon American government as merely a change from one imperial master to another. During the World War the nationalistic sentiment grew, as in the rest of the world. The principle of self-determination of small nations had an inevitable appeal to the Porto Ricans. The political parties were republicans, socialists, and unionists. The last group constituted about half the votes; the other two divided the other half about equally. The unionists controlled the legislature. The name "unionist" grew out of local factors and did not refer to the policy of the party. Unionists were in favor of independence or some form of autonomy, although the exact degree of independence desired might differ with individuals. The term which became current was "associated free state." Campbell of Kansas introduced a bill of this nature in the United States Congress. One of the outstanding features was the election of the governor, who would have the right to appoint his own department heads. The United States would have a resident commissioner in the island. The general scheme closely resembled the British precedents, which were just then very much in evidence through the creation of the Irish Free State.

These were the conditions accompanying the return of the Republicans to power in the United States. Harding appointed as governor, in reward for his campaign services, E. Mont Reily, a political worker from Kansas City. He had scarcely landed, in the summer of 1921, before he was in controversy with the Porto Ricans. Political turmoil was continuous. The legality of Reily's appointments was attacked. His recall was demanded. Impeachment proceedings in the Porto Rican legislature were attempted. Formal charges were made before the House in Washington by the resident commissioner, who insisted on an investigation. Reily finally resigned on February 16, 1923, and on March 12 Horace M. Towner of Iowa was appointed by Harding to fill the vacancy. No further serious difficulties were experienced in the island, but the free-state movement continued.

The nationalism of Porto Rico took advantage of the advertising possibilities of Lindbergh's Caribbean flight in the winter of 1927–1928 and of the meeting of the Sixth Pan-American Conference at Havana. A concurrent resolution was passed by the legislature which was a welcome to Lindbergh and an appeal to Coolidge. Lindbergh acted as messenger in delivering this document to the President: "The message of Porto Rico to your people is: 'Grant us the freedom that you enjoy, for which you struggled, which you worship, which we deserve, and you have promised us.'"

After Coolidge's speech before the Sixth Pan-American Conference at Havana in January, 1928, the president of the senate and the speaker of the house of the Porto Rican legislature sent a telegram congratulating him on the speech and asking that he recommend to Congress that they enact those sentiments. If it is impossible to do more,

we ask to be allowed to be constituted as a free state, concerting thus with your great republic such good and fraternal relations as may be necessary for the mutual welfare of the United States and

Porto Rico and to the dignity of our citizens. Justice and nothing but justice is what we ask, as citizens of America, as faithful Christians, and as children of the Almighty God that gave us the same inalienable rights your great republic knew how to invoke when declaring for independence at the memorable convention at Philadelphia.

A telegram was sent to the Pan-American Conference at Havana on January 22, 1928, which repudiated the press reports that independence was asked for:

We do not ask the Conference to intervene in domestic affairs of the American Union, but to express its solidarity and sympathy with aspirations of Porto Rico to full political and financial self-government in harmony with President Coolidge's opening speech.

Another telegram, of February 13, was sent to the President and to the Senate and House by the lower house of the Porto Rican legislature.

Porto Rico recommends ["demands" in the House and Senate telegrams] that the principles involved in these words [Lincoln's "government of the people etc."] be applied to our island in the form of public institutions, recommending to Congress the approval of bills introduced by our resident commissioner providing for the election of the governor of Porto Rico by the vote of her people at the elections of 1932 and enabling our people to formulate our own constitution in accordance with several memorials presented to Congress by our legislative Assembly.

Coolidge sent a single reply to the whole series of communications, addressing it to Governor Towner. He said that Porto Rico enjoyed a more liberal government than ever before in its history, and that the United States had made no promises to it which had not been fulfilled. "The Porto Rican government at present exercises a greater degree of sovereignty over its own internal affairs than does the government of any state or territory of the United States." The President then quoted a description of how bad conditions had been in the island before the coming of the United States. He recounted statistics to prove in dollars and cents what American rule had done for Porto Rico. But the Porto Ricans were not impressed by the array of figures or conciliated by his tone of impatient superiority. The President failed to consider the psychological factors, which are so important in such a situation.

The legislature replied that they looked for association with the United States, not for independence, "but association implies equality, coördination — not subordination. Equality and a perfect association would be feasible by means of the form of government suggested, leaving it to future progress to determine the shaping of the final form of association between the United States and Porto Rico."

Another answer appeared in *Current History* for May, 1928. It was written by Felix Cordova Davila, resident commissioner of Porto Rico in Washington. Davila attacked the statement of Coolidge that Porto Rico "exercises a greater degree of sovereignty . . . than . . . any state or territory of the United States." The Constitution, he pointed out, applies to the states. The Federal government exercised only powers delegated by the states, and residuary powers were retained by the states. The Constitution placed no limit on the power which might be exercised by Congress over Porto Rico. So many bills affecting Porto Rico were introduced in each Congress that "we in Porto Rico are so uneasy when Congress is in session that the adjournment of Congress is for Porto Rico a great relief." The actual powers of Porto Rico were analyzed. The governor and the president had absolute veto power; in the states a two-thirds vote might override a governor's veto. The appointed governor prepared the budget and might veto any item of an appropriation bill. The appointed auditor controlled accounts. The executive was appointed, not elected as in the states. The governor did not even know the language of the people he ruled. The commissioner of education was appointed by the president, and the legislature had no voice in the education of their children; the people controlled these matters in the states.

The organic law of Porto Rico might be changed at any time by Congress; in the states the people made and amended their own constitutions at will. The Congress taxed Porto Rico without representation, and in the war required compulsory military service without representation. "The first deals with rights of property; the second, with the sacred rights of life." This exchange of ideas had no practical result except that it set forth the different points of view. The President's answer on the Porto Rican question had already been given in his annual message to Congress on December 6, 1927: "As it is not contemplated that any change should be made immediately, the general subject may well have the thoughtful study of the Congress."

The Virgin Islands

The desire for a naval base in the eastern end of the Greater Antilles was an important element in United States policy after the Civil War. Attempts were made in 1867 and 1902 to purchase the Virgin Islands. The World War crisis forced the issue, and a treaty was signed on August 4, 1916, for the purchase of St. Thomas, St. John, St. Croix, and some smaller islands for $25,000,000. Ratifications were exchanged on January 17, 1917. An emergency-government act was approved on March 3, 1917. All civil, military, and judicial powers were vested in the governor and such other persons as should be appointed by the president. Army and navy officers might be appointed. Danish local laws, where not in conflict with this act, were to remain in force. They could be amended or repealed by the colonial council with the approval of the president. Free trade was established between the islands and the United States and its possessions in goods which were the products of these territories. Local taxes were continued as under Danish law. An export duty of $8 a ton was levied on sugar. This act made no mention of the civil and political rights of the residents. An act of

February 25, 1927, conferred citizenship on all children born after January 17, 1917, and on all Danish subjects who did not make a declaration to the contrary. The export duty on sugar was reduced from $8 a ton to $6.

Conclusion

These brief sketches of Caribbean countries outline the main features of United States policies in that area. In Central America interest lay primarily in stability, conditioned by the problems of security of the Panama Canal and of the route of the proposed Nicaragua canal. Investments and economic interests were relatively small in money value, although a considerable number of citizens were involved. The value of investments did not necessarily measure the solicitude they aroused in the protecting country. In the Greater Antilles, United States interests were more evenly divided between naval and economic considerations. From the military point of view those islands formed the first, or outer, line of naval defense for the southern coast of the United States, and especially for the Canal. Each of the great water passages from Florida to the Virgin Islands was commanded by the United States, and all possibility of a foreign foothold in that region was eliminated.

The Caribbean policy came into the campaign of 1920 to some degree. Harding said:

Nor will I misuse the power of the Executive to cover with a veil of secrecy rejected acts of unwarrantable interference in domestic affairs of the little republics of the Western Hemisphere such as in the past few years have not only made enemies of those who should be our friends, but have rightfully discredited our country as their trusted neighbor.

His record in Cuba, Haiti, Santo Domingo, Nicaragua, and Panama showed little departure in general policy from that pursued by the Wilson administration. During the period from 1923 to 1925 there was a tendency toward withdrawal, and conciliation was in evidence in Nicaragua, Cuba, Santo Domingo, and Mexico, although a more aggressive trend was followed in relations with Panama. Blakeslee attributed this policy to Hughes. However, it should be pointed out that it coincided with the advent of Coolidge, with the recovery from the crisis of post-war deflation, and with the policy of conciliation attending the preparations for the presidential election of 1924. After 1925 a more aggressive attitude was assumed in Nicaragua and Mexico along with the completion of the Panama treaty of 1926. Just what effect Hughes's resignation and Kellogg's appointment had on this change was uncertain. One difference was clear, however: there was more friction and irritation in Kellogg's conduct of foreign relations than under the Hughes administration.

A natural question presents itself as to whether the United States policy was justified. Any answer depends upon the point of view. From the standpoint of the United States, orderly government was established and preserved, economic interests were promoted, and naval security was fully guaranteed. In this sense there could be but one answer for the average American. But this was imperialism pure and simple. From the standpoint of the population of the Caribbean countries the answer was not so clear. When a backward country was developed by foreign capital, the interest on the investments, profits, and salaries, as well as the product of the industry, left the country. The permanent benefits to the people of the country were small. The greater the proportion of foreign capital invested, the smaller the benefits to the people. The absentee landlord and the absentee industrialist were not interested in the country beyond the scope of their business. The population to a great degree was kept in the condition of laborers, at the lowest possible wages. The one-crop system was imposed on such countries as Cuba and Santo Domingo. Taxation was usually relatively light on the foreign holdings and relatively heavy on the native, with his low standards of living and low wages.

Such countries must remain economically dependent for an indefinite time, and in the meantime the foreigner drained the land of its productivity and natural resources. It was doubtful if the character of the people was materially bettered by artificial stimulation of their wants in imitation of the standards of the United States. The foreign governmental methods and industrial organization increased the technical requirements and complicated the adjustments of native life very rapidly, whereas the educational and cultural levels of the people developed slowly. It was at least open to argument whether the gap between the standards of training and ability required to manage the new government and economic organization, on the one hand, and the level of development of the people, on the other, was not wider in 1928 than in 1900. Were the backward peoples catching up, or were they falling farther and farther behind the pace set by modern civilization? Whether in the sphere of influence of the United States in the Caribbean or in that of some other imperial nation, it was only with outside support that the existing conditions of their artificial civilization could be maintained, even after years of development. It was an artificial stage of existence and was superimposed upon them.

SELECTED BIBLIOGRAPHY

General

DUNN, R. W. American Foreign Investments. The Viking Press, 1926.

LATANÉ, J. H. A History of American Foreign Policy. Doubleday, Doran and Company, Inc., 1927.

BLAKESLEE, G. H. The Recent Foreign Policy of the United States. The Abingdon Press, 1925.

HUGHES, CHARLES E. The Pathway of Peace. Harper & Brothers, 1925.

Mexico

HACKETT, C. W. The Mexican Revolution and the United States, 1910–1926. World Peace Foundation, Pamphlet Series, IX, No. 5.

   This should be supplemented by Hackett's articles each month in *Current History*.

RIPPY, J. F. The United States and Mexico. Alfred A. Knopf, Inc., 1926.
This is the only one-volume survey of the whole field of United States relations with Mexico. Very reliable.

Central America

MUNROE, DANA G. The Five Republics of Central America. Carnegie Endowment for International Peace, Division of Economics and History, 1918.
YOUNG, J. P. Central American Currency and Finance. Princeton University Press, 1925.
COX, I. J. Nicaragua and the United States, 1909–1927. World Peace Foundation, Pamphlet Series, X, No. 7.
This should be supplemented by C. W. Hackett's articles each month in *Current History*.

STIMSON, H. L. American Policy in Nicaragua. Charles Scribner's Sons, 1927.
In this book Stimson gives his personal story of his mission to Nicaragua.

Cuba

CHAPMAN, CHARLES E. A History of the Cuban Republic. The Macmillan Company, 1927.
JENKS, L. H. Our Cuban Colony. The Vanguard Press, 1928.

Haiti

DOUGLAS, P. H. "American Occupation of Haiti," *Political Science Quarterly* (June–September, 1927), Vol. XLII, pp. 228–241, 368–396.
KNIGHT, M. M. "Haiti's Progress under American Protection," *Current History* (June, 1926), Vol. XXIV, pp. 351–358.
Both this and the preceding article are competent short studies of the question and may serve as a sound introduction to the mass of periodical literature, the most of which must be read with the greatest caution. The New York *Nation* for June 6, 1928, brought out an important aspect of Haiti news. The Associated Press correspondent for Haiti was formerly H. P. Davis, author of "Black Democracy," and later Frank Evans, an officer in the Marine Corps and head of the Haitian gendarmerie. At an earlier time Evans served in the United States as a publicity man for the Marine Corps. The United Press correspondent was Captain Craigie of the Marine Corps, also a former publicity man for that branch of the service.

Santo Domingo

KNIGHT, M. M. The Americans in Santo Domingo. The Vanguard Press, 1928.
This is an unusually sound piece of work in a field where there is almost nothing reliable. It takes into account the effect of American occupation on the people of Santo Domingo, as well as the interests of the United States in the island.

CHAPTER XXX

POLITICAL POLICIES: THE WESTERN
HEMISPHERE (Concluded)

South America

BEFORE the World War the United States did not extend to South America any body of positive policies similar to those applied to the Caribbean area. Those countries were more remote, and the arguments of military defense and economic interest were not so clear. Furthermore, the states of the southern continent were relatively more stable politically than the semitropical and tropical Caribbean states. After the World War some tendencies indicated a more positive interest in that region, on lines which resembled some aspects of Caribbean policy. Argentina, Brazil, and Chile had become powerful and progressive republics. Brazil was tropical, but the other two lay in temperate latitudes more nearly similar to the United States. The Pacific coast and the interior to the north of these presented very formidable natural handicaps. The mountain ranges extended almost to the coast. The interior plateaus were extremely high. The transportation difficulties were all but insuperable. The tropical possessions across the eastern ranges of mountains on the eastern watershed had little connection with the highlands, which were the centers of civilization and of economic activity. The lands along the whole Pacific coast were immensely wealthy in minerals which were essential to the world. The difficulties of exploitation were such that only enterprises with large capital could be successful. This meant foreign capital, especially in the tropical latitudes, where the people possessed little accumulated wealth.

431

Bolivia

Bolivia possessed great tin deposits and produced nearly one third of the world's supply. The production was dominated by United States capital. Approximately 40 per cent of Bolivian revenue was derived from tin. There was some gold, but more silver and copper. It was the world's chief source of bismuth, which was British-controlled. Oil after the war rivaled tin in political importance; not that oil was produced, but control of the deposits was considered essential for the future. The Standard Oil Company of New Jersey came to dominate the field. The more or less familiar drama of a weak nation trying to conserve these resources by nationalizing the subsoil and limiting the size of holdings was played out to the end. The limitations were evaded, and the government royalty was reduced from 12 and 15 per cent to 11 per cent. These oil resources lay to the east of the mountains, and the outlet was to the Atlantic. Transportation was the greatest need of the country in order to bind it together and make possible its development under the handicaps imposed by nature. The sanitation of cities was another serious problem. The sanitation loan of 1920 presents an example of another angle of foreign investments which became more and more frequent. It was what is called a tied investment, since it required that the materials used in construction must be American. This type of requirement made business, through the bankers' activities, for many branches of American enterprise.

The most important of the loans of capital to the Bolivian government was the Stifel-Nicolaus loan (made in 1922) of $33,000,000 at 8 per cent, running twenty-five years. The bonds were not redeemable before 1937, and then at 105. The security for the loan included about half the total revenue in 1922 and about two thirds in 1925. For the service of the loan a Permanent Fiscal Commission was created, as stipulated in the contract, composed of three members, two of whom were nominated by the bankers. This commission was authorized to collect the taxes pledged to the loan. One of the bankers' commissioners was to be a director of the national bank. These conditions were more than the situation warranted; but through an earlier blunder the government had given the banker group an option on future loans. The bankers took advantage of their option and of Bolivia's need. English money was offered as low as 5 per cent, but Bolivia could not accept. The bonds were taken at 92 and 93 and sold to the public at 101. The purpose of the loan was to refund the public debt and to build highways and railroads. The relation of the United States government to the loan was obscure. It did not appear in the contract, as in the Salvador contract. Since the loan was made after the Department of State had inaugurated its policy of supervising loans, it was natural to assume that it had official sanction. Some writers made very positive statements regarding the alleged share of the department in the negotiations, but there was not enough specific evidence available to be dogmatic on the question. The total amount of American investments in Bolivia in 1927 was estimated at nearly $100,000,000, of which some $50,000,000 was in tin and oil.

Peru

Peru presents many natural characteristics similar to those of Bolivia. American investments increased from about $50,000,000 before the World War to $100,000,000 in 1925. Copper production was largely American. The Vanadium Corporation of America produced about 92 per cent of the world's supply of that metal. About 90 per cent of the oil production in 1925 was controlled by the Standard Oil Company of New Jersey. Government construction of roads and sanitation projects were largely in the hands of the Foundation Company of New York. Here, again, appeared the now familiar institution — the collection agency. For the loan of

$7,000,000 issued in 1924 the government pledged revenues as security. These were to be collected by an agency controlled by the Foundation Company. The Peruvian army was being assisted by a French advisory mission, and the navy by a naval mission from the United States.

Chile

Chile presented quite a different aspect both politically and economically. American investment in 1912 was estimated at $15,000,000; by 1925 it was expanded to about $400,000,000. This was represented by holdings in copper, iron, nitrates, industrials, and in the public debt. In contrast to the sister republics to the north, outside control of finances did not appear.

TACNA-ARICA

The Tacna-Arica dispute between Peru and Chile grew out of the treaty of Ancón of 1883, one of the treaties closing the war between Chile and her neighbors, Peru and Bolivia. The disputed provinces were to continue in the possession of Chile, but after ten years a plebiscite was to determine their permanent status. The matter remained an open controversy, as the plebiscite was never held. An appeal was made by both Peru and Bolivia to the League, but many considerations intervened. Direct negotiations were attempted in December, 1921. The United States intervened on January 18, 1922, offering its good offices. A conference was held at Washington in which the issue between Peru and Chile was defined and the United States was chosen as arbiter to interpret the plebiscite section of the treaty of Ancón and immediately related matters. The award was rendered on March 4, 1925. It decided in favor of holding the plebiscite, and the Plebiscitary Commission of three — one appointed by Chile, one by Peru, and one (the president of the commission) by the United States — was set up to prepare and administer the settlement.

The work of the commission was hampered by controversy. First Chile refused to coöperate; then Peru. General Pershing served for the United States until January, 1926, when he was relieved by General Lassiter. The commission finally terminated its activities in June, 1926, when Lassiter published a report criticizing Chile for improper conduct relative to the attempted plebiscite.

In the meantime negotiations had been transferred to Washington (April 15, 1926) in order to arrive at some other solution. Three different general proposals were discussed: neutralization; division between Peru and Chile, giving Tacna and the port of Arica to Peru; and sale to Bolivia, the proceeds to be divided between the disputants. This last proposal had much in its favor from the standpoint of the larger interests of all concerned, as Bolivia felt the lack of an outlet over her own territory to the sea. The outstanding difficulty, however, was the fact that her foreign-loan obligations and the pledging of her revenues made such an addition to her financial obligations a matter of doubtful public policy. The interest of the United States in the settlement of the question was more than a matter of Pan-American idealism: a peaceful settlement which would remove these disturbing factors from the international politics of western South America was of serious economic concern to the United States. The possible effect of a second "war of the Pacific" on the relations between the United States and these three South American nations is beyond prediction, and such a war might yield most unexpected results. It is not overstating the matter to point out that political interest in any geographical area was in direct proportion to the economic and military importance of such an area to the United States. This explains the tendency to extend into South America policies similar to those of the Caribbean area.

THE PAN-AMERICAN CONFERENCES

The Fifth Pan-American Conference was held at Santiago, Chile, in 1923. At this meeting the conflict of the points of view of the United States and Latin America was much in evidence. The sincerity of the disarmament policy of the United States was attacked because of the assistance given to Brazil in reorganizing her navy. The statement that the Monroe Doctrine would be interpreted by the United States alone became the subject of severe criticism. Steps were also taken to reorganize the Pan-American Union in the direction of an American League of Nations. This would incidentally limit the influence of the United States in the union. The American government found it expedient to yield on some points. The presidency of the governing board was made elective instead of being vested permanently in the Secretary of State of the United States, and any country might be represented by a special delegate in the absence of the regular minister accredited to the United States. In practice the elective presidency went to the American secretary, although the international agreement authorized the election of any other member. A plan for an American League of Nations, presented by President Brum of Uruguay, was postponed to the next conference. This plan would go farther than the reorganization of the Pan-American Union and would restrict United States control even more. Naturally it was not received with enthusiasm by the American delegation. The agenda of the conference included many subjects, but only four treaties were completed: the registration of trademarks, publicity of customs documents, provision for special conferences, and a peace treaty providing that all questions not settled diplomatically be submitted to an American commission for investigation, no military measures to be taken in the interim. This peace treaty was essentially an adoption of the principle of the Bryan treaties by the Pan-American Union.

The Sixth Pan-American Conference was held at Havana, Cuba, on January 16 and February 20, 1928. In some respects the United States could not look forward to it without misgivings, since the question of reorganization was to come up, and the Caribbean policy of the United States had aroused heated opposition throughout Latin America. However, the conditions immediately surrounding the meeting were unusually favorable. Lindbergh was making his good-will flight round the coasts of the Caribbean. President Coolidge attended the conference in person. This was a unique event. The reception of the President was a typically Latin-American ovation and provided a most cordial setting for the opening sessions. The location of the meeting at Havana, just outside the borders of the United States, where American influence was particularly strong, lent an atmosphere of conciliation. By contrast one can imagine the effect had the meeting been at Buenos Aires, where the United States good-will flyers had been received in silence only a short time before. The importance of Hughes as head of the United States delegation could hardly be overestimated. These factors contributed to the result, although they did not fully explain the friendly feeling.

When the question of reorganization was presented, Hughes accepted the principle that the governing board should be composed of such representatives as the governments might appoint, and that such appointment might devolve upon diplomatic representatives, just as though the United States had never opposed it. This was an important reversal in policy. The proposal of rotation in the office of president was defeated. The attempt to enlarge the scope of the Union to include political subjects was also defeated. In both these votes Latin-American states for the most part voted with the United States. Two important peace resolutions were adopted approving compulsory arbitration of differences of a juridical character and condemning wars of aggression.

The problem of preparing a codification of international law was first acted upon in 1901 at the conference held in Mexico City. Results were extremely slow. A convention on private international law was adopted at Havana by all states except the United States, and agreement was reached on some subjects of public international law. An international aviation treaty was adopted, and in it the United States insisted upon reservation of the right to regulate all air traffic in the vicinity of the Panama Canal Zone and of American fortifications in the Caribbean. It was not that the United States refused to permit airways across the Zone: its insistence was upon the right to specify the airways and to establish prohibited districts in order to prevent the discovery of military secrets which might be of advantage to enemies. The Pan-American motor highway and the Pan-American railroad were favorably considered.

In view of the hostile demonstrations throughout Latin America directed at the Caribbean policy of the United States, it was expected that these questions would be aired at Havana. Instead they were not mentioned in any definite manner. Indirectly, however, certain principles involved were discussed heatedly in connection with the problems of international law. In spite of attempts to shelve it, a resolution concerning the right of one nation to intervene in the affairs of another was presented. It was one of the few matters that aroused excitement. No agreement could be reached, and, as often happens when embarrassing questions arise, it was deferred to the next conference.

The questions which came nearest to causing disaster were those of tariff and quarantine. The fight was led by Dr. Pueyrredon, the Argentine ambassador to Washington. That country produced cattle, corn, wheat, wool, and flax-seed, the same articles as the United States farmer. High tariffs were imposed upon these products by the United States. The tariff on Cuban sugar had been increased in 1921 and 1922. Other American producers clamored for further protection on bananas from Caribbean countries and on tomatoes, peppers, etc. from Mexico. The regulations of the United States against Argentine meat were interpreted as an economic discrimination for the sole purpose of excluding competition. Argentina was taking exactly the same stand against the United States on the meat question as the United States had taken forty-five years earlier against Europe. The Latin-American proposal was directed primarily at the United States and was to the effect that the Pan-American Union take action to suppress or reduce high tariffs in order to establish greater freedom of trade, and to supervise the application of sanitary quarantine against plant and animal products. Mexico and Venezuela supported Argentina in the discussion. A deadlock threatened when Dr. Pueyrredon declared that he would not sign any convention that did not provide for the desired action on tariff and quarantine. His government eventually intervened and designated another member as head of the delegation, thus avoiding the definite crisis.

It was impossible to evaluate the real results of the conference without further developments. The most significant element which appeared immediately was the fact that Latin America was badly divided. On every controversial question, including intervention and tariff, there were a substantial number of states that supported the United States.

CANADA

The reorientation of Canada was one of the very important results of the World War as it affected the relations of the United States. Before the war Canada was thought of primarily as one of the dominions of the British Empire, whose interest lay with the mother country and her European interests. The newer view recognized that in many respects Canada had more in common with the United States than with Great Britain. The problem of the Pacific in 1921 forced this view into the foreground. Canada insisted on Oriental exclusion and the termination of the Japanese alliance. The Washington Conference of 1922 averted a crisis in the British Empire as well as in the Pacific. Canada, in fact, came to be looked upon so much as an American nation that there were numerous suggestions that she be included in the Pan-American Union. United States relations involved many questions of importance to both nations. Canada furnished nickel and wood pulp for paper. The proposed Great Lakes–Atlantic waterway project involved important international entanglements. The numerous boundary problems in earlier years led to a valuable experiment beginning in 1909. By treaty an International Joint Commission was created as a permanent organization to which disputes might be referred. Hughes suggested at Havana that such commissions would be valuable among the other American states as a step toward permanent peace.

CONCLUSION

As all discussions of the policies of the United States in the Western Hemisphere begin with the Monroe Doctrine, so they also end with it. The Monroe Doctrine, understood in its original sense (which is still the more popular sense) as a dictum to Europe "Thou shalt not" was for the most part outgrown. After the World War there seemed to be little occasion for anxiety that any non-American power would attempt to establish itself in the Western Hemisphere. To the average American, however, the Monroe Doctrine had become such a habit — or mental disease — that it had become a necessity to the adequate expression of the national ego. The corollaries of the doctrine — or, in other words, the Monroe Doctrine interpreted in the sense of "the United States must look after Latin America" — were never before so vital to imperial United States as after the World

War. The only valid question that could be raised here was whether it was necessary, after all, that the United States be imperial.

SELECTED BIBLIOGRAPHY

DUNN, R. W. American Foreign Investments. The Viking Press, 1926.

KEENLEYSIDE, H. L. Canada and the United States. Alfred A. Knopf, Inc., 1929.

MARSH, M. A. The Bankers in Bolivia. The Vanguard Press, 1928.

STUART, G. H. The Tacna-Arica Dispute. World Peace Foundation, Pamphlet Series, X, No. 1, 1927.

CHAPTER XXXI

POLITICAL POLICIES: EUROPE

THE most pressing problems in European relations after the armistice were emergency or transitional activities pending the making of the permanent peace. The impending conflict between isolation and international coöperation hampered even this participation in European affairs. When the Harding administration took office the policy was to take no part in European political questions; that is, in those which did not affect American interests. This was in accordance with a literal interpretation of the Monroe Doctrine as it applied to Europe. Hughes drew a distinction between political questions on the one hand and economic questions on the other. The American government was vitally interested in the latter field on account of the position of the United States in the monetary world. Distinctions could be drawn on paper between things political and economic, but in practice the economic implications were found to be present in almost all. The distinction was useful primarily for political purposes as a convenient means of conciliating the extreme isolationists. A distinction was also drawn between Europe and the League of Nations, which was fully as vague.

The Harding administration set out to make separate peace settlements with Germany, Austria, and Hungary. There were two groups of claims against the German government: the claims of American citizens for destruction of property and the costs of the army on the Rhine. The Germans had two groups of claims against the United States: property in the possession of the alien-property custodian and property requisitioned or sold, such as patents, ships, and a radio station.

In the Treaty of Versailles the United States had made no

442

demands for indemnity either in colonies or in money, but the claims indicated above against Germany and her allies were recognized. The administration of the German reparations to the Allied and Associated Powers was vested in a body called the Reparations Commission.

In the joint resolution terminating the war with Germany and Austria (approved July 2, 1921) it was provided that all property was to be retained until "suitable provision" should be made for meeting the claims of Americans against the German and Austrian governments, and all rights of the United States provided in the Versailles treaty were claimed for the United States.

The separate treaties with Germany, Austria, and Hungary were signed on August 25, August 24, and August 21, respectively, were ratified by the Senate on October 18, and were proclaimed during October and November, 1921. Mixed commissions were provided to fix amounts. An agreement dated August 10 worked out the details and fixed April 9, 1923, as the final date for filing claims. A total of approximately $1,500,000,000 in claims was filed. Of these, only $120,000,000 were awarded.

In the meantime German payments under the Versailles treaty broke down. France undertook to collect by force. Finally, a proposal for a commission of experts (apparently suggested by the United States government) was accepted. The experts worked out the so-called Dawes Plan for collecting reparations. The American members of the commission which drafted it were probably suggested by the United States government, but they were nominally appointed by the Reparations Commission. Isolation was rapidly breaking down; and the next steps were the London and Paris financial conferences (1924 and 1925), where the proceeds of the experts' plan were allocated among the powers. The United States was officially represented in both these meetings, and was assigned 55,000,000 marks a year on costs of the army on the Rhine and $2\frac{1}{2}$ per cent, or not to exceed 45,000,000 marks a year, on claims. These payments, as specified in the final protocol of January 14, 1925, began September 1, 1926.

The other side of the question was the policy of the United States in regard to German and other enemy property. The policy of the government in seizing and requisitioning enemy property during the war was in itself a matter of doubtful propriety under the principles of international law. The joint resolution of July 2, 1921, was an outright infraction both of international law and of traditional United States policy. The first step toward the return of alien property was the act of March 4, 1923, providing for the payment of German claims under $10,000 and for a payment of $10,000 on all larger claims, together with the interest to that date. During 1926 a plan for payment of the remainder was prepared by the Treasury Department. It was known in Congress as the Mills bill. In support of this measure Winston, Under Secretary of the Treasury, urged action, championing the sanctity of private property in time of war. He insisted that it was highly important for the United States to support this principle loyally, because the United States was a creditor nation and American investments in foreign countries in time of war must be protected. The Treasury plan was rejected by Congress, but a substitute was passed and was approved by the President on March 10, 1928. It set aside from certain German payments a fund from which the American claims against Germany were to be paid. Property of the nationals of Germany, Austria, and Hungary was to be returned. Payments to Germans for requisitioned property were to begin on the basis of an increased valuation not to exceed $100,000,000. Austrian and Hungarian property was to be returned on deposit with the Treasury of the amount of American claims against those states. It should be emphasized that this act was merely a plan of settlement and an authorization to proceed in accordance with the specifications. It would take several years for the plan to be executed, and it might break down before the settlement was completed.

FOREIGN DEBTS

During the war the United States advanced loans to the Allied powers in large amounts, and some credits were advanced after the armistice. The question of interallied debts was excluded from the settlements made at the Peace Conference, and in 1921 no steps had been taken by the United States toward adjusting the debts owed by foreign governments. Various plans were suggested — complete cancellation, partial cancellation, and payment in full. The American position was payment in full. Harding asked Congress for authority to negotiate adjustments of the principal and defaulted interest in his annual message of December 6, 1921. Congress passed an act, approved on February 9, 1922, creating a commission of five members, with the Secretary of the Treasury as chairman. They were authorized to refund or to convert principal and interest into bonds "in such form and of such terms, conditions, date of maturity, and rate of interest, and with such security, if any, as shall be deemed for the best interests of the United States of America," provided the maximum time of maturity should not exceed June 15, 1947, and the minimum rate of interest $4\frac{1}{2}$ per cent. Bonds of one government should not be exchanged for those of another. The life of the commission was limited to three years.

The terms of this act did not provide an adequate basis for settlement, and the British settlement was authorized by a special act (approved on February 28, 1923) and on different terms. The agreement extended the payments over a period of sixty-two years, and in effect provided for partial cancellation of the debt. This law increased the membership of the commission to eight, not more than four of the members to be of any one political party. Later an act of June 21, 1925, extended the life of the commission two years. By the time the commission expired (February 9, 1927) settlements were reached with thirteen countries for $11,500,000,000.

Only four countries had not made agreements — Russia, Greece, Austria, and Liberia. The agreements with France and Yugoslavia were not ratified. Subsequently settlements were made with Greece and Liberia. The major settlements were adjusted to spread over a period of sixty-two years. It was estimated that the settlements canceled 23 per cent of the British debt, 46 per cent of the Belgian debt, 52 per cent of the French debt, and 75 per cent of the Italian debt.

RELATIONS WITH RUSSIA

The Russian revolution occurred on March 15, 1917, and the provisional government was recognized by the United States on March 22. In November, 1917, the Bolsheviki came to power by revolution. They proceeded to confiscate land and public resources and to repudiate all debts contracted by previous governments. The United States refused to recognize the Soviet régime because it did not have the sanction of the Russian people, because it refused to respect its international obligations, and because it carried on revolutionary activity in the United States against the American government. The particular items of international obligations repudiated by the Soviet government were $187,000,000 in loans of the United States to the provisional government, $75,000,000 in bonds sold in the United States, and American property confiscated to the amount of $443,000,000. The position of the United States government was generally supported by the public, including the American Federation of Labor, which rejected at its annual meeting on October 12, 1926, a resolution favoring recognition. On the other hand, Senator Borah advocated recognition. Many of the leading governments of the world recognized the Soviet régime, but none of them secured a recognition of repudiated debts or compensation for confiscated property.

RELIEF ACTIVITIES

The record of American relations with Europe would be incomplete without a summary of relief activities covering the ten-year period. Part of this contribution to European rehabilitation was provided by the government, and the remainder by voluntary contributions of the people through relief organizations. The first four years, 1918–1922, called primarily for emergency relief. The United States government advanced $100,000,000 to be administered by the American Relief Association in Europe. This was under the direction of Herbert Hoover. Relief in Russia in 1921 was supplied partly from a government appropriation of $20,000,000 and partly from the Red Cross and other sources to the extent of $60,000. The next six years, 1922–1928, were somewhat different. The emergency requirement of the major countries had been met. Much of the remaining work was in the Balkan area and the Near East. The two leading agencies were the Near East Relief Committee and the Jewish Joint Distribution Committee. The former cared for orphans and refugees over a period of thirteen years, expending a total of $105,000,000; the latter carried on both emergency and construction relief among the Jewish people, expending $70,000,000, and proposed a continuation of their activities for another ten years on a basis of $1,000,000 per year. One of its outstanding experiments was the settlement of Jewish families on farm land in Russia.

SELECTED BIBLIOGRAPHY

HOUGHTON, N. D. Policy of the United States and Other Nations with Respect to the Recognition of the Russian Soviet Government, 1917–1929. International Conciliation Pamphlets, No. 247, 1929.

SCHUMAN, FREDERICK L. American Policy toward Russia since 1917. International Publishers, 1928.

BUELL, R. L. Europe: A History of Ten Years. The Macmillan Company, 1928.

JAQUITH, H. C. "Ten Years of American Relief Activities Abroad," *Current History* (February, 1929), Vol. XXIX, pp. 733–736.

CHAPTER XXXII

INTERNATIONAL POLICIES

The United States and the League of Nations

AFTER the defeat of the League of Nations in the United States Senate, the government was under the necessity of formulating a working policy for dealing with international problems. Harding had made many unwise and contradictory pledges during the campaign, and these undoubtedly embarrassed the administration in its conduct of foreign relations. It is impossible to explain the reasons for the early phases of policy toward the League or to place the responsibility exactly. Did the policy represent the personal convictions of President Harding or of Hughes, his Secretary of State, or did it represent the dictation of certain party leaders? The situation must be accepted for the time being without explanation.

The Knox resolution [1] declaring the end of the war reserved to the United States all the rights and benefits of the treaty of peace with Germany, and the resolution of ratification of the separate treaty with Germany forbade the president to participate in League activities or to appoint representatives on League commissions or organizations acting under its auspices without the consent of Congress. It is said that during the first weeks of the Harding administration communications from the League were not even answered, the government refusing to recognize its existence. This attitude was impossible to maintain; and a subterfuge was resorted to by which the United States was represented in the League activities by unofficial observers or, in some cases, by private

[1] Compare page 67.

individuals who were appointed to important positions with the approval of the American government. In regard to the unofficial observers Hughes stated the simple facts when he said : "They are unofficial simply in the sense that they are not and cannot properly become members of the League organization or committees. But, so far as our government is concerned, they represent it just as completely as those designated by the president always have represented our government in the conferences and negotiations which he properly authorizes in the conduct of our foreign relations." The extreme attitude of the Senate really defeated itself. Instead of that body's exercising its constitutional control over appointments and treaties during these early years, it had little or no voice in these matters where they concerned League activities. Unofficial observers were appointed without its consent, and the policies they were instructed to insist upon in international conferences were largely beyond its control.

The isolated position of the United States was gradually modified ; instead of ignoring the League as it had in 1921, by 1924 and 1925 it was participating officially in the London conference, in the Paris financial conference for adjusting payments under the Dawes Plan, and in the opium conference of 1924–1925. The last part of 1924 seems to mark the turning point. In 1925 Congress appropriated money to pay the United States' share of expenses arising out of the second opium conference and the Conference on Traffic in Arms. Europe recognized from the first the impossibility of the satisfactory conduct of international affairs without the coöperation of the United States, and gradually the American government came to realize that American interests required a measure of active coöperation with the League, although without membership. To these American policies was given the euphemistic name "coöperation without entangling alliances."

SOCIAL POLICY

Social and humanitarian questions of international character were handled by two types of organizations after the war. The first type, in point of time, was the international bureaus and unions, which were of pre-war origin; the second was the League of Nations, which represented a much broader scope of activities and a more complete machinery of administration. The Covenant of the League provided that the League should take over the independent bureaus and unions with the consent of the parties thereto, and but for the opposition of the United States many of them would have been absorbed or affiliated. In 1921 the League took steps to organize its health activities. The International Office of Public Health, created in 1907, found itself unable to coöperate directly because of the unwillingness of the United States to permit any organization of which it was a member to become attached to the League. Later the Permanent Health Organization of the League was formed, and indirectly through a mixed committee coöperated with the International Office of Public Health, and an American was appointed to the Standing Health Committee. This isolationist policy of the United States on social and humanitarian questions was not permanent. There was a gradual modification of attitude until in the opium conferences of 1925 the United States was officially represented. This broader policy was applied also to some other questions, but American participation even under these conditions was limited.

ECONOMIC POLICY: SELF-GOVERNMENT FOR BUSINESS

International economic questions presented a somewhat more difficult problem from the standpoint of American international policy and were of more vital importance to international peace. As one writer has put it: "Economic problems have taken the place of religion and of dynasty as offering the greatest danger of future wars, and misunderstanding and bitterness of spirit among business men are therefore doubly dangerous." To the adjustment of these problems through international action there are two methods of approach: through machinery of economic self-government and through the political machinery of states acting internationally.

Among business men two extreme points of view were represented in foreign policies. One group was extremely nationalistic, aggressively imperialistic, and was constantly appealing to the government to assist in the promotion of business abroad; the other was internationally minded and threw its influence on the side of the international accords which form the basis of good will among the powers. It was one of the peculiarities of the American situation that many of the most important contributions to world peace and stability came from the broader-minded business men, often conservatives in politics, rather than from the professional liberals such as Borah, Johnson, Norris, and La Follette, whose stock in trade was the protection of the "poor people" from the exploitation of Wall Street and the international banker. It was the second type of business man that supported the League of Nations and the International Chamber of Commerce.

The International Chamber of Commerce was created as an instrumentality of better understanding and self-adjustment among the business men of the world — a kind of business men's league of nations. Beginning in 1906 there were occasional congresses of chambers of commerce, but in 1919 the Chamber of Commerce of the United States took steps toward a meeting for the creation of a permanent international body. This meeting was held in Paris in 1920, and the permanent organization was effected. Membership consisted of national chambers of commerce and trade associations with one vote each. Associate membership of firms or individuals was provided, but without a vote. Head-

quarters were located at Paris, with permanent resident commissioners. The subjects considered by the organization
cover much the same range as those considered by governments in conducting foreign economic policies.

The ideas of this newer type of business man were illustrated by Victor M. Cutter, president of the United Fruit
Company, writing in *Current History* for October, 1927:

> The greatest and most complicated problem is international
> commerce. In the final solution it will be placed upon a just and
> sound basis, not by the judicial acts of the governments concerned,
> but by the establishment of intimate and friendly relations between
> manufacturers. Twenty years ago there were those who preached
> economic independence; today the folly of this doctrine is apparent
> to everyone. We have created a demand for so large a proportion
> of manufactured products which we must import that we lose our
> independence upon this count alone. . . . Foreign trade today means
> a full and free contact with all the countries of the world, and it
> means that our viewpoint must change from a national to an inter-
> national one. It has been proved time and time again that there is
> little use in bolstering up foreign trade by imperialism.

General Tasker H. Bliss expressed his opinion in *Foreign
Affairs*:

> It is the business men of a few great nations that will decide most
> future questions of peace and war. Can they not decide them in a
> business way? Can they not establish a working rule that will
> guarantee a fair distribution of the natural products of the world —
> that will assure their supply of coal, iron, copper, oil, or what not
> in the markets of the world without the constant apprehension of
> political interference? If they can they can do more than anything
> else to check war for the indefinite future.

COMMERCIAL ARBITRATION

Trade disputes between business men of different nationalities were an important source of international economic
friction, one that was met to a certain degree by instruments
of economic self-government. Many business men of several
countries adopted the method of arbitration of such disputes

through their own machinery rather than through appeals to the national courts of one of the parties. The International Chamber of Commerce indorsed the plan at its London meeting in 1921 and took steps to provide machinery and rules of procedure. The Economic Committee of the League of Nations drafted a protocol on commercial arbitration which was adopted by the Assembly on September 26, 1927, and opened to all nations for signature.

The Chamber of Commerce of the United States very early made an arbitration agreement with Argentine business men at Buenos Aires, and the Pan-American Financial Conference of 1920 indorsed this type of procedure. Agreements were later made with Brazil, Colombia, Ecuador, Panama, Paraguay, and Uruguay. In the United States a conference of trade bodies under the auspices of the Department of Commerce (November 15, 1921) recommended Federal legislation to legalize arbitration and the negotiation of treaties to extend it. The United States Arbitration Act of February 12, 1925, gave legal recognition to arbitration clauses in both foreign and domestic contracts. The awards within American jurisdiction would be confirmed and, if necessary, enforced by the Federal courts.

Economic Policy: Political Regulation

Economic disarmament, it was often pointed out, must precede military disarmament, and nations must substitute for the promotion of national trade some form of international regulation. The post-war political movement in that general direction had its beginnings in Wilson's third point: "The removal, so far as possible, of all economic barriers and the establishment of an equality of trade conditions among all the nations." In a modified form this idea went into the Covenant of the League. The Peace Conference avoided the most vital questions of economic equality, in part, at least, because the United States was not prepared to sacrifice certain national economic policies. The whole problem was therefore postponed, to be adjusted later by the League, and the League pursued these ends actively.

An important step taken by the League will serve to illustrate. In 1923 the Second General Conference on Communications and Transit at Geneva adopted a convention which prohibited discrimination in favor of nationals in import duties, tonnage dues, and preferential rail rates. It also authorized discrimination against any country following such discriminatory practices. This brings out the conflict between the discriminatory clauses in the Merchant Marine Act of 1920 and international law as recognized by the nations of the world in this multilateral treaty. The commercial treaty of 1925 with Germany, on the other hand, was in harmony with the international ideal.

The controversies over national control of raw materials were particularly conspicuous in the cases of oil and rubber. Various suggestions were advanced for solutions. One is illustrated by the oil controversy in the Near East. Exclusive control of different fields was attempted by several powers. The adjustment, after much argument, was the organization of the Turkish Petroleum Company on a plan which provided for the delivery of oil to four national groups — British, French, Dutch, and American. Thus international rivalry was eliminated, and each national group of companies was assured of its supply from the Irak fields by way of a Mediterranean port. Culbertson of the tariff commission advocated going much farther. His plan was to adjust raw-material problems and other commercial questions by means of multilateral treaties. Hoover also favored some form of international adjustment of these problems.

The regulation of air navigation was undertaken by an international air convention drafted by a committee of the Peace Conference in 1919. It provided that "contracting states recognize that every state has complete and exclusive sovereignty in the air space over its territory and territorial water." Each state granted freedom of passage to commercial aircraft except in certain prohibited areas for military defense and for public safety. Criminal jurisdiction followed the principles of admiralty law, being vested in the country of the ship's registry when acts were committed in the air; to this extent, it appears, there was a limitation placed upon "exclusive sovereignty." The Air Commerce Act of 1926 asserted the principle of sovereignty over air space but was silent on the question of criminal jurisdiction. The United States did not adhere to the international treaty; but in the proposed Panama treaty of 1926 the principles of the international air convention were recognized as applicable with respect to the joint control to be exercised over air commerce in Panama.

There are two lines of development relating to international electrical communications. The International Telegraph Convention of 1875 was drafted at St. Petersburg. A permanent bureau was established at Bern; and as telegraph problems developed, the convention and the regulations under its authority were revised. Only the United States, Mexico, Canada, China, and Peru were not members. The second line of development was a series of radio (wireless) conferences which began in Berlin in 1903. The first international convention was drafted in 1906 and was ratified by the United States; and a revised convention was drafted in 1912. Two choices of procedure were open after the war: to continue the separate regulation of wire and wireless or to combine all under one system. The first attempt was to follow the latter policy. A radio protocol which included all forms was signed by the United States, Great Britain, France, and Italy on August 25, 1919. A general conference was arranged to meet at Washington on October 8, 1920. Congress granted the necessary authority by an act of December 17, 1919. A draft convention was agreed upon, along with regulations which were later revised by a technical conference at Paris in 1925. On account of opposition to the draft convention a separate telegraph conference, a continuation of the St. Petersburg conferences, was held at Paris in 1925. The revised regulations, although relating primarily to the telegraph, covered some radio matters. The League had also considered the question from 1920 to 1925. By 1927 it was agreed to hold an International Radiotelegraph Conference at Washington under the authority of the radio convention of 1912. Seventy-eight governments were represented. The work of the conference was divided into two divisions: (1) a general convention and general regulations which would be adopted by all; (2) supplementary regulations which would apply only to the states that adhered to the International Telegraph Convention. In this way the conflict between the regulations, where they touched the overlapping between the two organizations, was adjusted. The tendency at this conference was to favor a return to the principle of the Washington Conference of 1920, which attempted to unify the regulation of both systems. The definition of radio communication adopted was "the transmission by radio of writing, signs, signals, pictures, and sounds of all kinds by Hertzian waves." The convention provided also that "an internal or national radio communication service which is likely to cause interference with other services outside the limits of the country in which it operates is considered as an international service from the viewpoint of interference."

The broadest step that was taken to arrive at a better understanding of international economic problems in general was the meeting of the International Economic Conference at Geneva on May 4, 1927, under the auspices of the League of Nations. Forty-seven nations were represented, including the three greatest nonmembers of the League — the United States, Russia, and Turkey. The conference was peculiarly constituted. It was not made up of diplomatic representatives of the governments concerned, but rather of individuals chosen for their knowledge of the problems involved. It was thought by the Council of the League that a conference so constituted could act with greater freedom and that the result of the meeting would be of greater benefit in sounding the possibilities of future agreements to be undertaken later through the regular diplomatic channels. The work of the conference was done by three commissions: industry, commerce, and agriculture. No definite recommendations on the subject of cartels were made by the industry commission. The commerce commission urged the removal of prohibition upon imports and exports, condemned special privileges to state-controlled enterprises which compete with private business, and advised an international agreement to govern the treatment of foreigners and foreign enterprises. The agriculture commission urged the farmers to adopt better scientific methods, urged an international campaign against animal and plant diseases, approved the extension of coöperative marketing, and advocated greater freedom of movement of agricultural products in international trade. In justifying the economic conference as a method of meeting such problems, a French representative in the League of Nations Assembly presented an argument which is difficult to answer: "It [the Assembly] will vote for it with confidence, because the bitter experience which we have undergone — and which must never be allowed to occur again — proves to all that the course on which we are embarking is at least a priori better than that we have already followed."

BACKWARD COUNTRIES

The three generally recognized views regarding the relations between the so-called advanced and backward countries were independence, imperialism, and the mandatory system. It was only natural that the backward countries themselves should insist upon complete independence. No matter how inefficiently they might govern themselves, they preferred self-management to outside interference. A political maxim

which once had great currency was that a people could
attain real political stability only through self-development,
even though the attainment was at the price of years or
even generations of bloodshed and disorder. Did not Europe
evolve in that way? So long as consideration was limited
strictly to a view of the backward peoples these theories
were probably sound; the difficulty, however, was that there
had developed a conflict between two widely different stages
of civilization, and the backward countries were involved,
whether they consented or not, in the destinies of the more
powerful civilizations.

The natural result of the rivalries of national states for
raw materials and markets, for military security, and for
world power was national imperialism. Disorder and disease seemed to call for outside interference. The mission
of national culture and religious zeal impelled the imposition
of the "superior civilization" upon the "inferior." However
altruistic the imperial state declared itself to be, the rivalries
and suspicions of the contending powers kept the world in a
state of uncertainty where recurring crises threatened to precipitate world war. Eventually world war came, in 1914.

In the course of discussion of post-war reconstruction of
the world on a new basis the mandatory system was evolved.
Its purpose was to place the backward peoples under a
guardianship subject to international supervision. It was
hoped thereby to eliminate suspicion, rivalries, and exploitation of helpless peoples, with the ultimate goal in view of
preparing the mandate for self-government.

During the treaty fight of 1919–1920 the policy of the
United States Senate respecting mandates was clearly enunciated in the form of an absolute refusal to participate in the
responsibilities involved. The League assigned the mandates
for territories then in question without the participation of
the United States. In the Yap controversy the United States
refused to accept the action of the League. The outcome of
the dispute was a treaty with Japan by which the United

States consented to the mandate, but reserved for itself equal rights with the treaty powers under the peace treaty without assuming any of the responsibilities. This policy was subsequently extended in a series of treaties in which the United States gave consent to other mandates under the League. The United States was thus isolated as the most "backward" of the great imperial powers because of its refusal to participate in the experiment of international administration of backward areas as a substitute for national imperialism, and because of its rejection of the League of Nations and its opposition to the Pan-American League plan.

MILITARY DISARMAMENT

Economic disarmament, could it have been attained even approximately during the first decade after the World War, would undoubtedly have contributed much to military disarmament. Both movements made some advance during the period, but it was slow and uncertain. The nationalist reaction, national economic self-sufficiency, and military security were formidable obstacles. Wilson, in his Fourteen Points, approached the question from the standpoint of reduction of armaments to a standard of "domestic safety." In the Covenant of the League the standard indicated was "national safety," "taking into account the geographical situation and circumstances of each state." The League created its permanent advisory commission in 1920 and also a commission on reduction of armaments, later called the Coördination Commission. Work was undertaken on the private manufacture of arms, on the interchange of information concerning armament, on trade in war materials, on chemical and bacteriological warfare, on the limitation of national expenditures for armament, on international control of armaments, and on the extension of the principles of the Washington naval treaty, and a protocol was drafted for the pacific settlement of international disputes. These activities led to the meeting of the Preparatory Disarmament Commission of 1926 to 1927 to prepare the way for a conference on general disarmament — land, sea, and air.

THE UNITED STATES AND THE LEAGUE PROGRAM

The administration clearly defined the position of the United States on certain of the points indicated above. It opposed discussion of the question of the private manufacture of arms so long as the question of government manufacture was not included. In 1922 the Washington Conference drafted a treaty outlawing chemical warfare, which was not ratified, and in the League conference on international trade in arms the United States insisted that a similar prohibition must be included. The limitation of national expenditures for armament was disapproved as impractical, and international control over armament in any form was absolutely refused.

CHEMICALS AND THE SUBMARINE

Very soon after the war, proposals for disarmament were complicated by a reversal of military opinion, and to a certain extent public opinion, on chemical warfare and the submarine. During the war the Allied and Associated Powers denounced the use of these weapons by the Germans as a reversion to barbarism. That these weapons were most effective, however, was a fact that could not be overlooked. After the war many naval authorities, especially in France and the United States, began the defense of the submarine. Admiral Sims was conspicuous among these in the United States. Military medical authorities later announced that the evil effects of gas were greatly exaggerated. The chemical-warfare services of the United States and of other powers ended by declaring that gas was the most effective and humane instrument of war in use by modern armies — effective in that more men could be incapacitated for immediate service than by any other weapon, humane in that it resulted in fewer fatalities and less serious after effects than any other. This contention was supported by use and experiment which seemed to prove that nonlethal gases had proved more effective than poison gases. These new points of view complicated the evolution of limitation of all armament projects.

THE WASHINGTON CONFERENCE

The first important act of the United States on the question of armament after the defeat of the League of Nations in the Senate was the move made by Harding in calling a conference on the limitation of armaments. The defeat of the League obligated the new administration to take some action as a substitute. The British Empire was faced with the problem of the renewal of the Japanese alliance and the adjustment of the Pacific problem of its dominions. The result was the linking of the limitation of armament with Pacific and Far Eastern problems when the formal invitations were issued on August 11, 1921, to the major powers. Although nine powers interested in the Pacific attended the conference, only five — the United States, the British Empire, Japan, France, and Italy — participated in the treaties for the limitation of armament. Limitation was placed upon capital ships, upon aircraft carriers, and upon the size of cruisers. In a second treaty, use of gas was outlawed, and submarines were placed under the limitation that they were not to be used as commerce destroyers. In a third treaty a pledge was given that fortifications and naval bases in the Pacific, with certain exceptions, were not to be strengthened.

THE LEAGUE AND THE WASHINGTON CONFERENCE

The League urged that the principles of the Washington naval-limitation treaty should be extended to other states, but opposition to the fixed-ratio plan defeated the attempt.

The plan of the American government assumed that all branches of the naval service were of equal value regardless of geographic location or other factors conditioning security. France held that as a matter of national military policy submarines were her most important naval unit. The British Empire placed emphasis on cruisers. These differences had in the beginning, at Washington, played an important part in making impossible the extension of the 5 : 5 : 3 ratio to all classes of vessels. When the scope of the plan was extended to include all powers, the plan was doomed.

THE THREE-POWER NAVAL CONFERENCE AT GENEVA

When it seemed to President Coolidge early in 1927 that the Preparatory Disarmament Commission was not arriving at what he considered satisfactory results in considering land, water, and air armaments together, he suggested a conference of the powers signatory of the Washington naval treaty to discuss the extension of the limitation of armaments. Italy and France declined; Great Britain and Japan accepted. The wording of the notes, however, was of great importance. In refusing the invitation France pointed out that the United States would "not be astonished to see French opinion preoccupied with its duties as a member of the League of Nations and with its moral obligations toward all the powers which form part of it." France furthermore stated that "an attentive study of the American proposals has convinced the Government of the republic that in their present form they risk compromising the success of the task already commenced at Geneva with the active help of the representatives of the American Government." The French reply to a second American note was even more pointed. It concluded as follows: "For us it is a question of probity toward the League of Nations. Considering the spirit in which the delegations have favorably received our proposals, we cannot let any doubt arise as to the sincerity of our efforts." The

British note of acceptance closed with this significant statement: "They would, however, observe that the relation of such a conversation to the proceedings of the Preparatory Commission at Geneva would require careful adjustment."

The three powers met at Geneva from June 20 to August 4 without arriving at any agreement. The United States persisted in its policy of extending the ratio plan to other classes, placing limits upon the total tonnage in each class and upon the maximum size of guns and torpedo tubes; its interest lay in the 10,000-ton cruisers. The British insisted upon a cruiser policy which seemed to be an expansion of naval armament rather than a limitation; their interest lay in a large number of smaller cruisers of the 7500-ton type. If the conference did not accomplish anything more, it brought home to the American people a broader comprehension of the nature of the program for the limitation of armaments, and of the difficulties attending it. When the League failed to secure satisfactory results, its failure was hailed in the United States by anti-League elements as simply another proof that it was a failure anyway. When the American plan failed so ignominiously, it was necessary to find another explanation.

It is valuable to make some comparisons between the Washington and Geneva conferences on naval limitation. At the time of the Washington Conference the League was barely established and its future was uncertain. The United States had refused to deal with the League, and the powers were anxious for American coöperation. Harding's program for the limitation of armaments was linked with the British necessity of a Pacific settlement to conciliate the empire and with the necessity of readjusting the Japanese alliance. An understanding of the Washington Conference is impossible unless one appreciates the British influence. The other Allied powers also were interested in a stabilization of the Far East in the light of the situation which had developed during the World War. In 1921 the United States was engaged in the largest naval building program in the nation's history, one which would radically disturb the historic balance of naval power. The conference applied the limitation primarily to capital ships, whose prestige was seriously compromised at the time by submarines and airplanes. Lastly, all the powers concerned made substantial sacrifices in one form or another to accomplish the result. Conditions seemed to demand a settlement that would disarm suspicion, if not ships, and check the threatened competition in naval armament.

At the time of the three-power conference at Geneva the League had proved itself by six years of work, and the major obligations of the member states were to the League. The notes of the British Empire and France took the view that the work of the League conference must take precedence, and that the work of an independent conference must be subordinated to, and coördinated with, the larger work of the League. The representatives of the United States were already taking part in the work of the League's Preparatory Disarmament Commission, and what could the United States contribute to a three-power conference which it could not contribute to the League conference? The Geneva conference did not have linked with it any other problems which would bring pressure to bear in favor of some kind of compromise settlement. No great naval building programs of a threatening nature were in progress. Extension of a fixed ratio to other major naval craft was impossible because geographical location determines the value of different arms of the service, and naval experts do not fully agree even then. Lastly, in any limitation agreement along American lines the United States would not be making any sacrifice, as the limit set would permit the United States to build up to it. With the other major powers the situation was quite different: they would have to sacrifice what, from their point of view regarding national security, would be the strongest branch of their naval service.

THE UNITED STATES AND THE WORLD COURT

The receipt by the United States of a certified copy of the protocol of signature of the World Court was acknowledged on August 15, 1921. American action, however, was delayed until early in 1923, when Harding asked Hughes for a formal opinion on the matter. Hughes's letter of February 17, 1923, to Harding laid down as the basis of American policy that the United States should adhere to the protocol of signature, with the Hughes reservations:

I. That such adhesion shall not be taken to involve any legal relation on the part of the United States to the League of Nations or the assumption of any obligations by the United States under the Covenant of the League of Nations constituting Part I of the treaty of Versailles.

II. That the United States shall be permitted to participate through representatives designated for the purpose and upon an equality with other states, members respectively of the Council and Assembly of the League of Nations, in any and all proceedings of either the Council or the Assembly for the election of judges or deputy judges of the Permanent Court of International Justice, or for the filling of vacancies.

III. That the United States will pay a fair share of the expenses of the Court as determined and appropriated from time to time by the Congress of the United States.

IV. That the Statute for the Permanent Court of International Justice adjoined to the Protocol shall not be amended without the consent of the United States.

Harding submitted the protocol to the Senate in a special message of February 24, 1923. No action was taken. He repeated his approval of the Court in a public address at New York on April 24 and at St. Louis on June 21, 1923. The recommendation was renewed in Coolidge's first annual message of December, 1923. In the meantime (June, 1923, to June, 1924) the existing arbitration treaties with Great Britain, France, Japan, Portugal, Norway, the Netherlands, and Sweden were being renewed, with a provision for considering the possibility of referring disputes to the Court after the adhesion of the United States to the protocol. In the summer of 1923 the American members of the Permanent Court of Arbitration at the Hague nominated a candidate for judge to succeed Ruy Barbosa. It appeared that the administration assumed that the adhesion of the United States was practically certain.

Outside official circles the Court was indorsed by most of the leading public men: Elihu Root, former Justice J. H. Clarke, E. M. House, A. L. Lowell, G. W. Wickersham, and others. At the Senate committee hearings held on April 30 and May 1, 1924, individuals and organizations of all kinds appeared in favor of American adherence. Wickersham spoke for the American Bar Association, Edgar Wallace for the American Federation of Labor, Walker D. Hines for the Chamber of Commerce of the United States, Bishop Brent for the Federal Council of Churches, and others for numerous church and religious organizations and national women's organizations. In the voluminous testimony presented, a point made by Wickersham was especially striking in view of the opposition to the Court. He pointed out that the submission of any case to the Court was purely voluntary on the part of the United States as provided in the statute; furthermore, that all arbitration treaties to which the United States was a party provided especially that before a case could be submitted to any arbitral tribunal a special treaty must be made covering the case in question and must be ratified by the Senate. It was clear that no matter what the future might hold for the Court, the Senate had the opportunity to veto the submission of any case not only to this court but to any other; and even if its consent were given, such conditions might be attached in any particular case as would protect the interests of the United States to the satisfaction of the Senate.

Lodge brought forward a plan of his own which was introduced into the Senate on May 8, 1924. It would direct the president to take steps to call the Hague Conference to draft a plan for a world court. The next day Coolidge made it known that his position was not changed. The situation was unusual, as this was a presidential year and Coolidge was a candidate for nomination for a second term. Lodge was chairman of the Committee on Foreign Relations and one of the most powerful Republican party leaders. Why should he come out in opposition to Coolidge's policy on the eve of the national nominating conventions? Wickersham said, "No such piece of buffoonery has ever been brought forward by a responsible statesman." Few newspapers indorsed the idea. The plan was given such a cold reception that Lodge withdrew it before the committee had an opportunity to vote upon it.

Senator Pepper (Pennsylvania, Republican) introduced resolutions which were designed to separate the Court from the League. The first was presented on April 7, and a more extreme one on May 22. The latter was a composite plan so constituted that it was hoped it could be used as a basis for bringing together the Republican factions.

In the World Court fight for ratification there was a division of opinion which in many respects resembled the League contest of 1919–1920. For purposes of classification the different views can be conveniently arranged in four groups. The administration stood for ratification with reservations which were primarily interpretative. The purpose of these was to make clear that in entering the Court the United States was not entering into legal relations with the League, and that the American position in the Court was on a basis of equality with the other members. Lenroot (Republican) and C. A. Swanson (Democrat) were leaders of this element in the Senate. The second group would go one step farther and, by amendment, separate the Court from the League. Pepper was one of the leaders of this group until late in the contest. The third faction went still farther. It repudiated the Court altogether, as merely an organ of the League, and proposed immediate steps for the organization of a totally new court under American leadership. The Lodge plan belonged to this class. The fourth class was the irreconcilables, the "battalion of death," who were opposed to any world court under existing conditions and especially the "League Court," as they named it. Borah and Johnson, Republicans, and Reed of Missouri, Democrat, were the most conspicuous leaders in this group.

A large number of resolutions were presented, but interest centers around those reported by the Committee on Foreign Relations. The second Pepper resolution was reported from committee by Pepper by a vote of 10 to 6. Johnson of California and the Democrats were recorded against it. Senator Swanson introduced (May 5) a resolution which followed the recommendations of the administration. It was defeated in committee by a vote of 8 to 10, but was presented as a minority report. In addition to the Hughes-Harding reservations, it contained the following provision:

The signature of the United States to the said protocol shall not be affixed until the powers signatory to such protocol shall have indicated, through an exchange of notes, their acceptance of the foregoing reservations and understandings as a part and a condition of adhesion by the United States to the said protocol.

The irony of the situation lay in the fact that a Republican administration, elected on a platform of opposition to the policy of the Democratic administration, was relying upon a Democrat, even upon a Wilson Democrat, to take the lead in advocating the administration's program of ratification of the Court statute against the President's own party. The conditions were such, however, that the Senate took no action; and the parties entered the presidential campaign without a test of strength and without the open factional strife within them (especially the Republican party) which a vote on the Court issue would inevitably have engendered.

The Republican party platform in 1924 indorsed the Court and favored "the adherence of the United States to this tribunal as recommended by President Coolidge." The Democratic platform renewed its declaration of confidence in both the League and the Court. At the meeting of the Congress following his reëlection Coolidge again recommended (December 3, 1924) the adherence of the United States to the Court

upon the conditions stated in the recommendation which is now before the Senate, and further that our country shall not be bound by advisory opinions which may be rendered by the Court upon questions which we have not voluntarily submitted for its judgment. This would provide a practical and convenient tribunal before which we could go voluntarily, but to which we could not be summoned, for the determination of justiciable questions when they fail to be resolved by direct negotiations.

In his inaugural address (March 4, 1925) he said:

Where great principles are involved, where great movements are under way which promise much for the welfare of humanity by reason of the very fact that many other nations have given such movements their active support, we ought not to withhold our own sanction because of any small and inessential difference, but only upon the ground of the most important and compelling fundamental reasons. . . . The weight of our enormous influence must be cast upon the side of a reign, not of force but of law; and trial, not by battle but by reason.

In the meantime the House of Representatives had expressed its opinion definitely in favor of the ratification of the protocol by a vote of 301 to 28. This action had no effect, of course, except as an expression of the opinion of the House. Senator Swanson introduced his resolution again on March 5, with the addition of a fifth reservation intended to cover Coolidge's recommendation of the previous December. This new reservation held:

5. That the United States shall be in no manner bound by any advisory opinion of the Permanent Court of International Justice not rendered pursuant to a request in which it, the United States, shall expressly join in accordance with the statute for the said Court adjoined to the protocol of signature of the same to which the United States shall become signatory.

The Swanson resolution was referred to the Committee on Foreign Relations. It had not been reported on March 13, when a motion was adopted through the coöperation of the party floor leaders Curtis and Robinson to the effect "that on December 17, 1925, the Senate in open executive session proceed to the consideration of Senate Resolution 5 submitted by Mr. Swanson, etc." The vote was 77 to 2. This left a long interval in which many readjustments might be made. It was announced in the press that a "diplomatic school" would be conducted during the summer and that a "nation-wide campaign to instruct the American people in the foreign affairs of the United States will be undertaken this summer by the men who shape its international destiny." Coolidge, Kellogg, Swanson, and King of Utah would lead the pro-Court propaganda; Pepper, the independents; and Borah, Johnson of California, and Reed of Missouri the irreconcilable opponents of the Court.

Propaganda for and against the Court was conducted by organizations and individuals. Misrepresentation concerning these propaganda agencies was so extreme that it was very difficult to arrive at any definite conclusions. The League of Nations Nonpartisan Association was very active; and opponents of the Court charged that but for this "artificial" propaganda, supported by big business and the international banker, sentiment in favor of the Court would have collapsed in the United States.

The campaign for outlawry of war was a subordinate element in the Court controversy. Senator Borah had introduced an outlawry resolution in the Senate on December 20, 1922, but it had not been pushed. The propaganda was organized in succeeding years; and an American Committee for the Outlawry of War was established with headquarters in Chicago, with S. O. Levinson as chairman. It was indorsed by Presbyterians, Methodists, Unitarians, and others. In August, 1924, a formal statement of principles was issued which was similar to the Borah resolution. Coolidge, in his speech of acceptance on August 14, 1924, expressed approval of the principles involved in the plan.

The plan was to declare aggressive warfare an international crime, to codify international law, and to create an international court with compulsory jurisdiction over all controversies arising among nations. This is the source of Borah's position that the United States should not enter an international court until there was a codification of international law. On July 14, 1925, the supporters of outlawry of war and of the World Court announced the so-called "harmony plan" as a compromise program. It provided, on the basis of the Harding-Coolidge reservations, for the entrance of the United States into the Court for a period of two years. If at the end of that time no steps had been taken to outlaw war by treaty agreement, the United States would be free to reconsider its relations with the Court. This plan was taken to the country, by religious leaders especially; but nothing came of it, as the pro-Court element grew strong enough to ratify the protocol without these additional conditions.

Coolidge, in his third annual message of December 8, 1925, discussed the Court at length. He said in part:

If we are going to support any court, it will not be one that we have set up alone or which reflects only our ideals. Other nations have their customs and their institutions, their thoughts, and their methods of life. If a court is going to be international, its composition will have to yield to what is good in all these various elements. Neither will it be possible to support a court which is exactly perfect, or under which we assume absolutely no obligations. If we are seeking that opportunity, we might as well declare that we are opposed to supporting any court.

The debate opened, according to schedule, on December 17. An Associated Press dispatch indicated the alignment as follows:

Once more the mantle of leadership for favorable Senate action fell upon the shoulders of a Democratic spokesman. In opposition stood a determined phalanx of irreconcilables under the captaincy of a Republican chairman of the Foreign Relations Committee. Holding the balance was a group whose leaders had been the "mild reservationists" of the fight over the League.

There was little that was new in the debates as they dragged through the succeeding weeks and filled about three hundred pages of the *Congressional Record*. There were some important differences of personnel. Senators Lodge, Knox, and Brandegee were dead. The Committee on Foreign Relations was in the hands of Borah, a man who was as uncompromising in this contest as Lodge had been in the battle over the League. He offered three additional reservations: (1) that no force or economic sanctions were to be used to enforce decisions, (2) that the Court should not perform any function not designated in the statute, and (3) a reaffirmation of the traditional policy on nonentanglement in foreign politics. He declared that the Court was tied to the League by twenty-two sections of the statute. Pepper, in the interest of party harmony, came over to the support of the administration program and was severely denounced by Borah. Formerly Pepper had advocated severing the Court completely from any connection with the League. On January 6, 1926, Reed of Missouri moved to investigate propaganda in support of the Court and the debt pacts. He charged that J. P. Morgan and foreign countries were working together to secure cancellation of debts in order to clear the way for huge private loans, and that monied interests were behind the World Court scheme. The opposition contended that the resolution was designed merely to delay action on the Court. It was defeated 56 to 16. Reed then denounced the refusal "to investigate insidious foreign propaganda when it might disturb the 'sacred international bankers.'"

The next complication was the certainty that the tax bill would be reported from committee before a vote would be had on the Court. One or the other of these major measures would have to wait. An obvious filibuster developed. There was a clear two-thirds majority in favor of the Court, but the little group of irreconcilables refused to permit a vote. Robinson, Democratic floor leader, announced that if a vote was not had the next day a cloture petition would be circulated. It was presented that night before the close of the session and was signed by forty-eight senators — twenty-four Republicans and twenty-four Democrats. Reed fought the measure in the bitterest of attacks; Swanson reminded him that he had voted for the cloture rule himself when it had been adopted, and presented the record of the occasion. The rule was invoked on January 25 by a vote of 68 to 26. This limited each senator to one hour, after which time a vote must be taken. The vote was had on January 27, and resulted in 76 for adherence to the Court and 17 against. Among those voting for the ratification were forty Republicans and thirty-six Democrats. In opposition were fourteen Republican irreconcilables, two Democrats (Reed of Missouri and Blease of South Carolina), and one Farmer-Labor vote. The irreconcilables then announced that they would appeal the question to the voters in the election then approaching. The first victim selected was Senator McKinley of Illinois, who was up for renomination in the primaries. Reed and Borah were active in the Illinois campaign.

The resolution of ratification adopted included the following reservations and understandings:

1. That such adherence shall not be taken to involve any legal relation on the part of the United States to the League of Nations or the assumption of any obligations by the United States under the treaty of Versailles.

2. That the United States shall be permitted to participate through representatives designated for the purpose and upon an equality with the other states, members, respectively, of the Council and Assembly of the League of Nations, in any and all proceedings of either the Council or the Assembly for the election of judges or deputy judges of the Permanent Court of International Justice or for the filling of vacancies.

3. That the United States will pay a fair share of the expenses of

the Court as determined and appropriated from time to time by the Congress of the United States.

4. That the United States may at any time withdraw its adherence to the said Protocol and that the Statute for the Permanent Court of International Justice adjoined to the Protocol shall not be amended without the consent of the United States.

5. That the Court shall not render any advisory opinion except after due notice to all states adhering to the Court and to all interested states and after public hearing or opportunity for hearing given to any state concerned; nor shall it, without the consent of the United States, entertain any request for an advisory opinion touching any dispute or question in which the United States has or claims an interest.

The signature of the United States to the said Protocol shall not be affixed until the powers signatory to such Protocol shall have indicated, through an exchange of notes, their acceptance of the foregoing reservations and understandings as a part and a condition of adherence by the United States to the said Protocol.

Resolved further, As a part of the act of ratification that the United States approve the Protocol and Statute hereinabove mentioned, with the understanding that recourse to the Permanent Court of International Justice for the settlement of differences between the United States and any other state or states can be had only by agreement thereto through general or special treaties concluded between the parties in dispute; and

Resolved, further, That the adherence to the said Protocol and Statute hereby approved shall not be so construed as to require the United States to depart from its traditional policy of not intruding upon, interfering with, or entangling itself in the political questions of policy or internal administration of any foreign state; nor shall adherence to the said Protocol and Statute be construed to imply a relinquishment by the United States of its traditional attitude toward purely American questions.

It should be noted that in the final form there are substantial changes from the original Swanson resolution. The fifth reservation was introduced by Swanson in a modified form on January 23, 1926, shortly before the final vote, to conciliate the more extreme factions. The first part of the reservation embodied Coolidge's view that cases in which the

United States possesses an interest should not be submitted for advisory opinions without its consent. This would place advisory opinions on the same basis as cases submitted to the Court for judgments. This, in fact, was the practice as laid down by the Court in the Eastern Karelia case. The American reservation merely made it a matter of permanent agreement. The last part of the reservation, asserting the right of the United States to a voice in requests for advisory opinions in which an interest was claimed, was a radical addition. This brings forward an important controversy over the interpretation of the statute and the Covenant. Which document gave rise to advisory opinions, or were they authorized by both? Article 14 of the Covenant stated, "The Court may also give an advisory opinion upon any dispute or question referred to it by the Council or by the Assembly." Article 36 of the statute, in defining the jurisdiction of the Court, stated that "the jurisdiction of the Court comprises all cases which the parties refer to it and all matters especially provided for in treaties and conventions in force." The Covenant specifically mentioned advisory opinions, and the statute was framed under authority of this article of the Covenant; so the logical approach to the question would be that Article 36 of the statute would embrace advisory opinions as a matter provided for by a treaty in force. On this point, however, there was the widest disagreement in the United States, some holding that the statute did not authorize advisory opinions at all.

The American argument against permitting advisory opinions at all was based not only on the language of the statute but also on the contention that advisory opinions were political rather than judicial in character and therefore were certain to involve the Court in the political controversies of the League, which alone could ask advisory opinions. It was held that this destroyed the judicial character of the Court. In consideration of American legal practice this was a peculiar view, since advisory opinions were authorized in eleven states of the United States — seven by constitutional provision and four by statute.

During the World Court fight there was much talk, among certain critics of the Court, of the League's failure to accept the original draft of the statute providing for compulsory jurisdiction in respect to certain classes of legal cases. The advisory commission submitted a recommendation for the codification of international law, a task which was to be carried out in connection with the establishment of the Court. Although it was an ideal to be striven for, it was considered by the League as not immediately practicable. The compulsory clause, which might be voluntarily assumed by any power, had not been ratified by any major power. It was not ratified or even considered as a serious possibility by the American government.

Not only did the Senate refuse to ratify the compulsory agreement, but in the resolution of ratification it included the traditional paragraph specifically prohibiting the submission of cases without its consent. Whether acceptance by the League of the proposal to codify international law would have changed the attitude of the Senate remained a matter of speculation. The Senate, as Hughes pointed out, had given no intimation of a change; in fact, what action it did take indicated the opposite trend.

Copies of the Senate resolution of ratification were forwarded by Secretary Kellogg to each of the states signatory to the statute with a request that answer should be made in accordance with the terms of the resolution. A copy was forwarded also to the secretary-general of the League at Geneva. The matter was considered in the Council of the League of Nations. Sir Austen Chamberlain for Great Britain suggested that a conference should be arranged in which the United States should meet with the signatory states and arrange an agreement. He advanced three reasons for this course. The statute was a multilateral treaty; therefore it should properly be varied by another multilateral agreement to which all the original signatories should be parties, rather than by an exchange of notes. Next he pointed out that the reservations affected the rights of members of the Court; finally, that the fifth reservation "is capable of bearing an interpretation which would hamper the work of the Council and prejudice the rights of members of the League, but it is not clear that it is intended to bear any such meaning." On March 18 the Council adopted a resolution as proposed by Chamberlain.

Invitations to a conference to be held at Geneva on September 1, 1926, were forwarded on March 29 to the members of the Court and to the United States to arrange an agreement between them. Individual states were asked to inform the United States of their desire for unity of action. The news of this attitude on the part of the League aroused intense hostility among the anti-Court elements in the United States. They declared that it confirmed their contention that the Court was controlled by the League. The United States declined the invitation on April 17 rather sharply. Kellogg took the ground that "the reservations are plain and unequivocal, and according to their terms they must be accepted by an exchange of notes." He had "no authority to vary this mode of procedure or to modify the conditions and reservations or to interpret them." He expressed his disapproval of the action of the Council; and declared that if any machinery was necessary to put the United States reservations into effect, it would more properly be considered after ratification. If, however, the signatories wished to consult among themselves, he could have no objections. Forty states met as scheduled at Geneva, the sessions lasting from September 1 to September 23.

The American reservations were accepted substantially with the exception of the second part of the fifth. The conclusions of the conference were embodied in a final act signed by the delegates. The states signing agreed to make this final act the basis of their replies to the United States notes. Annexed to the final act was a draft protocol, embodying the attitude of the conference, to serve as a basis of negotiation with the United States. When this multilateral treaty was ratified, America's adherence would become effective. This was the plan originally proposed by the Council, but it would be arrived at by a different route.

The conference at Geneva was faced with a difficult problem. First they had to interpret the meaning of the reservations of the United States before a policy could be formulated or machinery worked out to make it effective. Kellogg's blunt declaration that "the reservations are plain and unequivocal" and that he had "no authority . . . to interpret them" was quite at variance with the facts. Examination of the debates in the Senate reveals that the leading senators who had been responsible for the form given to the reservations differed substantially among themselves as to their interpretation and effect. The discussions at Geneva revealed that there was a lack of understanding, especially in America, of the difficulties involved from the standpoint of international law, particularly those difficulties associated with the use of multilateral treaties such as were at issue. Furthermore, when the Department of State received the answers of the forty-eight states, it would be compelled to interpret the reservations in order to determine what conditions the United States had imposed and whether these conditions had actually been complied with. Why not interpret them before the replies were made rather than after and thus facilitate the effecting of an agreement? It was not to be expected, and it would have been highly improper, that the members of the Court as an international body should accept the reservations as a blank check, in which the United States would be free to fill in afterwards from time to time whatever interpretations it saw fit to make.

The discussions held at Geneva indicated a very sincere desire on the part of the powers there assembled to meet the wishes of the United States. The protocol provided that the manner in which the consent of the United States to requests for advisory opinions should be given was to be worked out through agreement with the council of the League of Nations, and that "should the United States offer objection to an advisory opinion being given by the Court, at the request of the Council or the Assembly, concerning a dispute to which the United States is not a party or concerning a question other than a dispute between States, the Court will attribute to such objection the same force and effect as attaches to a vote against asking for the opinion given by a member of the League of Nations either in the Assembly or in the Council."

The November elections of 1926 in the United States brought serious defeats to the Republicans. In his Armistice Day address in Kansas City, Coolidge announced that he would not ask the Senate to modify its position. Thus the United States remained out of the Court. The anti-Court press announced in connection with the elections that the World Court was defeated at the polls, as several World Court senators were defeated for reëlection either at the primaries or at the general election. Such generalizations were, however, misleading. There were thirty-two senators to be elected in 1926. Of the pro-Court senators ten were defeated and fifteen elected; of the anti-Court senators five were reëlected and two were defeated. On the assumption that the World Court was the deciding issue in these elections, anti-Court sentiment determined the result for fifteen senators and pro-Court sentiment the result for seventeen. This left a margin of two in favor of the Court. However, in examining the local issues in the several states where senators were to be elected, there was good reason to believe that the World Court was not the decisive issue. In two outstanding contests—for instance, Illinois and North Dakota—the agricultural issue seemed to have been the more decisive factor.

The position of the irreconcilables presented some matters of interest, if not of humor. Inasmuch as these men had invaded Illinois for the express purpose of punishing McKinley for his vote for the World Court, when Smith defeated McKinley they immediately claimed the victory. After the results of the primary were announced Reed said:

> The result in Illinois can be attributed to Senator McKinley's vote for the World Court. . . . Clearly the voters were determined to adhere to the policies of Washington. They will not tolerate any interference with American rights by foreign powers, and they have no desire to interfere with the policies of other countries so long as our rights are not invaded. The American voter has not been inoculated with the damnable virus of internationalism.

A Smith campaign slogan was "America first — no World Court." Smith was looked upon as a defender of the policies of the great George Washington. However, this was before Reed as chairman of the Senate committee investigating campaign funds (especially Republican funds) had decided that it was a corrupt use of money that elected Smith in Illinois and Vare in Pennsylvania. Apparently the voters were inoculated with the "damnable virus" of gold. It was primarily through the influence of Reed and his committee that the "slush-fund twins" were excluded from the seats in the Senate to which they had been legally declared elected. The World Court served as an explanation at one time; corruption at another. Reed, his irreconcilable friends of both parties, and the people in general were satisfied with both explanations, and memories are short where self-interest points the way.

The election of 1926 did decide one important question. A group of insurgent Republicans had been excluded from the party as a result of their bolting the party in 1924. After the 1926 elections the regular Republicans found themselves with one member less than the Democrats. The four insurgent members, who were anti-Court, held the balance of power between the parties. For political reasons the conclusion of the whole business was obvious: drop the Court and invite the insurgents back into the fold to make a

Republican majority, a move which was soon accomplished. It was only in this indirect manner that the elections of 1926 defeated the World Court. It was exaggerated nationalism and partisan politics that defeated ratification.

When Congress met in December, 1927, after additional changes in alignment owing to the filling of vacancies, the make-up of the Senate was 48 Republicans, 47 Democrats, and 1 Farmer-Labor member. The death of a New Mexico senator after Congress met reduced the Democrats to forty-six and, by appointment of a new senator, increased the Republicans to forty-nine. A majority still depended upon the insurgents. Furthermore, a presidential election was in the offing, and it would not be expedient to reopen party factional conflicts. The situation therefore did not indicate the early revival of the World Court question.

Wilson assumed the responsibility for the defeat of the reservations to the Covenant of the League of Nations — reservations which were unacceptable to the states in the League; Coolidge accepted such reservations to the statute of the World Court, shifting the responsibility for rejection of the American reservations to the states which were members of the Court. In both cases the conditions of American adherence were excessive and would have destroyed the principle of equality of states so far as that principle was embodied in these documents. In both cases the results were the same — defeat.

Even though the United States has refused to adhere to the statute, it should be remembered that it is one of the powers to which the Court is always open. If a dispute should arise it might, with the consent of the Senate (a consent which would be required in any case), be submitted to the Court for adjudication. The membership of the League includes nearly all the nations of the world; so does the membership of the Court. The League and the Court are, in the last analysis, the nations of the world organized to accomplish particular purposes or objects. The League is the instrument of political action; the Court is the instrument of judicial action. An organization is neither better nor worse than its members; and if these organizations cannot be trusted, can these same nations organized under certain so-called American plans be trusted?

Root has summarized the problem of international organization with reference to the Court in such a way that it may very well serve as a conclusion of this discussion:

The question what kind of an institution for international benefit should be attempted is not a thing to be reasoned out from an American point of view, or from a French point of view, or from a Japanese point of view. It is to be solved by ascertaining what beliefs and opinions all the different nations hold in common and basing the new institution upon those beliefs and opinions, not including in the make-up of the new institution anything because Americans alone think it better, or French alone think it better, or Japanese alone think it better. These common beliefs and opinions are few and simple, and new international institutions must accordingly be very simple in their origin if they are to continue. Thousands of elaborate schemes for the prevention of war have been produced in the United States within the last few years; most of them have been quite worthless because the authors completely overlooked the differences of opinion and modes of thought and feeling in other countries, differences which would prevent acceptance of the proposed scheme, and if it were accepted would prevent its operation. The process of finding what it is worth while to try to do internationally is a good deal like the old problem of finding the greatest common denominator which used to be so tedious when we were children. The question presented by a proposal of an international institution is not whether it is the best institution conceivable. It is whether the proposed institution would be useful so far as it goes and whether there is any practical probability of getting fifty odd nations to agree to a better institution.

The important thing is to get the right kind of institution started, even though it be in the most rudimentary form. There is one unfailing characteristic of human nature which comes into play when an institution is once started. It is that after an institution is established and is conspicuous and universally known, it enters into the basis of thought of the people who have to do with the subjects to which it relates. People begin to think differently about such subjects. They begin to think that way, and if the institution is so conducted as to command confidence within its original limited scope, it grows naturally and inevitably because the fundamental idea being no longer a novelty and being accepted, enlargements and improvements of the idea are soon readily accepted.

POLITICAL ARBITRATION AND CONCILIATION

The arbitration treaties in force after the World War were usually called the Root treaties; they dated for the most part from the Roosevelt administration. They were very limited in scope inasmuch as they made the following provision:

Differences which may arise of a legal nature, or relating to the interpretation of treaties existing between the two Contracting Parties, and which it may not have been possible to settle by diplomacy, shall be referred to the Permanent Court of Arbitration established at the Hague by the Convention of the 29th of July, 1899, provided, nevertheless, that they do not affect the vital interests, the independence, or the honor of the two Contracting States, and do not concern the interests of third parties.

In each individual case the agreement to arbitrate must be ratified by the Senate; the Senate had insisted upon this as a matter of prerogative. The scope of the treaty was so limited as to be practically worthless, and the requirement of Senate ratification of each separate agreement meant that the treaty had no legal binding force. Whatever value there may have been in these documents was derived from their psychological influence as statements of public policy on the part of the participants. The term of the treaties was five years, and they were renewed from time to time.

President Taft attempted to carry arbitration to a point where it would be practical. The first article of these Taft-Knox treaties was as follows:

All differences hereafter arising between the High Contracting Parties, which it has not been possible to adjust by diplomacy, relating to international matters in which the High Contracting

Parties are concerned by virtue of a claim of right made by one against the other under a treaty or otherwise, and which are justiciable in their nature by reason of being susceptible of decision by the application of the principles of law or equality, shall be submitted to the Permanent Court of Arbitration established at the Hague by the convention of October 18, 1907, or to some other arbitral tribunal as may be decided in each case by special agreement.

The point of particular difficulty in this proposal was the determination of the limits of justiciable questions. For this purpose a joint high commission was to be established which should decide respecting the classification of individual cases. The treaties were defeated in the Senate by objection to the commission as unconstitutional and by the addition of the clause making it necessary to submit each case to the Senate for consent to arbitrate.

These two groups of treaties had to do with arbitration. The next attempt was the Bryan "cooling off" treaties, which abandoned the effort to secure the consent of the Senate to any effective arbitration treaty. These treaties set up machinery of conciliation to supplement arbitration. The language of the first article of the French treaty, which varied in some of the other treaties, was as follows:

Any disputes arising between the Government of the United States of America and the Government of the French Republic, of whatever nature they may be, shall, when ordinary diplomatic proceedings have failed and the High Contracting Parties do not have recourse to arbitration, be submitted for investigation and report to a Permanent International Commission, constituted in the manner prescribed in the following article.

The parties agreed not to resort to force during such investigation and before the report was made.

The commissions referred to were to be permanent, in order that when a dispute arose the machinery for handling it should already be constituted. Jessup summed up the status of the treaties and the commissions to 1928 as follows: "Twenty-one of these treaties were concluded, but with respect to only ten of these were the contemplated permanent commissions ever created, and with respect to only two have the places on these commissions been filled when vacancies occurred."

Such was the pre-war background of United States policy in these fields. The defeat of the League of Nations marked the reaction. In the post-war period no new departures were taken in conciliation until 1928. During 1923, treaties were negotiated with the five Central American states. They provided for the submission to commissions of inquiry of disputes "regarding questions of fact relative to failure to comply with the provisions of any of the treaties or conventions existing between them and which affect neither the sovereign and independent existence of any of the signatory republics, nor their honor or vital interests." The Bryan treaties had included all disputes; these limited conciliation to nearly the same scope as the Root arbitration treaties. The Bryan treaties provided for permanent commissions; in these the commissions had to be established for each dispute after it arose. In both these respects the Hughes treaties were a distinct step backward.

During the same year (1923) the Fifth Pan-American Conference at Santiago drafted a peace treaty. It was of the unlimited type of conciliation treaty similar to the Bryan treaties. It provided that two permanent commissions were to be created, one in Washington and one in Montevideo, to receive applications for inquiries; that in each case arising a commission of inquiry should be created; that the report must be rendered within one year, and no party to the dispute should make military preparations or engage in any hostile act within six months thereafter; and that the commissions must be chosen from American states (this requirement differed from the Bryan treaties, which permitted selection of Europeans).

The World Court episode from 1923 to 1926 has already been given in detail. It involved an attempt to bring the

United States into line with post-war world developments in the adjudication of international disputes as distinguished from arbitration. The action of the Senate demonstrated again the same reaction as in the field of conciliation.

Thus far the trend of post-war developments was in a backward direction. The year 1928 worked some change. The Root arbitration treaty with France expired on February 27, 1928. Instead of merely extending it for another five years, as had previously been done, a new treaty was negotiated. This was signed on February 6, 1928, the one hundred and fiftieth anniversary of the French alliance, and was ratified by the Senate. It was a curious mixture of three ideas: outlawry of war in the preamble, conciliation in the first article, and arbitration and adjudication in the second.

The first article was almost identical with the first article of the Bryan treaty with France. The second was almost identical with the article quoted from the proposed Taft-Knox treaty. It even contained the proviso that in each case the agreement to arbitrate must be ratified by the Senate. It is obvious that thus far there was nothing unusual in the treaty. The exceptions in the third article were somewhat different. The terms "independence," "honor," and "vital interests" were omitted. The exception of the interest of third parties remained from the Root treaty. The reservation of the Monroe Doctrine dated from the Hague conventions. The exclusion of domestic questions was reminiscent of the League controversy. The French reservation of League obligations was new. By an exchange of notes it was agreed that the exceptions in the third article applied only to action under the second, and did not affect the unlimited conciliation proviso of the first. These provisions are clearly little different from pre-war policy. The reservations did not go so far as the Senate had gone in the Root treaties, but they went even farther than the Senate had gone in the Taft treaties. Nothing radical or even new was involved in the treaty itself. The thing which excited the public was the declaration contained in the preamble indorsing the principle of outlawry of war. A preamble, of course, had no binding force; so the declaration was nothing more than an amiable gesture so far as the purpose of the treaty was concerned. In the public mind it was confused (possibly for political purposes) with a parallel movement proposing to outlaw war by international agreement. It seemed quite certain, in view of the conferences between the Department of State and the Senate Committee on Foreign Relations, that the outlawry preamble was of importance politically to secure the support of Senator Borah, chairman of the Senate committee. Furthermore, party solidarity on the eve of a presidential election was a most desirable consideration.

The Pan-American Conference at Havana, January 16 to February 20, 1928, adopted two peace resolutions. The first declared that "the American republics desire to express their condemnation of war as an instrument of national policy in their mutual relations," and resolved that they "adopt compulsory arbitration as the means to be employed for the pacific settlement of their international differences of a juridical character." Within a year delegates were to be sent to a conference in Washington to draft "a convention for the realization of this principle with the minimum of exceptions considered indispensable to safeguard the independence and sovereignty of the State." The second resolution declared "(1) that every act of aggression is considered illegal and is therefore declared forbidden; (2) that the American states shall employ all pacific means to settle the disputes which may arise between them."

The international conference of American states on conciliation and arbitration provided in the former resolution met at Washington, December 10, 1928, to January 5, 1929. Two treaties were drafted. The arbitration treaty contained in its preamble a condemnation of war as an instrument of national policy, and Article I bound the ratifying states to submit to arbitration all cases "which are juridical in their nature" when they could not be settled by diplomacy. The definition of juridical character was the same as that incorporated in the Covenant and in the statute. Two exceptions were made: domestic questions and disputes involving states not parties to the treaty. The second, or conciliation, treaty provided for the submission to conciliation, according to the machinery set up in the treaty of May 3, 1923, of "all controversies of any kind which may arise between them for any reason and which may not have been possible to settle through diplomatic channels." Thirteen states signed the treaties with reservations; and seven, including the United States, signed without.

RENUNCIATION OF WAR, OR OUTLAWRY OF WAR

The world background for the renunciation of war must begin with the League of Nations. In Article 12 of the Covenant, members of the League pledged themselves not to resort to war without recourse first to peaceful methods of settlement of disputes, and then not until three months after the award or report. They further promised, in Article 13, not to go to war against a member that complied with such award or decision. If a member made war in violation of its covenants, it should be deemed "to have committed an act of war against all other members of the League," who agreed to establish an economic blockade, and the Council should make recommendations respecting military measures. These commitments involved two things: the pledge not to resort to war without recourse first to peaceful settlement, and the establishment of machinery of enforcement or international police measures to require obedience to international obligations and the keeping of the peace. Indirectly war seemed to be legalized in case peaceful methods of settlement failed to render any decision. The World Court provided further means of peaceful settlement by extending the principles of the League's policy.

The Covenant of the League served as a starting point for the extension of the post-war peace movement. On October 2, 1924, the Assembly of the League adopted a "Protocol for the Pacific Settlement of International Disputes" and opened it for the signature of the nations. The preamble was as follows:

Animated by the firm desire to insure the maintenance of general peace and the security of nations whose existence, independence, or territories may be threatened;

Recognizing the solidarity of the members of the international community;

Asserting that a war of aggression constitutes a violation of this solidarity and an international crime;

Desirous of facilitating the complete application of the system provided in the Covenant of the League of Nations for the pacific settlement of disputes between states and of insuring the repression of international crimes; and

For the purpose of realizing, as contemplated by Article 8 of the Covenant, the reduction of national armaments to the lowest point consistent with national safety and the enforcement by common action of international obligations . . .

Article 1 pledged the signatories to undertake to incorporate amendments into the Covenant in line with the provisions of the protocol and, in the meantime, to accept the protocol as binding. Article 2 was as follows:

The signatory powers agree in no case to resort to war either with one another or against a State which, if the occasion arises, accepts all the obligations hereinafter set out, except in the case of resistance to acts of aggression or when acting in agreement with the Council or the Assembly of the League of Nations in accordance with the provisions of the Covenant and of the present Protocol.

By Article 3 the jurisdiction of the Permanent Court of International Justice was accepted as binding. Article 10 declared that "every state which resorts to war in violation of the undertakings contained in the Covenant or in the present Protocol is an aggressor." "In event of hostilities having broken out, any state shall be presumed to be an aggressor, unless a decision of the Council, which must be taken unanimously, shall declare otherwise," if it has violated obligations assumed under the League. "Apart from the cases dealt with in paragraphs 1 and 2 of the present Article [the obligations referred to above], if the Council does not at once succeed in determining the aggressor, it shall be bound to enjoin upon the belligerents an armistice, and shall fix the terms, acting, if need be, by a two-thirds majority and shall supervise its execution. Any belligerent which has refused to accept the armistice or has violated its terms shall be deemed an aggressor." In this document there was a definite outlawry of war, and an extension of the machinery of adjudication and conciliation and the machinery of enforcement of the obligations. It should be further noted that the protocol contemplated a reduction of armament as a consequence, and that the preparatory work looking to a conference on reduction of armament — land, sea, and air — accompanied and followed this action. The adoption of this document by the Assembly and its ratification by the governments involved were two very different things. Ratification failed; but the principles were not given up and were revived from time to time in later conferences.

The next important step was the Locarno Conference and agreements (October 5 to October 16, 1925). The major treaty of the group may be used to illustrate the results:

ARTICLE 2. Germany and Belgium, and also Germany and France, mutually undertake that they will in no case attack or invade each other or resort to war against each other.

This stipulation shall not, however, apply in the case of —

1. The exercise of the right of legitimate defense. . . .

2. Action in pursuance of Article 16 of the Covenant of the League of Nations.

3. Action as a result of a decision taken by the Assembly or by the Council of the League. . . .

ARTICLE 3. In view of the undertakings entered into in Article 2 of the present treaty, Germany and Belgium and Germany and

France undertake to settle by peaceful means and in the manner laid down herein all questions of every kind which may arise between them and which it may not be possible to settle by the normal methods of diplomacy.

The relation of the Locarno settlements to the League of Nations was clearly recognized in the preamble, which stated that the supplementary guaranties were "within the framework of the Covenant of the League." It was further understood that these treaties were to pave the way for the admission of Germany to the League. The nations that were parties to the Locarno settlements were Germany, Great Britain, Belgium, Italy, Poland, and Czechoslovakia.

The United States was the only great power which was not a party to one or more of these post-war commitments regarding war. It is only in the light of the European background that the American movement for renunciation of war can have any meaning. The origins of the American movement for outlawry of war have already been discussed in connection with the World Court controversy. The matter was revived as a live issue by the message addressed to the American people by Briand, the French premier, on April 6, 1927, on the occasion of the anniversary of the entrance of the United States into the World War. Briand announced his willingness to negotiate a treaty with the United States "to outlaw war" ("to use an American expression") between the two countries.

The renunciation of war as an instrument of national policy is a conception already familiar to the signatories to the Covenant of the League of Nations and of the treaties of Locarno. Every engagement entered into in this spirit by the United States toward another nation, such as France, would contribute greatly in the eyes of the world to broaden and strengthen the foundations on which the international policy of peace is being erected.

This statement illustrates beyond a doubt what Briand had in mind. He wished the United States to renounce war in the same manner in which the signatories of the above-named treaties had. There is no evidence that he had any intention of going beyond what those treaties had provided. It is understood that his message was inspired by James T. Shotwell, of Columbia University.

The most immediate reaction in the United States was among private individuals interested in international peace. These men, possibly with information from behind the scenes, saw more in Briand's statement than did the general public : they saw a conciliatory gesture at the period of crisis during the disarmament discussions, and an assurance of good will to the American Legion's meeting, which was to be held in France during the summer. Nicholas Murray Butler wrote a letter to the *New York Times* on April 26 emphasizing the importance of Briand's statement. On April 29 the American Foundation presented a plan for such a treaty with France as was suggested, and Shotwell published one on May 31. The first was broad in its scope ; the second was limited. The Shotwell plan followed closely the Locarno statement on "outlawry," the Bryan treaties on conciliation, and the Root treaties on arbitration ; in other words, it resembled the Franco-American arbitration treaty signed on February 6, 1928. In reality neither plan was an outright outlawry of war.

On June 20, 1927, the French submitted a draft treaty "to outlaw war" between the two nations which had definitely in mind the Locarno pacts in Europe.

ARTICLE I. The High Contracting Powers solemnly declare, in the name of the French people and the people of the United States of America, that they condemn recourse to war and renounce it respectively as an instrument of national policy toward each other.

ARTICLE II. The settlement or the solution of all disputes or conflicts, of whatever nature or of whatever origin they may be, which shall arise between France and the United States of America shall never be sought by either side except by pacific means.

On November 22 Senator Capper announced his intention to introduce a resolution indorsing, first, a formal renunciation of war by agreement with such nations as would accept ;

secondly, a declaration defining an aggressor nation as one which "having agreed to submit to arbitration, begins hostilities without having done so." President Coolidge was reported (November 25) as believing that outlawry of war was impractical and of doubtful efficacy, because Congress alone can declare war and no treaty engagement can deprive Congress of its constitutional rights. A declaration by Congress, he said, would be helpful only in the sense that it would aid in creating a sentiment for world peace. Senator Borah was quoted the same day as being of the opinion that peace resolutions would make little impression on Congress in view of pressing domestic questions and the presidential election. He was reported the day after as declaring that a scheme for outlawing aggressive warfare was impracticable, since there could be no definition of an aggressor nation.

A conference between Secretary Kellogg and the Senate Committee on Foreign Relations was held on December 21. Obviously something had been going on behind the scenes which brought action. On the following day Borah declared in favor of a multilateral treaty to outlaw war. On December 28 Kellogg addressed a note to France in which he said:

It has occurred to me that the two governments, instead of contenting themselves with a bilateral declaration of the nature suggested by M. Briand, might make a more signal contribution to world peace by joining in an effort to obtain the adherence of all the principal Powers of the world to a declaration renouncing war as an instrument of national policy.

The French reply, which was delivered on January 5, 1928, accepted in principle the renunciation of "all war of aggression" and "the settlement of differences of whatever nature" by pacific means. The two parties would agree to "bring this treaty to the attention of all states and invite them to adhere." Kellogg was not satisfied with the French note on two points and expressed his dissent in a note dated January 11. First, the contemplated treaty should be negotiated with the principal powers instead of asking their adherence

to a Franco-American treaty; secondly, the limitation of
the proposal to aggressive war was not in harmony with
Briand's draft of June 20, 1927, nor with the American
proposal. The French reply to this was dated January 21:

> Its suggestions on January 5 pertaining to the terms of the multi-
> partate treaty were inspired by a formula which has already obtained
> the unanimous adhesion of all Powers members of the League of
> Nations and which, moreover, could be accepted by them in respect
> to the United States, as it had already been accepted among them-
> selves.
>
> The Government of the Republic in all circumstances without
> reservation has declared itself ready to associate itself with any
> declaration tending to denounce war as a crime and to institute
> international sanctions susceptible to preventing or suppressing war.
> Its feeling in this respect has not changed. Its position remains
> the same.

Kellogg's next communication was dated February 27. He
expressed his belief that the Covenant of the League of Nations did not stand in the way of the desired end, and called
attention to the fact that the Pan-American Conference had
just adopted an unqualified "condemnation of war as an
instrument of national policy." "If, however, such a declaration were accompanied by definitions of the word 'aggressor'
and by exceptions and qualifications stipulating when nations
would be justified in going to war, its effect would be very
greatly weakened and its positive value as a guaranty of
peace virtually destroyed."

The negotiations were obviously becoming seriously involved in verbiage, inconsistencies, and pretenses. The Covenant recognized the right of self-defense, and also provided
definitely for the use of military measures under certain
conditions to enforce the obligations of the League. If the
Covenant was not repugnant to the unqualified renunciation
of war, there was then no avoiding the admission that
Kellogg's proposed renunciation of war was qualified. If
it was qualified, then what were the mental reservations?
Furthermore, the positive declaration that the United States

disapproved the use of the term "aggressor" was in direct conflict with its action at Havana in connection with the Pan-American Conference. The United States approved the resolution for the unqualified renunciation of war, as Kellogg pointed out to France; but it also approved the companion resolution declaring "that every act of aggression is considered illegal and is therefore declared forbidden," and about this Kellogg was silent.

The meeting of the Council of the League made it convenient for the French government to consult with the other powers regarding the American proposal. The exact nature of the conferences is not known, but they were apparently satisfactory. The French answer was sent under date of March 30. Kellogg's inconsistencies in regard to the aggressor nation did not escape comment, and the note attempted to explain the American charge that the French government was inconsistent in proposing unconditional renunciation of war in the draft treaty of June 20, 1927, and conditional renunciation in the recent negotiations. The gist of the argument was that a bilateral treaty with the United States alone was a different matter from a multilateral treaty such as they were then discussing. Subject to four understandings, France was willing to proceed with the negotiations with the other powers mentioned (namely, Great Britain, Germany, Italy, and Japan), with a view to agreeing on a draft multilateral treaty. Firstly, it should include all world powers on a basis of absolute equality; secondly, violation of the agreement by one party should automatically release all the others; thirdly, according to Kellogg's assurances the treaty would not deprive the signatories of the right of legitimate defense.

If such is the attitude of the American Government on these three fundamental points, and [fourthly] if it is clearly understood in a general way that the obligations of the new compact should not be substituted for or prejudice in any way previous obligations contained in international instruments such as the Covenant of the League of Nations, the Locarno agreements, or treaties guaranteeing neutrality whose character and scope cannot be modified thereby, then the differences of opinion which have appeared in the course of previous phases of the negotiations have to do more with words than with the reality of the problem facing the two governments today.

Agreement was reached between the two governments to proceed with the negotiations with the four powers named. The United States submitted the proposal formally in identical notes dated April 13, together with a draft treaty. The French government also submitted a draft treaty, which was released for publication on April 21. In these draft treaties the two governments adhered to their respective points of view, the United States in the unqualified form and France in the qualified form.

The exact meaning of the American unqualified renunciation of war was finally explained to the public in an address delivered by Secretary Kellogg before the American Society of International Law on April 28. After stating the position of France on six named points, he answered each separately:

1. *Self-defense.* "There is nothing in the American draft of an antiwar treaty which restricts or impairs in any way the right of self-defense. The right is inherent in every sovereign state and is implicit in every treaty. Every nation is free at all times and regardless of treaty provisions to defend its territory from attack or invasion, and it alone is competent to decide whether circumstances require recourse to war in self-defense. . . . "

2. *The League Covenant.* "The Covenant imposes no affirmative primary obligation to go to war. . . . There is, in my opinion, no necessary inconsistency between the Covenant and the idea of an unqualified renunciation of war. . . ."

3. *The treaties of Locarno.* The renunciation-of-war treaty would give "a double assurance that the Locarno treaties would not be violated by recourse to arms."

4. *Treaties of neutrality.* "The United States is not informed as to the precise treaties which France has in mind, and cannot therefore discuss their provisions. . . ."

5. *Relations with a treaty-breaking state.* As a matter of law the "violation of a multilateral antiwar treaty through resort to war by

one party thereto would automatically release the other parties from their obligations to the treaty-breaking state. . . ."

6. *Universality.* It was planned that all nations should be parties, but it is preferable not to postpone the coming into force of such a treaty until all have ratified it.

In the light of this address it appears that France and the United States were in agreement that the states concerned would be taking the pledge with reservations, and they were in essential agreement as to the nature of the reservations, with the possible exception of the second and the sixth. The explanation of self-defense was most inclusive and would undoubtedly comprehend the Monroe Doctrine and such policies as the United States had repeatedly defined in previous years as purely defensive. The statement with regard to [the League was misleading. Such obligation to go to war as the Covenant implied was in the nature of international police for the enforcement of international obligations. Kellogg, as Secretary of State, directed the pacification of Nicaragua, which Coolidge insisted was not war but merely the exercise of such necessary international police functions as devolve upon the United States in the Western Hemisphere. The common action of the powers in enforcing the obligations of lawbreaking states under the Covenant of the League would have in international law a status as an act of international police functions which could not possibly attach to the unilateral action of the United States under the Monroe Doctrine. No one for a moment understood that Kellogg advocated the renunciation of the Monroe Doctrine or the Caribbean policies of the United States. The essential difference between the position of the United States and that of France was, in the last analysis, that the United States would take the pledge with mental reservations and France would take it with written reservations.

The difference between the two, however, was important. France would define the reservations in advance of any particular crisis in order that the principles agreed upon in friendly conference might be applied in time of tension; the United States would leave the definition of reservations until national passions had been aroused by a crisis, and then the interpretation would of necessity be a unilateral application of the mental reservations. France associated the declaration of policy closely with the means of enforcement of international commitments as already provided for by the League. The United States was merely making a declaration of policy without respect to any sanctions or penalties. It was the characteristic American policy of participating in the formulation of international policies and then refusing to assume any responsibilities for their execution. The participation of the United States in several international conferences after the war through unofficial observers, who insisted on being heard but refused to sign the resulting treaties, exasperated Europeans. Their criticism was that the United States placed too much emphasis on national rights and not enough on national duties.

The replies of the powers to the notes of the United States of April 13 were favorable. The British reply, however, requires some comment. It restated, without dissent, essentially the points considered by the United States and France, but advanced one important elaboration. Chamberlain, for Great Britain, made the following restatement of established British foreign policy:

. . . there are certain regions of the world the welfare and integrity of which constitute a special and vital interest for our peace and safety. . . . Their protection against attack is to the British Empire a measure of self-defense. It must be clearly understood that His Majesty's Government in Great Britain accept the new treaty upon the distinct understanding that it does not prejudice their freedom of action in this respect. The Government of the United States have comparable interests any disregard of which by a foreign power they have declared that they would regard as an unfriendly act. His Majesty's Government believe, therefore, that in defining their position they are expressing the intention and meaning of the United States Government.

In his note of June 23 notifying the powers of the favorable reception of the draft treaty, Kellogg restated from his address of April 28 his understanding of the treaty and made no objection to the British interpretation. This introduced his reservations officially into the record of the negotiations. A second draft of the treaty, with a revised preamble, was submitted in the note of June 23. This was the draft finally accepted by the powers. Chamberlain, in his acknowledgment of this note, again stated his view in regard to policies of regional defense. "The General Treaty for the Renunciation of War" was formally signed at Paris on August 27, 1928. The text of the two essential articles follows:

ARTICLE I. The High Contracting Parties solemnly declare in the names of their respective peoples that they condemn recourse to war for the solution of international controversies, and renounce it as an instrument of national policy in their relations with one another.

ARTICLE II. The High Contracting Parties agree that the settlement or solution of all disputes or conflicts of whatever nature or of whatever origin they may be, which may arise among them, shall never be sought except by pacific means.

In his sixth and last annual message to Congress (December 4, 1929) Coolidge declared that "the observance of this Covenant, so simple and so straightforward, promises more for the peace of the world than any other agreement ever negotiated among the nations." He insisted that it did not deprive the United States of the right of self-defense and did not bind it to take any action in case the treaty were violated. Kellogg, the Secretary of State, and Borah, the chairman of the Senate Committee on Foreign Relations, advanced the same view. In the course of the session the treaty became closely linked with the fifteen-cruiser bill. The peace people wanted the renunciation of war, the big-navy group wanted the cruisers, and there were others who wanted both. *The Chicago Tribune* had declared editorially on June 16, 1928, that "Kellogg's peace treaties are bunk. If they have any effect it will be to chloroform American preparedness while in no way deterring the voracious nations of Europe and Asia." On January 2, 1929, an agreement was reached to put the treaty on renunciation of war ahead of the cruiser bill in the Senate; but the discussions of the two measures were closely associated during the next few weeks. There was little positive opposition to the treaty, but some senators doubted whether it contributed much toward peace. At least, as Swanson put it, "it marks an advance for peace, not a retreat. It will be beneficial in crystallizing and increasing the sentiments of the people of the world for peace." Those who opposed it were opposed to it only because it contained no statement recognizing the right of self-defense and the Monroe Doctrine. In their judgment this defect might be remedied either by an interpretative reservation attached to the resolution of ratification or by a report made by the Committee on Foreign Relations. Coolidge let it be known that he wanted the treaty as it stood, without reservation or interpretation. White House breakfasts ensued, at which the President discussed the measure with senators, but to no avail. The refusal to permit the interpretative committee report brought a vigorous attack on the treaty by Reed of Missouri on January 11. On the next day Senator Bingham had twenty-four signatures to a round robin asking for the interpretative report from the committee. Enough more votes were asserted to be available to make over one third. Reed presented a resolution on January 14 calling upon the committee for the report. The next day, without a vote on the resolution, Borah brought in the report to the effect that it was the opinion of the committee that the treaty did not impair the right of self-defense; that since the Monroe Doctrine was regarded as a part of the nation's defense the treaty did not preclude the right to maintain that doctrine as interpreted by the United States. The treaty was ratified on the same day by a vote of 81 to 1. The *Kansas City Star's* correspondent closed his account of the day's events with the following paragraph:

Thus renouncing war the Senate will take up tomorrow its unfinished business, which is the bill authorizing the construction of fifteen 10,000-ton cruisers and appropriating $270,000,000 for the same.

On January 17, 1929, Coolidge signed the treaty in the presence of his whole cabinet. The cruiser bill was passed and was signed by the President on February 13 as a companion measure. Senator Capper was not satisfied with renunciation of war. On February 11 he moved a resolution authorizing the president to place an embargo on shipment of arms to a nation violating the renunciation treaty, and further proposed a multilateral treaty to secure the coöperation of other powers to this end. In imposing these sanctions another step would be taken toward an actual outlawry of war. The resolution was not passed, however.

In conclusion, what did the United States proposal of renunciation of war mean to members of the League of Nations or to signatories of the Locarno agreements? It meant little if any practical extension of the obligations those nations had already assumed when the proposal was understood in the light of Kellogg's explanations and Borah's interpretative report; and since it contained no provision for enforcement, it did not go as far in that respect as the earlier treaties. What did it mean to the United States? It meant much; for, with the exception of Russia, the United States was the only great power that had made no pledges of peace similar to those made in 1920 and afterwards by the rest of the world. In that respect it was a distinct change in policy and a means by which the irreconcilable nationalists might reconcile themselves to limited American participation in world peace. It gave the United States the satisfaction of the appearance of leadership in world peace. What did it mean from the standpoint of the world? Inasmuch as the United States had repudiated the League and the World Court, the renunciation of war might serve as a formula by which the qualified adherence of the United States to world-peace commitments would be secured. The treaty was not, strictly speaking, outlawry of war, although that was the term in current use in the United States. "Outlawry of war" meant not only renunciation but also enforcement. It was therefore a step toward outlawry as an ideal and a goal; it embraced practically the whole world, including the United States, and therein lay its ultimate significance.

THE CODIFICATION OF INTERNATIONAL LAW

There were two widely differing views on the question of codification of international law. One placed the emphasis on the future and the building up of a body of new international law in keeping with the post-war status of international relations. The method for achieving this purpose would be through the activities of the League and other international bodies, and it would take the form of multilateral treaties, such as those respecting traffic in arms, air and electrical communications, opium, and prohibitions and restrictions on imports and exports, as well as decisions of the Assembly and Council and of arbitral bodies. In a sense the League would become an international legislative body. The other view placed the emphasis on the past and the utilization of the body of pre-war international law. The method of procedure would be the creation of commissions of specialists who would bring together past practices and correlate these. In the process, of course, much that was new would inevitably be incorporated into the various codes.

The refusal of the United States to join the League was a serious handicap to the first mode of procedure, but nevertheless much was done. The League did not view the second method with much favor during its first years. The Covenant did not provide for codification, and Root's suggested amendment was rejected. The advisory commission of jurists who drafted the statute of the World Court provided for compulsory jurisdiction over justiciable questions and predicated such jurisdiction upon a recommendation for the codification of international law. The recommendation of the advisory commission was, however, rejected by the League. It was not until September, 1924, that the Assembly, on the motion of Sweden, provided for a codification commission. A preliminary list of subjects was prepared, was forwarded by the Secretariat to the states of the world (both members and nonmembers) for examination and reply, and, on the basis of this information, a report was made to the Council. Early in 1927 a report was rendered on seven subjects which seemed suitable for codification. Additional subjects were yet under consideration.

The attitude of the United States government can best be judged by its reply to the League proposals, the essential part of which follows. The reply was dated October 12, 1926.

It is the view of the Government of the United States that international arrangements on the general subjects of : (1) Nationality, (2) Territorial Waters, (3) Diplomatic Privileges and Immunities, (4) Responsibility of States in respect to Injury caused in their Territory to the Persons or Property of Foreigners, which are the first four subjects mentioned in the communication of the Secretary-General, would serve a useful purpose and would therefore be desirable, and that there would be no insuperable obstacles to the concluding of agreements on these subjects. The Government of the United States is not prepared at this time to state whether all the points mentioned in the questionnaires on the subject referred to would yield to regulation by international agreement, nor does it desire to express an opinion regarding the desirability or possibility of regulating all other points by international agreement until it has had opportunity to make a more intensive study of them than it has yet done. The details would seem to be proper matters for discussion in any negotiations which may ensue.

With respect to the fifth subject, namely, procedure for the concluding and drafting of treaties, the Government of the United States perceives no real necessity for the regulation of these subjects by international agreement. It would seem that the determination of the procedure of international conferences might well be left to the discretion of the delegates representing the Governments participating in such conferences and that the procedure for the drafting and concluding of treaties might be left for determination by the parties negotiating them.

With regard to the sixth subject enumerated in the communication of the Secretary-General, namely, Piracy, it is the view of the Government of the United States that piracy, as that term is known in international law, is so nearly extinct as to render of little importance consideration of that subject as one to be regulated by international agreement.

With respect to the seventh subject, namely, Exploitation of the Products of the Sea, the Government of the United States is of the opinion:

1. That international regulation of certain fisheries, such as those of whales, is desirable and should be realizable.

2. That information as to the status of fisheries for most of the true fishes is not sufficiently complete to admit of the formulation of regulations at the present time.

3. That in most cases particular fisheries may best be regulated by treaties between the nations most directly concerned.

4. That investigations to determine the need for and character of regulations to sustain the various fisheries should be encouraged; and

5. That an international conference is desirable to consider the problem of conserving the whale.

REVIVAL OF THE WORLD-COURT ISSUE

Before the campaign of 1928 an attempt was made to re-open the question of ratification of the World Court protocol. Senator Gillett of Massachusetts presented a resolution urging the resumption of negotiations for an understanding on the United States reservations. This was answered by Representative Tinkham of the same state, who announced his intention to introduce a resolution looking toward the withdrawal of the offer of ratification. This incident left no appreciable trace on the campaign of 1928. The Republican platform was silent on the subject.

Borah, the chairman of the Senate Committee on Foreign Relations, had led the fight against the Court on the ground that there had been no outlawry of war and no codification of international law. The possible removal of these two important objections to participation appeared certain during the winter of 1928–1929. Was it not logical to reopen the World Court question? A story was carried in the press on November 25, 1928, to the effect that Coolidge had initiated another inquiry among the powers regarding United States adhesion.

The Council of the League of Nations set up a commission of jurists in 1928 to determine whether amendments to the statute of the World Court were desirable in the light of eight years of experience. Elihu Root was selected as one of the members and accepted on January 7, 1929. It was reported that he visited Hoover in Washington on January 11 and received his approval of the project to reopen the question of ratification by the United States. In February a note was addressed to the powers concerned by the American government. On March 9 the authority of the commission of jurists was enlarged by action of the League Council to include the question of American adhesion. Two days later a formula presented by Root was accepted by the commission as a basis of discussion. On the subject of advisory opinions it outlined the procedure to be followed: First, requests for advisory opinions would be communicated in advance to the United States government by the League of Nations; secondly, the United States would then indicate its attitude on the request; thirdly, in case of objection on the part of the United States an attempt would be made to arrive at an agreement on the statement of the question to be submitted; fourthly, if no agreement could be reached and the advisory opinion was insisted upon, the United States might withdraw from the Court. The Root formula, with slight modifications in its language, was accepted by the commission. Before it could become effective, however, it would have to be accepted by the Council of the League, by the members of the Court, and by the United States Senate.

SELECTED BIBLIOGRAPHY

CULBERTSON, W. S. International Economic Policies. D. Appleton and Company, 1925.

BASSETT, J. S. The League of Nations. Longmans, Green & Co., 1928.

HUGHES, CHARLES E. The Pathway of Peace. Harper & Brothers, 1925.

BLAKESLEE, G. H. The Recent Foreign Policy of the United States. The Abingdon Press, 1925.

BUELL, R. L. Europe: A History of Ten Years. The Macmillan Company, 1928.

HOWARD-ELLIS, C. The Origin, Structure, and Work of the League of Nations. Houghton Mifflin Company, 1928.

MILLER, D. H. The Geneva Protocol. The Macmillan Company, 1925.

MILLER, D. H. The Peace Pact of Paris. G. P. Putnam's Sons, 1928.

SHOTWELL, JAMES T. War as an Instrument of National Policy. Harcourt, Brace and Company, 1929.

League of Nations Yearbooks. World Peace Foundation Pamphlet Series, Boston.

Publications of the League of Nations and of the Permanent Court of International Justice are handled in the United States by the World Peace Foundation, 40 Mount Vernon Street, Boston.

International Conciliation Pamphlets of the Carnegie Endowment for International Peace.

Periodical material, which is indispensable, includes *Current History*, *The American Journal of International Law*, *Foreign Affairs*, and the Information Service of the Foreign Policy Association.

◄ PART FOUR ►

Politics and Political Theories

CHAPTER XXXIII

POLITICAL PARTIES AND POLITICS

IT IS the purpose of this chapter to summarize political developments after the World War, with particular reference to the problem of political parties. The presidential election of 1920 as it involved the issue of the League of Nations has been discussed and needs only to be mentioned here. The platforms of the major parties are summarized so far as possible in the order in which the planks appeared. Totally unrelated subjects were found side by side, and closely related or interdependent questions were often completely separated. The platforms might be reorganized and classified according to subject matter; but such a change would convey a false impression of orderly thinking and procedure, and this was, with rare exceptions, entirely foreign to party deliberations. In some cases it would reveal in too glaring a manner the inconsistencies and omissions in party promises. It is a commonplace that the platforms of the party of which one is not a member can never be taken seriously. To anyone but a rank partisan it is evident that the platforms of neither party can be accepted as the repository of historical truth. Inasmuch as compromise was one of the most prominent aspects of political coöperation among conflicting elements, the positive promises of the party were drafted in such a manner as to attract as many votes as possible and alienate as few as possible.

THE REPUBLICAN PLATFORM, 1920

The Republican platform of 1920 denounced the Democratic party for unpreparedness for both peace and war. It promised that the Republicans would restore constitutional government, and that the Federal government would not encroach upon the states. They contended that Democratic foreign policy had not been based upon principle and denounced Wilson's Mexican policy, the suggestion of the Armenian mandate, and the policy of the League of Nations.

The Republicans took the credit for such reconstruction legislation as was enacted after the war, and promised an agricultural program. They charged that the President had defeated national economy, had vetoed the budget law, and had failed to reform taxation, and they laid the high cost of living to the inflation of the currency. They complained that profiteering was allowed, and claimed that the Federal Trade Commission was hostile to the best interests of business. They advocated highways, conservation, reclamation, a strong army, a strong navy, women's suffrage, Federal aid to education (particularly physical education) and Federal control of Federal money spent for such purposes, a greater centralization of Federal functions, a child-labor law, a public-health program, a women's bureau, and the Americanization of Hawaii.

THE REPUBLICAN NOMINATION, 1920

The Republican presidential possibilities were manifold. Hiram Johnson was a radical in domestic politics and was opposed to the League. Leonard Wood was considered to represent the Roosevelt tradition; he was not so radical as Johnson, but he was opposed to the League as it stood. Governor Lowden of Illinois was a business man and an agriculturalist. Senator Harding from Ohio, a conservative, a reservationist on the League question, was a representative of the senatorial group which was powerful in the party. An item in the *New York Times* immediately after Roosevelt's death reported that Harding was most talked of as the next choice of the party. Hoover, whose reputation was linked with relief work in Europe and with the food administration during the war, occupied a peculiar position in the early stages of the preconvention campaign. Both parties claimed him. He was undoubtedly the most popular candidate in the field; but when he declared for the Republican party he was dropped, of course, by the Democrats. The *Literary Digest* poll indicated his outstanding popularity when the convention met; but among the old-guard politicians he meant nothing and was ignored. Senator Lodge, the temporary chairman, delivered the keynote speech — a denunciation of everything Wilsonian. This was symbolical of what was to come. Whoever was nominated must be acceptable to the senatorial clique and share their resentments. When the inevitable deadlock ensued, the choice of Harding was made by a little group of politicians in private conference. The deal was merely ratified by an obedient and confused convention. Harding was an affable politician, but not a statesman. During his service in the Senate his name was never associated with any important measure. The choice for vice president was Calvin Coolidge, who had made a reputation as governor of Massachusetts during the Boston police strike.

THE DEMOCRATIC PLATFORM, 1920

In their platform of 1920 the Democrats pledged their "adherence to the fundamental progressive principles of social, economic, and industrial justice." They advocated the League of Nations. They stood for tax reduction and reform, for economy (which they declared the Republicans had blocked), as well as for reconstruction legislation, which was necessary to reduce the high cost of living. The Democrats had enacted an agricultural program, as well as labor legislation. They declared that "labor is not a commodity, it is human," and they opposed compulsory arbitration of labor disputes. They indorsed women's suffrage, maternity and infancy legislation, assistance to education, and care of disabled soldiers. They upheld the transportation and communication policies of the Federal government, but declared that the Republicans had prevented an adequate transportation act dealing with railroads. They approved government supervision of business and Wilson's Mexican policy, and extended sympathy to Ireland and to Armenia. They declared that Porto Rico should eventually be made a state, that Alaskan resources should be developed, that Philippine independence should be granted, and that the homestead act should be extended to Hawaii. Asiatic immigration should be excluded. They denounced Republican corruption, especially the Michigan election scandal, which had given the Republicans the majority in the Senate.

THE DEMOCRATIC NOMINATION, 1920

The Democratic convention was uneventful. There was no outstanding personality to take over the leadership of Wilson. Attorney-General Palmer, W. G. McAdoo, former Secretary of the Treasury, and Governor J. M. Cox, of Ohio, were leading possibilities. McAdoo alone had proved ability of presidential caliber. On the forty-fourth ballot Cox was nominated as a compromise. Franklin D. Roosevelt, Assistant Secretary of the Navy, was named for vice president.

Two radical minority parties should be mentioned, but they did not play an important part in the campaign. The Socialists nominated Eugene V. Debs for the fifth time. Debs conducted his campaign from the Federal Penitentiary at Atlanta, where he was imprisoned because of his activ'ties in opposing the war. The Farmer-Labor party attempted to combine these two irreconcilable elements. La Follette refused the nomination, and it fell to P. P. Christensen, of Utah.

THE CAMPAIGN, 1920

An unusual combination of elements influenced the campaign and counted against the Democrats, the party in power. Wilson's personality and his policy of ratification of the Covenant of the League of Nations without reservations reacted against Cox. The high cost of living and the economic collapse of 1920, especially among the agricultural classes, was charged to the administration. Race prejudices, especially Irish and German, were exploited to punish the party in power. Lastly, the liberal program of the Wilson administration was contrary to the spirit of the prevailing conservative and reactionary tendencies of the post-war period.

There was little enthusiasm for the Republicans, but there was strong opposition to the Democrats. As William Allen White put it: "In 1920 the people voted their resentments." Everything seemed to conspire to heap up grievances against the party in power. If the Democrats could have been defeated without electing the Republicans, the country would have been well satisfied. Another aspect of the lack of interest in the Republican campaign was the difficulty of raising money. The party was left with a huge deficit, which was paid off with difficulty before the next election, and then only through the generosity of Harry Sinclair, the beneficiary of the lease of the Teapot Dome naval reserve.

The result of the election was not unexpected. The popular majority given to Harding was 6,998,964. He polled 61.6 per cent of the popular vote to Cox's 34.9 per cent. The electoral vote was 404 to 127. Even Tennessee went Republican, the first break in the solid South since reconstruction.

THE HARDING-COOLIDGE ADMINISTRATION

The inauguration of Harding passed without any unusual features. His cabinet was, however, an unusual combination of Republican factions: Charles E. Hughes (New York), Secretary of State; Andrew W. Mellon (Pennsylvania), Secretary of the Treasury; J. W. Weeks (Massachusetts), Secretary of War; Harry M. Daugherty (Ohio), Attorney-General; Will H. Hays (Indiana), Postmaster-General; Edwin Denby

(Michigan), Secretary of the Navy; Albert B. Fall (New Mexico), Secretary of the Interior; H. C. Wallace (Iowa), Secretary of Agriculture; Herbert Hoover (California), Secretary of Commerce; J. J. Davis (Pennsylvania), Secretary of Labor. Hughes, Mellon, and Hoover were soon recognized as the real framework of the administration. Harding died on August 2, 1923. He thus escaped the humiliation which would have been his lot. Already charges of corruption in the administration were becoming ominous. Vice President Coolidge was immediately inaugurated and undertook to weather the storm which was breaking on the eve of a presidential election.

Under the leadership of Thomas J. Walsh of Montana (Democrat) in the Senate, scandals in connection with the leasing of oil reserves to Harry Sinclair and E. L. Doheny were uncovered. Proceedings were instituted in 1924 to cancel the lease to the Elk Hills reserve granted to Doheny, and that to the Teapot Dome reserve granted to Sinclair. Indictments were returned against the two and Secretary Fall, in June, 1924, for bribery and conspiracy to defraud. Fall had accepted a loan of $100,000 from Doheny and $25,000 from Sinclair, according to evidence then available. Later it was found that his relations with Sinclair involved much more. Denby, as Secretary of the Navy, was forced by circumstances to resign. Although the scandal was not definitely attached to him, it occurred in connection with naval reserves while he was the responsible head of the department. Will Hays had resigned early in the administration; but when investigations into campaign funds were started in 1924, questionable conduct was alleged in connection with his management of the campaign of 1920 while chairman of the Republican National Committee. In 1928 much more was uncovered.

The administration of the Department of Justice was long under fire. In March, 1924, when Daugherty refused the Senate committee access to official files in connection with investigations regarding corruption in his department, Coolidge dismissed him. He was the last of the so-called "Ohio gang." One of the most unsavory scandals was that which involved C. R. Forbes, director of the Veterans' Bureau. Forbes was indicted in February, 1924, shortly before the nominating convention, and later was convicted of corruption, especially in the administration of hospitals and supplies for disabled veterans of the World War.

The exposures just preceding the campaign and during it might possibly have been too great a load for the Republicans to carry if Harding had been in the executive chair. The change in presidents and the rapid shifts in cabinet and other executive positions tended to give the impression that even if there had been corruption, the administration had been cleansed and the Republican house set in order. The argument of the party man was to ask what better proof need be given of the fundamental purity of the Republican party. Moreover, the unimpeachable integrity of such members as Hughes and Hoover never served an administration better than in 1924.

THE REPUBLICAN PLATFORM, 1924

In the Republican convention of 1924 the old guard was subordinated. The President's faction was in the minority; but it was in a position to dictate, and it was generally understood that the platform really represented the President's views on most points. The open differences between the President and Congress over legislation and appointments were temporarily in the background. The platform opened with a tribute to Harding. The Republicans stressed economy in government and the reduction of the debt, and maintained that this accomplishment "presents a record unsurpassed in the history of public finance." They declared that taxes had been reduced, but charged that the Democrats had prevented reform. They indorsed the tariff act of 1922. They approved international action to prevent war, entrance into the World Court, and limitation of armament, and held that policies with respect to Mexico and the Tacna-Arica dispute were successful. They enumerated the agricultural legislation already enacted, and promised further legislation. They approved Federal participation in highways, the child-labor amendment, the eight-hour day, and vocational education. They condemned the Railroad Labor Board and compulsory arbitration of labor disputes. They maintained that public utilities should be regulated, but that there should be no government ownership. In dealing with the coal problem they denied that the government had power to regulate the price, but insisted that profiteering should be prevented. Their policy included the promotion of the merchant marine and inland waterways. They declared that disabled veterans should receive "increasing solicitude." They indorsed conservation of natural resources and advocated a Department of Education. A pledge was made to draft material resources as well as men in case of war. They advocated the encouragement of commercial aviation, and promised that the army and navy should not be weakened. They denounced corruption and approved restriction of immigration.

THE REPUBLICAN NOMINATION, 1924

The nomination of a Republican candidate for president presented no difficulties in 1924, and Coolidge was chosen on the first ballot. The selection of a vice president was not so easy. No one seemed to command substantial and determined support. The final choice was Charles G. Dawes.

THE DEMOCRATIC PLATFORM, 1924

In their platform of 1924 the Democrats praised the Wilson administration and denounced the corruption of the Republicans. They declared that the tariff was written in the interest of monopolies and that it prevented development of foreign trade. They defended the income tax, which had been designed originally to lay the burden of taxation upon those who are most able to pay. They denounced the "nuisance taxes" and sales taxes as a burden on the consumer, and declared that the tariff and railroad rates deprived the farmer of both profits and markets. They promised a policy of international coöperation, competitive tariff, lower costs of transportation, completion of the waterway systems, co-operative marketing, rural credits, and the like. They insisted that the Transportation Act must be rewritten, and that the Muscle Shoals policy must be fulfilled. They contended that contraction of currency had bankrupted the farmer. They approved reclamation and improvement of highways. They maintained that mining was suffering in the same way as agriculture. They declared that the government should own and operate the merchant marine, that the anthracite-coal industry should be regulated, that the states were primarily responsible for education, that congressmen should not be permitted to sit in Congress after they were defeated for reëlection, that campaign funds should be regulated, that the narcotic trade should be suppressed. "We demand that the states in the Union shall be preserved in all their vigor." Policies regarding Asiatic immigration, the Philippines, and Alaska were similar to those of 1920. They condemned the Lausanne treaty for its alleged bartering of Armenia for the Chester oil concession. They indorsed disarmament, and declared that "war is a relic of barbarism and . . . justifiable only as a measure of self-defense." They asserted that the draft in case of war should be applied to wealth as well as to men. They stressed freedom of race and religion, and declared that "the Democratic party pledges all its energies to the outlawing of the whole war system," and that "there is no substitute for the League of Nations as an agency of peace." They indorsed deep waterways from the Great Lakes to the Gulf and to the Atlantic, flood control, and power development, and condemned the Federal Trade

Commission for failure to prevent or prosecute monopolies. They favored development of aviation. They declared that "labor is not a commodity," and that child life and women should be protected. With respect to Latin America they said, "God made us neighbors — justice shall keep us friends."

THE DEMOCRATIC NOMINATION, 1924

The Democratic convention was one of the most unusual in the history of the party. The planks on the Ku-Klux Klan and the League touched the emotions and deepest-seated prejudices of the delegates and of the country. The crude, provincial New York mob in the galleries antagonized the South and the West. The clear-cut anti-Klan plank was defeated by a majority of 4.3 votes. The outspoken League plank was defeated 353.5 to 742.5. There were numerous candidates, but the contest settled down to a long-drawn-out duel between McAdoo and Smith. The debate on the Klan plank put the convention in a bitter mood. McAdoo reached 530 votes on the sixty-ninth ballot, somewhat less than a majority and far less than the necessary two thirds. Smith reached his greatest strength on the seventy-seventh ballot with 367 votes. The first break came on the ninety-third ballot, when John W. Davis rose from 68 votes to $205\frac{1}{2}$. He was nominated on the hundred and third ballot. The convention had lasted sixteen days. Smith was conservative, Eastern, a Tammany member, a Catholic, and "wet," all of which were anathema to a large part of the West and South. McAdoo was relatively liberal, Protestant with Klan support, and "dry." Davis was a liberal conservative, Eastern, for the League, Protestant, and "dry" (or relatively so); in other words, Davis was a compromise. The second place on the ticket went to Governor Charles Bryan of Nebraska, a radical Westerner and the brother of William J. Bryan.

THE PROGRESSIVE PARTY, 1924

A new Progressive party was launched during July, with La Follette as candidate and Senator Burton K. Wheeler (Montana, Democrat) as second on the ticket. The party was indorsed by the Socialist party, the Farmer-Labor party, and the American Federation of Labor. La Follette made a statement of his principles which served as a platform. He declared that "the great issue before the American people today is the control of government and industry by private monopoly," and pledged a house-cleaning in the administrative departments, the preservation of natural resources, the revision of the water-power act and the minerals-leasing act. He maintained that the nation's water power should be owned by the government, that the Transportation Act should be repealed, and that government ownership should be established. He advocated the reduction of taxation on individual incomes, a program of rigid economy, the reduction of military expenditures by $800,000,000, and the collection of war debts from foreign countries. He condemned the Mellon tax plan, and advocated a constitutional amendment which would authorize Congress to enact a statute over a judicial veto and would authorize the election of Federal judges for fixed terms by a direct vote of the people. He denounced the tariff of 1922, and declared that the Federal Reserve system and the farm-loan system were to be liberalized to provide credit on fair terms to agriculture, that coöperative enterprises should be promoted by appropriate legislation, and that railroad rates on agricultural products should be reduced to about pre-war levels. He maintained that the use of injunctions in labor disputes should be abolished; that labor and the farmer should be free to organize and bargain collectively; that the child-labor amendment should be ratified; that adjusted compensation should be provided for veterans; that the sales tax was a means of imposing burdens on the poor; that the Great Lakes waterway should be built to the sea; and that the sovereignty of the people is supreme over all, and with the people should lie the final decision in national policy. The foreign policy of financial imperialism was denounced as "contrary to the will of the American people, destructive of domestic development, and provocative of war." He maintained that there should be outlawry of war, abolition of conscription, drastic reduction of armaments, and the guaranty of a public referendum on peace and war.

THE CAMPAIGN, 1924

The course of the campaign was uneventful. The differences between Republican and Democratic platforms and candidates were too small to arouse enthusiasm. There were no real issues; in fact, the country was not interested in issues. The Democratic party was demoralized by the New York convention. On the other hand, there was little enthusiasm for La Follette. His support was mostly in the nature of a protest by a minority against the old parties. The popular vote for Coolidge was 15,718,789, or 54.1 per cent; for Davis 8,378,962, or 28.7 per cent; and for La Follette 4,822,319, or 17.2 per cent. The electoral vote was 379 for Coolidge, 139 for Davis, and 13 for La Follette.

THE COOLIDGE ADMINISTRATION

In the Congress elected in 1924 the party alignment was clearly in favor of the Republicans. The Senate contained 50 Republicans, 5 La Follette men, 40 Democrats, and but 1 Farmer-Labor man; the House contained 232 Republicans, 15 La Follette men, 183 Democrats, 3 Farmer-Labor men, and 2 Socialists. The La Follette Republicans were read out of the party as the penalty for their bolt in the campaign. The majorities of 1924, however, were not so great as those of 1920, and in this respect they were significant of the general trend. The administration party was in no sense united. The internal differences became conspicuous at times, as in the controversies over confirmation of appointments. For the President's own party to refuse to confirm the Warren appointment to the cabinet was without precedent. This was only the most conspicuous of Coolidge's differences with the Senate, — differences which began almost from the time of his accession to the presidency. Other important disagreements occurred over legislation, taxation, army and navy establishment, veterans' legislation, water power, agriculture, etc., and the World Court.

In the Congress elected in 1926 the administration Republicans were in important instances defeated for the Senate. When it came time to organize in December, 1927, the numbers stood 48 Republicans, including insurgents, 47 Democrats, and 1 Farmer-Labor. The Republican organization invited the insurgents back into the party, and naturally they made conditions, which meant return under practically their own terms. The insurgents, therefore, held the balance of power.

During the summer of 1927, which the President spent in South Dakota, he faced an important decision: Should he ask for the nomination in 1928? There was little doubt that he could have it for the asking. If nominated, he would be charged with violating the third-term precedent. It was quite possible that he could not be elected. Even if he was elected, it was almost certain that it would be without a working majority of regular Republicans in Congress. Various attempts were made to force the issue, but Coolidge took his time. On August 2 he handed the newspaper correspondents a slip of paper containing the single sentence "I do not choose to run for president in 1928." There were some who insisted on "drafting" Coolidge, but he repeated his refusal. This opened the field for various aspirants.

THE REPUBLICAN PLATFORM, 1928

In the drafting of the Republican platform of 1928 the women's organizations got little satisfaction, and the Federation of Labor received only the vaguest of pledges. The farmers carried the fight for the equalization-fee plank to the floor of the convention, but were defeated 817 to 267. The issue for modification of prohibition was carried to the floor also and defeated. The platform was not so much a statement of future policies as a summary of past legislation, and was approved by the convention without change.

Coolidge and Republican policies were given unqualified indorsement. The Republicans asserted that "economy has been raised to the dignity of a principle of government"; that the record of the Treasury was unsurpassed in debt reduction, tax reduction, and tax and tariff reform; that "the protective tariff is as vital to American agriculture as it is to American manufacturing"; that foreign trade increased because the American people could buy; and that foreign debts were refunded and German claims adjusted. They approved the foreign policy of the administration — outlawry of war, protection of American interests abroad, and support to American trade — and they pledged themselves to aid and assist in the perfection of international law and the settlement of international disputes. They recounted the agricultural measures under the Republican régime, and promised reorganization of marketing, assistance in diversification, and the creation of a Federal Farm Board to promote the establishment of stabilization corporations. They promised that they would seek to stabilize the coal-mining industry, and that highway appropriations would be continued. The labor plank was indefinite; but they indorsed collective bargaining, and admitted that there were some instances where the injunction had been abused and had given "rise to a serious question for legislation." They approved railroad and merchant-marine legislation and the flood-control bill. They declared that radio policy was to foster education, entertainment, and business; that the waterways policy was to be continued; and, while emphasizing the authority of the states, that public utilities were to be regulated. They praised the Republican conservation policy, particularly in respect to oil and water power, and declared that the Eighteenth Amendment was to be enforced. They denounced corruption in government, declaring that "economy, honesty, and decency in the conduct of political campaigns are a necessity. . . . The campaign of 1924 complied with all these requirements." Full accounts were to be published every thirty days, beginning with August 1, and final accounts five days before the election, and they insisted that there must be no deficit at the end of the campaign. They approved reclamation, aviation, and immigration policies, and declared that naturalization should be limited to those who are loyal to American institutions, and that the navy was to be supported to the full ratio under the treaty limitations. They indorsed Hawaiian and Alaskan policies, approved the continuance of the policy of 1924 which admitted women to a share in the management of the party, advocated the adoption in time of war of the draft of material resources as well as man power, and recommended that Indian affairs should be investigated. They declared that the efforts "to have the Federal government move into the field of state activities never has had and never will have the support of the Republican party."

THE REPUBLICAN NOMINATION, 1928

Before the meeting of the convention it was clear that Hoover was the favorite; and when the Pennsylvania delegation announced its support at the beginning of the sessions, he was assured of approximately seven hundred votes, a safe majority. Lowden, in accordance with his previous pledge, withdrew from the contest when the party failed to adopt the equalization-fee plank as a part of its agricultural program. The other contenders were Watson of Indiana, Goff of West Virginia, Norris of Nebraska, and Curtis of Kansas; but their chances were hopeless. Among these Curtis received the strongest support, a fact which seemed to be the determining element in his choice as candidate for vice president. Herbert Hoover was nominated as candidate for president on the first ballot by an overwhelming majority.

The Democratic Platform, 1928

The Democratic platform of 1928 opened with a tribute to the memory of Woodrow Wilson. The Democrats declared that they favored the revival of the spirit of local self-government and the preservation of states' rights, and they denounced Republican corruption in extreme language. They pledged the party to efficiency and economy in administration and to reorganization of government, and promised reform in banking in order to prevent speculation. They denounced the Republican policy of taxation as relieving those best able to pay and withholding reduction from those least able to pay, and promised a tariff which would maintain legitimate business and wage standards, would restore the tariff commission to its original status of a fact-finding body, and would permit effective competition and insure against monopoly. Their measure of adequate protection was the "actual differences between the cost of production at home and abroad, with adequate safeguard for the wage of the American laborer." They declared, further, that the Republican party had done little for agriculture over a period of fifty years; that the party had made promises repeatedly and had as often broken them. The Democrats promised an agricultural program which would place agriculture on an equality with other industries and would include credits to coöperatives, a Federal Farm Board, adjustment of taxes, and the encouragement of coöperatives. They held that the

surplus problem should be solved without curtailing production, and they pledged the party "to an earnest endeavor
to solve this problem of the distribution of the cost of dealing
with the crop surpluses over the marketed units of the crop
whose producers are benefited by such assistance." They
promised a program that would solve also the condition of
the mining industry. They promised a constructive foreign
policy based on outlawry of war, freedom from entangling
alliances, protection of American rights, noninterference in
the affairs of other nations, and restoration of the United
States to leadership in international arbitration and limitation of armaments. They indorsed the policy of encouragement of waterways, water transportation, flood relief, and
declared that the water-power act should be enforced strictly,
that water-power sites should be protected in the public interest, and that natural resources should be conserved. They
declared that no injunctions should be granted in labor disputes except upon proof of threatened irreparable injury and
after notice and hearing, and that the injunction should be
confined to those acts which directly threaten irreparable
injury. They urged that methods be found to prevent unemployment, that public works should be constructed during
times of unemployment, that children should be protected
through infancy and childhood, that women should receive
equal pay for equal work, and that restriction of immigration
should be maintained. They emphasized that policies respecting radio should preserve freedom of speech and prevent monopoly. They pledged "an honest enforcement of
the Eighteenth Amendment and all other provisions of the
Federal Constitution and all laws enacted pursuant thereto."
They condemned excessive campaign costs and promised
full publicity. They advocated that the merchant marine
be kept in operation, but they opposed monopoly, favoritism,
and sacrifices in the sales of ships. They maintained that
"the Federal government should offer to the states such
counsel, advice, research, and aid as may be made available

through our schools in view of our national needs." They declared that "during the last seven years, under Republican rule, the antitrust laws have been thwarted, ignored, and violated so that the country is rapidly becoming controlled by trusts and sinister monopolies. . . . Honest business, no matter what its size, need have no fears of a Democratic administration. The Democratic party ever will oppose illegitimate and dishonest business." They advocated that the traditional methods of self-government should be granted to Hawaii and Alaska and that Philippine independence should be granted. They pledged that the health activities of the government should be enlarged in order to stamp out contagious diseases and ascertain remedies for cancer, infantile paralysis, and the like.

THE DEMOCRATIC NOMINATION, 1928

The Democratic nomination in 1928 was practically a foregone conclusion by the time the convention met. On the first ballot Alfred E. Smith, governor of New York, was nominated for president. Joseph T. Robinson of Arkansas was nominated for vice president. The bitter fight in the platform committee over the liquor question had been adjusted by the compromise plank on enforcement. On the day following the nomination Smith sent a telegram to the convention approving the platform except that he restated his position on the liquor question. He pledged enforcement of the existing law, but declared that he would use his influence to secure a change in the law. He was opposed to the return of the saloon, however. In this way, instead of quieting the liquor issue, as the convention had hoped to do, the candidate reopened the whole question. The fact that Smith was a Catholic had already embarrassed his candidacy. The combination of the two questions, prohibition and religion, handicapped him in the West, where otherwise discontent indicated a possible revolt against the Republican party, and in the Democratic-Protestant South, where normally it was expected that a Democratic candidate would receive unquestioned support.

THE CAMPAIGN, 1928

The Democratic candidate delivered his speech of acceptance at Albany on August 22. He did not depart from the platform or add to it on any essential point except on prohibition. On that subject he declared for enforcement, but stated that his influence would be used to secure modification of the Eighteenth Amendment. During the latter part of September he made a tour beyond the Mississippi. This was the real opening of his campaign. His first speech was delivered at Omaha on September 18. He discussed agriculture along the lines of the platform, indorsing the equalization fee in principle. The second speech was at Oklahoma City (September 20), on the subject of religious intolerance. In his third speech, at Denver on September 22, he discussed the water-power question, stating that the government, national or state, must own the power site and the generating plant. At Helena (September 24) he attacked the Republican record on oil leases and on conservation of natural resources. The later speeches of Smith's tour added nothing new. During a southern tour he outlined at Louisville on October 13 his tariff position, indorsing clearly the protective tariff. At Sedalia he attacked the economy record of the Republican administration. The remaining six major speeches were primarily restatements of matter from earlier addresses, but gave considerable time to prohibition in answer to Hughes. At no time did Smith make more than a general reference to foreign policies.

The Republican candidate delivered his speech of acceptance at Palo Alto on August 11. It also followed closely the views expressed in the party platform. He pointed out, however, some interpretations which were of importance to his coming campaign. The past years, he declared, had been a reconstruction period and must be evaluated from that standpoint, but the problems of the future were problems of construction. In stating the objectives of government he said: "Economic advancement is not an end in itself. . . . Our purpose is to build in this nation a human society, not an economic system." On August 21, at West Branch, Iowa, his birthplace, Hoover discussed primarily waterways in their relation to agriculture. The next speech was at Newark, on September 17. Tariff was the subject, analyzed in its bearing on different economic groups — the laborer, the farmer, and the manufacturer. It was the most commonplace speech of his campaign, since he followed closely the orthodox Republican traditions. In a speech at Boston on October 15 he discussed foreign trade and foreign economic policies. At New York (on October 22) his theme was the principles underlying government according to the American tradition: private rather than public conduct of business, government regulation of public utilities, free competition in business, individual liberty, and political equality. On his return trip to the Pacific coast he spoke at St. Louis, on November 2, on the constructive side of government. In this speech he summarized his whole theory of government as applied to existing conditions. He took as his premise the view that the United States had developed a unique political, economic, and social system, based on essentially new principles — equality of opportunity and freedom of the individual — and that the preservation of these principles requires the government to take constructive action in three fields: in great undertakings in public works, in fostering policies of social betterment, and "in broadening the assistance of the government to the growing efforts of the people to coöperation among themselves to useful social and economic ends." Beginning with his speech of acceptance Hoover had included some reference to this question of economic self-government in most of his speeches during the campaign, but there was little popular understanding of the significance of the new theory of economic and social control.

The campaign of 1928 was unique in the history of presidential elections. National radio hook-ups carried direct to the people every important event from the broadcasting of the proceedings of the nominating conventions to the announcement of the election returns. Both parties, beginning in the middle of September, presented daily radio programs both morning and evening. The total radio bill for both parties was over $1,250,000.

The election of November 6, 1928, registered 444 electoral votes for Hoover and 87 for Smith. The popular vote was 21,429,109 for Hoover, 15,005,497 for Smith, and 267,835 for Norman Thomas, the Socialist candidate. These figures are only approximate, since official figures are not available for all the states. It was estimated that 75 per cent of the eligible voters participated, which testified to the unusual popular interest in the campaign. The Congress elected was constituted as follows: Senate, 55 Republicans, 39 Democrats, 1 Farmer-Labor man, and 1 seat vacant; the House, 269 Republicans, 165 Democrats, and 1 Farmer-Labor man. Hoover's speeches indicated that a turning point had come in public policies. Hoover was one of the very few Americans who came to the presidency with a reasoned theory of government which he proposed to make the basis of a definite administration program.

CHAPTER XXXIV

FACTORS IN RECENT AMERICAN HISTORY:
AN INTERPRETATION

TEN years of United States history have been reviewed. What is the significance of the decade, its relation to the past, and the promise of the future? The history of the United States is not the story of an isolated unit revolving in space and evolving a peculiar and unique civilization. Fundamentally, American civilization is only an aspect of modern Western civilization, and is actuated by the same basic heritages — political, economic, social, religious, and cultural. In this respect United States history is only a chapter in a larger theme — the expansion of Europe. The American environment produced, however, some highly important variations on the theme, and the variations were not exactly harmonious. Too much emphasis has been placed upon some of the variations and too little upon the underlying unities.

Industrialism as a factor in modern history was the product of capitalism and of power — steam, electricity, and gas — applied to the machinery of production, transportation, and communication. In Europe the traditional date for its emergence was the latter part of the eighteenth century; in the United States it came during the two decades preceding the Civil War.

Individualism also was a factor in the transition from medievalism to modernism, and was one of the outstanding characteristics of the modern period. In the medieval world, rights inhered in the group or institution — the clergy, the nobility, the guild, the town, and the like. The individual enjoyed rights only as a member of such a group. The idea that rights inhered in an individual just because he was a man was a product of the modern age. In seventeenth-century England there was advocacy of the rights of Englishmen. This was a stage in advance of the medieval concept of group rights. In the eighteenth century there emerged the generally accepted doctrine of the natural rights of man: that man possessed rights not because he was a member of a group or a subject of some nation, but because he was a man. The logical conclusion of this doctrine was that government could not justly infringe upon these God-given rights. One of the first acts of the French Revolution was to draft a Declaration of the Rights of Man. In the English colonies the patriot leaders discarded the doctrine of the rights of Englishmen and incorporated into the Declaration of Independence the newer doctrine that "we hold these truths to be self-evident, that all men are created equal; that they are endowed by their Creator with certain inalienable rights; that among these are life, liberty, and the pursuit of happiness." It was this doctrine of individualism which became one of the fundamental factors in American history. Before the Civil War this found expression in what was called the laissez faire theory of government: that government was best which governed least, and which interfered least with the free development of the individual; or, to put it in another way, what was good for the individual was good for the group.

Democracy as a factor in modern history must be understood not in the present-day sense, but rather as the evolution of responsible popular government. By the term "responsible government" is meant not any particular *form* of government but rather a principle of government. The principle might find expression in various forms of institutions, and any standard of measurement of the degree of responsibility was a matter of relativity. The absolute kingship was responsible government in contrast to feudal disorder, and formed the first link in the chain of the evolution of modern democracy. Monarchy gave way to constitutional monarchy, and this in turn to parliamentary government, as in England under the two-party system, or on the Continent in the bloc system, or in the United States in the presidential system. The nineteenth century placed emphasis also upon the extension of political privileges to all. The government formed under the American constitution was not democracy in the nineteenth-century sense. It was an aristocratic republic. It was a government of the better classes as respects both voting and office-holding. Jeffersonian democracy recognized the common people as competent to decide which of the better classes should rule them. Jacksonian democracy asserted the right of the common man both to vote and to hold office. That was the extent of the development of democracy before the Civil War.

Nationalism, the fourth of the factors chosen to illustrate this discussion, also underwent a long process of evolution. World empire of the Medieval Church and the Holy Roman Empire gave way to the new force. Nationalism in the early modern period was illustrated by the examples of England and France, and in more recent times by Italy and Germany. In both these latter cases the unification had been attempted by means of sentiment, propaganda, and persuasion, but to no avail; and finally, between 1860 and 1870, they were both unified by a process of blood and iron. In America essentially the same procedure was followed. In 1783 Great Britain had recognized the independence of thirteen independent states. These states formed a loose confederation, and then a closer one; but they still retained certain rights, delegating only enumerated powers to the central government. Then for nearly seventy years a debate went on: states' rights versus nationalism. This was the bone of contention in the bank question, roads, tariff, public lands, and finally slavery. Sentiment, propaganda, and persuasion failed to settle the issue, and finally, in 1861, an appeal was taken to the high court of blood and iron. The decision, rendered upon the battlefield, was in favor of nationalism. Lincoln, Bismarck, and Cavour were a great triumvirate. What Germany and Italy did with the victory of nationalism is a part of European history. What the United States did with the victory is one of the central themes of later American history.

During the years preceding the Civil War the foundations of the industrial system had been laid; during the conflict industrial-urban America unseated agricultural America and took control. This shift in balance of power from country to town unchained momentous consequences. The concentration of undue economic power in the hands of a few individuals produced a popular reaction which demanded the regulation of this power by the government in order to protect the public interest. In so doing the traditional concept of individualism was fundamentally modified. Economic and social restraints were imposed. The political axiom that what is good for the individual is good for the group was questioned and then altered. Democracy began to take on a new meaning. Laissez faire theories were at least partly discarded. A government responsible to the whole electorate required the industrial system and associated social evils to submit to government. In this manner the scope and meaning of democracy were enlarged. The freedom of the individual to develop his opportunities was still the basis of action; but the government was called upon to assume very definite responsibilities for preserving conditions where this freedom would continue to function. A strongly centralized government became the agency for the exercise of these powers. This reconstruction of the Federal government took place during the first twenty-five years following the Civil War. Thus the victory of nationalism was written into the Constitution by the Fourteenth Amendment, was recognized by the Supreme Court in 1886 and after, and was asserted by Congress in a long series of laws which reached their climax in such acts as the Interstate Commerce Law of 1887, the Anti-trust Act of 1890, and several measures of social legislation. These changes marked the close of the first era after the Civil War. Having once indorsed the new principles, the only question of the future was the extent and the manner in which they should be exercised.

Between 1887 and the World War there was no essential modification in the direction of change. Industrialism presented its problems in a more intensified form, and the progressive theory of public interest was extended at the expense of laissez faire theory. The individual was subjected to such restraints as would have been inconceivable to Americans fifty years earlier. The accepted theory of democracy demanded a sweeping exercise of regulatory powers. Industry, however, did not submit to control without a struggle. If government was to regulate, then business felt that such exercise of powers should be wielded by friends of business rather than by its enemies. The intrenchment of the so-called "vested interests" in government called forth a popular movement for the reform of the machinery of democracy: the secret ballot, the direct election of senators, the direct primary, the presidential-preference primary, the initiative, the referendum, and the recall. It was hoped that these instruments would restore the government to the people and make it responsible to their will.

During the pre-war period certain other factors began to enter largely into the story. Industrialism developed to a point where domestic markets were unable to absorb the output, and foreign markets were sought. Raw materials were needed from abroad to feed domestic factories. American nationalism also sought a wider field of expression. Europe underwent a revival of neomercantilism and of imperialism during the eighteen-seventies. This same impulse was felt in America, and after 1880 the United States embarked upon the road of over-sea imperialism. In close conjunction with imperialism there was a development of internationalism.

The Civil War had been a vindication of American stability which, with the growth of American economic interests, dictated the inclusion of the United States in the system of international coöperation. By the time of the World War the United States was taking an active part in international government as it then existed.

The World War introduced a new situation. After nearly every great war at least two fundamentally different points of view are presented respecting reconstruction. One attempts to evaluate the changes wrought by the war and to formulate a policy in keeping with the new era. Unless this view is supported by unusual leadership it fails to accomplish its purpose. The tide of events, for a time at least, is almost invariably in the opposite direction. The period after the World War is no exception. The second point of view demands a return to pre-war conditions, to put everything back as it was; and, coupled with this, it demands a reversal of all war policies disapproved by the public. The important considerations of logic and consistency do not enter into the situation. This view represents a complete failure on the part of its proponents to grasp the significance of the events through which they have lived. Its supporters are those people who forget nothing and learn nothing. In many respects there is no period of which people know less than the period through which they have lived. "Back to normalcy" became the slogan, while "Less government in business" typified reaction against pre-war progressive measures and opposition to the exercise of war powers. Nevertheless this reaction introduced the conservative revolution and opened the way for novel developments which could not possibly have been anticipated. There was no logical body of conservative principles at hand to take the place of the discarded progressive principles except the traditional nineteenth-century theories of laissez faire, individualism, and nationalism. These were made to serve in the emergency as best they could. It was probably fortunate that there was no personality sufficiently powerful to impose a literal interpretation of them upon the country. The policy of drift and opportunism made the transition less abrupt and damaging. It also made possible the evolution of practical adjustments by a process of experimentation. The next step was the process of rationalizing what had been done as a justification for the future. It yet remained to be seen to what extent a system of political theory could be evolved. As for the progressives, the World War marked the passing not only of progressive theory, but also of progressive leadership. As the progressives were out of power they did not enjoy the opportunity of evolving a readjustment through the process of trial and error. The policy of drift did not furnish them with the materials for a revised theory of government. The student of American life must recognize that the World War closed one era in American history and inaugurated another.

Industrialism was one of the most obvious and inescapable facts of the period. It would scarcely be an exaggeration to compare the history of the decade to a drama written around a single character. The pre-war period was skeptical of industrialism in many of its aspects; but after the war, industrial prosperity became the keynote of public policy. Instead of regulating or breaking up industrial combination, the government promoted it. There was no interference with business; government assisted it. The public now held industrial securities on a large scale and was therefore interested in the profits of industry.

The post-war period brought several distinct changes in the problems of the individual and democracy. The long campaign for woman's rights resulted in the adoption of woman suffrage by constitutional amendment in 1920. The effect of this departure was problematical, particularly since few women voted. The tendencies of popular government as respects the voting of men and women are illustrated by the

figures showing a decline in voting after 1896. In that year
82.8 per cent of the qualified voters cast a ballot; in 1900,
77 per cent; in 1904, 67.6 per cent; in 1908, 67.2 per cent;
in 1912, 62.8 per cent; in 1916, 70.3 per cent; in 1920, 49.3
per cent; and in 1924, 51.1 per cent. The male vote was de-
clining, but it was the woman suffrage amendment which
caused the sharp decline in 1920. It is obvious that in Federal
elections the decisions at the polls after the World War could
not claim a clear majority of all voters. Theoretically democracy is a government by the majority, while in practice in the
United States it was a government by the active but small
minority.

Democracy has been thought of primarily in terms of
political privileges. Obviously the ideals of the eighteenth
and nineteenth centuries in respect to these matters were
achieved in full by 1920. The later nineteenth century and
the twentieth placed more emphasis on economic and social
interpretations. These features of the problem involve the
search for a means of establishing and preserving a balance
between the individual and the public interest. Democracy
had been too much concerned with the rights of the individual,
and society was left to muddle along as best it could. Was
the historic concept of the individual important enough to
require sacrifice of the interests of society? In the ox-team
stage of civilization the individual could do relatively little damage to society. In an industrial age complicated by
high-speed transportation and communications the individual
might easily become a menace to society. It is significant
that the only great challenge to democracy from any rival
theory of government came from those systems of political
thought which went to the opposite extreme and vested rights
in society — Socialism, Bolshevism, and Fascism. In these
systems the individual was granted privileges — not rights
— to the extent that the group might deem expedient.

Two general methods were evolved in the attempt to solve
the problem of the relation between the individual and the

group in a democracy,— namely, government regulation and self-government. Pre-war democracy experimented primarily with government regulation. There can be no question that it accomplished much. There is also a certain justice in criticisms of its operation. It was inevitable that much antagonism and hostility should develop between the regulative power and business. Such a spirit tended to defeat the purpose of control for the benefit of the public. There was constant question as to just where regulation became mere interference.

The conservative reaction after the war questioned not only the ability of government to exercise intelligent regulation, but expressed a distrust of direct democracy which was designed to insure that such regulation should be effective. Such machinery as the initiative, the referendum, the recall, and the primaries practically passed out of the current political vocabulary. The meeting of state legislatures each biennium raised the question of the repeal of the primary laws or of their modification. Woman suffrage did not add an appreciably higher quality to the political expression of mass intelligence, nor did it contribute permanency or continuity to the proverbial fickleness of public opinion. The presidential primary proved a farce in practice. The initiative, the referendum, and the recall, for the most part, fell into disrepute and disuse.

At least three outstanding factors contributed to this situation. In the first place, there was the tendency for historic development to express itself in periods of action and reaction. This is an obvious fact in history, but no adequate explanation has ever been made as to why this happens. In the second place, even the most ardent progressive had to admit that neither government regulation nor direct democracy accomplished what was expected of it. Such benefits as were contributed could be preserved only through modified application of these devices. This inescapable fact necessarily placed the progressives on the defensive. Finally, there was the distrust of democracy itself, not only in the United States but the world over. In the United States it was expressed in reaction against government regulation and direct democracy; in Europe it manifested itself in Bolshevism in Russia, Fascism in Italy, dictatorship in Spain, and in less drastic forms in other countries.

With respect to this last point a fuller consideration is in order. Several peculiar factors underlay the questioning of democratic equalitarianism in the United States. One point of development was the intelligence tests applied to a large part of the army during the World War. These were followed up after the war by psychologists and pseudo-psychologists and educators. The results of the tests indicated that only a relatively small part of the population possessed intelligence above that of a child eleven or twelve years old. Another factor was the glorification of the successful business man, which placed a premium upon achievement of economic success and power. Still another factor was the expert, a product of modern specialized training, who was set apart from the common run of men. The logical outcome of such factors when applied to the practice of government was a reversion from the principle of democratic equality to that of a limited ruling class invested with authority because of mental superiority or of other means of exercising power. Numerous writers declared that civilization faced a choice from two alternatives: either democracy must be abandoned in favor of some form of dictatorship, or else the theory of democracy must be modified to recognize the leadership of the so-called superior classes. The historical student must always remember that in this case, as well as in other historic movements, democracy is not static, but has constantly been undergoing change as to form, content, and meaning. Further changes were and still are inevitable. The only question which can be raised legitimately concerns the form that they will take.

The parts played by government regulation and direct

democracy were therefore markedly less or else different in the post-war period than formerly, but both continued in a modified form. The adoption by the Federal Trade Commission of the new methods of procedure, stipulations and trade-practice conferences, continued the government supervision of business but changed its character drastically. It is possible that in the long run the changes even extended effective government regulative powers, although critics of the new policies held the opposite view.

The attempt to withdraw government from business regulation had unexpected results. The doctrine of laissez faire and individualism could never bring a return to those conditions envisaged by the Grant era in the persons of Rockefeller, Carnegie, Vanderbilt, and Gould. Industrialism was to them a battle of individual captains of industry. For the post-war period a different background had been created through the growth of organizations of business men in trade associations and the like. Business was standing on the basis of organized groups. Hoover overstated the facts somewhat before the Chamber of Commerce of the United States in May, 1926, when he said, "There is scarcely an individual in our country who does not belong to more than one of them." This exaggeration, however, serves to emphasize a fact that was not generally appreciated. These groups, as Hoover pointed out, "represent a vast ferment of conscious coöperation," and a majority of them "recognize a responsibility to the public as well as to their own interest." It was obvious that some agency must regulate and coördinate the parts of the economic machine. If the regulative functions were not to be exercised by government, they must be exercised by other agencies — in reality by another kind of government. The idea of economic self-government was not wholly new, and few recognized what was happening; but many persons acted in accordance with facts as a practical necessity without realizing the contradictions between their professions and their actions. A few leaders, like O'Leary of the Chamber of Commerce of the United States, argued the matter fully before business men. As the restrictions of political government were withdrawn or relaxed, the organized agencies of business expanded and gradually came to occupy new fields of activity. Political government stood as an agency of last resort, or as a coördinating medium between political, economic, and social functions of society, or as a clearing house for information, or (as in the agricultural coöperative movement) as an agency for encouraging and assisting that industry to help and to govern itself. Although the system of self-government was incompletely developed by 1928, yet it was clear that the concept of democracy must be enlarged to include economic self-government as well as political government.

Any system of government regulation is said to build up a system of bureaucracy. Coolidge said at Williamsburg, on June 5, 1926, "Of all forms of government, those administered by bureaus are about the least satisfactory to an enlightened and progressive people." W. G. McAdoo said at one time that self-government was merely exchanging political bureaucracy for the bureaucracy of associations of corporations; either case was bureaucracy, but in the former the people had control. Bureaucracy was condemned in the platforms of both political parties, but there seemed to be little understanding of the problems involved.

In continental Europe there was a separate body of administrative law applied by a system of administrative courts. In England there was no such separate system. American law followed English principles, and while laissez faire theories were predominant no serious question was raised. The adoption of a policy of government regulation of economic and social activities introduced the absolute necessity of administrative agencies. The first outstanding example was the Interstate Commerce Commission in 1887; but the first Wilson administration created commissions for most other branches of economic life. In spite of the failure of most Americans to recognize the fact, these commissions constituted a system of administrative courts and developed the beginnings of a system of administrative law. Possibly the failure to recognize the real significance of these bodies was responsible for granting them powers which were not properly judicial in character. It is certain that the attempt to impose common-law procedure in some of these commissions instead of permitting them to formulate their own procedure seriously hampered their operation. Common-law procedure dealt primarily with cases involving individuals, and was designed to protect individuals. Administrative law must place the emphasis upon the execution of public policy for the general good. Hoover understood the problem, at least partly, when he advocated the reorganization of the commissions in order to leave them judicial powers only; but Hoover was an exception among public men. The denunciation of these bodies as bureaucracy was totally beside the point. The character and powers of these courts may be modified by law, but it is inconceivable that these administrative agencies could be abolished. To vest their functions in cabinet departments would mean merely that similar agencies and law would be developed there. A half-century of evolutionary developments could not be suddenly discarded.

Nationalism, with its expansion into national imperialism, was a dominant factor during the nineteenth and early twentieth centuries. Internationalism modified these factors, but the extent of the limitations imposed upon national sovereignty were not clearly apparent. The League of Nations marked a positive change. International government was set up in coördination with national government. Each international agreement following the establishment of the League further extended the authority of the international body and extended a corresponding limitation upon the national state. World history would appear to be an evolution upon a larger scale of a conflict that is similar in many respects to that between states' rights and nationalism in the history of the United States.

The period after the World War was referred to by some writers as the "new medievalism." Although the term is not adequate, nevertheless it is very suggestive. The medieval period emphasized group rights, and the modern period individual rights; but the recent period attempted a compromise between the two. The medieval ideal of state was a world organization, the modern ideal was the national state; but the post-war ideal was a compromise which attempts to coördinate the two.

This chapter has dealt primarily with abstractions; but it is essential to a proper understanding of historical processes to examine and interpret the factors that underlie the tangible material facts and personalities. This discussion makes no pretense of finality, but it should be sufficient to stimulate thought. A single decade of history does not often record such far-reaching changes as those of the first ten years after the World War. It must be viewed as more than just a multiplicity of events, although mere bulk and confusion may be the more superficial impression of many who have participated in it. The student of the period is indelibly impressed with the fact that it was an economic age. The emphasis was strongly on things material. This emphasis must not be permitted to obscure the less obvious factors, however, which become significant when placed in perspective.

APPENDIX A

THE TEXT OF THE COVENANT OF THE LEAGUE OF NATIONS

THE HIGH CONTRACTING PARTIES,

In order to promote international co-operation and to achieve international peace and security

by the acceptance of obligations not to resort to war,

by the prescription of open, just and honourable relations between nations,

by the firm establishment of the understandings of international law as the actual rule of conduct among Governments, and

by the maintenance of justice and a scrupulous respect for all treaty obligations in the dealings of organised peoples with one another,

Agree to this Covenant of the League of Nations.

ARTICLE 1

Membership and Withdrawal

The original members of the League of Nations shall be those of the Signatories which are named in the Annex of this Covenant and also such of those other States named in the Annex as shall accede without reservation to this Covenant. Such accession shall be effected by a Declaration deposited with the Secretariat within two months of the coming into force of the Covenant. Notice thereof shall be sent to all other Members of the League.

Any fully self-governing State, Dominion, or Colony not named in the Annex may become a Member of the League if its admission is agreed to by two-thirds of the Assembly, provided that it shall give effective guarantees of its sincere intention to observe its international obligations, and shall accept such regulations as may be prescribed by the League in regard to its military, naval, and air forces and armaments.

Any Member of the League may, after two years' notice of its intention so to do, withdraw from the League, provided that all its international obligations and all its obligations under this Covenant shall have been fulfilled at the time of its withdrawal.

ARTICLE 2

Executive Organs

The action of the League under this Covenant shall be effected through the instrumentality of an Assembly and of a Council, with a permanent Secretariat.

ARTICLE 3

Assembly

The Assembly shall consist of Representatives of the Members of the League.

The Assembly shall meet at stated intervals and from time to time as occasion may require at the Seat of the League or at such other place as may be decided upon.

The Assembly may deal at its meetings with any matter within the sphere of action of the League or affecting the peace of the world.

At meetings of the Assembly each Member of the League shall have one vote, and may not have more than three Representatives.

ARTICLE 4

Council

The Council shall consist of Representatives of the Principal Allied and Associated Powers, together with Representatives of four other Members of the League. These four Members of the League shall be selected by the Assembly from time to time in its discretion. Until the appointment of the Representatives of the four Members of the League first selected by the Assembly, Representatives of Belgium, Brazil, Spain, and Greece shall be members of the Council.

With the approval of the majority of the Assembly, the Council may name additional Members of the League whose Representatives shall always be members of the Council; the Council with like approval may increase the number of Members of the League to be selected by the Assembly for representation on the Council.

The Council shall meet from time to time as occasion may require, and at least once a year, at the Seat of the League, or at such other place as may be decided upon.

The Council may deal at its meetings with any matter within the sphere of action of the League or affecting the peace of the world.

Any Member of the League not represented on the Council shall be invited to send a Representative to sit as a member at any meeting of the Council during the consideration of matters especially affecting the interests of that Member of the League.

At meetings of the Council, each Member of the League represented on the Council shall have one vote, and may have not more than one Representative.

ARTICLE 5

Voting and Procedure

Except where otherwise expressly provided in this Covenant or by the terms of the present Treaty, decisions at any meeting of the Assembly or of the Council shall require the agreement of all the Members of the League represented at the meeting.

All matters of procedure at meetings of the Assembly or of the Council, including the appointment of Committees to investigate particular matters, shall be regulated by the Assembly or by the Council and may be decided by a majority of the Members of the League represented at the meeting.

The first meeting of the Assembly and the first meeting of the Council shall be summoned by the President of the United States of America.

ARTICLE 6

Secretariat and Expenses

The permanent Secretariat shall be established at the Seat of the League. The Secretariat shall comprise a Secretary General and such secretaries and staff as may be required.

The first Secretary General shall be the person named in the Annex; thereafter the Secretary General shall be appointed by the Council with the approval of the majority of the Assembly.

The secretaries and staff of the Secretariat shall be appointed by the Secretary General with the approval of the Council.

The Secretary General shall act in that capacity at all meetings of the Assembly and of the Council.

The expenses of the Secretariat shall be borne by the Members of the League in accordance with the apportionment of the expenses of the International Bureau of the Universal Postal Union.

ARTICLE 7

Seat, Qualifications of Officials, Immunities

The Seat of the League is established at Geneva.

The Council may at any time decide that the Seat of the League shall be established elsewhere.

All positions under or in connection with the League, including the Secretariat, shall be open equally to men and women.

Representatives of the Members of the League and officials of the League when engaged on the business of the League shall enjoy diplomatic privileges and immunities.

The buildings and other property occupied by the League or its officials or by Representatives attending its meetings shall be inviolable.

ARTICLE 8

Reduction of Armaments

The Members of the League recognise that the maintenance of peace requires the reduction of national armaments to the lowest point consistent with national safety and the enforcement by common action of international obligations.

The Council, taking account of the geographical situation and circumstances of each State, shall formulate plans for such reduction for the consideration and action of the several Governments.

Such plans shall be subject to reconsideration and revision at least every ten years.

After these plans shall have been adopted by the several Governments, the limits of armaments therein fixed shall not be exceeded without the concurrence of the Council.

The Members of the League agree that the manufacture by private enterprise of munitions and implements of war is open to grave objections. The Council shall advise how the evil effects attendant upon such manufacture can be prevented, due regard being had to the necessities of those Members of the League which are not able to manufacture the munitions and implements of war necessary for their safety.

The Members of the League undertake to interchange full and frank information as to the scale of their armaments, their military, naval, and air programmes and the condition of such of their industries as are adaptable to warlike purposes.

ARTICLE 9

Permanent Military, Naval, and Air Commission

A permanent Commission shall be constituted to advise the Council on the execution of the provisions of Articles 1 and 8 and on military, naval, and air questions generally.

ARTICLE 10

Guarantees against Aggression

The Members of the League undertake to respect and preserve as against external aggression the territorial integrity and existing political independence of all Members of the League. In case of any such aggression or in case of any threat or danger of such aggression the Council shall advise upon the means by which this obligation shall be fulfilled.

ARTICLE 11

Action in Case of War or Threat of War

Any war or threat of war, whether immediately affecting any of the Members of the League or not, is hereby declared a matter of concern to the whole League, and the League shall take any action that may be deemed wise and effectual to safeguard the peace of nations. In case any such emergency should arise the Secretary General shall on the request of any Member of the League forthwith summon a meeting of the Council.

It is also declared to be the friendly right of each Member of the League to bring to the attention of the Assembly or of the Council any circumstance whatever affecting international relations which threatens to disturb international peace or the good understanding between nations upon which peace depends.

ARTICLE 12

Disputes to be submitted for Settlement

The Members of the League agree that if there should arise between them any dispute likely to lead to a rupture, they will submit the matter either to arbitration or to inquiry by the Council, and they agree in no case to resort to war until three months after the award by the arbitrators or the report by the Council.

In any case under this Article the award of the arbitrators shall be made within a reasonable time, and the report of the Council shall be made within six months after the submission of the dispute.

ARTICLE 13

Arbitration or Judicial Settlement

The Members of the League agree that whenever any dispute shall arise between them which they recognise to be suitable for submission to arbitration and which cannot be satisfactorily settled by diplomacy, they will submit the whole subject-matter to arbitration.

Disputes as to the interpretation of a treaty, as to any question of international law, as to the existence of any fact which if established would constitute a breach of any international obligation, or as to the extent and nature of the reparation to be made for any such breach, are declared to be among those which are generally suitable for submission to arbitration.

For the consideration of any such dispute the court of arbitration to which the case is referred shall be the Court agreed on by the parties to the dispute or stipulated in any convention existing between them.

The Members of the League agree that they will carry out in full good faith any award that may be rendered, and that they will not resort to war against a Member of the League which complies therewith. In the event of any failure to carry out such an award, the Council shall propose what steps should be taken to give effect thereto.

ARTICLE 14

Permanent Court of International Justice

The Council shall formulate and submit to the Members of the League for adoption plans for the establishment of a Permanent Court of International Justice. The Court shall be competent to hear and determine any dispute of an international character which the parties thereto submit to it. The Court may also give an advisory opinion upon any dispute or question referred to it by the Council or by the Assembly.

ARTICLE 15

Disputes not submitted to Arbitration or Judicial Settlement

If there should arise between Members of the League any dispute likely to lead to a rupture, which is not submitted to arbitration in accordance with Article 13, the Members of the League agree that they will submit the matter to the Council. Any party to the dispute may effect such submission by giving notice of the existence of the dispute to the Secretary General, who will make all necessary arrangements for a full investigation and consideration thereof.

For this purpose the parties to the dispute will communicate to the Secretary General, as promptly as possible, statements of their case with all the relevant facts and papers, and the Council may forthwith direct the publication thereof.

The Council shall endeavour to effect a settlement of the dispute, and if such efforts are successful, a statement shall be made public giving such facts and explanations regarding the dispute and the terms of settlement thereof as the Council may deem appropriate.

If the dispute is not thus settled, the Council either unanimously or by a majority vote shall make and publish a report containing a statement of the facts of the dispute and the recommendations which are deemed just and proper in regard thereto.

Any Member of the League represented on the Council may make public a statement of the facts of the dispute and of its conclusions regarding the same.

If a report of the Council is unanimously agreed to by the members thereof other than the Representatives of one or more of the parties to the dispute, the Members of the League agree that they will not go to war with any party to the dispute which complies with the recommendations of the report.

If the Council fails to reach a report which is unanimously agreed to by the members thereof, other than the Representatives of one or more of the parties to the dispute, the Members of the League reserve to themselves the right to take such action as they shall consider necessary for the maintenance of right and justice.

If the dispute between the parties is claimed by one of them, and is found by the Council, to arise out of a matter which by international law is solely within the domestic jurisdiction of that party, the Council shall so report, and shall make no recommendation as to its settlement.

The Council may in any case under this Article refer the dispute to the Assembly. The dispute shall be so referred at the request of either party to the dispute, provided that such request be made within fourteen days after the submission of the dispute to the Council.

In any case referred to the Assembly, all the provisions of this Article and of Article 12 relating to the action and powers of the Council shall apply to the action and powers of the Assembly, provided that a report made by the Assembly, if concurred in by the Representatives of those Members of the League represented on the Council and of a majority of the other Members of the League, exclusive in each case of the Representatives of the parties to the dispute, shall have the same force as a report by the Council concurred in by all the members thereof other than the Representatives of one or more of the parties to the dispute.

ARTICLE 16

Sanctions of Pacific Settlement

Should any Member of the League resort to war in disregard of its covenants under Article 12, 13, or 15, it shall *ipso facto* be deemed to have committed an act of war against all other Members of the League, which hereby undertake immediately to subject it to the severance of all trade or financial relations, the prohibition of all intercourse between their nationals and the nationals of the covenant-breaking State, and the prevention of all financial, commercial, or personal intercourse between the nationals of the covenant-breaking State and the nationals of any other State, whether a Member of the League or not.

It shall be the duty of the Council in such case to recommend to the several Governments concerned what effective military, naval, or air force the Members of the League shall severally contribute to the armed forces to be used to protect the covenants of the League.

The Members of the League agree, further, that they will mutually support one another in the financial and economic measures which are taken under this Article, in order to minimise the loss and inconvenience resulting from the above measures, and that they will mutually support one another in resisting any special measures aimed at one of their number by the covenant-breaking State, and that they will take the necessary steps to afford passage through their territory to the forces of any of the Members of the League which are co-operating to protect the covenants of the League.

Any member of the League which has violated any covenant of the League may be declared to be no longer a Member of the League by a vote of the Council concurred in by the Representatives of all the other Members of the League represented thereon.

ARTICLE 17

Disputes involving Nonmembers

In the event of a dispute between a Member of the League and a State which is not a Member of the League, or between States not Members of the League, the State or States not Members of the League shall be invited to accept the obligations of membership in the League for the purposes of such dispute, upon such conditions as the Council may deem just. If such invitation is accepted, the provisions of Articles 12 to 16 inclusive shall be applied with such modifications as may be deemed necessary by the Council.

Upon such invitation being given, the Council shall immediately institute an inquiry into the circumstances of the dispute and recommend such action as may seem best and most effectual in the circumstances.

If a State so invited shall refuse to accept the obligations of membership in the League for the purposes of such dispute, and shall resort to war against a Member of the League, the provisions of Article 16 shall be applicable as against the State taking such action.

If both parties to the dispute when so invited refuse to accept the obligations of membership in the League for the purpose of such dispute, the Council may take such measures and make such recommendations as will prevent hostilities and will result in the settlement of the dispute.

ARTICLE 18

Registration and Publication of Treaties

Every treaty or international engagement entered into hereafter by any Member of the League shall be forthwith registered with the Secretariat and shall as soon as possible be published by it. No such treaty or international engagement shall be binding until so registered.

ARTICLE 19

Review of Treaties

The Assembly may from time to time advise the reconsideration by Members of the League of treaties which have become inapplicable and the consideration of international conditions whose continuance might endanger the peace of the world.

ARTICLE 20

Abrogation of Inconsistent Obligations

The Members of the League severally agree that this Covenant is accepted as abrogating all obligations or understandings *inter se* which are inconsistent with the terms thereof, and solemnly undertake that they will not hereafter enter into any engagements inconsistent with the terms thereof.

In case any Member of the League shall, before becoming a Member of the League, have undertaken any obligations inconsistent with the terms of this Covenant, it shall be the duty of such Member to take immediate steps to procure its release from such obligations.

ARTICLE 21

Engagements that remain Valid

Nothing in this Covenant shall be deemed to affect the validity of international engagements, such as treaties of arbitration or regional understandings like the Monroe Doctrine, for securing the maintenance of peace.

ARTICLE 22

Mandatory System

To those colonies and territories which as a consequence of the late war have ceased to be under the sovereignty of the States which formerly governed them and which are inhabited by peoples not yet able to stand by themselves under the strenuous conditions of the modern world, there should be applied the principle that the well-being and development of such peoples form a sacred trust of civilisation and that securities for the performance of this trust should be embodied in this Covenant.

The best method of giving practical effect to this principle is that the tutelage of such peoples should be entrusted to advanced nations who by reason of their resources, their experience or their geographical position can best undertake this responsibility, and who are willing to accept it, and that this tutelage should be exercised by them as Mandatories on behalf of the League.

The character of the mandate must differ according to the stage of the development of the people, the geographical situation of the territory, its economic conditions, and other similar circumstances.

Certain communities formerly belonging to the Turkish Empire have reached a stage of development where their existence as independent nations can be provisionally recognised subject to the rendering of administrative advice and assistance by a Mandatory until such time as they are able to stand alone. The wishes of these communities must be a principal consideration in the selection of a Mandatory.

Other peoples, especially those of Central Africa, are at such a stage that the Mandatory must be responsible for the administration of the territory under conditions which will guarantee freedom of conscience and religion, subject only to the maintenance of public order and morals, the prohibition of abuses such as the slave trade, the arms traffic, and the liquor traffic, and the prevention of the establishment of fortifications or military and naval bases and of military training of the natives for other than police purposes and the defence of territory, and will also secure equal opportunities for the trade and commerce of other Members of the League.

There are territories, such as South-West Africa and certain of the South Pacific Islands, which, owing to the sparseness of their population, or their small size, or their remoteness from the centres of civilisation, or their geographical contiguity to the territory of the Mandatory, and other circumstances, can be best administered under the laws of the Mandatory as integral portions of its territory, subject to the safeguards above mentioned in the interests of the indigenous population.

In every case of mandate, the Mandatory shall render to the Council an annual report in reference to the territory committed to its charge.

The degree of authority, control, or administration to be exercised by the Mandatory shall, if not previously agreed upon by the Members of the League, be explicitly defined in each case by the Council.

A permanent Commission shall be constituted to receive and examine the annual reports of the Mandatories and to advise the Council on all matters relating to the observance of the mandates.

ARTICLE 23

Social and Other Activities

Subject to and in accordance with the provisions of international conventions existing or hereafter to be agreed upon, the Members of the League :

(*a*) will endeavour to secure and maintain fair humane conditions of labour for men, women, and children, both in their own countries and in all countries to which their commercial and industrial relations extend, and for that purpose will establish and maintain the necessary international organisations ;

(*b*) undertake to secure just treatment of the native inhabitants of territories under their control ;

(*c*) will entrust the League with the general supervision over the execution of agreements with regard to the traffic in women and children, and the traffic in opium and other dangerous drugs ;

(*d*) will entrust the League with the general supervision of the trade in arms and ammunition with the countries in which the control of this traffic is necessary in the common interest ;

(*e*) will make provision to secure and maintain freedom of communications and of transit and equitable treatment for the commerce of all Members of the League. In this connection, the special necessities of the regions devastated during the war of 1914–1918 shall be borne in mind ;

(*f*) will endeavour to take steps in matters of international concern for the prevention and control of disease.

ARTICLE 24

International Bureaux

There shall be placed under the direction of the League all international bureaux already established by general treaties if the parties to such treaties consent. All such international bureaux and all commissions for the regulation of matters of international interest hereafter constituted shall be placed under the direction of the League.

In all matters of international interest which are regulated by general conventions but which are not placed under the control of the international bureaux or commissions, the Secretariat of the League shall, subject to the consent of the Council and if desired by the parties, collect and distribute all relevant information and shall render any other assistance which may be necessary or desirable.

The Council may include as part of the expenses of the Secretariat the expenses of any bureau or commission which is placed under the direction of the League.

ARTICLE 25

Promotion of Red Cross and Health

The Members of the League agree to encourage and promote the establishment and co-operation of duly authorised voluntary national Red Cross organisations having as purposes the improvement of health, the prevention of disease, and the mitigation of suffering throughout the world.

ARTICLE 26

Amendments

Amendments to this Covenant will take effect when ratified by the Members of the League whose representatives compose the Council and by a majority of the Members of the League whose Representatives compose the Assembly.

No such amendment shall bind any Member of the League which signifies its dissent therefrom, but in that case it shall cease to be a Member of the League.

ANNEX

I. ORIGINAL MEMBERS OF THE LEAGUE OF NATIONS SIGNATORIES OF THE TREATY OF PEACE

United States of America	Cuba	Nicaragua
Belgium	Ecuador	Panama
Bolivia	France	Peru
Brazil	Greece	Poland
British Empire	Guatemala	Portugal
Canada	Haiti	Rumania
Australia	Hedjaz	Serb-Croat-Slovene State
South Africa	Honduras	Siam
New Zealand	Italy	Czecho-Slovakia
India	Japan	Uruguay
China	Liberia	

STATES INVITED TO ACCEDE TO THE COVENANT

Argentine Republic	Norway	Spain
Chili	Paraguay	Sweden
Colombia	Persia	Switzerland
Denmark	Salvador	Venezuela
Netherlands		

II. FIRST SECRETARY-GENERAL OF THE LEAGUE OF NATIONS

The Honourable Sir James Eric Drummond, K.C.M.G., C.B.

APPENDIX B

THE TEXT OF THE STATUTE OF THE PERMANENT COURT OF INTERNATIONAL JUSTICE

Article 1. A Permanent Court of International Justice is hereby established, in accordance with Article 14 of the Covenant of the League of Nations. This Court shall be in addition to the Court of Arbitration organized by the Conventions of The Hague of 1899 and 1907, and to the special Tribunals of Arbitration to which States are always at liberty to submit their disputes for settlement.

CHAPTER I

ORGANIZATION OF THE COURT

Article 2. The Permanent Court of International Justice shall be composed of a body of independent judges, elected regardless of their nationality from among persons of high moral character, who possess the qualifications required in their respective countries for appointment to the highest judicial offices, or are jurisconsults of recognized competence in international law.

Article 3. The Court shall consist of fifteen members: eleven judges and four deputy-judges. The number of judges and deputy-judges may hereafter be increased by the Assembly, upon the proposal of the Council of the League of Nations, to a total of fifteen judges and six deputy-judges.

Article 4. The members of the Court shall be elected by the Assembly and by the Council from a list of persons nominated by the national groups in the Court of Arbitration, in accordance with the following provisions.

In the case of Members of the League of Nations not represented in the Permanent Court of Arbitration, the lists of candidates shall be drawn up by national groups appointed for this purpose by their Governments under the same conditions as those prescribed for members of the Permanent Court of Arbitration by Article 44 of the Convention of The Hague of 1907 for the pacific settlement of international disputes.

Article 5. At least three months before the date of the election, the Secretary-General of the League of Nations shall address a written request to the Members of the Court of Arbitration belonging to the States mentioned in the Annex to the Covenant or to the States which join the League subsequently, and to the persons appointed under paragraph 2 of Article 4, inviting them to undertake, within a given time, by national groups, the nomination of persons in a position to accept the duties of a member of the Court.

No group may nominate more than four persons, not more than two of whom shall be of their own nationality. In no case must the number of candidates nominated be more than double the number of seats to be filled.

Article 6. Before making these nominations, each national group is recommended to consult its Highest Court of Justice, its Legal Faculties and Schools of Law, and its National Academies and national sections of International Academies devoted to the study of law.

Article 7. The Secretary-General of the League of Nations shall prepare a list in alphabetical order of all the persons thus nominated. Save as provided in Article 12, paragraph 2, these shall be the only persons eligible for appointment.

The Secretary-General shall submit this list to the Assembly and to the Council.

Article 8. The Assembly and the Council shall proceed independently of one another to elect, firstly the judges, then the deputy-judges.

Article 9. At every election, the electors shall bear in mind that not only should all the persons appointed as members of the Court possess the qualifications required, but the whole body also should represent the main forms of civilization and the principal legal systems of the world.

Article 10. Those candidates who obtain an absolute majority of votes in the Assembly and in the Council shall be considered as elected.

In the event of more than one national of the same Member of the League being elected by the votes of both the Assembly and the Council, the eldest of these only shall be considered as elected.

Article 11. If, after the first meeting held for the purpose of the election, one or more seats remain to be filled, a second and, if necessary, a third meeting shall take place.

Article 12. If, after the third meeting, one or more seats still remain unfilled, a joint conference consisting of six members, three appointed by the Assembly and three by the Council, may be formed, at any time, at the request of either the Assembly or the Council, for the purpose of choosing one name for each seat still vacant, to submit to the Assembly and the Council for their respective acceptance.

If the Conference is unanimously agreed upon any person who fulfils the required conditions, he may be included in its list, even though he was not included in the list of nominations referred to in Articles 4 and 5.

If the joint conference is satisfied that it will not be successful in procuring an election, those members of the Court who have already been appointed shall, within a period to be fixed by the Council, proceed to fill the vacant seats by selection from among those candidates who have obtained votes either in the Assembly or in the Council.

In the event of an equality of votes among the judges, the eldest judge shall have a casting vote.

Article 13. The members of the Court shall be elected for nine years.

They may be re-elected.

They shall continue to discharge their duties until their places have been filled. Though replaced, they shall finish any cases which they may have begun.

Article 14. Vacancies which may occur shall be filled by the same method as that laid down for the first election. A member of the Court elected to replace a member whose period of appointment had not expired will hold the appointment for the remainder of his predecessor's term.

Article 15. Deputy-judges shall be called upon to sit in the order laid down in a list.

This list shall be prepared by the Court and shall have regard firstly to priority of election and secondly to age.

Article 16. The ordinary Members of the Court may not exercise any political or administrative function. This provision does not apply to the deputy-judges except when performing their duties on the Court.

Any doubt on this point is settled by the decision of the Court.

Article 17. No Member of the Court can act as agent, counsel or advocate in any case of an international nature. This provision only applies to the deputy-judges as regards cases in which they are called upon to exercise their functions on the Court.

No Member may participate in the decision of any case in which he had previously taken an active part, as agent, counsel or advocate for one of the contesting parties, or as a Member of a national or international Court, or of a Commission of inquiry, or in any other capacity.

Any doubt on this point is settled by the decision of the Court.

Article 18. A member of the Court can not be dismissed unless, in the unanimous opinion of the other members, he has ceased to fulfil the required conditions.

Formal notification thereof shall be made to the Secretary-General of the League of Nations, by the Registrar.

This notification makes the place vacant.

Article 19. The members of the Court, when engaged on the business of the Court, shall enjoy diplomatic privileges and immunities.

Article 20. Every member of the Court shall, before taking up his duties, make a solemn declaration in open Court that he will exercise his powers impartially and conscientiously.

Article 21. The Court shall elect its President and Vice-President for three years; they may be re-elected.

It shall appoint its Registrar.

The duties of Registrar of the Court shall not be deemed incompatible with those of Secretary-General of the Permanent Court of Arbitration.

Article 22. The seat of the Court shall be established at The Hague.

The President and Registrar shall reside at the seat of the Court.

Article 23. A session of the Court shall be held every year.

Unless otherwise provided by rules of Court, this session shall begin on the 15th of June, and shall continue for so long as may be deemed necessary to finish the cases on the list.

The President may summon an extraordinary session of the Court whenever necessary.

Article 24. If, for some special reason, a member of the Court considers that he should not take part in the decision of a particular case, he shall so inform the President.

If the President considers that for some special reason one of the members of the Court should not sit on a particular case, he shall give him notice accordingly.

If in any such case the member of the Court and the President disagree, the matter shall be settled by the decision of the Court.

Article 25. The full Court shall sit except when it is expressly provided otherwise.

If eleven judges can not be present, the number shall be made up by calling on deputy-judges to sit.

If, however, eleven judges are not available, a quorum of nine judges shall suffice to constitute the Court.

Article 26. Labor cases, particularly cases referred to in Part XIII (Labor) of the Treaty of Versailles and the corresponding portion of the other Treaties of Peace, shall be heard and determined by the Court under the following conditions:

The Court will appoint every three years a special chamber of five judges, selected so far as possible with due regard to the provisions of Article 9. In addition, two judges shall be selected for the purpose of replacing a judge who finds it impossible to sit. If the parties so demand, cases will be heard and determined by this chamber. In the absence of any such demand, the Court will sit with the number of judges provided for in Article 25. On all occasions the judges will be assisted by four technical assessors sitting with them, but without the right to vote, and chosen with a view to insuring a just representation of the competing interests.

If there is a national of one only of the parties sitting as a judge in a chamber referred to in the preceding paragraph, the President will invite one of the other judges to retire in favor of a judge chosen by the other party in accordance with Article 31.

The technical assessors shall be chosen for each particular case in accordance with rules of procedure under Article 30 from a list of "Assessors for Labor cases" composed of two persons nominated by each Member of the League of Nations and an equivalent number nominated by the Governing Body of the Labor Office. The Governing Body will nominate, as to one half, representatives of the workers, and as to one half, representatives of employers from the list referred to in Article 412 of the Treaty of Versailles and the corresponding Articles of the other Treaties of Peace.

In Labor cases the International Labor Office shall be at liberty to furnish the Court with all relevant information, and for this purpose the Director of that Office shall receive copies of all the written proceedings.

Article 27. Cases relating to transit and communications, particularly cases referred to in Part XII (Ports, Waterways and Railways) of the Treaty of Versailles and the corresponding portions of the other Treaties of Peace, shall be heard and determined by the Court under the following conditions:

The Court will appoint every three years a special chamber of five judges, selected so far as possible with due regard to the provisions of Article 9. In addition, two judges shall be selected for the purpose of replacing a judge who finds it impossible to sit. If the parties so demand, cases will be heard and determined by this chamber. In the absence of any such demand, the Court will sit with the number of judges provided for in Article 25. When desired by the parties or decided by the Court, the judges will be assisted by four technical assessors sitting with them, but without the right to vote.

If there is a national of one only of the parties sitting as a judge in the chamber referred to in the preceding paragraph, the President will invite one of the other judges to retire in favor of a judge chosen by the other party in accordance with Article 31.

The technical assessors shall be chosen for each particular case in accordance with rules of procedure under Article 30 from a list of "Assessors for Transit and Communications cases" composed of two persons nominated by each Member of the League of Nations.

Article 28. The special chamber provided for in Articles 26 and 27 may, with the consent of the parties to the dispute, sit elsewhere than at The Hague.

Article 29. With a view to the speedy dispatch of business, the Court shall form annually a chamber composed of three judges who, at the request of the contesting parties, may hear and determine cases by summary procedure.

Article 30. The Court shall frame rules for regulating its procedure. In particular, it shall lay down rules for summary procedure.

Article 31. Judges of the nationality of each contesting party shall retain their right to sit in the case before the Court.

If the Court includes upon the Bench a judge of the nationality of one of the parties only, the other party may select from among the deputy-judges a judge of its nationality, if there be one. If there should not be one, the party may choose a judge, preferably from among those persons who have been nominated as candidates as provided in Articles 4 and 5.

If the Court includes upon the Bench no judge of the nationality of the contesting parties, each of these may proceed to select or choose a judge as provided in the preceding paragraph.

Should there be several parties in the same interest, they shall, for the purpose of the preceding provisions, be reckoned as one party only. Any doubt upon this point is settled by the decision of the Court.

Judges selected or chosen as laid down in paragraphs 2 and 3 of this Article shall fulfil the conditions required by Articles 2, 16, 17, 20, 24 of this Statute. They shall take part in the decision on an equal footing with their colleagues.

Article 32. The judges shall receive an annual indemnity to be determined by the Assembly of the League of Nations upon the proposal of the Council. This indemnity must not be decreased during the period of a judge's appointment.

The President shall receive a special grant for his period of office, to be fixed in the same way.

The Vice-President, judges and deputy-judges shall receive a grant for the actual performance of their duties, to be fixed in the same way.

Traveling expenses incurred in the performance of their duties shall be refunded to judges and deputy-judges who do not reside at the seat of the Court.

Grants due to judges selected or chosen as provided in Article 31 shall be determined in the same way.

The salary of the Registrar shall be decided by the Council upon the proposal of the Court.

The Assembly of the League of Nations shall lay down, on the proposal of the Council, a special regulation fixing the conditions under which retiring pensions may be given to the personnel of the Court.

Article 33. The expenses of the Court shall be borne by the League of Nations, in such a manner as shall be decided by the Assembly upon the proposal of the Council.

CHAPTER II

COMPETENCE OF THE COURT

Article 34. Only States or Members of the League of Nations can be parties in cases before the Court.

Article 35. The Court shall be open to the Members of the League and also to the States mentioned in the Annex to the Covenant.

The conditions under which the Court shall be open to other States shall, subject to the special provisions contained in treaties in force, be laid down by the Council, but in no case shall such provisions place the parties in a position of inequality before the Court.

When a State which is not a Member of the League of Nations is a party to a dispute, the Court will fix the amount which that party is to contribute toward the expenses of the Court.

Article 36. The jurisdiction of the Court comprises all cases which the parties refer to it and all matters specially provided for in Treaties and Conventions in force.

The Members of the League of Nations and the States mentioned in the Annex to the Covenant may, either when signing or ratifying the protocol to which the present Statute is adjoined, or at a later moment, declare that they recognize as compulsory, *ipso facto* and without special agreement, in relation to any other Member or State accepting the same obligation, the jurisdiction of the Court in all or any of the classes of legal disputes concerning:

(*a*) The interpretation of a Treaty.

(*b*) Any question of International Law.

(*c*) The existence of any fact which, if established, would constitute a breach of an international obligation.

(*d*) The nature or extent of the reparation to be made for the breach of an international obligation.

The declaration referred to above may be made unconditionally or on condition of reciprocity on the part of several or certain Members or States, or for a certain time.

In the event of a dispute as to whether the Court has jurisdiction, the matter shall be settled by the decision of the Court.

Article 37. When a treaty or convention in force provides for the reference of a matter to a tribunal to be instituted by the League of Nations, the Court will be such tribunal.

Article 38. The Court shall apply:

1. International conventions, whether general or particular, establishing rules expressly recognized by the contesting States;

2. International custom, as evidence of a general practice accepted as law;

3. The general principles of law recognized by civilized nations;

4. Subject to the provisions of Article 59, judicial decisions and the teachings of the most highly qualified publicists of the various nations, as subsidiary means for the determination of rules of law.

This provision shall not prejudice the power of the Court to decide a case *ex aequo et bono*, if the parties agree thereto.

CHAPTER III

Procedure

Article 39. The official languages of the Court shall be French and English. If the parties agree that the case shall be conducted in French, the judgment will be delivered in French. If the parties agree that the case shall be conducted in English, the judgment will be delivered in English.

In the absence of an agreement as to which language shall be employed, each party may, in the pleadings, use the language which it prefers; the decision of the Court will be given in French and English. In this case the Court will at the same time determine which of the two texts shall be considered as authoritative.

The Court may, at the request of the parties, authorize a language other than French or English to be used.

Article 40. Cases are brought before the Court, as the case may be, either by the notification of the special agreement or by a written application addressed to the Registrar. In either case the subject of the dispute and the contesting parties must be indicated.

The Registrar shall forthwith communicate the application to all concerned.

He shall also notify the Members of the League of Nations through the Secretary-General.

Article 41. The Court shall have the power to indicate, if it considers that circumstances so require, any provisional measures which ought to be taken to reserve the respective rights of either party.

Pending the final decision, notice of the measures suggested shall forthwith be given to the parties and the Council.

Article 42. The parties shall be represented by Agents.

They may have the assistance of the Counsel or Advocates before the Court.

Article 43. The procedure shall consist of two parts: written and oral.

The written proceedings shall consist of the communication to the judges and to the parties of cases, counter-cases and, if necessary, replies; also all papers and documents in support.

These communications shall be made through the Registrar, in the order and within the time fixed by the Court.

A certified copy of every document produced by one party shall be communicated to the other party.

The oral proceedings shall consist of the hearing by the Court of witnesses, experts, agents, counsel and advocates.

Article 44. For the service of all notices upon persons other than the agents, counsel and advocates, the Court shall apply direct to the Government of the State upon whose territory the notice has to be served.

The same provision shall apply whenever steps are to be taken to procure evidence on the spot.

Article 45. The hearing shall be under the control of the President or, in his absence, of the Vice-President; if both are absent, the senior judge shall preside.

Article 46. The hearing in Court shall be public, unless the Court shall decide otherwise, or unless the parties demand that the public be not admitted.

Article 47. Minutes shall be made at each hearing, and signed by the Registrar and the President.

These minutes shall be the only authentic record.

Article 48. The Court shall make orders for the conduct of the case, shall decide the form and time in which each party must conclude its arguments, and make all arrangements connected with the taking of evidence.

Article 49. The Court may, even before the hearing begins, call upon the agents to produce any document or to supply any explanations. Formal note shall be taken of any refusal.

Article 50. The Court may, at any time, intrust any individual, body, bureau, commission or other organization that it may select, with the task of carrying out an inquiry or giving an expert opinion.

Article 51. During the hearing any relevant questions are to be put to the witnesses and experts under the conditions laid down by the Court in the rules of procedure referred to in Article 30.

Article 52. After the Court has received the proofs and evidence within the time specified for the purpose, it may refuse to accept any further oral or written evidence that one party may desire to present unless the other side consents.

Article 53. Whenever one of the parties shall not appear before the Court, or shall fail to defend his case, the other party may call upon the Court to decide in favor of his claim.

The Court must, before doing so, satisfy itself, not only that it has jurisdiction in accordance with Articles 36 and 37, but also that the claim is well founded in fact and law.

Article 54. When, subject to the control of the Court, the agents, advocates and counsel have completed their presentation of the case, the President shall declare the hearing closed.

The Court shall withdraw to consider the judgment.

The deliberations of the Court shall take place in private and remain secret.

Article 55. All questions shall be decided by a majority of the judges present at the hearing.

In the event of an equality of votes, the President or his deputy shall have a casting vote.

Article 56. The judgment shall state the reasons on which it is based.

It shall contain the names of the judges who have taken part in the decision.

Article 57. If the judgment does not represent in whole or in part the unanimous opinion of the judges, dissenting judges are entitled to deliver a separate opinion.

Article 58. The judgment shall be signed by the President and by the Registrar. It shall be read in open Court, due notice having been given to the agents.

Article 59. The decision of the Court has no binding force except between the parties and in respect of that particular case.

Article 60. The judgment is final and without appeal. In the event of dispute as to the meaning or scope of the judgment, the Court shall construe it upon the request of any party.

Article 61. An application for revision of a judgment can be made only when it is based upon the discovery of some fact of such a nature as to be a decisive factor, which fact was, when the judgment was given, unknown to the Court and also to the party claiming revision, always provided that such ignorance was not due to negligence.

The proceedings for revision will be opened by a judgment of the Court expressly recording the existence of the new fact, recognizing that it has such a character as to lay the case open to revision, and declaring the application admissible on this ground.

The Court may require previous compliance with the terms of the judgment before it admits proceedings in revision.

The application for revision must be made at latest within six months of the discovery of the new fact.

No application for revision may be made after the lapse of ten years from the date of the sentence.

Article 62. Should a State consider that it has an interest of a legal nature which may be affected by the decision in the case, it may submit a request to the Court to be permitted to intervene as a third party.

It will be for the Court to decide upon this request.

Article 63. Whenever the construction of a convention to which States other than those concerned in the case are parties is in question, the Registrar shall notify all such States forthwith.

Every State so notified has the right to intervene in the proceedings; but if it uses this right, the construction given by the judgment will be equally binding upon it.

Article 64. Unless otherwise decided by the Court, each party shall bear its own costs.

INDEX

Acceptance business and foreign trade, 323

Adjudication distinguished from arbitration, 70

Agricultural depression and reclamation policy, 253

Agriculture, tariff revision, 114–115; Federal Reserve system and credit, 117; representation on the Federal Reserve Board, 122; rural retardation, 227; World War expansion, 228; prices, 228; depression of 1920–1921, 228–229; policies, 229–233; Joint Commission of Agricultural Inquiry, 229; Farm Bloc, 229; National Agricultural Conference, 230; National Industrial Conference Board, 230; Chamber of Commerce of the United States, 230; International Economic Conference, 231; Wilson, Harding, and Coolidge, 231; economic theory, 232; emergency policies, 233; railroad rates, 234; tariff, 234; marketing legislation, 234–247; standards and grading of products, 234; control of central markets, 234–235; cotton futures act, 235; grain futures act, 235; packers and stockyards act, 235; perishable products markets, 235; coöperative marketing, 235–236; credit problem, 236; long-time credit, 237–238; short-time credit, 238–239; intermediate credit, 239–241; War Finance Corporation, 240; surplus problem, 242–244; McNary-Haugen bills, 243–244; Farm Board, 243–244; campaign of 1928, 245–246; farm recovery, 246; Agricultural Code enacted, 1913–1929, 247; coöperative extension system, 247; market news service, 247

Air commerce act of 1926, 156; foreign clauses, 345–346

Air mail, inaugurated, 153; legislation, 154; postage, 154–155; transfer to private operation, 154–155; foreign service, 344–345

Alaska, 367–368

Alien property held by the United States, 444

Allied debts, American policy at Peace Conference, 32; settlement, 445–446

American Farm Bureau and agricultural bloc, 229

American Federation of Labor, membership, 211; attitude toward shop committee, 217

Arbitration, commercial, domestic, 204–205; foreign, 452–453

Arbitration, in the Covenant, 19; distinguished from adjudication and mediation, 70; treaties renewed with a World Court provision, 465; Root treaties, 483; Taft treaties, 483–484; treaties with Central American states, 485; treaty with France, 1928, 486–487; Pan-American Conferences, 487; Washington Conference of American States in 1929, 487

Argentina, tariff difficulties with, 306

Armistice, with Germany, 11–12; with Austria, 12; reaction after, 13, 15

Arms, traffic in, 362–363

Army, policy, 351–357; reorganization act of 1920, 353; decreases to 1923, 355; increases after 1926, 355–356; air policy, 360–361

Assistance to business, 87

Austria, Peace Treaty of 1919, 67; Peace Treaty with United States, 442–443; American claims against, 442–444

Automobile, developments, 139; numbers, 139; accidents, 142; uniform model state laws, 142; regulation, 142–145; relations with railroads, 143–144; investiga-

571

Trust business and national banks, 122–126

Virgin Islands, 426–427

Wallace, H. C., secretary of agriculture, 231
War expenditures, 93
War Finance Corporation, agricultural credit, 230, 233, 240; created, 322
War legislation, attempted repeal, June, 1920, 62; termination, March, 1921, 67
Warehouse act, 234
Washington Conference, Far East policies, 365–366; limitation of naval armament, 460–462; gas warfare outlawed, 461; naval treaties and the League of Nations, 461–462
Washington Conference of American States, 1929, 487–488
Water-power policy, 258–265; act of 1920, 260–261
Watson-Parker act, 132–133
Wealth, national, 174; rural versus urban, 227
Wheat, foreign criticism of price control, 316
Whitley plan, 215
Wickersham, G. W., criticism of peace by joint resolution, 62; defense of World Court, 466
Wilson, Woodrow, attitude toward European War, 5; first public endorsement of League of Nations, 5; naval appropriations act, August 29, 1916, 6; war-aims notes of December 18, 1916, 6; war-aims address, January 22, 1917, 6; Fourteen Points, 7–9; Four Principles, 9–10; Four Objects, 10; Five Particulars, 11; war aims as a basis of peace, 11–12; armistice, 11–12; election of 1918, 12; annual message, 1918, 13–14; censorship removed, 14; government control of cables, 14; mission to Europe, 14; preparation for Peace Conference, 14; secret treaties, 15–16; arrival in Europe, 16; evolution of ideas regarding peace and the League, 17–18; provisions of the Covenant,

18–20; origins of Covenant, 20–23; first draft of a Covenant, 21; World Court omitted from first draft of Covenant, 21; Smuts plan for a League, 22; later drafts of a Covenant, 22–23; World Court restored to League discussions, 23; return with draft of the Covenant, 26; Metropolitan Opera House address, 27; amendments to the Covenant, secured, 28–29; French security treaty, 29; international trade policies at Peace Conference, 32–34; views on further amendment of Covenant after signature of the Peace Treaty, 36; call for a special session of Congress, 36; presented Peace Treaty to the Senate, 40; defense of Treaty, 43; appeal to the country, 44; illness, 44; letter to Hitchcock, November 19, 1919, 46; Jackson Day dinner letter, January 8, 1920, 51; acceptance of Hitchcock reservations, 53; correspondence with Hitchcock regarding reservations presented to Democratic caucus, 56; letter to Hitchcock, March 8, 1920, 59; dismissal of Lansing, 59; treaty returned by Senate, 60; letter to Oregon Democrats, 63; memorial tablet at Geneva, 69; laissez faire theories, 86; government assistance to business, 87; economy, 90; budget bill, 90; internal revenue policy, 95–96; tariff policy, 105–107; railroad policy, 127–128; highway policy, 139–141; inland waterway policy, 146; aviation policy, 155; electrical communications policy, 159; business regulation, 194; agricultural policy, 231; reclamation policy, 251; forest policy, 254; veto of national prohibition act, 271–272; veto of emergency tariff, 301; raw materials policy, 314; compulsory military training, 352; Philippine policy, 369; Colombia, 403–404; Porto Rico, 422; disarmament policy, 459
World Court, omitted from Wilson's first draft of Covenant, 21; re-

𝕿𝖍𝖊 𝕬𝖙𝖍𝖊𝖓𝖆𝖚𝖒 𝕻𝖗𝖊𝖘𝖘

GINN AND COMPANY · PROPRIETORS · BOSTON · U.S.A.

13:29